How to Start, Finance
and Operate
YOUR OWN BUSINESS

How to Start, Finance and Operate YOUR OWN BUSINESS

by James L. Silvester

Foreword by Senator Paul Trible

Lyle Stuart Inc.   Secaucus, New Jersey

Published by Lyle Stuart, Inc.
120 Enterprise Ave., Secaucus, N.J. 07094
Published simultaneously in Canada by
Musson Book Company,
A division of General Publishing Co. Limited
Don Mills, Ontario

Address queries regarding rights and permissions
to Lyle Stuart, Inc., 120 Enterprise Ave.,
Secaucus, N.J. 07094

Manufactured in the United States of America

5   4

Library of Congress Cataloging in Publication Data

Silvester, James L.
    How to start, finance, and operate your own business.

    1. New business enterprises.   I. Title.
HD62.5.S56   1984   658.1'1   84-50
ISBN 0-8184-0347-0

FOREWORD

Do you want to start your own business?

Then you need the information this book can provide. As someone who participates daily in the representative process which is the hallmark of our national government, I am keenly aware of the limits to what government can do. While we can in some cases encourage, and in other cases provide information, and in certain limited cases direct action, we cannot create.

Only you can do that. I fervently hope you do. We all know that it is so-called "small businesses" which create jobs, which provide services, which strengthen communities, which are a critical element of the mysterious condition called "prosperity."

Yet I think we need to go a step beyond the phrase "small business" and think in terms of a particular type of small business—what I would call "Infant Business." The moment an idea moves from the dream stage in your mind to the planning stage, then I think you are an infant business. Now the challenge is to bring you forth into a productive small business.

James Silvester gives you the tools to help move you from being an infant business to a small business. In our society, each of us has the opportunity to create a small business. If you've picked up this book, you no doubt have the motivation. This book will help provide the third element you need—the knowledge to do so.

The combination of the opportunity our society provides and your motivation and knowledge will be what determines if our nation prospers. As George Gilder said about the processes of our economy:

> This is a drama most essentially not of measurable money and machines, aggregates and distributions, but of mind and morale. Above the vast architecture of production, and surrounding it, is a statistically invisible

atmosphere of moods and ideas, a phantasmagoria of images and visions of the future, which either admit, or eclipse, the sustaining light and power of the sun: the life-giving faith in the possibility that free enterprises can prevail among the unpredictable forms of wealth in the unknown world to come.

Paul Trible
United States Senator from Virginia

PREFACE

This book is designed as a guide for those individuals seeking to be in business for themselves and those existing enterprises searching for new opportunities. Chapter I specifically deals with people who have not yet started their own businesses. It attempts to convey to prospective entrepreneurs the characteristics needed to be successfully self-employed.

Chapter II shows how an individual or existing firm may evaluate business opportunities so as to avoid potentially dangerous mistakes commonly made because sufficient analysis is lacking.

Chapter III deals with different sources of managerial assistance available to the small business community.

Chapter IV explains the importance of proper legal structure in fulfilling the objectives of owners and managers.

The nature of business funding arrangements in different situations is described in Chapter V. It also outlines the use of capital relative to the profit-making function and shows how to determine funding needs.

Chapter VI specifically reviews the nature of business funding and the various types of capital involved. In addition, traditional and non-traditional financial outlets are broadly described.

The details concerning the construction of the "all important" business plan is discussed in Chapter VII. An inadequate plan will be rejected without question. There are standards that must be considered.

Chapter VIII reviews the particulars in dealing with funding sources. Producing an excellent business plan isn't enough. The plan must be presented verbally in a confident and convincing manner keeping in mind that hard give-and-take negotiations will occur.

Chapter IX explains the need for sound management practices when operating a business in today's tough environment. Certain managerial techniques are identified and reviewed.

Chapter X explains some of the important elements to consider when starting and funding a service, retail, wholesale, or manufacturing business.

The book ends with chapter XI, which magnifies the sources listed in chapter VI by homing in on specific government programs directed at small firms and the individual investment preferences of many private funding outlets.

NOTE: Neither the author nor the publisher will be held liable for any transactions with any person, proprietorship, partnership, corporation, or association listed in this book. It is believed that all names, addresses, and telephone numbers listed in this book are accurate as of the time of printing, although no guarantee can or will be made.

ACKNOWLEDGMENTS

I dedicate this book to my wife, children, mother, sister, and deceased father. Without their support and encouragement, this project would not have been possible.

Acknowledgment must also be given to all those fine students and friends who helped in gathering the pertinent information contained herein.

Research Directors:
Roy Carper III
Lara Davis
Fredrick Koerner
Steven Orndoff
Leslie Watada
Elizabeth Wray

Typist
Janet Heishman
Diana Rytter

Researchers:
Gary Bageant
Kay Balcer
Pam Bell
Terry Bennett
Elaine Dawkins
Marjorie Edmondson
William Eyles
Cecelia Farland

Carol Frederiksen
James Freeman
Brad Funkhouser
Anne Goldstein
Tania Gomez
Robert Greatorex
Peggy Hess
Valerie Hubbard
Laura Johnson
Daphne Manuel
Shawn Martin
Carl Myers
Rosalia Petrosino
Eleni Peyser
Shirley Prosser
Sue Robinson
Myrna Shirley
Judith Slaughter
Karl Witsberger
Karin Zeek

CONTENTS

INTRODUCTION

A New Emphasis

It's a relief to note that a large contingent of public and private economists, academicians, and journalists are currently acknowledging the vital role of small businesses in the total economy. Many of these experts believe that government should do more to foster small business vitality and growth. In fact, some call it our economic salvation. Recently, a futurist (trend analyst) appeared on the ABC late night television show "The Last Word" and proclaimed that small business entrepreneurs will lead us back to economic prosperity in the 80's. There is reason to believe this is true.

Recent studies conducted by major universities, think tanks, congressional committees, and the U.S. Small Business Administration have revealed that most of the economic growth over the last ten years can be traced to the small business community. The same studies concluded that small firms are accountable for about 50 percent of the country's output and most of the growth in employment over the same period. To illustrate this point, one can turn to a research study conducted by MIT Professor David Birch which concluded that between 1969 and 1976, approximately 82 percent of all the new jobs created in the U.S. were the result of small business activity. To top all this off is the fact that most new innovations over the last century have originated in the research departments of small businesses or by individual entrepreneurs. These facts have given reason to call the small business sector, which comprises nearly 95 percent of all private firms in the country, the "vital majority."

For too many years small firms were looked upon as an insignificant part of our economic life and largely ignored by representative governments. A decade ago the catchword was "Big Is Better" and much of the country's tax policies and resources were shifted in favor of giant corporations at the expense of small businesses and prospective entrepreneurs. Society has paid the price of this approach. It is safe to say that a strong correlation exists between the nation's emphasis on large corporate organizations and its general economic decline. Without a doubt, many giant firms are stagnate and drifting without focus or resolve. Most cannot compete in the international marketplace and are severe drags on the U.S. economy

Many of these large concerns are attempting to maintain the status quo against enlightened politicians who would emphasize free trade and shift the country's resources, either wholly or partially, back to the more productive small business sector. If they are successful in their lobbying efforts and reverse this new direction, it would condemn the United States to continued economic stagnation and compromise our standing as a world leader. In addition, it must never be forgotten that American political freedoms are directly linked to the survival of the entrepreneur as a vital force in society.

James L. Silvester
Shenandoah College
School of Business Administration
Winchester, Virginia 22601

Chapter I

ARE YOU THE TYPE
It's Important to Know

The New Wave

The 1980's have been called the "Decade of the Entrepreneur" for good reason. Despite severe economic conditions and the highest level of business failure since the Great Depression, more people are pursuing self-employment than at any time in our country's history, as evidenced in Table 1. Self-satisfaction, desire for independence, limited job opportunities, and layoffs seem to be the main reasons why individuals are seeking to be their own bosses.

Know Your Limitations

The lure of self-employment should be tempered with a keen sense of reality and facts. Most new businesses fail within the first three years of operation, according to numerous studies conducted by private groups and the Small Business Administration. Researchers have concluded that most of these failures were due to poor business practices on the part of the entrepreneur. In addition, the studies found that many individuals seeking the self-employment option are not cut out for the task. Some people think they can beat the odds by buying an established business that has been in operation for some time or by purchasing a franchise. True, it will increase your chances somewhat in the beginning, but if you fail to use sound business techniques, and/ or lack the necessary personality traits, then the possibility of success in any business endeavor is greatly diminished.

Whether you are starting a new business or buying an existing operation, you must ask yourself the following question which could reveal potential problem areas: Do I have what it takes? Most small businesses are risky at best, but your chances of success are improved if you realistically understand the difficulties involved and work out as many of them as you can before jumping in with both feet.

TABLE 1

New Business Incorporations

1965	203,897
1966	200,010
1967	206,569
1968	233,635
1969	274,267
1970	264,209
1971	287,577
1972	316,601
1973	329,358
1974	319,149
1975	326,345
1976	357,766
1977	436,170
1978	478,019
1979	524,565
1980	533,520
1981	581,661
1982	281,458*

*Through June.

NOTE: These figures do not include new businesses that were started as sole proprietorships or partnerships. If they were, the numbers would exceed 1 million.

SOURCE: By permission of Dun & Bradstreet Credit Services, a company of The Dun & Bradstreet Corporation.

Studies by the U.S. Small Business Administration have concluded that most successful entrepreneurs display common characteristics. They are as follows:

DRIVE

...Responsibility—ability to make sure things get done

...Persistence—willingness to see things finalized

...Health—having physical and mental stamina

...Initiative—ability to take charge when necessary and be the first to act

...Vigor—having the limitless vitality needed to suceed

THINKING ABILITY

...Originality—ability to create new ideas and approaches

...Creativity—ability to think and explore in unorthodox ways; also initiative

...Critical Sense—ability to make intelligent comparison and comment

...Analytical Sense—ability to reason in practical, theoretical and abstract terms

HUMAN RELATIONS ABILITY

...Sociability—ability to get along with others, including peers, in a number of settings (home, work, politics, international relations, etc.)

...Cooperation—willingness to work with others in a constructive manner

...Tactfulness—ability to hold or water-down discomforting comments or actions

...Cheerfulness—willingness to laugh and smile even when the going gets rough

...Consideration—ability to appreciate the value of other people's time and money

...Personal Relations—ability to get along with people who are close

...Ascendency—ability to govern and control wisely without excessive ego involvement

...Emotional Stability—having appropriate maturity level for the task

...Cautiousness—ability to give serious evaluation before taking risk; successful entrepreneurs avoid gambling, they are moderate risk takers

COMMUNICATIONS ABILITY

...Oral Communications—ability to speak in a clear, concise, and logical manner

...Verbal Comprehension—ability to listen, absorb, and understand others' conversation

...Written Communication—ability to write in a clear, concise, and logical way

TECHNICAL KNOWLEDGE

...The information a manager possesses about the physical process of producing the goods or services.

...The ability to use the information in a useful manner.

If it can be determined that you possess most of the above-mentioned traits or can acquire them if deficiencies exist, then your chance of success in a small business is greatly enhanced. In your comparison, try to avoid overly optimistic estimates of yourself. Be candid about your personality traits and abilities. It is better to learn now that you are not suited for self-employment before investing time, money, and hard work in something that is doomed to fail from the beginning. Economic and emotional scares can be avoided if you heed the warning signals.

Additional insight into self-evaluation can be gained by answering the questions in Table 2. Again, honest appraisal is called for to insure accuracy in defining yourself. Remember, you are risking your time and hard-earned dollars.

If most of the checks are on the left-hand side of the table, then your chances of small business success are reasonable. Make sure that these positive answers were not a result of wishful thinking. Checks found in the center or on the right-hand side of the table should be carefully examined to determine if these weaknesses can be overcome. Perhaps, in the short term, you should hire associates and/or consultants whose strong points compensate your weak areas. Many of your weak traits can probably be corrected through education and training. But that is a long-term consideration. If you are weak in too many areas, it is in your best interest not to pursue self-employment any further.

TABLE 2

RATING SCALE FOR PERSONAL TRAITS IMPORTANT TO A BUSINESS PROPRIETOR

INSTRUCTIONS: After each question place a check mark on the line at the point closest to your answer. The check mark need not be placed directly over one of the suggested answers because your rating may lie somewhere between two answers. Be honest with yourself.

ARE YOU A SELF-STARTER? _____

| I do things my own way. Nobody needs to tell me to get going. | If someone gets me started, I keep going all right. | Easy does it. I don't put myself out until I have to. |

HOW DO YOU FEEL ABOUT OTHER PEOPLE? _____

| I like people. I can get along with just about anybody. | I have plenty of friends. I don't need anyone else. | Most people bug me. |

CAN YOU LEAD OTHERS? _____

I can get most people to go along without much difficulty.	I can get people to do things if I drive them.	I let someone else get things moving.

CAN YOU TAKE RESPONSIBILITY? _____

I like to take charge of and see things through.	I'll take over if I have to, but I'd rather let someone else be responsible.	There's always some eager beaver around wanting to show off. I say let him.

HOW GOOD AN ORGANIZER ARE YOU? _____

I like to have a plan before I start. I'm usually the one to get things lined up.	I do all right unless things get too goofed up. Then I cop out.	I just take things as they come.

HOW GOOD A WORKER ARE YOU? _____

I can keep going as long as necessary. I don't mind working hard.	I'll work hard for a while, but when I've had enough, that's it!	I can't see that hard work gets you anywhere.

CAN YOU MAKE DECISIONS? _____

I can make up my mind in a hurry if necessary, and my decision is usually o.k.	I can if I have plenty of time. If I have to make up my mind fast, I usually regret it.	I don't like to be the one who decides things. I'd probably blow it.

CAN PEOPLE TRUST WHAT YOU SAY? _____

They sure can. I don't say things I don't mean.	I try to be on the level, but sometimes I just say what's easiest.	What's the sweat if the other fellow doesn't know the difference.

CAN YOU STICK WITH IT? _____

If I make up my mind to do something, I don't let anything stop me.	I usually finish what I start.	If a job doesn't go right, I turn off. Why beat your brains out?

HOW GOOD IS YOUR HEALTH? _____

I never run down.	I have enough energy for most things I want to do.	I run out of juice sooner than most of my friends seem to.

SOURCE: U.S. Small Business Administration.

Unorthodox Characteristics

A. David Silver, a noted venture capitalist and author, who manages a venture capital firm in New Mexico, contends in his new book, *The Entrepreneurial Life: How to Go for It and Get It* (John Wiley and Sons, New York), that many successful entrepreneurs experience a number of common difficulties in early life that may account for their later achievements. These difficulties include "educational arrest, lack of social interaction or motivation, sickly in nature, less wealth than peers, and small physical build." In addition, Silver suggests that venture capitalists prefer adult entrepreneurs who suffer from "guilt," especially the kind of guilt derived from "divorce." They feel it is a highly "motivating" factor. Also, individuals experiencing guilt in their "marriages" are considered good prospects. Silver also implied in an April 19, 1978, article published by the periodical *Chicago Business*, that successful entrepreneurs tended to be dominated by "achievement oriented mothers" and have "extraordinary sex drives."

It should not be implied that the aforementioned characteristics are necessary in order to be successful in your own business. It is obvious that many people have made a go of their businesses without having a single characteristic mentioned in this section. What should be remembered is that some who have made it through self-employment had experienced stumbling blocks in earlier years, thereby providing a foundation to face the difficult choices encountered in starting and managing a business.

In addition, keep in mind that Mr. Silver was referring to venture capitalists, who tend to be a unique breed unlike other funding sources. These financiers pursue people and opportunities quite different from the typical Joe or Jane running the average small business. Generally, venture capitalists will invest only in firms and entrepreneurs that are geared for fast growth. They want to make big bucks and feel it takes a certain type of individual to accomplish this task. Chapter VI provides more discussion about venture capitalists.

Not All Peaches and Cream

Once it is determined that you possess most of the necessary traits to run a small business and can deal with deficiencies that exist, you must consider the pros and cons of self employment before committing time and energy beyond this point. There are some distinct negative aspects of running your own business. They are highlighted below:

— Constantly Changing Buying Motives of Potential Customers— Rapid inflation and disinflation, compressed economic cycles, unanticipated trends, etc., can have a significant impact on a small firm.

— Number of Business Failures—The failure rate for small businesses is at an all-time high, obviously reflecting the current severity of the recession.

— Possibility of Losing Money—Where you find potential reward the possibility of risk is always present. An individual can lose a considerable amount of money if the business is a losing proposition and he fails to bail out in time to cut large losses.

— Psychological Damage—Business failure can produce negative psychological effects that may haunt someone for a long time to come. Some will completely avoid a second try at self-employment.

— Long Hours—Contrary to popular belief, most successful entrepreneurs put in 12-hour days. Most work as hard as corporate executives.

— Medium Income—Successful small business people make, on the average, about the same as a mid-level manager in a large corporation.

— Income Variation—Income derived from your own business will be less regular than the receipt of a salary or wage from an employer. If you are starting a new business, the first six to twelve months might be bad because the operation is normally functioning at a loss. Even after business income is generated, variations in profits can be expected because of many factors (seasonal business, slow accounts receivables, heavy inventories, etc.).

Keep in mind that where you find disadvantages in any situation, positive aspects will also surface. In keeping with this notion, below are listed the advantages in pursuing self-employment.

— Independence—Self-employment provides a degree of personal and economic freedom not found when working for somebody else.

— Economic Security—Many individuals feel that economic security can be gained through self-employment. Given the high level of employee cutbacks in large and medium-sized firms, sometimes self-employment becomes the only alternative. Some see it as insulation against future layoffs. Consequently, many business executives and hourly workers are seriously pursuing small business opportunities. Many are already running sideline businesses hoping to someday generate a full-time operation.

— Potential Profit—Where you find the potential for risk, profit opportunities also exist.

— Quality of Life—Many individuals find a high degree of fulfillment in self-employment. Some successful entrepreneurs have reported an enhanced self-image and positive attitude along with other psychological rewards.

— Good Economic Environment—With the recession almost over and economic expansion underway, it is an ideal time to be starting a small business. This is even more true of service enterprises which comprise most of the nation's small firms. The service field is expected to be the fastest growing sector of the economy.

— Consumer and Business Confidence Is Up—Buyers and sellers are very positive about the country's economic prospects at this point. If it continues, economic growth will follow suit.

— Lower Inflationary Expectation—For the time being, inflation is under control and that is a positive note to investors, managers, and consumers. High inflation erodes confidence in the economy and recession normally follows in order to correct spiraling prices.

— New Emphasis on Small Firms—As mentioned in the introduction, governments are starting to realize the importance of the small business sector to the whole economy. Consequently, more governmental resources and favorable tax legislation will be directed to the small business community. Someday in the near future the entrepreneur will be seen, not as an enemy to be wiped out, but as our economic salvation.

Chapter II

EVALUATING BUSINESS OPPORTUNITIES
Protection Against Disaster

Take Time and Investigate

When seeking to start a business or buy an existing operation, investigation and analysis should be given high priority. It is surprising to note the many well-intentioned opportunity seekers, both individuals and companies pursuing expansion, who fail to properly examine prospective investment possibilities. The consequence of this inadequate investigation is generally financial hardship. In some cases, horror would be a better term to use.

Many reasons can be given for the lack of proper evaluation before jumping in with both feet. The primary ones are quite obvious. Lack of knowledge to conduct proper investigation and analysis and/or the inability to pay for professional help to do the necessary work tend to be cited as the major stumbling blocks. Impulsiveness and lack of patience are also dangerous motivations that can stymie adequate examination. Inappropriate or insufficient investigation will lead to predictable circumstances that include but are not limited to the following situations:

— underestimation of capital needs
— overestimation of market potentials
— underestimation of competition
— inappropriate location
— acquisition of obsolete equipment

— acquisition of unanticipated business debts and claims
— questionable business reputation that may take years to correct

Spend the time to investigate and analyze all possible aspects of a business proposition. Failure to do so could result in financial disaster, not to mention the negative psychological effects that can leave an individual or organization scared for a long time to come.

Which Way to Go

What business opportunity should I pursue? This is a question generally answered before you know your suitability for self-employment. It is something that should be carefully examined up to the very minute before committing yourself to any course of action.

A good starting point would be an evaluation of your experience and background. This would include your education, employment history, and hobbies. Compare your achievements with what you like to do. The more knowledge and experience you possess that can be used in operating a business, the greater are your chances of success.

So it is wise to pick a field that you know something about. Make sure you like operating in that area. Dislike and lack of enthusiasm for the business you choose will probably lead to failure. You might consider working for another small business, in your area of interest, in order to learn the ropes.

Your road to business ownership can lead in four directions, each having unique pros and cons. One can purchase a firm already in business or start from scratch. Acquiring a franchise is another possibility, which incorporates the features of a start-up and existing operation. For example, when purchasing a franchise you are basically paying for the right to market an already established product or service owned by somebody else (the franchisor). Under your franchise agreement, you (the franchisee) will be expected to market the product/service successfully. The fourth road to ownership is limited to a few individuals. Someday you might be lucky enough to inherit a business. Since this possibility is remote for most people, its advantages and disadvantages will not be discussed.

Purchasing an Existing Operation

There are positive factors to consider in buying an existing business. Occasionally a going concern may be available at a bargain price because the owner is anxious to sell. Investigation by you and your attorney or accountant should determine the owner's exact reasons for selling. Even though the price seems low, other factors might make the deal a costly endeavor.

Buying an existing operation reduces the time and cost associated with establishing a new business. Your customer base is already established and much of the leg work associated with starting out is already completed. In addition, the previous owner might convey some helpful tips and experiences in operating the business, thereby reducing the time involved in the learning process. You might consider hiring the former owner full or part time. The most important advantage in buying an existing firm is longevity. Simply put, the longer a business has been around, the greater are its chances for continuance. Research has concluded that a business surviving past ten years stands a good possibility of being around for a long time. Table 3 illustrates this fact.

TABLE 3

AGE OF BUSINESS FAILURE—1981

Age In Years	Percentage Of Total Failures
Five Years Or Less	49.1
Six To Ten Years	30.7
Over Ten Years	20.2

SOURCE: "The Business Failure Record." By permission of Dun & Bradstreet Credit Services, a company of The Dun & Bradstreet Corporation.

Where you find positive aspects in a given situation, negative ones will also surface. Buying an existing operation can provide pitfalls to potential entrepreneurs. You may pay too much for the business because of inflated estimates of worth. Current inventories and accounts receivables (customer accounts) may be dated. The firm's equipment might be in poor condition but overstated in value for selling purposes. Customer relations (goodwill) might be in bad shape and the firm's present location may not be the best. Refer to Table 4 for causes of business failure.

Your lawyer and accountant should assist you in identifying negative conditions that may exist before purchasing an existing enterprise. Conducting an independent financial audit by a CPA of your choice should be mandatory. After the audit is completed, ask the CPA to analyze the financial statements carefully. In addition, request that the

TABLE 4

Apparent Causes 1981	Percent	Manufacturers	Wholesalers	Retailers	Construction	Commercial Services	All
NEGLECT							
Due to	Bad Habits	0.1	0.4	0.1	0.2	0.1	0.2
	Poor Health	0.1	0.4	0.2	0.2	0.2	0.2
	Marital Difficulties	0.1	—	0.1	0.1	—	0.1
	Other	0.1	0.1	0.3	0.1	0.1	0.2
FRAUD							
On the part of the principals, reflected	Misleading Name	—	0.1	0.0	—	0.1	0.0
	False Financial Statement	0.1	0.3	0.1	0.0	0.1	0.1
by	Premediated Overbuy	0.1	0.1	0.0	—	—	0.0
	Irregular Disposal of Assets	0.2	0.3	0.0	0.0	0.1	0.1
	Other	—	—	0.0	0.0	0.1	0.0
LACK OF EXPERIENCE IN THE LINE	Inadequate Sales	58.2	58.9	60.9	63.6	50.4	59.4
LACK OF MANAGERIAL EXPERIENCE	Heavy Operating Expenses	32.5	25.6	21.9	21.5	29.9	24.7
UNBALANCED EXPERIENCE	Receivables Difficulties	11.9	12.1	2.4	9.1	5.0	6.4
	Inventory Difficulties	5.4	10.9	11.6	1.0	0.8	6.9
INCOMPETENCE	Excessive Fixed Assets	4.7	1.9	2.7	1.9	5.6	3.1
	Poor Location	0.5	0.7	4.2	0.5	1.5	2.2
Evidenced by inability to avoid conditions which resulted in	Competitive Weakness	14.7	16.9	17.9	14.7	15.7	16.3
	Other	3.6	2.3	1.8	8.0	2.4	3.5
DISASTER	Fire	0.3	0.1	0.2	0.0	0.2	0.2
	Flood	0.1	—	0.0	—	—	0.0
Some of these occurences could have	Burglary	0.1	0.1	0.0	—	0.1	0.0
been provided against through insurance	Employees' Fraud	—	0.1	0.0	—	—	0.0
	Strike	0.1	0.2	0.0	0.0	0.0	0.1
	Other	0.1	0.1	0.2	0.2	0.0	0.1
REASON UNKNOWN		8.1	7.5	9.3	9.9	16.5	10.1
Percent Of Total Failures		13.2	10.2	41.0	21.5	14.1	100.0

Because some failures are attributed to a combination of apparent causes, the totals of these columns exceed the totals of the corresponding columns on the left.

Source: "The Business Failure Record." By permission of Dun & Bradstreet Credit Services, a company of The Dun & Bradstreet Corporation.

assets listed by the seller be verified to determine true worth. These services will cost you several hundred dollars, but the cost is minimal compared to what you could lose in a bad deal. Talking to former, present, and potential customers of the business in question might reveal some interesting insights. Table 5 outlines most of the pros and cons in buying an existing business.

TABLE 5

BUYING AN ESTABLISHED BUSINESS

ADVANTAGES
   Suppliers already established
   Existing community goodwill
   Established customer base
   Location known to be adequate
   Facilities are existent
   Regulatory requirements have already been met
   Credit relationships have already been established
   Some inventories and supplies may be on hand
   Many growing pains have been overcome
   Proven employees

DISADVANTAGES
   Ownership changes can result in loss of community goodwill and customers
   Current policies may be difficult to break because of precedents established by former owners
   Existing employees may resist change
   Equipment may be in poor condition and/or obsolete
   Present location may not be the best and moving is or will be required

Starting a New Business

The advantages in starting your own business from scratch are many. You can avoid unpleasant precedents that might be established by another owner relating to vendors, customers, bankers, and creditors. Starting anew will insure some discretion over the location of the new enterprise, product/services to be marketed, employees hired, accounting and tax procedures used, etc. A new firm, with a unique product or service, may be the first to exploit a market in an area, thereby gaining a strong foothold against potential competitors.

A start-up situation can prove to be equally discouraging for a number of reasons. A lot of ground work is involved in acquiring business licenses and permits, establishing relations with suppliers, buying equipment/supplies, etc. Also, new firms generally lack a customer base to support operations initially and confidence and goodwill take time to build. In addition, credit by suppliers and banks may be slow in coming until you become established and prove your ability to pay. Finally, most new enterprises fail within the first three years of operation due to business and managerial incompetence on the part of the entrepreneur (refer to Table 4). Also, Table 6 lists most of the advantages and disadvantages in starting a small business from scratch.

TABLE 6

STARTING A BUSINESS

Many entrepreneurs prefer to start a small business and build it themselves from the ground floor up. There are unique advantages to this approach, but pitfalls also exist. Careful examination is warranted before moving in this direction.

POSITIVE FACTORS
  Suppliers can be evaluated and chosen fresh.
  Credit connections are new and can be nurtured from the beginning.
  The latest equipment, supplies, and inventories can be picked according to exact requirements and specifications.
  Client contacts and relationships are new. Negative precedents can be avoided from the beginning.
  The development of community goodwill is wide open, with the possibility of developing a unique image.
  The optimum location can be identified and acquired or leased.
  Financial records can be tailored to exact needs.

NEGATIVE FACTORS
  Starting a business entails a greater risk than buying an existing operation.
  Capital and credit may be more difficult to obtain, given the lack of operating histories and/or the inexperience of the people involved.
  Starting and organizing will require time and energy.
  Positive customer and community reaction may be slow in coming.
  Supplemental income may be needed until the business begins to turn profits.
  Needed employees may be difficult to lure initially, given financial constraints in the early years of operation.

The Franchising Route

Franchising, another road to business ownership, has distinct pluses worth noting. The product/service is established and, in some cases, customer goodwill has already been achieved. Many franchise organizations will provide partial start-up funding and credit after operations begin as well as local, regional, and national promotion assistance. In addition, your limited experience and/or education can be supplemented with the franchisor's extensive knowledge in a product or service area if management training and follow-up assistance is provided. Also, affiliation with some franchisors will allow for cost savings in purchasing supplies and equipment due to combined buying power of the franchisees through the franchise organization. The more reputable franchisors will recommend or require certain layouts, displays, facilities, property, business techniques, etc. It is wise to adopt these since most have proven successful in actual operation by other franchisees.

Taking the franchise route can cause you some headaches. Freedom to set your own prices and change or alter the product/service line may be limited. The degree of limitation will depend upon the franchisor. You will have to split your sales revenues with the franchise organization and payments vary anywhere between one and 20 percent of gross sales, with four being the average. Also, many franchisors require a lot of paperwork from their franchisees. If the above-mentioned situations haven't scared you yet, the franchise contracts might. They tend to be long, complex, and, in some cases, vague. Many questionable points may be diluted or hidden in legal terminology. See that your attorney reads the contract document to insure that the franchisor cannot evade its promises and responsibilities under the terms of the franchise agreement. Make sure that the organization is not expecting unreasonable demands in the form of up-front fees, percentage paybacks, limiting controls, etc.

High front fees can be discouraging for anyone pursuing the franchise alternative. Many of the better-known franchisors require that you have a couple of hundred thousand dollars before getting the franchise. That's only half the cost. They will lend you the rest. But don't be fooled by low fees either. It may mean that the franchise organization is not providing adequate support functions after operations commence.

Once you have narrowed your choice down to a particular franchise, additional evaluation is needed. The federal government and many states require franchise organizations to provide detailed information about their operations to prospective franchisees. This data is provided to assist you in making your decision. Even though the federal government has gone to extreme lengths to insure credibility within the franchise industry through disclosure requirements, indiscretions still exist. Question the franchisor concerning costs, business policies, contract terms, etc. Verify the answers with current franchisees. Talking to individuals associated with the franchise organization (as franchisees) will provide a valuable source of information. Don't ask the franchisor for references. Seek out the franchisees yourself so as to insure unbiased comments.

Find out if the franchise organization is reputable and delivers what is promised. Make sure that the franchisor is really on your side. In addition, call or write the National Better Business Bureau, 230 Park Avenue, New York, New York 10017, and the Better Business Bureau in the city where the franchise headquarters is located. Ask for a report on the company.

It is wise to consider a few questions before spending countless hours on a serious franchise evaluation. Therefore, the following questions are designed to provide an initial insight into what constitutes a reputable franchise organization. The answers you receive may save you time, money, and grief.

1) Were promises made concerning enormous profits?
2) Were promises made concerning minimal effort?
3) Were promises made concerning getting rich quick?
4) Was the franchisor more interested in making a sale than making the franchisee successful?
5) Was pressure exerted to sign a purchase contract?
6) Was pressure exerted to sign a purchase contract based upon the franchisor's threat that the "so-called" opportunity would not be available tomorrow?
7) Does the franchisor constantly pursue in order to make a sale? (Telephone, mail, showing up without an appointment, etc.)
8) Did the franchisor refuse or evade any direct questions?
9) Were the franchisor's answers to questions stated in vague terms?
10) Did the franchisor refuse or evade questions relating to references (other franchisees that can be asked for their opinions)?
11) Did the franchisor hedge on questions concerning training and assistance programs made available to franchisees? Did the answers lack specifics in reference to dates, length of assistance, trainers, etc.?
12) Did the franchisor hesitate to agree on having the franchisee's attorney available to ask questions and/or review the franchise contract?

If the answer to any of the aforementioned questions is "yes," serious consideration should be given before doing business with the franchisor. Once the differences are resolved to your satisfaction, if possible, and the initial research facts are in order, proceed by conducting a comprehension evaluation of the franchise deal by answering the questions that appear on pages 34 through 37. This should assist you in determining whether the franchise organization and agreement is right for you. In addition, several good books have been published by private and government organizations on the subject of franchising. Drop a note and ask for information. Several of these provide extensive information on franchise organization:

Franchise Opportunities Handbook
Superintendent of Documents
U.S. Government Printing Office
Washington, D.C. 20402

Franchise Index/Profile
Superintendent of Documents
U.S. Government Printing Office
Washington, D.C. 20402

Directory of Franchising Organization
Pilot Books
347 Fifth Avenue
New York, New York 10016

The Franchise Annual Handbook and Directory
Info Press, Inc.
736 Center Street
Lewiston, New York 14092

IFA Membership Directory
International Franchise Association
1025 Connecticut Avenue, N.W.
Suite 1005
Washington, D.C. 20036

Investigate Before Investing: Guidance For Prospective Franchisees
International Franchise Association
1025 Connecticut Avenue, N.W.
Suite 1005
Washington, D.C. 20036

Franchise firms that you feel are not acting appropriately should be reported to a number of private and public organizations. They are:

National Franchise Association Coalition
P.O. Box 366
Fox Lake, Illinois 60020

International Franchise Association
1025 Connecticut Avenue, N.W.
Suite 1005
Washington, D.C. 20036

Franchise and Business Opportunities Program
Federal Trade Commission
Washington, D.C. 20580

National Better Business Bureau
230 Park Avenue
New York, New York 10017

Better Business Bureau in the city where the franchise headquarters is
located.

In addition, many states maintain agencies that monitor franchise
organizations. If you have problems, write to the State Corporation
Commission in your state capital.

Questions to Answer Affirmatively
Before Going Into Franchising

Check if answer is "yes"

The Franchisor

1. Has the franchisor been in business long enough (5 years or
   more) to have established a good reputation?   _____

2. Have you checked Better Business Bureaus, Chambers of
   Commerce, Dun and Bradstreet, or bankers to find out about
   the franchisor's business reputation and credit rating?   _____

3. Did the above investigations reveal that the franchisor has a
   good reputation and credit rating?   _____

4. Does the franchising firm appear to be financed adequately so
   that it can carry out its stated plan of financial assistance and
   expansion?   _____

5. Have you found out how many franchisees are now operating?   _____

6. Have you found out the "mortality" or failure rate among
   franchisees?   _____

7. Is the failure rate small?   _____

8. Have you checked with some franchisees and found that the
   franchisor has a reputation for honesty and fair dealing among
   those who currently hold franchises?   _____

9. Has the franchisor shown you certified figures indicating exact
   net profits of one or more going operations which you have
   personally checked yourself?   _____

10. Has the franchisor given you a specimen contract to study with
    the advice of your legal counsel?   _____

The Franchisor
11. Will the franchisor assist you with:
    a. A management training program? _____
    b. An employee training program? _____
    c. A public relations program? _____
    d. Obtaining capital? _____
    e. Good credit terms? _____
    f. Merchandising ideas? _____
    g. Designing store layout and displays? _____
    h. Inventory control methods? _____
    i. Analyzing financial statements? _____
12. Does the franchisor provide continuing assistance for franchisees through supervisors who visit regularly? _____
13. Does the franchising firm have an experienced management trained in depth? _____
14. Will the franchisor assist you in finding a good location for your business? _____
15. Has the franchising company investigated you carefully enough to assure itself that you can successfully operate one of its franchises at a profit both to it and to you? _____
16. Have you determined exactly what the franchisor can do for you that you cannot do for yourself? _____

The Product or Service
17. Has the product or service been on the market long enough to gain good consumer acceptance? _____
18. Is it priced competitively? _____
19. Is it the type of item or service which the same consumer customarily buys more than once? _____
20. Is it an all-year seller in contrast to a seasonal one? _____
21. Is it a staple item, in contrast to a fad? _____
22. Does it sell well elsewhere? _____
23. Would you buy it on its merits? _____
24. Will it be in greater demand five years from now? _____
25. If it is a product rather than a service:
    a. Is it packaged attractively? _____
    b. Does it stand up well in use? _____
    c. Is it easy and safe to use? _____
    d. Is it patented? _____
    e. Does it comply with all applicable laws? _____
    f. Is it manufactured under certain quality standards? _____
    g. Do these standards compare favorably with similar products on the market? _____
    h. If the product must be purchased exclusively from the franchisor or a designated supplier, are the prices to you, as the franchisee, competitive? _____

Check if
answer
The Franchise Contract   *is "yes"*

26. Does the franchise fee seem reasonable?   _____

27. Do continuing royalties or percent of gross sales payment
    appear reasonable?   _____

28. Are the total cash investment required and the terms for
    financing the balance satisfactory?   _____

29. Does the cash investment include payment for fixtures and
    equipment?   _____

30. If you will be required to participate in company-sponsored
    promotion and publicity by contributing to an "advertising
    fund," will you have the right to veto any increase in
    contributions to the "fund?"   _____

31. If the parent company's product or service is protected by
    patent or liability insurance, is the same protection extended to
    you?   _____

32. Are you free to buy the amount of merchandise you believe
    you need rather than required to purchase a certain amount?   _____

33. Can you, as the franchisee, return merchandise for credit?   _____

34. Can you engage in other business activities?   _____

35. If there is an annual sales quota, can you retain your franchise
    if it is not met?   _____

36. Does the contract give you an exclusive territory for the length
    of the franchise?   _____

37. Is your territory protected?   _____

38. Is the franchise agreement renewable?   _____

39. Can you terminate your agreement if you are not happy for
    some reason?   _____

40. Is the franchisor prohibited from selling the franchise out from
    under you?   _____

41. May you sell the business to whomever you please?   _____

42. If you sell your franchise, will you be compensated for the
    goodwill you have built into the business?   _____

43. Does the contract obligate the franchisor to give you con-
    tinuing assistance after you are operating the business?   _____

44. Are you permitted a choice in determining whether you will
    sell any new product or service introduced by the franchisor
    after you have opened your business?   _____

45. Is there anything with respect to the franchise or its operation
    which would make you ineligible for special financial assist-
    ance or other benefits accorded to small business concerns by
    federal, state, or local governments?   _____

46. Did your lawyer approve the franchise contract after he studied
    it paragraph by paragraph?   _____

47. Is the contract free and clear of requirements which would call
    upon you to take any steps which are, according to your
    lawyer, unwise or illegal in your state, county, or city?   _____

Check if
answer
is "yes"

The Franchisor

48. Does the contract cover all aspects of your agreement with the franchisor?
49. Does it really benefit both you and the franchisor?   _____

Your Market

50. Are the territorial boundaries of your market completely, accurately, and understandably defined?   _____
51. Have you made any study to determine whether the product or service you propose to sell has a market in your territory at the prices you will have to charge?   _____
52. Does the territory provide an adequate sales potential?   _____
53. Will the population in the territory given you increase over the next 5 years?   _____
54. Will the average per capita income in the territory remain the same or increase over the next 5 years?   _____
55. Is existing competition in your territory for the product or service not too well entrenched?   _____

YOU—The Franchisee

56. Do you know where you are going to get the equity capital you will need?   _____
57. Have you compared what it would take to start your own similar business with the price you must pay for the franchise?   _____
58. Have you made a business plan—for example:
    a. Have you worked out what income from sales or services you can reasonably expect in the first 6 months? The first year? The second year?   _____
    b. Have you made a forecast of expenses, including a regular salary for yourself?   _____
59. Are you prepared to give up some independence of action to secure the advantages offered by the franchise?   _____
60. Are you capable of accepting supervision, even though you will presumably be your own boss?   _____
61. Are you prepared to accept rules and regulations with which you may not agree?   _____
62. Can you afford the period of training involved?   _____
63. Are you ready to spend much or all of the remainder of your business life with this franchisor, offering his product or service to the public?   _____

SOURCE: U.S. Small Business Administration.

Franchising has created opportunities for thousands of American entrepreneurs. Many of these individuals could not have pursued self-employment without the introduction and growth of the franchise concept. But the franchise route does not guarantee success by any means. Even with the backing of a strong and reputable franchisor, success can only be achieved by hard work and the intelligent use of time and money.

Look Before You Leap

Before venturing into self-employment, an individual must conduct adequate investigation to insure that a business being started or purchased stands a chance of success. Information concerning various aspects of internal and external conditions facing a prospective owner must be sought and candidly scrutinized. Lack of data or the unwillingness to pursue questions can lead to disaster.

Below are described the more common considerations that should be addressed when contemplating entrepreneurship. Approach each one with an open mind and try to avoid personal bias that may cloud the facts.

MARKET

Determine the ability of the market to carry all existing businesses serving it and prospective firms considering an introduction. There are occasions where a new or existing business can be so efficient and well managed, relative to its competitors, that it can survive in an overly competitive or declining market and, in some cases, even prosper. When analyzing the market as the only seller with a new product or service, make sure a real need is present before committing resources. Only through the use of statistical analysis can these conclusions be reached. Examining data in reference to community growth patterns, levels of economic activity, traffic counts, etc., may reveal some interesting facts. Opinion surveys may also prove useful. Part of Chapter VII deals with estimating market conditions relative to sales forecasting.

COMPETITIVE CONDITIONS

Evaluate the degree of competition within the marketplace in question. How many competitors exist? Who are they? Where are they located? What are their strengths and weaknesses? Who is growing, stagnating, declining, and why?

REGULATORY ENVIRONMENT

In some cases, fortunes are made or lost depending upon the actions of local government officials. Changing zoning regulations and patterns, alterations of traffic flows, changes in building codes, decisions concerning public transportation and parking, etc., can have a significant effect on any business. Many motels and restaurants have met with demise due to the redirection of traffic flows. Most local communities have short- and long-range growth plans. It is wise to study these plans carefully and ask local officials questions regarding the existing or potential location.

Also, keep in mind the impact of existing and potential state and federal government regulations. Examination of these is of paramount importance. Seeking the advice of officials representing agencies charged with any regulatory responsibilities may be wise.

HUMAN RELATIONS

Before purchasing an existing operation, look into the current state of employee relations. Negative attitudes on the part of needed and hard to replace workers may be compromising the firm's existence. If starting a business, it would be wise to examine the general nature of employee relationships which may be common within local areas. Many business owners interact and establish informal standards. It is amazing how consistent these standards can be from business to business in the same community.

PRIOR CLAIMS

In reference to buying a business, always have an attorney investigate any legal claims that may exist against the operation before purchasing. Unpaid taxes, wages, bills, and/or mortgage liabilities can exist and are usually passed on to the new owner upon acquisition.

PHYSICAL FACILITIES

Physical condition of all buildings and equipment should be given careful consideration before purchasing a business. Professional appraisers can determine the fair value of tangible assets. Obsolete and inefficient facilities are normally expensive to replace, especially if an exorbitant price was paid initially for these assets.

PRODUCTS/SERVICES

Evaluate existing or future product/service lines. Determine the positive and negative features in relation to price, promotion, distribution, and competition.

ENVIRONMENTAL RISKS

Is the proposition in question susceptible to external uncontrollable events? If so, which ones and to what extent? For example, governmental actions, international events, or reactions by competitors may cause difficulties. Evaluate all facets of the environment and determine how the business in question will be effected. External threats are listed in Table 23 on page 154.

Buyer Beware

A seller always has a motivation for disposing of property. It may or may not be candidly revealed to prospective purchasers. This is why it's important that proper investigation be conducted into the reasons for selling. Hiring a competent consultant, accountant, or attorney can help in identifying and analyzing various aspects of the proposition. Surprising situations may be discovered that are not apparent to the untrained observer.

Below are listed some of the more common explanations for someone's selling out. Make sure the truth is known before committing time and money.

Wants to retire
Too old to pursue
Not interested anymore
Going back to the corporate world
Not making enough money
Loss of profits, sales, and/or markets
Sickness
Desires to relocate outside the immediate area
Wants to pursue other business endeavors
Competitive pressures
Tired of the problems and headaches associated with business ownership

Watch Out for the Lemon

A failing business can be easily detected if the right elements are examined and understood. Generally, an operation ceases to be viable for more than one specific reason, although it centers around a single broad deficiency—managerial incompetence on the part of owners and managers. Dun and Bradstreet, the well-known financial reporting firm, states that 92.1 percent of small firms that fail do so because of managerial ineptness. They further break down statistics to account for exact causes of demise, all relating to management deficiencies, which can be found by referring to Table 4 illustrated earlier in this chapter.

Below are mentioned some of the more specific reasons attributed to small business failure. If one or more of these conditions exists, it should be quite obvious to the professionally trained eye and may even be apparent to anyone taking a close look.

LACK OF MARKET POTENTIALS

Many businesses fail due to the lack of an adequate market for their products or services. Also, the total existing market may be contracting at a rate faster than the ability or willingness of the firm to react and shift emphasis. Only through sufficient market examination and evaluation can these threats be revealed. Chapter VII goes into detail about determining market potentials.

CAPITAL STARVATION

Many new businesses and existing enterprises tend to underestimate their capital requirements, thereby creating a capital squeeze somewhere down the pike, generally at an inopportune time. In many cases, adequate capital is present, but mismanagement of funds causes difficulties. These factors will affect the firm's ability to generate sales, thus adversely affecting profits. Many lenders and investors will simply be reluctant to advance and risk their money if these conditions prevail, probably forcing the closing or scaling back of operations.

HEAVY COMPETITION

Many entrepreneurs, before purchasing or starting a business, fail to account for competitive factors in the market to be served by their new operation. Severe competition can have a detrimental effect on any organization, forcing it to close, in many cases, before it gets off the ground. Consequently, a comprehensive examination is necessary to determine if existing and potential demand can support all firms currently serving the market and projected newcomers.

UNCONTROLLED GROWTH

Many businesses expand too quickly, thereby causing strains on their financial and/or managerial structures. Both large and small organizations fall victim to this deadly sin. Several large corporations have recently gone bankrupt because of expansion beyond their resource capabilities. Once profits begin to decline or evaporate, lenders and investors run for the hills. Growth should be planned well in advance, making sure that adequate resources are available to support endeavors before committing to expansion goals.

INAPPROPRIATE LOCATION

A bad location can be difficult to spot initially. Therefore, adequate investigation is necessary to determine the history of the location and whether it is suitable. How many businesses have been at the location in the past twenty years? What types of businesses were there? Why did they leave? Always conduct research concerning the location of an existing business being contemplated for purchase or the suitability of placing a business in a particular locale. Collecting information such as opinion surveys and analyzing data in reference to traffic counts and parking facilities will reveal considerable information about the viability of any location whether new or old.

DISASTROUS EVENTS

Is the business subject to catastrophic events that can drain its vitality and resources to the point where it cannot recover? Has it occurred before?

UNUSUAL AGREEMENTS

Examine the existence of any agreements the business has with present owners, employees, and third parties. Do these contracts compromise the present or future profitability of the enterprise? Can they be broken if the firm is purchased? Always have an attorney evaluate and comment on any agreements that may exist to insure flexibility in business operations. On some occasions, owners who are selling out may attempt to lock-in favored employees with contractual agreements, whereby the new owners cannot replace those workers for a given period of time.

What to Expect

If one or more of the conditions mentioned in the preceding section exists, expect any number of the following situations to prevail within a business.

— Uncontrolled Expenses—Costs may be increasing faster on a proportionate basis than sales revenues, thus eating into or eliminating profits and creating losses. Many business operations fail to maintain adequate accounting procedures that would alert management to excessive cost increases.

— Falling Profits—Consistently falling profits is probably an indication of deteriorating sales revenues or due to expenses increasing faster than sales on a relative basis.

— Accelerated Debt Service—If indebtedness becomes too great, the ability of the business to serve its debts becomes questionable. It may spell trouble in the near future. If this condition exists, the business will probably attempt to pay debts by borrowing additional funds (borrow from Peter to pay Paul), which is only a quick fix in most cases. Eventually, both Peter and Paul come collecting at the same time.

— Falling Sales—A steady trend of falling sales can produce negative consequences for any business. Normally, "expenses do not decline relative to sales," thereby squeezing or eliminating profit margins. In addition to the conditions reviewed in the previous section that could cause a decline in sales revenues, poor internal management in reference to product/service planning, market research, promotion efforts, and distribution can also result in declining sales.

If one or more of the just-mentioned conditions prevail within a business enterprise, the firm may have some degree of difficulty meeting its current obligations. Its liquid position, also known as working capital, may be deteriorated to the point where current bills can't be paid on time.

What Is the Fair Price?

There are two basic approaches used to determine the fair price for a business. The methods are described below.

BOOK VALUE/GOODWILL METHOD

This approach is simple to compute. Subtract the liabilities of the business (debts) from its assets. What's left over is called book value. It is assumed that if the assets of a business were sold and the debts paid in full, what would remain in the form of cash is the true money worth of an operation. In addition to computing this figure when selling a business, an intangible asset called goodwill is taken into account and given a dollar value. Goodwill is simply described as the reputation or positive condition achieved by a business because of sound management or, in some cases, just good fortune. Once goodwill is financially evaluated, the value established will be added to the book value in order to determine the selling price.

ANTICIPATED PROFIT METHOD

Many experts feel that using the book value and goodwill approach is inadequate and not a reliable indicator of true business worth. In fact, they support the contention that expected profits should dictate the selling price for a business. For example, in the real estate business, a house's value is not based upon the cost of materials (tangibles) and labor (intangibles) but is determined by what the market will pay for the structure.

When using this method, an estimation of future profits will need to be made. This can be done by examining past and current performance, present and anticipated market conditions, and environmental threats facing the business. After profits are projected, they can be compared against the selling price (potential investment) in order to determine an adequate value. To illustrate, suppose a buyer is interested in purchasing a business priced at $150,000. The potential buyer also wants to return his investment in 10 years, not counting salary draw. It has been determined that an average annual net profit of $14,000 can be generated by the business over the next decade. By using the simple formula shown below, the following conclusion can be determined.

$$\frac{\text{Purchasing Price}}{\text{Average Annual Net Profits}} = \frac{\$150,000}{14,000} = \begin{array}{c}10.7 \text{ years to} \\ \text{return investment}\end{array}$$

Obviously, the buyer must either accept a longer pay-back period or negotiate a lower price. Another factor that may enter into the discussion about price is the degree of risk inherent in the business proposition. A greater risk generally demands a faster pay-back and if average net income is set at $14,000 per year, the price of the business should come down to reflect those uncertainties. For example, a purchase price of $125,000 will be returned in 8.9 years as illustrated below:

$$\frac{\text{Purchase Price}}{\text{Average Annual Net Profits}} = \frac{\$125,000}{14,000} = 8.9 \text{ years}$$

Conversely, a lesser risk may demand a longer pay-back period because of the higher price demanded.

When using the net tangible asset/goodwill or anticipated profit methods, also seek the assistance of competent accountants and attorneys to help in assigning values and making projections. Profit estimation is reviewed in Chapter VII.

Using Financial Information

When analyzing business opportunities, serious consideration must be given to the "nuts and bolts" aspects. Financial information, when used and presented in proper format, can weed out the losers from the winners in short order. In addition, it may help to reveal the "right price" to pay for a business if acquisition is contemplated. When starting a business from the ground floor, financial data can be obtained to assist in determining the necessary capital base needed to begin and support operation until profits are generated. Once in operation, the information provided by financial statements can help insure sound fiscal management.

FINANCIAL STATEMENTS

Financial statements can say a whole lot about a firm's viability. Consequently, it is imperative to know the major financial statements generally available for evaluation purposes. First, the balance sheet is used to list a firm's assets and liabilities. These two major elements are further divided into sub-classifications (Current Assets, Non-Current Assets, Current Liabilities, Non-Current Liabilities, and Owners Equity). Second, the profit and loss statement, also known as the income statement, is used in listing and analyzing revenue and expense accounts to determine the firm's profitability. Third, a cash-flow statement is sometimes used as a supplement to the two major elements just mentioned. Its purpose is to get a closer look at how a firm manages liquid (cash) resources. Segments of Chapter VII, including Tables 18, 19, and 20, describe and illustrate these financial statements and discuss their functional purpose.

Financial information is useless without a means of comparison. A firm's financial statement should be compared to similar businesses and against the industry as a whole before attempts are made to analyze its performance. To accomplish this task, various accounts within the balance sheet and income statement can be divided into each other, thereby creating what are called financial ratios. Since ratios are compiled and published on many firms and industries by several research organizations, standards of comparison are easy to make for existing businesses. Some research outlets maintain ratios and cost information dealing with starting a new business.

An intense discussion of ratio analysis is way beyond the scope of this publication. It would be wise to write the Superintendent of Documents, U.S. Government Printing Office, Washington, D.C. 20402, and request copies of the following booklets. They cost $4.50 each.

Ratio Analysis for Small Business
Handbook of Small Business Finance

COMMON RATIOS USED TODAY

Ratio	*Used to Determine*
Current Assets / Current Liabilities	Cash position (ability to pay short-term debts)
Quick Assets / Current Liabilities	Cash position (ability to pay short-term debts)
Current Liabilities / Net Worth	Relationship between capital invested and short-term (year to year) debt obligations
Net Sales / Net Worth	How often capital is being recycled
Net Sales / Inventory	How many times inventory is turned over to generate sales
Fixed Assets / Net Worth	Relationship between invested capital and hard assets such as plant and equipment
Total Debt / Net Worth	Relationship between invested capital and all debt obligations
Net Profit / Net Sales	Rate of return on sales generated

Ratio	*Used to Determine*
Net Profit Net Worth	Efficient use of invested capital
Net Sales Working Capital	How much working capital should be maintained in relation to a given level of sales
Accounts Receivables Daily Credit Sales	If customer accounts are being paid according to terms

Table 7 contains an example of a ratio table compiled and published by Dun and Bradstreet. The ratios shown deal with general automotive repair shops ranging in asset size from $50,000 to $2,000,000 and above. The figure shown in parenthesis above each asset category is the number of firms giving financial information. Also, use the center number of the three given under each asset classification as a means of comparison. That is the median figure between the high and low numbers.

Appendix A contains a list of research organizations (names and addresses) offering financial ratios and other useful data to prospective entrepreneurs and current business owners. Information about specific types of businesses is available from these outlets and listed under each address.

Additional Insight

You might want to make some final considerations before pressing ahead with your plans. Answering the following questions might provide additional insights into your readiness for business ownership. If you have already decided to purchase a franchise, many of the following questions will be answered automatically by the franchise organization and/or previous series of questions. But it wouldn't hurt to go ahead and answer the questions for your own protection, just in case something was overlooked.

Consider these questions carefully before answering. Be honest and fair with yourself because it's your time and money at stake. Answer all that apply to your situation. Obviously, some will not. If you respond to most in a favorable way (yes) and feel comfortable with the rest, then the next step in the actualization of your own business involves obtaining capital.

TABLE 7

ECONOMIC SECTOR: SERVICES

SIC: 7538 GENERAL AUTOMO-
TIVE REPAIR SHOPS

	TO 50M	50-2MM	2MM+	TOTAL
CURRENT ASSETS	(1045)	(764)	(130)	(1939)
TO	4.55	6.11	4.50	5.12
CURRENT DEBT	1.95	3.01	2.25	2.34
(TIMES)	1.10	1.65	1.47	1.33
NET PROFITS				
ON	16.20	13.70	10.75	14.79
NET SALES	7.18	7.85	6.22	7.44
(PERCENT)	2.44	3.55	3.26	3.11
PROFITS				
ON	87.99	40.29	25.84	62.25
NET WORTH	42.74	21.44	10.91	27.98
(PERCENT)	16.71	10.96	5.33	11.45
PROFITS				
ON	182.14	106.07	57.10	144.58
WORKING CAPITAL	71.38	44.38	32.46	54.84
(PERCENT)	10.14	17.17	13.77	14.77
SALES				
TO	11.21	5.41	5.01	7.94
NET WORTH	6.13	2.90	1.96	4.22
(TIMES)	2.91	1.34	.55	1.82
SALES				
TO	20.00	11.49	11.08	16.38
WORKING CAPITAL	9.95	6.26	4.94	7.68
(TIMES)	3.35	3.02	2.19	3.06
COLLECTION PERIOD	26	36	36	31
	12	20	20	16
(DAYS)	5	9	9	7
SALES				
TO	40.0	25.0	21.3	33.3
INVENTORY	20.0	11.3	8.5	15.4
(TIMES)	10.0	5.6	4.5	7.5
FIXED ASSETS				
TO	112.3	79.0	70.2	94.6
NET WORTH	67.4	43.3	29.0	55.5
(PERCENT)	34.5	19.6	16.7	24.3
CURRENT DEBT				
TO	106.7	52.8	82.8	84.2
NET WORTH	36.8	24.2	27.1	30.0
(PERCENT)	9.7	7.5	6.1	8.3
TOTAL DEBT				
TO	204.4	101.8	102.3	144.8
NET WORTH	67.4	47.1	43.5	53.7
(PERCENT)	14.5	16.2	17.8	15.9
INVENTORY				
TO	97.8	96.7	118.5	98.4
WORKING CAPITAL	60.6	62.2	75.7	62.4
(PERCENT)	16.0	25.6	32.8	20.0
CURRENT DEBT				
TO	293.0	165.3	178.5	236.7
INVENTORY	131.3	81.9	95.6	100.0
(PERCENT)	47.7	38.0	45.1	42.8
FUNDED DEBTS				
TO	304.3	222.2	221.6	251.0
WORKING CAPITAL	101.4	81.0	62.2	87.3
(PERCENT)	12.5	22.2	9.4	18.2

SOURCE: By permission of Dun & Bradstreet Credit Services, a company of The Dun & Bradstreet Corporation.

ARE YOU THE TYPE?

Have you rated your personal qualifications using a scale similar to that presented earlier in this section?   _____

Have you had some objective evaluators rate you on such scales?   _____

Have you carefully considered your weak points and taken steps to improve them or to find an associate whose strong points will compensate for them?   _____

WHAT BUSINESS SHOULD YOU CHOOSE?

Have you written a summary of your background and experience to help you in making this decision?   _____

Have you considered your hobbies and what you would like to do?   _____

Does anyone want the service you can perform?   _____

Have you studied surveys and/or sought advice and counsel to find out what fields of business may be expected to expand?   _____

Have you considered working for someone else to gain more experience?   _____

WHAT ARE YOUR CHANCES FOR SUCCESS?

Are general business conditions good?   _____

Are business conditions good in the city and neighborhood where you plan to locate?   _____

Are current conditions good in the line of business you plan to start?   _____

WHAT WILL BE YOUR RETURN ON INVESTMENT?

Do you know the typical return on investment in the line of business you plan to start?   _____

Have you determined how much you will have to invest in your business?   _____

Are you satisfied that the rate of return on the money you invest in the business will be greater than the rate you would probably receive if you invested the money elsewhere?   _____

HOW MUCH MONEY WILL YOU NEED?

Have you filled out worksheets similar to those shown in Chapter V of this book?   _____

In filling out the worksheets, have you taken care not to overestimate income?   _____

Have you obtained quoted prices for equipment and supplies you will need?   _____

Do you know the costs of goods which must be in your inventory?   _____

Have you estimated expenses only after checking rents, wage scales, utility and other pertinent costs in the area where you plan to locate?   _____

Check if
answer
is "yes"

Have you found what percentage of your estimated sales your projected inventory and each expense item is and compared each percentage with the typical percentage for your line of business?   _____

Have you added an additional amount of money to your estimates to allow for unexpected contingencies?   _____

WHERE CAN YOU GET THE MONEY?

Have you counted up how much money of your own you can put into the business?   _____

Do you know how much credit you can get from your suppliers—the people you will buy from?   _____

Do you know where you can borrow the rest of the money you need to start your business?   _____

Have you selected a progressive bank with the credit services you may need?   _____

Have you talked to a banker about your plans?   _____

Does the banker have an interested, helpful attitude toward your problems?   _____

SHOULD YOU SHARE OWNERSHIP WITH OTHERS?

If you need a partner with money or know-how that you don't have, do you know someone who will fit—someone you can get along with?   _____

Do you know the good and bad points about going it alone, having a partner, and incorporating your business?   _____

Have you talked to a lawyer about it?   _____

WHERE SHOULD YOU LOCATE?

Have you studied the make-up of the population in the city or town where you plan to locate?   _____

Do you know what kind of people will want to buy what you plan to sell?   _____

Do people like that live in the area where you want to locate?   _____

Have you checked the number, type and size of competitors in the area?   _____

Does the area need another business like the one you plan to open?   _____

Are employees available?   _____

Have you checked and found adequate: utilities, parking facilities, police and fire protection, available housing, schools and other cultural and community activities?   _____

Do you consider costs of the location reasonable in terms of taxes and average rents?   _____

Is there sufficient opportunity for growth and expansion?   _____

Have you checked the relative merits of the various shopping areas within the city, including shopping centers?   _____

Check if
answer
is "yes"

In selecting the actual site, have you compared it with others? _____

Have you had a lawyer check the lease and zoning? _____

SHOULD YOU BUY A GOING BUSINESS?

Have you considered the advantages and disadvantages of buying a going business? _____

Have you compared what it would cost to equip and stock a new business with the price asked for the business you are considering buying? _____

HOW MUCH SHOULD YOU PAY FOR IT?

Have you estimated future sales and profits of the going business for the next few years? _____

Are your estimated future profits satisfactory? _____

Have you looked at past financial statements of the business to find the return on investment, sales and profit trends? _____

Have you verified the owner's claims about the business with reports from an independent accountant's analysis of the figures? _____

Is the inventory you will purchase a good buy? _____

Are equipment and fixtures fairly valued? _____

If you plan to buy the accounts receivable, are they worth the asking price? _____

Have you been careful in your appraisal of the company's good will? _____

Are you prepared to assume the company's liabilities and are the creditors agreeable? _____

Have you learned why the present owner wants to sell? _____

Have you found out about the present owner's reputation with his employees and suppliers? _____

Have you consulted a lawyer to be sure that the title is good? _____

Has your lawyer checked to find out if there is any lien against the assets you are buying? _____

Has your lawyer drawn up an agreement covering all essential points, including a seller's warranty for your protection against false statements? _____

SHOULD YOU INVEST IN A FRANCHISE?

Have you considered how the advantages and disadvantages of franchising apply to you? _____

Have you made a thorough search to find the right franchise opportunity? _____

Have you evaluated the franchise by answering the questions asked earlier in this section? _____

HAVE YOU WORKED OUT PLANS FOR BUYING?

Have you estimated what share of the market you think you can get? _____

Do you know how much or how many of each item of
merchandise you will buy to open your business?   _____

Have you found suppliers who will sell you what you need at a
good price?   _____

Do you have a plan for finding out what your customers want?   _____

Have you set up a model stock assortment to follow in your
buying?   _____

Have you worked out stock control plans to avoid over-stocks,
under-stocks, and out-of-stocks?   _____

Do you plan to buy most of your stock from a few suppliers
rather than a little from many, so that those you buy from will want
to help you succeed?   _____

HOW WILL YOU PRICE YOUR PRODUCTS AND SERVICES?

Have you decided upon your price ranges?   _____

Do you know how to figure what you should charge to cover
your costs?   _____

Do you know what your competitors charge?   _____

WHAT SELLING METHODS WILL YOU USE?

Have you studied the selling and sales promotion methods of
competitors?   _____

Have you studied why customers buy your type of product or
service?   _____

Have you thought about why you like to buy from some
salesmen while others turn you off?   _____

Have you decided what your methods of selling will be?   _____

Have you outlined your sales promotion policy?   _____

HOW WILL YOU SELECT AND TRAIN PERSONNEL?

If you need to hire someone to help you, do you know where to
look?   _____

Do you know what kind of person you need?   _____

Have you written a job description for each person you will
need?   _____

Do you know the prevailing wage scales?   _____

Do you have a plan for training new employees?   _____

Will you continue training through good supervision?   _____

WHAT OTHER MANAGEMENT PROBLEMS WILL YOU FACE?

Do you plan to sell for credit?   _____

If you do, do you have the extra capital necessary to carry
accounts receivable?   _____

Have you made a policy for returned goods?   _____

Have you planned how you will make deliveries?   _____

Have you considered other policies which must be made in your particular business?

Have you made a plan to guide yourself in making the best use of your time and effort?   _____

WHAT RECORDS WILL YOU KEEP?

Have you planned a system of records that will keep track of your income and expenses, what you owe other people, and what other people owe you?   _____

Have you worked out a way to keep track of your inventory so that you will always have enough on hand for your customers but not more than you can sell?   _____

Have you planned on how to keep your payroll records and take care of tax reports and payments?   _____

Do you know what financial statements you should prepare?   _____

Do you know how to use these financial statements?   _____

Have you obtained standard operating ratios for your type of business which you plan to use as guides?   _____

Do you know an accountant who will help you with your records and financial statements?   _____

WHAT LAWS WILL AFFECT YOU?

Have you checked with the proper authorities to find out what, if any, licenses to do business are necessary?   _____

Do you know what police and health regulations apply to your business?   _____

Will your operations be subject to interstate commerce regulations? If so, do you know to which ones?   _____

Have you received advice from your lawyer regarding your responsibilities under federal and state laws and local ordinances?   _____

HOW WILL YOU HANDLE TAXES AND INSURANCE?

Have you worked out a system for handling the withholding tax for your employees?   _____

Have you worked out a system for handling sales taxes? Excise taxes?   _____

Have you planned an adequate record system for the efficient preparation of income tax forms?   _____

Have you prepared a worksheet for meeting tax obligations?   _____

Have you talked with an insurance agent about what kinds of insurance you will need and how much it will cost?   _____

WILL YOU SET MEASURABLE GOALS FOR YOURSELF?

Have you set goals and sub-goals for yourself?   _____

Have you specified dates when each goal is to be achieved?   _____

Check if
answer
is "yes"

Are these realistic goals; that is, will they challenge you but at the same time not call for unreasonable accomplishments?   _____

Are the goals specific so that you can measure performance?   _____

Have you developed a business plan, using one of the SBA Aids to record your ideas, facts, and figures?   _____

Have you allowed for obstacles?   _____

WILL YOU KEEP UP TO DATE?

Have you made plans to keep up with improvements in your trade or industry?   _____

Have you prepared a business plan which will be amended as circumstances demand?   _____

SOURCE OF QUESTIONS: U.S. Small Business Administration.

Chapter III

SOURCES OF HELP
Ripe for the Picking

Help Galore

Few individuals are aware of the reservoir of assistance available from public and private organizations directed to the small business community. Taking advantage of these services may mean the difference between success and failure for many struggling businesses and entrepreneurs. Many of these informational outlets will help when evaluating business opportunities and specific propositions.

Where to Look

U.S. SMALL BUSINESS ADMINISTRATION (SBA)

One of the primary objectives of the U.S. Small Business Administration is to promote the economic well being of small firms and entrepreneurs. This is partly accomplished by providing an array of business and managerial assistance programs that are available upon request. The next several pages will be devoted to describing these non-financial services. Information concerning SBA financial assistance programs can be found later in the book.

SCORE (Service Corps of Retired Executives)—Retired business executives within this program offer advice to the small business community on a free basis. The combined experience of SCORE counselors spans the entire spectrum of American business. Volunteers meet with small business owners and prospective entrepreneurs to determine and discuss their difficulties. After careful consideration and evaluation, the counselor will formulate a plan of action designed to help minimize or eliminate the problem areas. In addition, the individual(s) requesting assistance will be guided through this sometimes difficult process. If the problem is extremely difficult or complex, several SCORE representatives may be asked to assist. Sometimes, other SBA and outside resources may be brought to bear. Currently, there are over 6,000 SCORE advisors located throughout the country.

ACE (Active Corps of Executives)—ACE is designed to supplement SCORE activities by providing business and managerial counseling on an on-going basis. Members of this organization are practicing executives, professionals, and academicians. Normally, ACE volunteers, numbering about 2,500, can provide the latest expertise that may not be available from SCORE chapters.

University Business Development Centers (UBDCs)—These organizations are established in tandem with the U.S. Small Business Administration to provide additional counseling services to the small business community. UBDC's are simply college- or university-based counseling centers utilizing institutional resources, including faculty and students. In addition, these centers muster community involvement and volunteers to accomplish their task of providing help to small firms and people wanting to start businesses. Appendix B provides a listing of current university business development centers.

Small Business Institutes (SBIs)—The U.S. Small Business Administration has contracted with over 400 colleges and universities to establish small business institutes. This program, although similar to the UBDC approach, does have distinct differences. Counseling services provided by SBI's are limited in one respect but more extensive in others. SBI student and faculty counselors are assigned to certain projects with the objective of providing detailed verbal and written recommendations to specific problem areas that a prospective entrepreneur or business owner may face. This approach enables students to experience real life business situations. The cost for this service is free to individuals or businesses seeking assistance.

Call Contracting Program—This SBA-financed program is designed to give free professional advice and expertise to small firms and individuals who qualify. The agency contracts with reputable and reliable accounting and/or consulting firms to carry out the objectives of this program. Generally, problems of a very difficult or technical nature are handled under call contracting.

Management Training—The SBA co-sponsors several types of training functions. Working in unison with private experts, the SBA provides courses, conferences, problem clinics, and workshops designed to deliver counseling services to local communities throughout the country. Checking with the regional SBA office can yield a schedule of events in particular areas served.

SBA Publications—The Small Business Administration has many free and inexpensive publications available to any individual upon request. These books and pamphlets provide valuable business and managerial tips on how to run a small business successfully. In addition, publications concerning the start-up of specific types of businesses are also available.

Free material is broken into three classifications which are as follows:

— Management Aids—These publications review procedures for handling operational and managerial difficulties.
— Starting Out Series—This information broadly describes the requirements for starting particular types of small businesses.
— Small Business Bibliographies—Specific information about major management functions is given in these reports.

The titles of these publications are reviewed in Appendix C located at the end of this book.

For sale, publications are broken into four categories. They are:

— Small Business Management Series—These detailed books deal with specific management problems faced by many start-up firms and existing operations.
— Starting and Managing Series—These publications yield specific and detailed information about starting and managing different types of small firms.
— Business Basics—This series of books attempts to teach various aspects of small business management.
— Nonseries Publications—These helpful publications deal with management topics but do not fall under any category listed thus far.

A listing of these publications can be found in Appendix D. Publications may be ordered by writing to the Superintendent of

Documents, U.S. Government Printing Office, Washington, D.C. 20402.

In addition, when seeking SBA managerial assistance services, call or write the field offices maintained by the agency. They are listed in Appendix E. They will send an assistance form that is to be completed and returned to the field office. This form is illustrated in Appendix F.

Department of Commerce

The U.S. Department of Commerce maintains an array of informational resources that are available to anyone. This department is constantly collecting economic, financial, and business data relating to the economy, different industries, states, and, in some cases, individual firms. Over the last decade, the Commerce Department has been heavily involved in the promotion of American products abroad. It has enormous amounts of data that can be used by domestic exporters when studying overseas markets. In addition, the department gets actively involved in setting up channels of distribution for any business (new or existing) wanting to exploit foreign market potentials. Department of Commerce field offices can be contacted for details concerning their publications and assistance programs. Refer to Appendix G for a listing of these offices.

The Minority Business Development Agency (MBDA), which is part of the Commerce Department, provides basic services to minority-owned firms. Their regional and district offices are listed in Appendix H. They will refer the entrepreneur to MBDA funded local offices providing services within certain geographic areas.

U.S. Federal Trade Commission (FTC)

The FTC was set up to protect consumers and businesses against firms that would promote restraint of trade and use unfair competitive methods. It publishes material on what constitutes illegal practices when conducting business. Write to the address below and request the publications concerning these matters. Knowing what to avoid initially may save many headaches later. Also, the publications might provide some insights into whether competitors are acting appropriately or not.

Federal Trade Commission
Washington, D.C. 20580

Governmental Procurement Assistance

The U.S. Small Business Administration provides help to small firms wishing to do business with the federal government through the SBA's procurement automated source system (PASS); a small firm's capabilities are matched to those government agencies requiring what the firm has to offer. Also, PASS will identify large companies that have obtained government procurement contracts and are in need of small sub-contractors to fulfill requirements in the agreements. Appendix I illustrates the PASS application form used by the SBA.

In addition, the U.S. Superintendent of Documents publishes the *Commerce Business Daily*, which reports most procurement opportunities available from Uncle Sam. Most of the PASS information received by the SBA is also contained in this publication. Therefore, subscribing to this daily report may be unnecessary. However, it does provide information on other opportunities that can be examined for potential exploitation. A subscription can be obtained by writing to:

Superintendent of Documents
Government Printing Office
Washington, D.C. 20402

The cost for the publication is broken down as follows:

$175 per year by 1st Class mail
$150 per year by 2nd Class mail
$ 90 for six months by 1st Class mail
$ 50 for six months by 2nd Class mail

Allow six weeks for delivery of the first issue.

Many state and local governments actively encourage small businesses to bid on their purchasing requirements. Contact their procurement offices for additional details. Also, foreign governments are always seeking American products and services. SBA and Department of Commerce field offices, listed in Appendices E and G, can provide assistance in reaching foreign government procurement offices located in the U.S. Contacting their embassies in Washington or consulate offices in major cities may also help.

Reading these publications will be of great help to you in under-standing governmental procurement procedures and may open up opportunities not apparent before.

U.S. INTERNAL REVENUE SERVICE

The IRS can provide information related to business taxation. It publishes many useful and free reports concerning the tax obligation of business enterprises. Some of the publications will assist in establishing the necessary accounting procedures for the proper handling and payment of taxes. Write or call the nearest IRS office and request the booklets needed. They are listed in Appendix K. IRS personnel will also answer questions personally.

STATE GOVERNMENTS

Most state governments are realizing the importance of small business activity to their economy. Many have developed assistance programs aimed at helping prospective entrepreneurs and existing small firms. Services may include managerial, procurement and/or funding help. The degree of assistance varies from state to state. To find out what may be available, write or call the offices listed in Appendix J for more information. Also, referring to Appendix L will give broad information about the services provided by different states.

LOCAL GOVERNMENTS

Most municipalities maintain records in reference to local economic activity. Statistics dealing with retail sales, personal income, construction permits, traffic counts, and growth patterns can be obtained and are useful when analyzing general business prospects or specific propositions. For example, when evaluating several possible store locations, traffic counts and area growth patterns should be carefully reviewed.

ACCOUNTANTS

In addition to their traditional role as bookkeeper and auditor, many accountants provide invaluable information and assistance relative to decisions concerning business propositions. Included below are some of the more common services that can be expected from most accountants.

— Of course, record keeping and auditing
— Corporate and individual tax planning

— Sales and income projection
— Budget construction
— Identification and exploitation of capital sources
— Construction of past, present, and pro forma (future) financial statements
— Cost containment analysis and procedures
— Determination and projection of working capital requirements
— Overall financial analysis

Although most are listed in the phone book, it is wise to consult a banker, attorney, or business consultant when seeking a suitable accountant. Bankers and lawyers are in constant contact with the accounting profession and they generally know the accountants that can provide adequate help at reasonable cost. A good approach is to seek out owners in similar lines of business and ask for advice. This can be the best source of reference available because of the direct contact between accountant and owner. In addition, there are two national, professional accounting associations that may provide referrals upon request. They are listed below. Also, try state associations. Many are more familiar with their membership than the national groups.

American Institute of Certified Public Accountants
1211 Avenue of the Americas
New York, New York 10036
(212) 575-6200

National Society of Public Accountants
1010 North Fairfax Street
Alexandria, Virginia 22314
(703) 549-6400

Accountants can save a tremendous amount of pain and expense if they are used wisely. Always have an accountant explore a prospective business proposition before purchasing, for obvious reasons cited earlier in the book. If already in business, you need accountants to evaluate any large investment decision contemplated. Even if a business has an internal accountant, outside opinion should be sought. It can be helpful in spotting difficulties that may not be apparent from the inside. The small price paid for the information is an investment if it helps avoid a bad deal which potentially could cause severe losses. Remember, it's better to pay a little now than a whole lot later.

Advertising Firms

Advertising agencies can be a source of marketing assistance overlooked by many existing firms and prospective entrepreneurs. Many agencies provide services over and above their traditional function of selling media. These include:

— Evaluation of marketing objectives
— Planning of advertising strategy and tactics
— Selection of correct media outlets
— Production of ad layouts and commercials
— Coordination and execution of strategy and tactics
— Evaluation of advertising results

Generally, small advertising accounts will have to pay for the additional services rendered over and above the cost of media purchased from the agency. However, larger accounts can expect some, if not all, of the aforementioned services, to be included as a part of the media fee paid. In other words, these services may be performed free of charge if large amounts of media are purchased.

Advertising agencies are located in the yellow pages of most phone books. In addition, talking to various media and other businesses may provide information concerning the services and reputation of various agencies. Also, several professional advertising associations might provide referrals upon request. The names and addresses are listed below.

American Advertising Federation
1225 Connecticut Avenue, N.W.
Washington, D.C. 20036
(202) 659-1800

American Association of Advertising Agencies
666 Third Avenue
New York, New York 10017
(212) 682-2500

Mutual Advertising Agency Network
8335 Jefferson Avenue
Detroit, Michigan 48214
(313) 821-0120

National Advertising Agency Network
14 East 48th Street
New York, New York 10017
(212) 355-7230

Referring to the publication entitled *Standard Directory of Advertising Agencies* will provide comprehensive information on most agencies, including their areas of specialty. This work can normally be found in a library. If not, write to the publisher and request the three-volume set. The cost is $157, at last word. It may seem expensive but consider the time and money associated with an extensive search.

National Register Publishing Company, Inc.
5201 Old Orchard Road
Skokie, Illinois 60077
(312) 470-3100

ASSOCIATIONS (TRADE AND PROFESSIONAL)

Trade and professional associations represent a specific group of businesses or individuals that find themselves in the same or similar line of business. Many trade associations maintain assistance programs designed to help and serve the firms they represent. Newsletters, seminars, toll free hotline, etc., are but a few services offered by many of these trade organizations. In addition, quite a few associations collect and analyze financial data in reference to the whole industry it serves as well as individual firms. This information is organized, and in many cases made available to members and prospective entrepreneurs wishing to enter the industry through a start-up operation or by purchasing an existing firm.

A list of trade and professional associations can be found by referring to the two publications given below. One or both should be found in most libraries. If not found, write or call the publishers for details and the cost to acquire the books.

Encyclopedia of Associations
Publisher—Gale Research Company
Book Tower
Detroit, Michigan 48226
(313) 961-2242

National Trade and Professional Associations of the United States
Publisher—Columbia Books, Inc.
        777 14th Street, N.W.
        Washington, D.C. 20005
        (202) 737-3777

There are many associations that represent the interest of the small business community in general. Some will provide useful information that could be utilized by an entrepreneur or existing firm when evaluating overall business conditions and trends and, in some cases, specific opportunities. These organizations are listed in Appendix M.

BANK OF AMERICA
The prestigious Bank of America constantly collects and analyzes data on the problems of starting a small business. These studies are made public through the bank's own publication called the *Small Business Reporter*. Individual reports on the businesses mentioned in Appendix N can be obtained by writing to the following address:

    Bank of America
    Department 3120
    P.O. Box 37000
    San Francisco, California 94137

CHAMBERS OF COMMERCE
Local chambers of commerce can provide valuable assistance to prospective entrepreneurs and existing small businesses. Besides facilitating interaction between local business people, civic groups, and professionals, CC's can be an important source of community contacts that could help any business. In addition, many chambers of commerce maintain small business committees that are used to promote and/or assist small firms within the area they serve. Also, some chambers have strong ties to the U.S. Small Business Administration and other governmental bodies, including state and local agencies that represent the interests of small enterprises.

Some chambers collect statistical data on the communities they serve and make this information publicly available. Facts concerning sales, income structure, growth patterns, etc., may be acquired so as to assist in the planning function. A listing of all chambers of commerce in the world can be obtained by referring to a publication entitled,

World Wide Chamber of Commerce Directory. If it cannot be found in a library, write the publisher mentioned below. The book costs less than $10, at last word.

Johnson Publishing Company, Inc.
P.O. Box 455, 8th and Van Buren
Loveland, Colorado 80537

COMPETITION

Competitors are almost always looked upon as "the enemy." However, with a little creative thinking, competitors can be viewed as a source of vital information. Some will candidly provide useful data upon being asked and others will not. Even if some competitors are strict about conveying ideas and information, their actions in the market place can reveal interesting particulars worth noting. For example, an unanticipated price hike may indicate that a competitor is experiencing unusually strong demand, falling profit margins, or increasing cost pressures. It may also signal a shift in marketing strategy or tactics. So, always ask questions, listen, and observe.

CUSTOMERS

Customers can yield valuable tips about the firm's image to the public at large. Many small business entrepreneurs have been shocked to hear the comments about their business from their clientele. Before starting a small business, it is wise to speak with potential customers. They might reveal some pros and cons that may not have been apparent upon initial or later evaluation. In reference to buying a going concern, seeking out current and potential customers could be an excellent way to gauge the viability of the enterprise being considered for acquisition.

FINANCIAL INSTITUTIONS

Local financial institutions have an intimate knowledge of the community they serve. Therefore, they can be an important source of information concerning business prospects. Many will help in analyzing financial data concerning the local economy and specific business opportunities. Most know what businesses can work in the community and which ones have a high chance of failure. Some even know which locations are good or bad for particular types of businesses.

FRIENDS, FAMILY, AND ASSOCIATES

Personal and professional relationships can yield valuable information even though extensive research is being conducted. Drawing on the combined experiences of friends, relatives, and associates can augment existing research efforts and in some cases fill knowledge vacuums that may exist. Soliciting advice can also bring to bear some interesting insights often under-emphasized or overlooked in the research endeavor. In some cases, it may provide profit opportunities, and in other situations, help avoid financial disaster.

U.S. presidents have been known to call on family members and friends when delineating major policy directions. John Kennedy constantly consulted his father on civil rights issues and Jimmy Carter drew on his mother and Southern friends for advice. Even his daughter, Amy, was consulted on nuclear arms questions.

Soliciting advice can be like picking peaches. Generally, a yield of good, average, and rotten fruit is collected. Therefore, when absorbing advice from friends, family, and/or associates, consider the source very carefully. Was previous advice and information solid and sound? If so, to what degree? If not, watch out.

INSURANCE COMPANIES

Insurance companies and their local agents can provide useful information relating to the reduction of liability under a number of conditions. Besides providing the traditional business insurance services such as casualty, health, and life protection, many are involved in the reduction of risks relating to defective products or services, non-payment of client accounts, international transactions, etc.

To find out which companies are involved in comprehensive risk reduction programs may require some time and energy. It may take time in finding the right kind of insurance combination required at a good price. Generally, calling local agents will reveal vital and necessary information. Again, talking to bankers, attorneys, accountants, and consultants will usually provide insight into the types of insurance required and where to find it.

Some insurance companies provide additional services to small firms and prospective entrepreneurs. These services can range anywhere from setting up pension and profit sharing plans to providing in-house consulting services on such things as cash-flow and resource management.

Legal Community

Attorneys are important in the business process and should be utilized when there are any doubts and/or unanswered questions about any proposition. An existing enterprise should use an attorney when examining situations that can have legal ramification either now or in the future. Start-up firms need to seek out legal assistance on matters such as legal structure, personal and business liabilities, permits, licenses, etc. Besides the items just mentioned, attorneys can help in the following areas:

— Analysis and evaluation of contracts
— Negotiation with investors, lenders, and suppliers
— Compliance with legal statutes and codes
— Defense in legal matters
— Identification of capital sources

Attorneys are listed in the yellow pages of the phone book. In addition, calling or writing the state bar association, which is usually located in the capital city of a particular state, will yield a list of lawyers located in a given area of that state, if requested. However, the best source of contact information concerning competent legal help will come from bankers, accountants, and business consultants. Most work with legal expertise on a regular basis and are in a position to know the best lawyer for a given situation. Also, try other businesses in a related field. Some good legal contacts may surface.

Consulting the publication entitled *The Lawyer's Register By Specialties and Fields of Law* may provide some helpful sources. If not located in a library, the book may be obtained by contacting the publisher at the address below.

Lawyer's Register Publishing Company
5325 Naiman Parkway
Cleveland, Ohio 44139

The cost is $49.50

Libraries (Public, Private and College)

Most large and medium-sized libraries maintain an array of business books and periodicals that can be helpful to any existing or prospective entrepreneur. In addition, some have learning resource centers with the latest in business-related audio and visual aids. Normally, cities with a population of around 5,000 have at least one library, although they generally lack adequate materials and facilities. There is an exception to this rule. Small towns harboring universities or colleges may have the advantage of the institution's library resources. Libraries within population centers exceeding 100,000 are more sophisticated and detailed in their information delivery capabilities. All things being equal, college and university libraries tend to be the best for business research purposes.

Many of the large state universities collect, assimilate, and publish an array of economic information on local areas within the state it serves. The quality of this data tends to be very high and can provide a small firm or prospective entrepreneur with valuable information when planning or analyzing opportunities.

PLANNING DISTRICTS
(ECONOMIC DEVELOPMENT CENTERS)

Many localities belong to planning districts. These districts maintain offices and are funded by one or more communities for the purpose of coordinating growth objectives. They gather, dissiminate, organize, and publish an array of data about the areas they serve. The information tends to be somewhat technical, but it can prove helpful to any firm or individual examining potentials within a locality. Market trends, population shifts, income patterns, activity in certain lines of business, are but a few of the types of information available from the office of a good planning district. Call the municipal manager of the local government to find out if such an organization exists and how to make contact if it does.

Some local governments call planning districts economic development companies or centers.

MANAGEMENT CONSULTANTS

Every business occasionally finds itself in a management situation that it cannot directly control or correct. When this condition prevails, a management consultant can be hired to help with the difficulties. In addition, a prospective entrepreneur may want to use a consultant to assist in the start-up phase of a new enterprise. Keep in mind that most of these consultants specialized in particular segments of management, although some generalists remain.

The management consulting profession is an unregulated industry requiring no certification. Consequently, many calling themselves consultants actually lack in the necessary education and expertise needed to be a good advisor. Given these circumstances, carefully examine the educational background and experience of any consultant before signing a service contract. Ask for client references and check them out thoroughly to insure the credibility and capability of the consultant.

Bankers, lawyers, and accountants can be excellent sources in providing contact with management consultants. Also, talking with potential or existing competitors may reveal some consultants willing to provide services in the area of business contemplated or currently being exploited. Another source of referrals are the professional associations that represent management consultants. Some maintain codes of ethics to enhance the credibility of their membership. These organizations are listed below.

Associations of Management Consultants
500 North Michigan Avenue, Suite 1400
Chicago, Illinois 60611
(312) 661-1700

Association of Consulting Management Engineers
230 Park Avenue
New York, New York 10169
(212) 697-9693

Institute of Management Consultants
19 West 44th Street
New York, New York 10036
(212) 921-2885

Society of Professional Management Consultants
16 West 56th Street
New York, New York 10019
(212) 586-2041

MARKETING CONSULTANTS

Like management problems, marketing difficulties can also surface demanding the attention of outside expertise. Market consultants should possess the same combination of education and experience as management advisors, except in different fields, of course. The types of assistance to expect from a marketing consultant include, but is not limited to, the following:

— Market research
— Market planning
— Mail order
— Direct mail
— Distribution
— Market testing
— Merchandising

Keep in mind that marketing consultants also tend to specialize in a particular field and a generalist may be difficult to locate. Checking the yellow pages of the phone books in larger cities will reveal some prospects. In addition, bankers, accountants, and attorneys may provide good contacts. The best leads are generally given by firms that are currently using or have employed a marketing consultant. When initially talking to consultants, always ask for background information and client references. Check the information out carefully to insure credibility. A bad consultant can be costly in terms of loss of time, markets, and money.

PERIODICALS

There are several excellent periodicals that serve the small business community. Reading and studying the contents contained within their covers can prove to be helpful to the individual wishing to start or buy a business. Also, existing enterprises can find useful material relating to the operational matters. Some of the information to be found in these publications include, but is not limited to, the following:

— Successful management techniques
— Dealing with lenders and investors
— Sources of capital
— Government assistance programs
— Marketing techniques and tips
— Bartering of goods and services
— Exporting

Appendix O contains the names and addresses of these small-business oriented periodicals.

Public Relations Firms and Consultants

These organizations and consultants provide publicity services to firms or individuals wishing to exploit the news value of particular business happenings. Publicity is usually an inexpensive means of creating an image and/or generating sales. However, the public relations (PR) function does have limits and it should never be viewed as a substitute for advertising. In fact, PR is normally seen as an extension of the marketing effort.

Public relations firms and consultants are listed in the yellow pages of phone books in large and medium-sized cities. However, the best sources of contacts include business consultants, bankers, accountants, lawyers, and other businesses who have used PR services. In addition, contacting the professional association listed below might provide some referrals. When talking to potential firms or consultants, always ask for background information and investigate thoroughly.

Public Relations Society of America
845 Third Avenue
New York, New York 10022
(212) 826-1750

Also, it is important to remember that many advertising agencies perform public relations services. When searching for advertising expertise, ask about PR functions as well.

Suppliers

Some vendors provide a wealth of information and help to new or existing businesses in the field they serve. A few suppliers will even go so far as to set up an entrepreneur in business by providing location, inventory, and financial assistance. Most do not go to those extremes, but many will help in one or more vital areas.

Constantly search for new suppliers. Evaluate their services and credit terms carefully. It is not unethical to play them against each other. In fact, it makes good business sense. Tell one or more suppliers that a better deal can be obtained elsewhere. Watch for their reactions. Some will bend and others will not.

Suppliers can be located in a set of publications known as *The Thomas Registers*. Most libraries have the volumes. If not available otherwise, they can be obtained by writing to the publisher whose address and phone number appears below. Inquire concerning information and the cost involved.

Thomas Publishing Company
One Penn Plaza
New York, New York 10001
(212) 695-0500

UNIVERSITIES AND COLLEGES

Many institutions of higher education have resources available for use by the small business community. Most college and universities maintain large numbers of books, magazines, and newsletters in the fields of business and economics that can be used for research or other related purposes. In addition, these institutions offer numerous classes which, if taken, may provide helpful information. Currently, over 300 business schools offer courses in "small business management" and/or "entrepreneurism." The U.S. Small Business Administration is compiling a list of these colleges and it should be available soon. A call to the regional SBA office may reveal how to get the list. Also, many business professors moonlight as free-lance, part-time consultants offering their expertise at rates normally below those charged by established consulting firms. They can be a source of valuable information.

Some business schools want their students to work on outside projects so as to allow them real-life experiences. Many schools make it a requirement. These colleges are always looking for challenging situations that can be used as a proving ground for their students. Generally, no fee is charged to the entrepreneur or small firm and these students can provide valuable talent in most problem situations.

Seminars and workshops are additional services provided by some institutes of higher education to existing businesses of all sizes and to prospective entrepreneurs. Topics can cover the entire business spectrum and the fees are normally low. Many of these interaction meetings are held in unison with the U.S. Small Business Administration, U.S. Department of Commerce, state or local chambers of commerce, or other bodies representing business interests.

Call the local college or university for details.

Chapter IV

CORRECT LEGAL STRUCTURE
Evaluation Is Necessary

Legal Forms of Organization

It is vitally important that entrepreneurs select the correct form of legal structure. Whether it is a new business just starting out or an existing operation, the legal form will determine to a great extent the way in which business is conducted, not to mention tax affairs. It will also affect the degree of freedom to operate within the total business environment.

Selecting the most appropriate form of legal organization is easier said than done. Many aspects must be examined, taking into account both personal and business considerations.

Five kinds of legal structure are in general use today. They are as follows: sole proprietorship, general partnership, limited partnership, corporation, and subchapter S corporation. Each has unique characteristics with certain advantages and disadvantages that need to be evaluated. Only the form which maximizes the interests of the entrepreneur and business should be selected.

SOLE PROPRIETORSHIP

Over 95 percent of all businesses in the country are classified as proprietorships. It is the simplest form of legal structure generally requiring only a local business license to operate. Normally, the owner also serves as manager. The primary advantages of this structure are as follows:

— Easy to form—Establishing a sole proprietorship is simple and inexpensive, requiring little or no government approval. Check with the local court clerk to determine if there are any licensing requirements.
— Owner keeps all of the profit—The owner is entitled to all profits generated by the business.
— Freedom from government regulation—Most government agencies direct their regulatory efforts toward large corporate entities, although the government paperwork requirement for small businesses has increased somewhat over the last decade. Whatever the case, small firms are expected to comply with all local, state, and federal regulations even though governmental policing is held to a minimum.
— Low Taxes—The owner of a sole proprietorship is taxed as an individual, at a rate normally lower than the corporate tax rate.
— Complete control—The owner makes all of the decisions and determines management policy.
— Quick decisions—Generally, one person can make quicker decisions than a number of individuals.
— Little working capital needed—In many cases, sole proprietorship can be operated with limited capital requirements.
— Easy to terminate—A sole proprietorship can quickly and easily cease operations without red tape.

Disadvantages of the sole proprietorship form of legal organization are listed below.

— Lack of continuity—If the owner becomes ill and/or dies, the business may terminate.
— Unlimited liability—The owner is legally responsible for all debts of the business without question. If the business fails and there are debts outstanding, creditors may sue the owner to satisfy their claims. The owner's personal assets could be at risk. Certain types of loss (physical, personal injury, theft, etc.) can be prevented by maintaining adequate insurance programs.
— Capital starvation—Some proprietorships have difficulty raising money because of the limited funding alternatives available to the legal form (only one owner, can't sell stock, etc.).
— Owner spread too thin—The owner has to wear many hats performing a number of diverse business functions (marketing, purchasing, bookkeeping, etc.).

— Lack of Expertise—Generally, a proprietorship is a "one person" show with limited experience in many facets of business operations and unable to attract needed expertise because of its small size and/or little growth potential.

— Difficult to transfer ownership—Selling all or part of a sole proprietorship can be equated to the difficulty in transacting real estate. In fact, many times real estate is involved.

GENERAL PARTNERSHIP

A partnership is defined by the Uniform Partnership Act "as an association of two or more persons to carry on as co-owners of a business for profit." Most general partnerships are evidenced by a written agreement called "Articles of Partnership." Though these articles are not required by law, most individuals involved in partnerships agree it is in the best interest of all to have a written agreement. In addition, the articles should be recorded with the clerk of the local court as a matter of public record for the protection of all individuals associated with the partnership. Articles of Partnership are designed mainly to spell out the contributions made by each partner to the business, whether by money or property, and the responsibilities of the partners in the firm. Table 8 lists the different types of partners that may be involved in partnership activities.

TABLE 8

TYPES OF PARTNERS

Ostensible (General) Partner—Active in the business and publicly known as being a partner.

Active Partner—Active in the business and may or may not be publicly known as being associated with the firm.

Secret Partner—Active in the firm but not presented publicly as a partner.

Dormant Partner—Inactive in the firm and not presented publicly as a partner.

Silent Partner—Inactive in the firm but can be presented as being associated with the partnership.

Nominal Partner—Not a partner in the firm but held out publicly to be a partner, usually for prestigious reasons. In some cases, these partners can be held liable for partnership activity if their names are used to represent the firm.

Subpartner—Not a partner but contracts with an active partner so as to participate in the partner's business and profits.

Limited Partner—Is not involved in managing the partnership, therefore his/her liability is limited to the amount invested and no more.

Below are some of the more common components of a general partnership agreement:

Name of the partnership
Its purpose
Date of formation
Its address
Name and address of partners
Duration of the partnership
Contributions made by each partner
How business expenses are handled
Division of profits and losses among partners
Duties and responsibilities of each partner
Salary and/or draw of each partner
Procedure for selling partnership interest
Method of accounting and recordkeeping
Handling the death of a partner
How to change the partnership agreement
How to handle disagreements
Dealing with absence and disability
Required and prohibited actions
Protection of remaining partners if a partner dies
Provisions for the retirement of partners

Advantages to the general partnership form of legal structure are mentioned below:

— Easy to form—Procedures and expenses are minimized.
— Enhanced capital availability—Two or more people will be providing and searching for capital. In addition, funding sources are more likely to entertain financing requests because of the broader capital base.
— Low tax rate—General partners are taxed as individuals. The individual tax rate is normally lower than that of a corporation.
— Broader management base—Two or more heads are better than one.
— Better quality employees—Partnerships tend to attract good employees because of the possibility of becoming a principal in the firm.
— Managerial flexibility—Generally, important decisions can be made quickly, although not as fast as in a sole proprietorship.
— Limited government interference—Like sole proprietorships, partnerships are normally free of extensive governmental scrutiny, although compliance with regulations is a must.

Disadvantages inherent in the general partnership include the following:

— Unlimited liability—The general partners are personally liable for the debts of the partnership. General partners can legally bind each other. This is why it is extremely important to know intimately the partners involved in the firm. Make sure all general partners are credible.
— Lack of continuity—Normally, a general partnership has a limited life and is terminated on the date specified in the Articles of Partnership or upon the death of a general partner. Termination can be avoided by stating in the articles that the partnership is perpetual.
— Divided authority—General partners may disagree, causing organization disharmony.
— Profits divided—Profits are shared by all general partners.
— Scarcity of suitable partners—Appropriate partners can be difficult to locate.

LIMITED PARTNERSHIP

Basically, limited and general partnerships share the same characteristics, with a few distinct differences worth noting. A limited partnership is defined as an association of at least one general partner and one limited partner. The limited partner is an individual who only invests capital and does not participate in managing the firm. In fact, the limited partnership form of business organization is viewed by many as a capital generating mechanism used quite frequently in real estate, oil and gas development, and mining deals. Very attractive tax benefits can be passed to investors involved in a limited partnership agreement.

The main thing to remember is that the general partner(s) in a limited partnership has unlimited liability for the debts of the business without question. On the other hand, limited partners are not liable for partnership debts if they do not participate in managing the business. Their personal assets are not at stake if the limited partnership incurs debts. They can only lose the amount invested and nothing more. Keep in mind that recent court rulings have determined that limited partners who actively get involved in management functions and affairs are not, in fact, limited partners and should be considered general partners, thereby assuming unlimited risk for the debts of the partnership.

If the limited partnership generates profits, the general partners are normally rewarded by receiving between one and 20 percent of all income produced after expenses are paid. The remaining 80 to 99 percent is divided among the limited partners. Percentages vary among different propositions.

CORPORATION

The corporation is the most complex legal structure discussed thus far. In 1819, Chief Justice Marshall defined a corporation as an "artificial being, invisible, intangible, and existing only in contemplation of the law." Consequently, the corporation is a legal entity separate from the people who own or operate it.

Corporations are normally formed subject to approval of the state government in the state in which the corporation will reside. If doing business in a number of states, the corporation needs to get the approval of each state and will be classified as a "foreign corporation" within those borders.

In order to form a corporation, an organizational meeting must take place. The organizer(s) must draft a corporate charter, also known as "Articles of Incorporation" which outline the powers and limitations of the proposed corporation. Table 9 shows an example of actual articles of incorporation that can be used by a Virginia corporation. The charter is then submitted to the secretary of state in the domicile state for approval. If the charter is disapproved, the secretary's office will probably recommend changes in the articles of incorporation so as to facilitate a positive decision. Table 9 illustrates an approved charter issued after articles of incorporation were submitted and accepted by the State of Virginia.

Typical articles of incorporation would include the following elements:

— Name of the corporation—Most states will not allow a corporation to pick a name similar to a corporate name already in existence, in order to avoid confusion. In addition, the name chosen may not be offensive or deceptive to the public. It is wise to call the State Corporation Commission or secretary of state to determine if the name selected can be used before submitting the articles of incorporation. Time and energy may be saved by avoiding disapproval and return of the articles. Some states will allow corporate organizers to reserve a name until the articles of incorporation are sent to the appropriate agency. Normally, there is a small fee for this service.

TABLE 9

ARTICLES OF INCORPORATION
of
Telemedia, Inc.

FIRST.—The name of this corporation is Telemedia, Inc.

SECOND.—Its registered office in the State of Virginia is located at *100 Anywhere Drive* in the City of *Winchester.* The registered agent in charge thereof is James L. Silvester who is a resident of the State of Virginia and who is a director of the corporation and whose business office is the same as the registered office of the corporation.

THIRD.—The purposes for which the corporation is organized are as follows:

A. To contract for and fund the development and production of television programs for distribution to cable television networks, on a syndicated basis to independent and major network owned and affiliated commercial television stations, to pay television systems, to public television stations and systems, and to such additional outlets as become available for programming. The Company intends to develop the ancillary marketing potential of these projects, and other projects independent of the television market, for distribution to the video disk and video cassette markets, audiocassette markets, records, radio, books, newspapers, and other print media, so as to enhance merchandising opportunities.

B. To do all other things lawful, necessary, or incident to the accomplishment of the purposes set forth above; to exercise all lawful powers now possessed by Virginia corporations of similar character; and to engage in any business in which a corporation organized under the laws of Virginia may engage except any business that is required to be specifically set forth in the articles of incorporation.

FOURTH.—The amount of the total authorized capital stock of this corporation is 50,000,000 common shares—par value .0003 cent per share, which equals fifteen thousand dollars ($15,000).

FIFTH.—The number of directors constituting the initial board of directors is *three,* and the names and addresses of the persons who are to serve as the initial directors are:

(Names and addresses are listed here)

SIXTH.—The directors shall have power to make and to alter or amend the By-Laws; subject to stockholders' rights under Section 13.1-24 of the codes of the State of Virginia; to fix the amount to be reserved as working capital, and to authorize and cause to be executed, mortgages and liens without limit as to the amount, upon the property and franchise of the corporation.

The By-Laws shall determine whether and to what extent the accounts and books of this corporation, or any of them shall be open to the inspection of the stockholders; and no stockholder shall have any right of inspecting any account, or book or document of this corporation, except as conferred by the law or the By-Laws, or by resolution of the stockholders.

The stockholders and directors shall have power to hold their meetings and keep the books, documents and papers of the corporation outside the State of Virginia, at such places as may be from time to time designated by the By-Laws or by resolutions of the stockholders or directors, except as otherwise required by the laws of the State of Virginia.

The object, powers, and purposes specified in any clause or paragraph herein above contained shall be construed as general powers conferred by the laws of the State of Virginia; and it is hereby expressly provided that the foregoing enumeration of specific powers shall in no wise limit or restrict any other power, object, or purpose of the corporation, or in any matter affect any general powers or authority of the corporation.

I, the UNDERSIGNED, for the purpose of forming a corporation under the laws of the State of Virginia, do make, file, and record these articles, and do certify that the facts herein are true; and I have accordingly hereunto set my hand.

DATED: _____   SIGNED: _____
                                            INCORPORATOR

— Purpose—The purpose for which the corporation was formed must be stated in precise terminology. Some states allow the use of broad language when stating corporate purpose, such as, "The purpose of the corporation is to engage in any lawful act or activity for which a corporation may be organized." However, most states want exact purposes clearly stated. Many corporate organizers use both approaches, for good reason. Making a specific statement of purpose will satisfy most states without question. In addition, others (such as funding sources) may look more favorably on the corporation if specific purposes are stated. Also, other states will be more willing to let the corporation do business within its borders without changing the corporate charter (articles of incorporation). A broad statement of purpose will give the corporation maneuvering room to expand into other profitable areas when opportunities arise.

— Life of the business—A statement of how long the corporation is to remain in business. It may be for months, years, or perpetuity. Some states will not require that this be answered, but will assume that the life is perpetual unless otherwise stated.

— Location—The address of the corporation's registered office must be stated. If the corporation wishes to incorporate in a state other than the one in which it resides, an office may be required in the other state. However, the establishment of the office can be avoided if the corporation appoints a "registered agent" in the state to act in behalf of its interests. The agent will be required to maintain certain corporate records and to accept communications between the state of incorporation and the corporation. Some states will require the agent representing the corporation to maintain an office. Some agents offer their services to many corporations wanting to incorporate in other states. Their fees for agent services are very reasonable. Call the State Corporation Commission or secretary of state in the state where incorporation is desired and ask for a list of registered agents.

— Incorporator(s)—The names and addresses of the incorporator(s) (organizers) need to be stated. Most states require that at least one incorporator be a resident of the state in which incorporation will take place.

— Capital Structure—The type of capital stock and the maximum amount authorized to be issued must be stated. The corporation must promulgate the number and class of shares to be offered. In addition, the privileges and limitations of each class of shares must be detailed in some states.

— Capital Requirement—Many states require a minimum capital infusion before the corporate charter (articles of incorporation) is approved.

— Preemptive Rights—A statement detailing the rights or restrictions of existing stockholders to purchase additional shares if issued by the corporation in proportion to their existing ownership interest before offering the new stock to prospective shareholders. Allowing preemptive rights gives existing shareholders the right to maintain their percentage control of the business.

— Initial Directors—The names and addresses of the individuals who will serve as initial directors must be given. These people serve until the first stockholder's meeting, after which they will either continue to serve or be replaced.

— Internal Affairs—A statement of how the corporation will be regulated. In most cases, by-laws are acknowledged as being the internal law of the corporation, and will be discussed below.

— Charter Changes—Procedures for changing the articles of incorporation should be stated even though it is defined in state law.

After the charter is approved by the state, stockholders need to have a meeting to adopt corporate by-laws and elect the board of directors. The board will in turn appoint the corporate officers. The by-laws are designed to serve as internal regulations that govern the operation of the corporation by establishing rights and limitations. Some by-laws will duplicate provisions of the articles of incorporation (charter) and state law. The most common by-laws used in corporation include, but are not limited to, the following:

— Address of the principal office. If preferred, all offices can be listed.
— Time, place, and required notification of annual stockholder meeting.
— Procedure for calling special stockholders' meetings.
— Required quorum and voting rights and limitations of stockholders.
— Number of corporate directors involved along with their compensation, if any. Lengths of terms of office, methods for electing and reelecting, and procedures for creating or dealing with vacancies on the board.
— Time, place, and required notification of regular board meetings.
— Procedures for calling special board meetings.
— Required quorum and voting rights and limitations of directors.
— Method of selecting corporate officers.
— Statement of major corporate officers (titles such as Chairman of the Board, Vice Chairman of the Board, President, Vice President, Treasurer, Secretary, etc.), including responsibilities and term of office.
— Procedures for creating new corporate positions and dealing with vacancies.
— Procedures for the issuance of stock.
— Form of stock certificate to use, including the terminology on the certificate.
— Procedures for handling stock transfers and record keeping.
— Procedure for the approval and issuance of dividends on a regular or irregular basis.
— Statement of the fiscal year.
— Sample of the corporate seal.
— Authorization to open financial accounts and sign checks.
— Procedures for issuing the annual statement and other periodic reports to the stockholders. Who's responsible.
— Steps and procedures for changing the by-laws.

The corporate form of legal structure has definite pros and cons. Advantages are listed below:

— Limited Liability—Stockholders are liable only for the amount of their investment, in most cases. In rare situations, stockholders may be at risk for more than the amount invested if the stock they purchase is assessable. Check the stock certificate. If it says "fully paid and assessable," liability may be greater than investment. However, most certificates read "fully paid and non-assessable" which means the risk is limited. Also, if the corporation is sued, stockholders are normally free of liability. However, managers may be subject to suit.

— Ease of Transferability—Ownership can be easily transferred by signing the stock certificate(s).

— Legal Entity—A corporation is a separate entity standing by itself, divorced from its owners and managers in the eyes of the law.

— Diversified Management—Some corporations have the ability to attract and draw on the skills of several individuals.

— Continuous Life—Corporations are generally perpetual in nature and can only be terminated by a vote of the stockholders. The state may revoke a corporate charter if laws are being broken by the corporation. Rarely, a corporation will elect to limit its life. This limitation must be stated in the articles of incorporation. If the corporation decides at a later date to be perpetual, the articles may be changed to reflect that wish.

— Ease in Raising Capital—Money can be generated by issuing shares of stocks and/or issuing bonds, in addition to the same funding methods available to other legal structures.

The corporate structure can present a number of difficulties to its owners and managers. Below are listed the most common:

— Government Interference—Corporations are more regulated than the other forms of legal organizations.

— Double Taxation—Corporations are taxed twice, in that they pay taxes on business income and then the stockholders must pay tax on their dividends. In addition, many states require corporations to pay a tax on their total capital.

— Corporate Formation—Starting a corporation is more difficult and usually more expensive than other legal forms.

— Charter Restrictions—The activities of a corporation may be limited by its articles of incorporation and laws not affecting other legal forms.

— Records—Normally, corporations require more bookkeeping responsibilities than do sole proprietorships or partnerships.

84 CORRECT LEGAL STRUCTURE

— Possible Liability—Many lenders will require the managers and major stockholders of a small corporation to endorse and guarantee loan agreements. This procedure may extend to other contractual agreements as well. This situation puts the personal assets of the managers and stockholders at risk.

It is not really difficult to form a corporation in most states. In fact, many entrepreneurs form their own without legal assistance, thereby saving hundreds or even thousands of dollars. Generally, states will assist in incorporation by providing booklets, forms, and samples to use in the process. Table 10 shows the sample "articles of incorporation" provided by the State of Virginia to prospective incorporators. Some states actually promote individuals to incorporate within their boundaries by using incentives. For example, Delaware, Nevada, and Wyoming are very popular incorporation states because of low capital taxes and a friendly attitude toward corporations. Also, these states have no corporate income taxes. Table 11 gives the names and addresses of the offices to contact in the above-mentioned states.

Normally, individuals can incorporate their businesses and expect no legal problems. There are instances in which the complexities of the business might necessitate an attorney being involved in the incorporation process. For example, a firm with many investors and/or engaged in interstate commerce might consider using legal assistance in putting the corporation together. The entrepreneur will have to decide for himself/herself if an attorney is needed. Whatever the case, most small business people should never pay over $300 in legal fees for incorporation services unless the business affairs of the business are complex. If self-incorporation is the desired approach, get a copy of the book, *How to Form Your Own Corporation Without a Lawyer for Under $50,* by Ted Nicholas. The publisher is Enterprise Publishing, Inc., located at 725 Market Street in Wilmington, Delaware 19801. It costs $14.95. This publication is considered the bible of self-incorporators, with over 750,000 in print. It includes ready-made forms to use along with the names, addresses, and fees for all state agencies involved in the incorporation process.

SUBCHAPTER S CORPORATION
A number of years ago, Congress recognized the need to increase the flexibility of small firms that use the corporate form of legal structure. Therefore, the subchapter S corporation was created and

TABLE 10

MODEL FORM FOR ARTICLES OF INCORPORATION

For a Virginia **stock corporation** for general business purposes

NOTE: This is designed as a model of the shortest permissible form of articles of incorporation; it contains all the required provisions. Other provisions may be added as desired in accordance with specific Sections of the Act to which reference should be made.

ARTICLES OF INCORPORATION
OF

_____

We hereby associate to form a stock corporation under the provisions of Chapter 1 of Title 13.1 of the Code of Virginia and to that end set forth the following:

(a)   The name of the corporation is

(b)   The purpose or purposes for which the corporation is organized are:

(c)   The aggregate number of shares which the corporation shall have authorized to issue and the par value per share are as follows:

CLASS AND SERIES	NUMBER OF SHARES	PAR VALUE PER SHARE OR NO PAR VALUE

NOTE: If there is to be more than one class of stock, the preferences, limitations and relative rights of the different classes should be set forth in this article.

(d)   The post-office address of the initial registered office is

_____, Virginia.
(Number)   (Street)   (Post Office)   (Zone)

The name of the city or the name of the county in which the initial registered office is located is_____

of_____ . The name of its registered agent is _____,

who is a resident of Virginia and who is a director of the corporation or who is a member of Virginia State Bar, and whose

business office is the same as the registered office of the corporation.

(e)   The number of directors constituting the initial board of directors is _____ and

the names and addresses of the persons who are to serve as the initial directors are:

Name   *Address*

Dated_____, 19_____.

_____

_____

_____

FEES ARE ON THE BACK OF THIS FORM   *Incorporators*

TABLE 11

Secretary of State
State of Delaware
Dover, Delaware 19901

Secretary of State
State of Nevada
Carson City, Nevada 89710

Secretary of State
State of Wyoming
Capitol Building
Cheyenne, Wyoming 82002

designed to permit closely held "small business corporations" to be treated as partnerships from a tax perspective, thereby eliminating double taxation. A standard corporation is taxed on two occasions. It must pay tax on its business income and then shareholders (owners) are taxed on the portion of net profits distributed and paid as dividends. Subchapter S provisions allow shareholders to absorb all corporate income or losses as partners and report it as individual taxpayers. In essence, the subchapter S corporation is not affected by corporate income taxes, thereby eliminating the double taxation feature of standard corporations. Aside from being treated as a partnership from a tax standpoint, the subchapter S and standard corporation share most of the same pros and cons, with a few exceptions.

A corporation must meet certain requirements before the subchapter S alternative becomes feasible. They are:

— The corporation must be a domestic entity (incorporated within the United States).
— The corporation can only have one class of stock.
— Only individuals or estates can be shareholders.
— The corporation cannot be part of another organization.
— The number of shareholders may not exceed 40.
— The corporation cannot have any nonresident alien shareholders.
— 20 percent or more of its revenue must be domestically generated.
— Dividends, interests, royalties, rents, annuities, and securities transactions cannot account for more than 20 percent of total revenues.

If the corporation meets all of the above requirements and wants to adopt the subchapter S option, it must do so within 75 days of starting business activity. In the case of an existing firm, adoption must be executed sometime within the initial 75 days of the firm's fiscal year. All shareholders in the business must give consent to electing the subchapter S structure. Their willingness will be evidenced by signing IRS Form 2553 which can be obtained by writing the local or regional IRS office. Table 12 illustrates this document. The adoption will remain effective until the corporation decides to cancel the status or the IRS revokes it because the firm has failed to maintain the required conditions. Cancellation will prevent the firm from adopting the subchapter S structure a second time in the near future. There is a waiting period of several years before the status can be renewed.

Subchapter S corporations do provide a few very attractive benefits to family corporations. Recent tax legislation has made it extremely advantageous to establish retirement programs under subchapter S provisions. In addition, family members who are shareholders can shift income from one member to another in order to minimize the tax bite. For example, a father in a high tax bracket can shift income to his son whose tax rate is lower, thereby reducing the tax burden on the whole family.

The major negative aspect of the subchapter S legal structure is its limitation on the number of shareholders it can assume (40 maximum). If the corporation is in an expansion mode and needs to raise additional funds over and above the financial capabilities of its present shareholders, the subchapter S status may have to be forfeited. The firm's management will need to evaluate the benefits of receiving the additional capital versus the cost of dropping the subchapter S form of legal organization. In addition, many states refuse to officially acknowledge the subchapter S form; therefore, corporate income or loss is not given preferential treatment under the income tax codes of the hostile state, although federal income tax advantages still exist.

Section 1244 Stock

Before forming a corporation it is wise to remember that certain tax incentives are available to make a business an attractive investment to prospective investors who may want to purchase stock (ownership) in the enterprise. When the directors have the first board meeting, they

TABLE 12

Form **2553** (Rev. October 1981) Department of the Treasury Internal Revenue Service	**Election by a Small Business Corporation** (Under section 1372 of the Internal Revenue Code) ▶ For Paperwork Reduction Act Notice, see instructions on back.	OMB No. 1545-0146 Expires 8-31-84

Note: This election under section 1372(a) to be treated as an "electing small business corporation" for income tax purposes can be approved only if all the tests in Instruction B are met.

Name of corporation (see instructions)	Employer identification number (see instructions)	Principal business activity and specific product or service (see instructions)
Number and street		Election is to be effective for tax year beginning (month, day, year)
City or town, State and ZIP code		Number of shares issued and outstanding (see instructions)
Is the corporation the outgrowth or continuation of any form of predecessor? . . . . . ☐ Yes ☐ No		Date and place of incorporation
If "Yes," state name of predecessor, type of organization, and period of its existence ▶		

If this election takes effect for the first tax year the corporation exists, complete A through H below, otherwise complete E through H.

A Date corporation first had shareholders	B Date corporation first had assets	C Date corporation began doing business	D Annual return will be filed for tax year ending (month)

E Name of each shareholder, person having a community property interest in the corporation's stock, and each tenant in common, joint tenant, and tenant by the entirety. (A husband and wife (and their estates) are treated as one shareholder. However, both must be listed below if both own interest in stock of the corporation.)	F Shareholders' Consent Statement. We, the undersigned shareholders, consent to the corporation's election to be treated as an "electing small business corporation" under section 1372(a). *(Shareholders sign and date below.)	G Stock owned		H. Social security number (employer identification number of estate or trust)
		Number of shares	Dates acquired	
1				
2				
3				
4				
5				
6				
7				
8				
9				
10				
11				
12				
13				
14				
15				

*For this election to be valid, the consent of each shareholder, person having a community property interest in the corporation's stock, and each tenant in common, joint tenant, and tenant by the entirety must either appear above or be attached to this form. (See instructions for column F.)

Under penalties of perjury, I declare that I have examined this election, including accompanying schedules and statements, and to the best of my knowledge and belief it is true, correct, and complete.

Signature and Title of Officer ▶   Date ▶

should consider the election of a section under the Internal Revenue Code (Number 1244) that allows an investor to treat a loss in "small business stock" as an ordinary instead of a capital loss, thereby enhancing its positive tax impact. In order for a corporation to qualify its shares as "section 1244 stock," it must approve the concept at the first director's meeting and before the issuances of any equity. Also, the shares issued can only be common stock and must be sold by the firm in exchange for money or property subject to a promulgated plan, with a few restrictions. Another legal limitation states that the amount of capital received for the shares may not exceed certain dollar limits that have been established.

Question Thyself

Before deciding what legal form to select, consider the following questions very carefully.

— What is the nature of liability from a personal standpoint?
— Would the business continue if the entrepreneur or other key principals of the firm became ill and/or died? Is it important that it does continue?
— Which legal structure would allow the greatest flexibility in management?
— Can additional capital be easily sought if needed?
— Can additional expertise be attracted if needed?
— Does the degree of regulation hamper business activity?
— What legal form can best fulfill the goals of the entrepreneur and business?

If in Doubt Look About

Many people lack the legal and accounting expertise needed to make a sound judgment about legal structure. Therefore, it is advisable to seek out the help of a competent tax attorney or certified public accountant (CPA) to insure the correct selection.

For Further Help

How to Form Your Own Corporation Without a Lawyer for Under $50, by Ted Nicholas. Enterprise Publishing, Inc., 725 Market Street, Wilmington, DE 19801. Price—$14.95

Tax and Business Organization Aspects of Small Business, by Jonathan Sobeloff. Joint Committee on Continuing Legal Education of The American Law Institute and The American Bar Association, 4025 Chestnut Street, Philadelphia, PA 19104

Selecting the Legal Structure for Your Firm. Free publication available from the U.S. Small Business Administration, P.O. Box 15434, Ft. Worth, Texas 76119. Ask for management aid number 231.

Incorporating a Small Business. Free publication available from the U.S. Small Business Administration, P.O. Box 15434, Ft. Worth, Texas 76119. Ask for management aid number 223.

Partnership Desk Book, by Burton J. Defren. Institute for Business Planning, IBP Plaza, Englewood Cliffs, NJ 07632.

Chapter V

NATURE OF SMALL BUSINESS FINANCING
Be Prepared

Capital and Small Business

That old maxim that suggests it takes money to make money is as true today as it was a century ago. Both new and existing businesses must have access to financial resources in order to take advantage of profitable situations that may arise. Funds are needed to market new products, pay vendors, meet payrolls, buy equipment, and extend credit to customers, just to mention a few business activities.

Money alone will not insure you a successful operation. Capital, like any resource, must be managed efficiently in order to maximize profits. Many cash rich firms have failed to turn profits because of poor or inadequate financial management. For example, a company that has large cash deposits on hand in a checking account, earning nominal interest income, may feel secure in the short term. But these are idle funds, not being used to generate revenues, which are vital in creating adequate profits.

Many new and operating small businesses suffer from undercapitalization and/or funds mismanagement. These afflictions are major causes of business failures. Generally, the end result is a capital squeeze forcing the owners to close down. The trick is to recognize the problem, early in the ball game, before it becomes reality and unmanageable, thereby avoiding the squeeze altogether.

Capital and the New Business

The capital requirements to start a new business will vary depending upon many factors. These need to be analyzed and investigated with great care so as to avoid underestimating financial resources needed to start and carry the business until profits are generated internally to support operations. For example, the type of operation you are starting will determine, to a great extent, your initial capital needs. A manufacturing operation will require more capital than a retail establishment. Wholesaling outlets tend to require more funds than service firms. Other items that need to be considered include location of the enterprise, current and projected economic climate, product/service to be offered, credit policies, etc.

A lot of thought and consideration should be given when studying your initial capital requirements. Many entrepreneurs, with good products and services, fail in their business attempts because of underestimating capital requirements in the beginning.

Tables 13 and 14 are provided courtesy of the Small Business Administration. If used correctly, they will provide you with estimates of capital needs to start any small business. It is advisable to have your lawyer and/or accountant assist you in completing the sheets. This will help in making accurate estimates. Once capital needs have been determined, the next step is to obtain the necessary funds to commence operation. These procedures will be discussed in Chapters VI-VIII.

Capital and the Existing Business

Many entrepreneurs fail to anticipate capital needs for present and future operations. Eventually, cash flow problems develop because of the undercapitalization and existing funds will prove inadequate in paying current obligations. This situation is not reserved exclusively for the small business person. Some large firms have met their demise because of failing to project funding needs. W.T. Grant, the giant discount chain, collapsed because it grew too quickly before uncovering sources of funds to finance the expansion. Cash flow problems developed that could not be reversed and the rest is history.

As a business expands, so do its capital needs. If growth increases faster than capital availability, a cash squeeze will occur causing financial hardship. Likewise, if the business is stagnant due to economic conditions and the availability of capital contracts, cash flow difficulties will ensue.

TABLE 13

ESTIMATED MONTHLY EXPENSES			
Item	Your estimate of monthly expenses based on sales of $ _____ per year	Your estimate of how much cash you need to start your business (See column 3.)	What to put in column 2 (These figures are typical for one kind of business. you will have to decide how many months to allow for in your business.)
	Column 1	Column 2	Column 3
Salary of owner-manager	$	$	2 times column 1
All other salaries and wages			3 times column 1
Rent			3 times column 1
Advertising			3 times column 1
Delivery expense			3 times column 1
Supplies			3 times column 1
Telephone and telegraph			3 times column 1
Other utilities			3 times column 1
Insurance			Payment required by insurance company
Taxes, including Social Security			4 times column 1
Interest			3 times column 1
Maintenance			3 times column 1
Legal and other professional fees			3 times column 1
Miscellaneous			3 times column 1
STARTING COSTS YOU ONLY HAVE TO PAY ONCE			Leave column 2 blank
Fixtures and equipment			Fill in table 14 and put the total here
Decorating and remodeling			Talk it over with a contractor
Installation of fixtures and equipment			Talk to suppliers from who you buy these
Starting inventory			Suppliers will probably help you estimate this
Deposits with public utilities			Find out from utilities companies
Legal and other professional fees			Lawyer, accountant, and so on
Licenses and permits			Find out from city offices what you have to have
Advertising and promotion for opening			Estimate what you'll use
Accounts receivable			What you need to buy more stock until credit customers pay
Cash			For unexpected expenses or losses, special purchases, etc.
Other			Make a separate list and enter total
TOTAL ESTIMATED CASH YOU NEED TO START WITH		$	Add up all the numbers in column 2

Source: U.S. Small Business Administration.

TABLE 14

LIST OF FURNITURE, FIXTURES, AND EQUIPMENT

Leave out or add items to suit your business. Use separate sheets to list exactly what you need for each of the items below.	If you plan to pay cash in full, enter the full amount below and in the last column.	If you are going to pay by installments, fill out the columns below. Enter in the last column your downpayment plus at least one installment.			Estimate of the cash you need for furniture, fixtures, and equipment
		Price	Downpayment	Amount of each installment	
Counters	$	$	$	$	$
Storage shelves, cabinets					
Display stands, shelves, tables					
Cash register					
Safe					
Window display fixtures					
Special lighting					
Outside sign					
Delivery equipment if needed					
TOTAL FURNITURE, FIXTURES, AND EQUIPMENT (Enter this figure also in table 13 under "Starting Costs You Only Have To Pay Once.")					$

Source: U.S. Small Business Administration.

TABLE 15

Cash Budget

(For three months, ending March 31, 19 _____)

	January		February		March	
	Budget	Actual	Budget	Actual	Budget	Actual
Expected Cash Receipts:						
1. Cash sales						
2. Collections on accounts receivable						
3. Other income						
4. Total cash receipts						
Expected Cash Payments						
5. Raw materials						
6. Payroll						
7. Other factory expenses (including maintenance)						
8. Advertising						
9. Selling expense						
10. Administrative expense (including salary of owner-manager)						
11. New plant and equipment						
12. Other payments(taxes, including estimated income tax; repayment of loans; interest; etc.)						
13. Total cash payments						
14. **Expected Cash Balance** at beginning of the month						
15. Cash increase of decrease (item 4 minus item 13)						
16. Expected cash balance at end of month (item 14 plus item 15)						
17. Desired working cash balance						
18. Short-term loans needed (item 17 minus item 16, if item 17 is larger)						
19. Cash available for dividends, capital cash expenditures, and/or short investments (item 16 minus item 17, if item 16 is larger than item 17)						
Capital Cash:						
20. Cash available (item 19 after deducting dividends, etc.)						
21. Desired capital cash (item 11, new plant equipment)						
22. Long-term loans needed (item 21 less item 20, if item 20 is larger than item 20)						

Source: U.S. Small Business Administration.

Capital needs arise because of many factors. Economic conditions on the local, state, or national level can cause revenues to temporarily decline, thereby making it difficult to meet obligations. Abnormal increases in accounts receivable (customer accounts) due to asset mismanagement and/or unexpected growth can cause a need for financial resources. Increasing inventory levels to support revenue growth and the purchase of new equipment to increase productivity will call for additional capital input. Purchasing merchandise before suppliers increase their prices and seasonal factors will increase the need to finance these inventories until sales are made and receivables collected. In addition, the exploitation of unexpected profit opportunities as they arise will call for capital over and above that which is normally available. Also, excessive withdrawal of earnings from the business and a reduction in credit or payment terms by suppliers will also increase capital needs.

Causes of capital shortages cannot be traced to any single event. There is a combination of factors that create the problems. Identification and positive reaction to these anticipated funding problems will insure proper cash flow and help avoid a potentially injurious capital squeeze. The cash budget in Table 15 will help project the capital needs for a business already in operation. The table, listing only three months, should be expanded to include an entire year, taking into consideration yearly objectives.

An accountant should assist when recording the projections. If expense records are maintained and posted to the table on a monthly basis, a comparison between budget estimates and actual expenditures can be made. Any variances that exist (differences between what was budgeted and actually spent) can be analyzed to determine the effects upon the financial structure of the business.

Chapter VI

UNDERSTANDING MONEY SOURCES
The Bank Isn't the Final Stop

Never Enough Money

Once you start or buy a small business, your need for capital is constant. Money is needed to finance current operations, expansion, seasonal inventories, and, in some cases, just to stay afloat. Unfortunately, traditional sources of funding for entrepreneurs have been less accommodating lately. Commercial banks, which supply over 65 percent of small business capital requirements, have downgraded their commitment to small firms. Many banks are raising service fees to small businesses above that which is charged their larger business customers. What's more, small firms usually are charged higher interest rates on loans than are larger businesses. Aspiring entrepreneurs, wishing to start their own businesses, have been left out in the cold almost completely. Banks claim that financing new, unproven enterprises is just too risky. To make matters worse, the U.S. Small Business Administration, which has come to be known as the lender of last resort, and other government funding outlets, have fallen victim to the Reagan budget ax.

Individuals wishing to start new businesses or expand existing operations do have alternatives when seeking capital beyond the traditional avenues of friend, family, self, and banks. Many of these are overlooked by entrepreneurs in the search process.

Capital Evolution

The capital needs of a business will be determined, to a great extent, by its stage of evolution. Each stage will demand different funding requirements. An understanding of these are needed in order to adequately project the need for financial resources.

- Seed Stage—This is capital to formulate an idea. The product or service is still on the drawing board being developed. At this stage market feasibility studies are conducted and examined. Most of this funding is provided by the entrepreneur and/or close associates, although it should be pointed out that some financial organizations have begun to fund businesses in the seed stage.

- Start-up Stage—This type of financing is used to get the new company off the ground. Product/service development is being completed and it has been determined that a market exists. Major emphasis is placed on developing managerial expertise, completing final market studies, projecting financial resources, etc. Generally, the product or service is not being marketed at this point.

- First Stage—This funding is provided to launch production of the product or service and to initiate marketing efforts.

- Second Stage—Capital is made available to finance initial cash flow and facilitate expansion of the new company. At this point, the company is not usually showing a profit. Money is needed to support inventories and accounts receivable (customer accounts) until sufficient profits are generated to support operations.

- Third Stage—Normally this money is provided to expand the business on a large scale. Sales are growing very rapidly and profits are being generated. Very little of the market for the firm's product or service has been exploited and funds are needed to support additional marketing endeavors, production, and working capital.

- Fourth Stage (also referred to as bridge financing)—This capital is used as interim financing until financial resources are obtained through a public offering of stock. At times, the bridge money is repaid out of the proceeds of the stock offering once executed. In this stage the company is attempting to make the transition from small firm to medium-size business. Subsequent public offerings can be made in order to continue expansion and growth.

- Acquisition Funding—Resources made available to allow a company to expand by purchasing other firms is an example of acquisition financing. Mergers and consolidations are common results of using this method of funding.

- Leverage Buyout—This financing technique can be used when the existing net assets of a company exceed its selling price. Since most companies are sold based upon a multiple of earnings, and that multiple has been decreasing over the last decade due to economic conditions, companies can be purchased by third parties utilizing assets as collateral for loans provided to these parties by financial outlets and/or previous owners. Management and employees can use this method to purchase their company. There have been cases reported where management teams have bought entire firms, using leverage techniques, without investing a penny of their own funds.

Capital Generation—Two Forms

Profits generated within a business can be used to finance various aspects of a firm's operation. This is referred to as *internal funding* and is an inexpensive source of money. Internal capital generation can be achieved in several ways. Cutting costs, selling surplus inventories and equipment, speeding up collection of accounts receivable, and retaining more profits in the business are a number of ways to augment internal capital.

In contrast, capital generated outside the business is called *external* financing. Outlets such as banks, suppliers, commercial finance companies, and investment bankers would be examples of sources external to the firm. Generally there are costs associated with this form of financing and they will be discussed later in this chapter.

Before utilizing external sources, a company should determine if its capital requirements can be met internally. Even though this may not generate all capital requirements needed, it will reduce dependency on external funding, thereby reducing interest costs and/or loss of control. Furthermore, the demonstrated capability to maximize internal capital will enhance the confidence of lenders and investors in the company and its management. This will increase their incentive to commit financial resources on a reasonable basis.

Utilizing internal funding can be costly at times. For example, selling assets to generate cash may have to be done at a loss; unloading certain fixed assets now may force the business to pursue costly sources of materials later on down the road; rigorous inventory reductions may cause stock shortages needed to generate production and/or sales; and the tightening of credit policies may result in loss of customers.

Generally speaking, a business that uses internal financing to the maximum will benefit from the approach. Although, this policy may have to be altered if at some point in the future external funding is needed, especially equity capital. Many equity investors are interested in dividend income. These investors may be discouraged if the firm's policies mandate reinvesting all net income in the business without rewarding investors in the form of dividends. Some speculative investors may be interested only in the capital gain potential of an investment (increase in the value of their investment) without expecting dividend income. Normally, investors expect both dividend yield and capital gains.

What Kind of Capital

When seeking funding alternatives for your small business, it is important to analyze carefully the purpose for which the capital will be used. This will determine the kinds of funds needed to carry out your objectives. Deciding what type of capital to employ can be a difficult task since many of the kinds of capital available, although different in name, can be used at the same time and for similar or identical purposes.

In general terms, there are two ways to fund a new or existing business. Many firms use a combination of these to finance operations. *Debt financing* is simply money borrowed from a lender, where you promise to repay the principal amount of the loan plus interest on agreed-upon terms, usually evidenced by a contract (loan agreement). *Equity financing* is somewhat different. This technique allows a business owner to exchange ownership in the firm for capital resources. These funds do not have to be repaid like a loan, but the equity investor will expect a return on investment in the form of stock dividends and/or capital gains upon selling the stock back to you or a third party. The major disadvantage to this form of financing is your loss of some control over the business because of the new owners.

Debt comes in several forms. A loan can be *unsecured,* in which no collateral is used to back the note. Your credit reputation is the only security available to the lender in this agreement. On the other hand, the *secured* loan is backed by some form of asset to insure the lender against loss due to nonrepayment. Even borrowers with good credit histories may be required to pledge assets occasionally due to economic conditions, bank policy changes, and industry shifts. Generally, it depends on the lender's perception of your financial condition. For example, if a prospective borrower's financial statements are in question as to ability to support a loan, the lender will be inclined to ask for collateral. The more common types of loan security are:

- Guarantor—This individual or firm guarantees payment of an obligation as evidenced by signing a contract (guarantor agreement).

- Endorsers—An endorser signs the obligation agreement and in some cases may have to post collateral. If the principal borrower defaults, the endorser is expected to pay.

- Comaker—A comaker is a principal in an obligation agreement. The borrower and comaker share joint responsibility.

- Accounts Receivable (Customer accounts)—These are commonly used as collateral on short-term loans. Repayment is made when customers pay on their accounts.

- Equipment—A lender will consider making loans against equipment that has been paid in full. The lender will determine the fair market value of the equipment and will lend up to a certain percentage (usually 60 percent) of that value.

- Marketable Securities (stocks and bonds)—Lenders will accept securities as collateral if they are readily marketable. Generally, financial sources will advance no more than 70 percent of the market value so as to protect against price declines. If the security prices drop below what the lender considers acceptable, then the borrower might have to post additional assets. These terms are spelled out in the loan contract.

- Real Estate—Most financial outlets consider real estate excellent collateral and will normally lend up to 90 percent of market value of the property.

- Savings Accounts—Certificates of deposit and savings accounts can be used to secure loans. The lender will hold the certificate or passbook as collateral with the right to the funds if default occurs. In most cases, lower rates of interest are offered on these loans because of the liquid nature of the pledged assets. These are commonly referred to as passbook or certificate loans.

- Chattel Mortgage—This instrument is somewhat like a real estate mortgage in that they both secure loans with property. In this case equipment is being used for collateral purposes. The lender will evaluate the present and future market value of the equipment and then advance funds amounting to something less than the present value. The business will be expected to make up the difference through a down payment and/or trade-in. If default occurs, the lender can foreclose on the equipment. The business must maintain the equipment and insure it against accidental loss.

- Insurance Policies—Lenders will accept life insurance policies as collateral for loans. They will advance up to the cash value of the policy and it must be assigned to them. When the terms of the loan contract are fulfilled, the policy can be reassigned back to its original status.

- Warehouse Merchandise—Financial institutions will lend up to a certain percentage of the market value of merchandise being stored in a bonded warehouse. The goods must be marketable and evidenced by a warehouse receipt, which is the collateral document used to secure the loan.

- Display Merchandise—Cars, appliances, furniture, etc., can be financed through a technique known as floor planning by using trust receipts as collateral. Lenders will advance funds against display merchandise, held in trust by the borrower, to be repaid when the items are sold.

- Leases—A lender holding a mortgage on property involved in a lease transaction may demand assignment of the lease such that rent payments are made directly to the lender. This will help insure loan repayments.

Collateral requirements and lender demands can place limitations upon your business activities. If the company is considered a good credit risk, limitations will be minimized. Conversely, a bad risk will be met with stiff conditions. Knowing the kinds of restrictions which a lender may demand will help you understand their possible effect on your business. Below are some of the more common loan restrictions used in lending transactions.

— Restriction of your ability to take on additional debt
— Limitation of the selling of accounts receivable and/or excess inventories to raise cash
— Prevention of dividend (earnings) pay-out beyond a certain level to insure that enough funds are left in the business to retire debt
— Maintenance of certain levels of working capital
— Necessity of supplying the lender with appropriate financial statements on a periodic basis

All lending restrictions are known as covenants and appear in the loan contract. Negative covenants limit the borrower's ability to act in certain areas without the permission of the lender. In contrast, positive covenants outline specifically the things which the borrower must do. The first three aforementioned loan restrictions are examples of negative covenants and the last two are positive.

When negotiating with lenders, keep in mind that they have three primary objectives. First and foremost on their minds is repayment of the loan. Lenders will evaluate a prospective borrower's ability to repay by analyzing the loan application and supporting documentation required to be completed. This will be explained in more detail in Chapter VIII. These forms will determine the ability to generate adequate cash to make loan payments without adversely affecting other organizational needs, such as working capital. Second, lenders are concerned with protecting their lending position. It is the nature of financial outlets to insure the money they lend with collateral agreements and loan restrictions (some were mentioned earlier). Third, lenders will attempt to charge the highest interest rate possible so as to maximize profits. Keep in mind that they are subject to market forces and must compete with other financial institutions. Letting them know that you have other alternatives might help in achieving a lower rate.

Before signing a loan agreement, make sure you and your attorney and/or accountant read the documentation carefully. No matter how desperate you are for the funds, make sure your interests are represented and protected. Attempt to negotiate terms that limit your restrictions. You will find· that lenders will bargain on certain loan conditions. Also, keep in mind that after the loan is made, many financial outlets will amend loan restrictions, on a periodic basis, depending upon the financial health of your business at the time. For example, if after a year into the loan your business is expanding and profits growing, some loan restrictions may be removed by the lender. You might be able to assume additional debt or sell your accounts receivable to generate cash. On the other hand, if your business deteriorates, additional security and limitations could be called for under the terms of the loan agreement. The point to remember is that lenders are flexible and will negotiate loan conditions.

Time factors are also important in understanding debt financing. In many cases these factors will determine the interest rate to be charged on a loan and whether collateral should be used.

Short-term borrowings are used to finance inventories and accounts receivable. When inventories are sold and outstanding accounts paid by customers, the loans are expected to be repaid. Many lenders will do this on either a secured or unsecured basis depending upon the business. Firms that have seasonal needs will generally have to operate on a secured basis. Some financial outlets offer borrowers *lines of credit*. These allow access to funds for short-term demands without having to apply for a loan every time the need arises. There is an upper limit that can be borrowed, established by the lender, based on the firm's ability to repay. Lines of credit, like all short-term credit, are expected to be paid in full within a period of one year.

Intermediate loans run longer than one year but less than five. These loans can be secured with collateral or can be unsecured, and are used to finance equipment purchases. *Long-term borrowings* extend beyond five years. They are collateralized and used to finance acquisitions, leveraged buyouts, and major plant expansions.

The specific kind of money used can also be distinguished by the source of repayment. As we mentioned earlier, short-term notes are paid from funds generated by retiring customer accounts and inventory turnover. Intermediate and long-term loans are repaid out of business earnings.

Evaluation of Capital Alternatives

In considering your funding situation, you must evaluate the implications of choosing a course of action. This can be accomplished by studying the factors listed below. Your reactions to these will determine, to some extent, the kinds of capital sources pursued.

- Risk—Lenders are always exposed to some degree of risk when they invest their funds. Likewise, the recipient of the capital is also at risk. Debt funds must be repaid in the form of principal and interest. This can place strains upon the cash flow of the company. If debt burden becomes too great, default is a possibility and with it a host of other problems such as credit denial, foreclosure, and maybe even bankruptcy. Even if you recover, your ability to raise funds in the future could be impaired. Lenders will either refuse to do business with you or will charge exceptionally high interest rates because they perceive you to be a questionable credit risk.

- Maneuverability—Many lenders will require that you place restrictions on the firm's assets. They may ask that you refrain from selling or borrowing against accounts receivable, equipment, and/or inventories. These limitations will be written into the loan contract. If you break the agreement, the lender may have the right to call in the loan or charge a higher rate of interest. Loan restrictions were discussed in detail on pages 103-104.

  Another example of reduced flexibility is the reliance on just a few sources of capital. Avail yourself of as many financial outlets as possible. This will enhance your access to funding when needed.

  In addition, relying too much on internal financing as opposed to external, and vice versa, could also prove to be restricting. Capital that is available and is not being utilized to generate sales, will result in loss of growth and profits.

- Cost—Capital costs are determined by their effects on business profits and the current owners. There are situations in which business profits could be higher if equity financing were used instead of debt. But since the current owners' profit participation would be diluted by taking on new stockholders, the equity alternative is rejected. For example, consider a firm that is comparing the cost of debt with that of equity financing. The company has the option of borrowing $50,000 at 16 percent interest or selling 20 percent of the stock to equity investors. Net income is expected to reach $100,000 this year and the company's effective income tax rate is 30 percent. The cost of debt in this case can be determined by using the following formula:

Cost of Debt to the Present Owners
  = Interest Rate × (1 − Effective income tax rate)
  = 16 × (1 − .30)
  = 16 × (.70)
  = 11.2%

Assuming a one-year loan to be repaid in one installment, the interest expense would equal $5,600, reducing net income to $94,400. Since debt is used, the present owners are entitled to all profits. If the equity alternative is used by the firm, net income would be $100,000 because no interest expense would be incurred. However, only $80,000 could be claimed by the present investors, since $20,000 would be directed to the new owners for their investment. This is generally viewed by the current owner as a cost of doing business and can be determined in the formula below:

Cost of Equity to the Present Owners
  $$= \frac{\text{Earnings Directed to New Investors}}{\text{Investment}}$$
  $$= \frac{\$20,000}{\$50,000}$$
  = .40 or 40%

Even though the equity alternative produces higher net income, it will probably be rejected due to the loss of control and earnings on the part of the current owners. The losses are a cost to them as evidenced in the computation above.

- Availability—A business may find that its preferred sources of capital have dried up for any number of reasons (economic conditions, industry status, international events, company factors, etc.). At this point, the firm must pursue other funding alternatives. For example, a company may be using retained earnings (internal financing) and short-term debt to finance operations. If a recession sets in and profits contract, internal funds will become strained. In addition, high interest rates, which usually accompany economic downturns, will discourage borrowing. The business might be forced to seek equity funding despite loss of control and earnings in order to survive.

- Control—Using debt and internal financing will not compromise control of the present ownership in most cases. If lenders do get nervous, they might demand a representation in the firm's management structure which could affect control somewhat. The use of equity financing will reduce the control of present owners. The degree of loss will depend on the amount of equity exchanged for capital. New firms will need to give more equity (ownership) for the same amount of funds than the more established companies with track records. Normally, equity investors are entitled to managerial voting rights in proportion to the stock they own in the business.

Where to Turn—Private and Government Outlets

The capital sources outlined in this section represent only a broad overview of what is available to small businesses and prospective entrepreneurs. Specific and detailed information regarding these financial outlets can be found in Chapter XI.

SELF

In the early stages of your business endeavors, capital may be hard to find. If this is the case, you might have to rely on personal resources to finance operations until you gain the trust of creditors.

There are a number of ways to tap your hidden wealth. You might consider using the money in your savings accounts and/or certificates of deposit. This prospect may be disquieting to you, but there is a way to borrow against these accounts without disturbing the funds. It's called "passbook borrowing" and bankers don't like to talk about it. You can borrow up to the amount that is on deposit using savings accounts and certificates of deposit as collateral. The unique feature to this alternative is the interest rates. According to current regulations, financial institutions can charge between 1 and 5 percent above the rate being paid on the accounts. Most charge 2 or 3 percent. For example, let's say you want to borrow $25,000 to finance a start-up business. You have $12,000 in your savings account paying 5½ percent and $20,000 in a certificate of deposit drawing a 13 percent rate. You can borrow the $12,000 from your savings account for approximately 8 percent with the additional $13,000 coming from your certificate account costing in the neighborhood of 16 percent. Your total cost of capital, about 13 percent, is well below that which is currently charged by financial outlets for small business lending purposes. Your savings and certificate accounts will remain intact, earning interest income. In fact, some or all of that interest income can be used to offset the interest charges against the passbook loan. If you use this approach the cost of the loan can be reduced to below 13 percent, depending upon the amount of interest income used. Of course, the money in your savings and certificate accounts will fail to grow in proportion to the amount of interest income utilized to reduce loan cost.

Another possibility you might want to consider is the cash value of your life insurance policies. This money can be borrowed and repaid over a long period of time. Loan rates vary among insurance companies, but generally run between 6 and 8 percent. You might wonder if this affects your life insurance coverage. It does to a degree. For example, if $10,000 is borrowed from your $50,000 life insurance policy and soon after something happens to you, those policies will only pay $40,000, minus interest charges incurred, to your estate. This assumes that you do not make any principal or interest payments. If you did, the amount paid would increase accordingly. So in essence, your insurance is reduced by the amount owed against the policy. It would be wise to purchase inexpensive term life insurance to cover the amount you borrow so as not to adversely affect your beneficiaries.

The house in which you live is another source of financing worth exploring. Equity you have built in your home can be borrowed by getting a second mortgage. Many lenders will advance up to 80 or 90 percent of the value of your home minus the first mortgage. Some will go as high as 95 and a few will lend up to 100 percent, although this is very rare. Lenders want to protect themselves against a dip in housing prices that could negatively affect their collateral position. These loans can run as long as 15 years, but most lenders prefer a seven- to ten-year payback period.

To illustrate how a second mortgage can be used, let's say that you purchased a house in 1972 for $30,000. Currently, its fair market value, as determined by a certified appraiser, is $70,000. The first mortgage amounts to $22,000. Your borrowing ability based upon the above information is calculated as follows:

$$85\% \text{ of } \$70,000 = \$59,500$$
$$- \quad \underline{22,000} \text{ first mortgage}$$
$$= \$37,500 \text{ equity available for borrowing}$$

FAMILY AND FRIENDS

Relatives and acquaintances might be willing to help in financing your business venture. They can raise funds in the same manner as yourself, which was described in the previous section. Keep in mind that these individuals expect to be repaid with interest and/or profits which can reduce your future earnings. Some may want the business to post collateral in the form of plant and equipment, inventories, accounts receivable, etc. Many will demand a "piece of the action," thereby diluting your control, although if investors do buy in, specific collateral does not have to be offered. Their investment is secured by the stock they own.

If you face any of the above situations, be ready with some answers. Offer your friends and relatives a reasonable interest rate on loans. A few may seek a chunk of the profits generated. Make sure that your future interest is protected. Agree that profits should reward their investment with an adequate return to a point. After that has been achieved, attempt to get their hands out of your pockets. If some want ownership, don't panic. Try to negotiate an agreement whereby you have the right to buy them out, at a profit of course, sometime in the future when you and the business can afford to do so. Management can also become a problem. Some of your friends and relatives, upon advancing funds, might feel compelled to help you run the business whether you like it or not. In some cases this cannot be avoided. If they own stock in the business, certain voting rights are guaranteed, in proportion to their investment, under state laws. Of course, if more than 50 percent of the stock is owned by you, control is in your hands. To avoid hard feelings, make sure it is made clear up front that you are the boss and interference in running the business will not be tolerated. A legal agreement outlining that requirement may be appropriate. Check with your attorney.

If at all possible, it is advisable to steer clear of family and friends for funding purposes. These sources can be less than amiable at times, creating more ill will than happy endings. In fact, these individuals can become adversaries very quickly, especially when it comes to money. They tend to do so more frequently than lenders/investors who are not acquainted with you on a personal basis. If no other financing alternative exists, the answer becomes academic. Take their money.

BANKS

Many large banks, located in metropolitan areas, are severing relationships with their small business clients. They cite risk factors and increasing costs of servicing small accounts as the primary reasons for the shift in emphasis. Most are at least raising service fees to small firms above those which are charged larger businesses. In addition, small businesses are charged higher interest rates on loans than are larger businesses. These changes will adversely affect entrepreneurs located in these areas, not to mention the whole American economy, although some banks, especially the ones found in smaller cities and rural areas, continue to provide financial services to small businesses and many are actively seeking new accounts.

Banks active in small business funding will either lend on a conventional basis or in tandem with a government agency. With conventional financing the bank utilizies its own funds without government involvement. Lending programs, including local, state, or federal entities, are normally in the form of loan participations involving direct government funds or loan guarantees. When an agency participates in a lending situation, part of the funds are advanced by the government and the remainder is supplied by the bank. Under guaranteed programs, banks that provide funds to businesses are protected against non-repayment to a certain percent of the loan amount (usually 90 percent). Banks like government-backed loans because the guaranteed portion can be sold to investors, in the secondary markets, for handsome profits. In addition, this frees capital to be used to make additional guaranteed loans to be sold at a profit. The lending process can be repeated continuously.

Banks offering conventional or government-sponsored loans to existing firms or start-ups will demand stiff collateral requirements in most cases. Business assets such as customer accounts, inventories, equipment, and land will have to be pledged in order to secure capital. Security in the form of personal assets might also be requested. Savings accounts, cars, residential property, jewelry, etc., can be used as collateral for business loans. Of course, tying up too many assets can adversely affect business operations. This was described earlier in the chapter. Remember, bankers have to compete for loans among themselves. Letting them know that other alternatives exist will probably bring collateral terms that can be tolerated.

Even though banks are one of the most conservative sources of capital available, they still supply 67 percent of small business funding needs. In the future, some of this burden will be shifted to other financial outlets more amiable to small firms. But for now, those seeking funds should locate banks actively involved with helping small enterprises and prospective entrepreneurs.

VENTURE CAPITAL COMPANIES

Venture capital firms are private concerns that pool the financial resources of wealthy individuals and organizations interested in making investments in small businesses. Some are subsidiaries of major corporations. Exxon and General Electric own venture capital companies. Recent federal legislation has provided tax benefits for venture capital outlets involved in funding projects. Consequently, this form of financing has increased dramatically, augmenting the money available to small enterprises and prospective entrepreneurs.

These firms will invest their capital in a number of ways. They might make loans, buy bonds (debt), or invest in companies by purchasing equity through stock ownership. A combination of the above may be used. Generally, their preferred approach is an equity purchase. Also, they might acquire bonds with equity kickers. In other words, the bond can be converted to stock ownership at the option of the investor.

Venture capital firms expect to receive an average of five times their original investment within five to seven years. This is why loans are not favored by venture capitalists. Small business loan rates seldom exceed 20 percent a year, in which case the return on investment would be somewhat less than is considered normal for the venture capital industry. At this point one might question the advantages of seeking out venture firms if they require such a large return. It must be remembered that a business receiving equity funds does not have to worry about principal and interest payments, which can make life easier in the early years of operation. The investor is expecting the business to grow rapidly and someday return a handsome profit. In most cases, before selling out, the venture firm will give the entrepreneur the option to purchase its interest in the business before offering it to a third party. The right of first refusal can be stipulated in the venture capital agreement.

Conversely, the disadvantage of equity participation is the loss of control. When ownership is exchanged for capital resources, the entrepreneur's ability to influence business affairs will be diluted. Investor input must be taken into consideration. The degree of loss will depend on several factors. Firms that have been in operation showing track records can normally convince venture capital firms to take less equity than if it was a start-up situation. Also, entrepreneurs providing a large portion of the money required for a start-up company can strike a better deal with venture capital organizations than entrepreneurs supplying little of their own personal funds. In any case, most of these financial outlets will not acquire more than 50 percent of the company receiving assistance. Therefore, ultimate control is left to the entrepreneur and managing team. Many venture firms will require that they be represented in management, but will make waves only if they feel it's in their best interest. Besides, these firms can provide valuable insight into running an operation successfully.

Venture capital companies will invest only in prospects that have bright futures and the potential for rapid growth. Small businesses such as gas stations, corner grocery stores, dry cleaners, etc., will not be able to pursue this alternative unless they plan to expand through chain operations.

Professional associations representing the venture capital industry are listed in Appendix P. They may provide valuable information concerning finding appropriate funding sources.

SMALL BUSINESS INVESTMENT COMPANIES (SBICs)

SBICs are private profit making concerns created under the Small Business Investment Act of 1958. Their primary goal is to provide financial resources to existing small businesses and prospective entrepreneurs. All SBICs that fall under the above act are licensed, regulated, and partially funded by the U.S. Small Business Administration. Some financial organizations call themselves small business investment companies but prefer not to fall under the jurisdiction of the SBA. They generally operate on the same basis as licensed SBICs with one exception. Low-interest government money, provided by the SBA, will not be available to them for relending purposes, thereby reducing their funding flexibility. Approximately 400 SBICs are in existence today across the nation.

Like venture capital companies, these financial outlets will invest in equity (stock), make loans, or buy bonds. They prefer to acquire debt as opposed to making equity investments because of their capital structure. Many SBICs borrow from the government and then relend to small businesses. If they make stock purchases, returns on their investment may be a long time coming. On the other hand, making loans and buying bonds will generate immediate income to pay the government for the funds borrowed.

SBICs prefer to finance small businesses with track records of at least six months or more. They will consider start-up situations in some cases. Only those prospects or firms that have promising futures are given consideration by small business investment companies.

Minority Enterprise Small Business Investment Companies (MES-BICs) provide funding specifically to minority-owned businesses. In addition, capital is made available to minorities interested in starting a new business or purchasing an existing operation. MESBICs are basically the same as SBICs. They are regulated and licensed by the U.S. Small Business Administration and receive part of their capital from the agency. Today over 125 are in existence.

Appendix Q contains a list of professional associations representing small business investment companies. Contacting them may result in funding contracts.

COMMERCIAL FINANCE COMPANIES

Many small businesses snubbed by banks can turn to commercial finance companies for help in certain areas. Even businesses experiencing financial difficulties can turn to these sources for assistance. Since these financial outlets tend to charge higher interest rates than banks, it is wise to try the banks first. If unsuccessful in that regard, a firm has the option of pursuing over 2,500 commercial finance companies now operating in this country.

Commercial finance companies will lend on a short- and/or intermediate-term basis with collateral always being required. For example, these companies will grant short-term (less than a year) loans using accounts receivable and inventories as collateral. Generally you can borrow up to 90 percent of the value of good receivables and 60 percent of inventory value. In addition, intermediate loans (one to five years) can be granted for equipment purchase. The finance company will collateralize the equipment for security purposes.

Leasing is another service offered by many commercial finance organizations. If a business is in need of some new equipment but lacks the necessary financial resources to purchase, lending is an alternative. The finance company will buy the equipment and lease it to the business. Monthly rental payments must be made that usually last three to seven years. The advantages to leasing are many. Little or no down payment is required; the equipment can be bought at the end of the lease agreement for a fraction of original cost; the business is

protected against obsolescence; leases do not appear as liabilities on
the financial statements of the business, thus not reducing its ability to
borrow for other reasons; and lease payments are fully deductible as
expenses. Other advantages are pointed out in Table 16.

TABLE 16

LEASING ADVANTAGES

- 100 percent financing—leasing generally requires little or no down payment
- preserves working capital that can be used for other revenue generating projects
- does not compromise control of the business
- does not disrupt existing financing arrangements
- lease payments are paid out of pre-tax revenues, thereby creating a tax write-off
  as opposed to purchasing capital equipment out of retained earnings (net income-
  dividends pay to investors, if any) and thereby losing important tax advantages
- lease liabilities are not generally reported on the firm's financial statements,
  thereby preserving its financial position
- provides the ability to obtain the latest and most efficient equipment that might
  not otherwise be available due to financial constraints
- facilitates the expansion or replacement of aging equipment
- provides a protection against inflation, since lease payments are made in current
  money
- provides protection against rapid obsolescence—if property becomes obsolete
  before the end of the lease period, it is generally possible to trade-up without
  much difficulty or cost
- after the lease term is completed, it is the responsibility of the leasing firm to
  dispose of the equipment
- the cost of leasing is higher than most other financing methods, but earnings on
  the capital that would otherwise be used outweigh the cost
- leasing can be used as an alternative or supplement to bank credit when
  borrowing conditions become too restrictive or uneconomical
- lease payments are entirely deductible as business expenses

Commercial finance companies can also factor (buy) accounts
receivable. They will purchase your receivables at a discount ranging
between one and 15 percent. Their fees are determined by a number of
considerations, including volume of sales, general quality of the firm's
customers, credit policies within the firm, and average size of an
account. The factoring procedure can be conducted on a non-notifica-
tion basis, which means customers are not aware that their accounts
have been sold. Factoring is believed to be a costly financial tool to be

utilized only if bank credit is unattractive or not available. There are some reasons to believe this may not be true. When evaluating expenses associated with factoring, you should carefully analyze the services being rendered. If receivables bookkeeping, collection, and credit risks are being assumed, either partially or wholly by the factor, internal costs associated with these functions will decrease in proportion to the increased participation of the factor. In addition, factoring service provides freed cash, otherwise tied up in receivables, that can be used to generate revenues. So, the elimination or reduction of the credit function within the business plus the profits created from unencumbered cash may make the factoring decision an attractive alternative or supplement to existing bank relationships. Table 17 outlines the advantage in dealing with a factor.

TABLE 17

ADVANTAGES TO FACTORING

- factors will collect accounts receivable

- factors will do all the bookkeeping relative to the credit function

- factoring can be used as a supplement or substitute to bank credit when borrowing conditions become too restrictive or uneconomical

- factors will conduct credit investigations on the firm's existing and prospective accounts. In fact, factors are experts in credit analysis. This will establish confidence in the ability to collect the accounts receivable.

- factors assume all the credit risks associated with accounts receivable

- factors allow firms to utilize all available cash for revenue generation. Banks may require that a business maintain compensating balances on hand (ranging between 5 and 15 percent of the loan amount). In addition, certain factoring arrangements can free cash that would otherwise be set aside to meet projected current obligations.

- factoring can actually enhance a firm's relationship with banks and other funding outlets. If lenders and investors are confident that a factoring organization will purchase the accounts receivable of a firm if the cash is needed, they will be more willing to provide assistance.

In addition, these commercial finance companies will advance funds for leveraged buyouts and acquisitions if sufficient collateral is made available. For example, a business might be interested in purchasing another firm but lacks the immediate financial resources to do so. A commercial finance company will fund all or part of the acquisition if enough collateral in the form of nonpledged (clean) assets is available in the firm to be acquired.

The two major associations representing the commercial finance industry are listed in Appendix R. They may provide information about funding outlets.

LIFE INSURANCE COMPANIES

Traditionally, life insurance companies have been very insensitive to small business funding needs. In fact, most of these firms prefer to invest in amounts of one million dollars or more per business deal. Obviously, this is beyond the financial requirements of most small enterprises. This is not to suggest that insurance companies should be forgotten as a viable source. Many of these insurers are starting to realize the profit potential in financing small businesses and some are currently active in providing funding programs. Most insurance companies will not entertain start-up situations. They prefer going concerns with profitable track records that have potential for future growth. Long-term lending is their favorite form of financing. The loans are expected to finance internal expansion. Funds can also be used for external growth through acquisition and leveraged buyouts.

PENSION FUNDS

Like insurance companies, pension funds prefer to finance only existing operations with attractive growth prospects. In fact, many insurers are partially pension funds. Start-up funding is avoided, with most consideration being given to long-term loans. Historically, these financial outlets have favored large businesses, but some are looking in the direction of small firms.

INVESTMENT BANKERS (UNDERWRITERS)

There are some investment banking houses that specialize in raising capital for small businesses with growth potential. They will make a *public offering* of securities in the business to the investment community. What happens, in fact, is that the underwriter (investment banker) sells stock and/or bonds for the small firm to individual investors willing to buy. Start-ups and existing firms can use this funding alternative to raise needed capital.

Underwriters will demand to be paid a minimum commission of 10 percent on the gross dollar amount they sell. In addition, fees called accountable and non-accountable expenses are charged, and they can be substantial. After everything is considered, the cost of raising capital through a public offering can exceed 35 percent of amount sought. In other words, raising $300,000 can cost in excess of $100,000. If the offering is unsuccessful (not enough money raised), any stock purchased must be returned to the investor for a refund. The underwriter will not charge you for those sales, but some expenses incurred will be passed on to the small firm or entrepreneur. All conditions of a public offering are normally covered in an underwriting agreement between the investment banker and the business to be financed. Attorneys for both parties should review this contract to determine if it suits the requirements of all involved.

In addition, an interstate public offering must be approved by the Securities Exchange Commission in Washington, D.C., and every state in which securities are sold. If the offering is intrastate (located within the confines of a particular state), only approval from that state is needed. The underwriter will take care of the details involved in notifying and registering with the appropriate government agencies.

SMALL BUSINESS ADMINISTRATION (SBA)

The U.S. Small Business Administration has been called the lender of last resort by small business advocates. One of its primary objectives is to help entrepreneurs secure financial resources to start businesses or expand existing operations. It is authorized to make participation loans and provide loan guarantees, and in some cases make direct loans to those firms classified as small by the agency. Consequently, many small businesses and prospective owners, frustrated by strained relations with their local bankers and economic conditions, have turned to the SBA for lending support.

To be considered for a loan, an individual or business firm must meet certain conditions. They are:

— must have adequate credentials
— must not be dominant in its field
— must comply with all federal employment laws
— must pursue traditional lending sources (only upon rejection by
    private lenders does the SBA alternative become a possibility)
— must be classified as small business by SBA size standards (these
    classifications are based on number of employees or the value of
    sales stated in dollars)

The criteria for determining if a business is small will vary depending upon the type of business. The specific criteria are as follows:

	Annual Sales	
Type of Business	*Not Exceeding*	
Retail	2-7.5 Million)	Limits will depend
Wholesale	9.5-22 Million)	on industry
Service	2-8 Million)	
General Construction	9.5 Million	
Special Trade Construction	1-2 Million	

Manufacturing firms are constrained by number of employees. The maximum employment level can be anywhere between 250 and 1,500 employees, depending upon type of industry.

These fundamental criteria are only the beginning. Many exceptions are allowed specific businesses and industries. The local SBA field office will prove helpful in determining which criteria apply to any business.

Assuming all SBA conditions are met, an entrepreneur can submit a business proposal to the agency for consideration. It will be carefully evaluated to determine positive and negative aspects. In the final analysis, if the project has merit (adequate market, good management, sufficient collateral, possibility of loan repayment, etc.), the SBA will offer a loan guarantee. It must be kept in mind that this is not a loan. The agency simply guarantees that a lender will be protected against default if funds are advanced to a small business concern. Up to 90 percent of the principal loan amount is covered for non-repayment to a maximum of $500,000; in other words, risk exposure is minimized. In addition, interest charges on these loans generally run a couple of points above the prime rate. It is hoped that the guarantees will induce lenders to advance the necessary financial resources to initiate and carry out the business project. Using the maximum guarantee limit, a loan for $555,555 can be granted with a 90 percent guarantee to the lender. A larger loan will reduce the guarantee below 90 percent and may increase lender resistance.

Even with a guarantee, some lending sources might balk for any number of reasons. Tight money, adverse economic climate, un-willingness to work with SBA, dislike for the business project, lack of collateral are some of the conventional comments made in rejecting a proposal. If this becomes the case, the SBA will offer to participate with the lending outlets. Under the participation program, the agency will advance some of the funds if the lender agrees to provide the remaining financial requirements. A minimum of 25 percent of the amount must be funded by the lender with the rest coming from SBA. The dollar amounts funded by the government cannot exceed $150,000. This will limit the funds available under the program to $200,000. The interest rate on the portion provided by the SBA will be less than the prevailing market, and the remaining balance funded by private lenders will carry the standard commercial rate (2 to 3 points above prime). Participation loans are the least common types of SBA funding because of the difficulty in getting private lenders and the SBA synchronized on individual business proposals.

If the participation offer is also refused by lending outlets, the SBA will consider making direct loans (utilizing agency resources) to start-ups and existing firms. The loans are made at attractive interest rates in amounts not to exceed $150,000. All participation and direct loans are made subject to the availability of funds.

There are some exceptions to SBA loan limitations. For example, under the SBA disaster programs, a borrower may exceed the official limits established for the general lending program discussed in this chapter. Also, the interest rate for direct loans to handicapped individuals is only 3 percent.

Unfortunately, the SBA has not escaped the Reagan budget ax. According to an official with the Richmond SBA Field Office, "funding for the direct and participation loans has come under severe scrutiny in the fiscal 1984 Federal Budget and beyond." The official did state that significant pressure was being exerted on the White House, by small business advocates in Congress and elsewhere, to increase funding levels. Whatever the case, loan guarantees will continue to be provided.

FARMERS HOME ADMINISTRATION (FmHA)

This agency falls under the jurisdiction of the U.S. Department of Agriculture. Its primary goal is to enhance the quality of rural life through upgrading the economic environment. This is accomplished by an array of funding programs to promote industrial, business, and agricultural development. It is the intention of the agency to provide supplemental financial support, augmenting the efforts of private lending sources, rather than competing with them. Under most FmHA programs, borrowers are required to pursue private funding when financially able to do so. The programs directed to agriculture are designed to build the family farm system, which is the economic base of many rural areas. Borrowers must be family-size operators, living on and operating the farm, at least on a part-time basis. Funding is available also for any type of agricultural activity. Business and industrial loans are made available to large and small businesses to promote economic development in communities with a population base below 50,000. Preference is given to applications for projects in open country, rural communities, and in towns of 25,000 people or less. These funds can be used to develop and finance business or industry, increase employment, and control or abate pollution. Within this broad framework, uses include, but are not limited to, the following:

— Business and industrial acquisition, construction, conversion, enlargement, repair, and modernization
— Purchasing and development of land, easements, right-of-ways, buildings, facilities, leases, materials, and custom feed lots
— Purchasing of equipment, lease-hold improvements, machinery, and supplies
— Start-up costs and working capital

FmHA will provide loan guarantees to private lenders who advance funds under its programs. The agency guarantees to limit any loss due to loan default to a certain percentage of the total amount involved (usually 90 percent). Interest rates are negotiated between the borrower and private lender unless the rate is mandated by statute. Insured loans are also offered. These funds are originated and made by the Farmers Home Administration directly. The agency sells the loans to private investors and insures repayment. Interest rates on insured funds are about the same as the current cost of federal borrowing. Some rates may be established by law.

Certain programs provide grants (which do not have to be repaid) and low interest loans to individual and organizations involved in certain agricultural pursuits. In addition, the FmHA provides emergency and disaster loan assistance to the farming community at very attractive interest rates.

FARM CREDIT ADMINISTRATION (FCA)

The Farm Credit Administration is an independent federal organization which oversees the nationwide farmer-owned and managed farm credit system. This network provides funding to the U.S. agricultural community through a number of programs. Federal Land Banks, located in most communities, supply long-term mortgage credit to purchase, enlarge, and improve farms. These banks will also finance mortgages on farm property and lend for other farming endeavors. Production Credit Associations, which are also supervised by FCA, make short- and intermediate-term loans for farm production, farm home, and/or farm family purposes. In addition, Cooperative Banks provide loan services to cooperatives supplying agricultural needs.

COMMODITY CREDIT CORPORATION (CCC)

This Department of Agriculture entity provides non-recourse loans for commodities stored on farms or in bonded commercial warehouses. This provides price support, thereby enabling farmers to carry out an orderly marketing program. In addition, this agency will financially assist farmers to expand or build farm storage facilities. Capital is also available to purchase drying equipment for use with stored commodities.

ECONOMIC DEVELOPMENT ADMINISTRATION (EDA)

The Economic Development Administration, which is part of the U.S. Department of Commerce, provides funding programs to businesses of all sizes. Start-up and existing firms are eligible to apply. EDA will consider only those requests that will have a positive impact upon areas designated as needing economic assistance. Its purpose is to enhance the earning levels of people within these areas by increasing job opportunities. EDA also provides assistance to firms, regardless of size, that have been adversely affected by foreign imports. The agency does not have funding limits, as is the case with the Small Business Administration. In fact, many firms that have exhausted SBA funds may turn to EDA for additional capital, although private funding outlets must be pursued first. Only after rejection by these firms does EDA funding become a possibility.

Sounds easy. Well, it's not. The EDA is a very tough cookie to deal with. Few funding requests are approved. The loan application procedure is long and cumbersome and conditions are numerous. Funding terms and restrictions prove to be too stringent for most firms. For example, the agency requires that at least 15 percent of the proposed project be funded by equity (ownership) or other secondary loans. One-third of the 15 percent must come from the state or organizations located within the community benefiting from the project. Also, loans used to finance capital purchases (buildings, land, equipment, machinery) cannot exceed 65 percent of the cost. In addition, an applicant for EDA funding must supply a large amount of the required working capital before a loan will be approved.

The agency will provide loan guarantees to lenders willing to fund borrowers. These arrangements also require collateral.

DEPARTMENT OF ENERGY (DOE)

The U.S. Department of Energy maintains funding programs directed to all businesses, regardless of size, operating in certain energy areas. In the past, the agency tended to favor large corporations. Recent evidence has shown that small firms are much more innovative than large ones, forcing the DOE to redirect some of its financial resources.

Most DOE programs provide grants to firms exploring ways to enhance domestic energy efficiency through conservation, new methods of energy utilization, and the development of alternative energy sources. This money does not have to be repaid. In addition, the department is providing loan guarantees to financial outlets lending to companies that develop new and old sources of coal. Guarantees run as high as 30 million dollars. DOE also has a similar program available to firms operating in the geothermal energy field. Up to 200 million dollars can be guaranteed.

MARITIME ADMINISTRATION

The Maritime Administration falls under control of the U.S. Department of Commerce. It provides an array of programs designed to aid large and small firms in the construction, reconstruction, or reconditioning of vessels in the American Merchant Marine. Most programs give direct payments to private ship owners. In one case, 45 million dollars was given just for a single ship. In addition, loan guarantees up to 126 million dollars per ship are offered to commercial lenders willing to provide funding.

NATIONAL OCEANIC AND ATMOSPHERIC ADMINISTRATION

Under the U.S. Department of Interior, this agency provides funding to assist in strengthening the domestic fishing industry. Loans are made to finance and refinance the cost of purchasing, constructing, equipping, maintaining, repairing, or operating new or used commercial fishing vessels or gear. Only American citizens with experience in the fishing trade are advised to apply.

U.S. GEOLOGICAL SURVEY

This Department of Interior agency encourages domestic mineral exploration by providing firms with direct government loans (up to $50,000).

BUREAU OF INDIAN AFFAIRS

The Bureau, which falls under the jurisdiction of the U.S. Department of Interior, offers programs to encourage the economic development of federal Indian reservations. Grants, direct government loans, and loan guarantees (up to one million dollars) are made available to Native Americans for this purpose.

EXPORT-IMPORT BANK (EXIMBANK)

The Export-Import Bank is an independent government agency established to promote American exports overseas. This is accomplished through a number of programs directed to firms involved in exporting and to commercial banks.

Eximbank can authorize the Foreign Credit Insurance Association (FCIA) to issue policies insuring exporters against political and/or commercial risks on short- and medium-term credit extended to foreign buyers. Insurance can be bought from banks participating in FCIA programs or directly from the Association. In addition, Eximbank itself will offer guarantees to U.S. businesses covering political and commercial risks involved in the performance of services overseas and in the leasing, consignment, or exhibition of U.S. goods abroad. The agency will also guarantee payment of medium-term export loans held by commercial banks. The aforementioned programs are designed to help U.S. exporters compete in the international marketplace. Without Eximbank-sponsored guarantees, many exporters would not offer foreign customers credit terms, thereby placing them at a competitive disadvantage with suppliers in other nations offering attractive terms. In short, Eximbank insurance programs provide reimbursement coverage to American exporters and bankers should foreign customers fail to pay.

Some lenders will advance only a certain amount of funds to finance exports. After this limit is reached, export money will be cut off or higher interest rates will be charged to international firms. Now, Eximbank will purchase export loans from commercial banks to provide additional capital, at reasonable interest rates, to firms wishing to sell overseas. Another program designed to facilitate U.S. exports

provides direct loans to overseas buyers of American goods and
services.

Overseas Private Investment Corporation (OPIC)

The Overseas Private Investment Corporation is an independent
federal agency that promotes U.S. investment abroad. It offers an array
of programs that can benefit American firms wishing to start new
operations or expand existing facilities in less developed nations. The
agency provides loan guarantees (up to 100 percent) to lenders that
assist organizations in exploiting international opportunities. Direct
loans are also made available. All funding programs are long term
(exceeding five years) in nature and commercial interest rates are
charged. Capital advanced under OPIC cannot finance more than 50
percent of the foreign venture. Therefore, additional money must be
provided from other sources.

Insurance programs are also offered to protect companies against
certain investment losses arising from operations in other countries.
The coverage reduces the risk associated with nationalization, war,
revolution, insurrection, civil strife, and currency inconvertibility.

Federal Reserve Board (FRB)

The Federal Reserve Board will offer loan guarantees to lenders who
financially assist firms engaged in producing goods or services for
national defense purposes. Specifically, its intention is to facilitate and
expedite the funding of contractors, subcontractors, and others engaged in operations deemed necessary for defense of the U.S. The
interest rates on these loans are low and 100 percent loan guarantees are
provided.

National Science Foundation (NSF)

The National Science Foundation provides grant money to assist
small firms conducting scientific research in the areas of new product/
process development. Some grants have exceeded one million dollars.
The money, which does not have to be repaid, is designed for basic
research and is not to be used to commercially market anything
created. After research and testing is conducted utilizing NSF resources, the firm is expected to have private funding available in order
to execute any marketing endeavors.

Given the scientific emphasis of NSF funding, only those small
companies that are technical in nature should seek this funding
alternative.

STATE DEVELOPMENT COMPANIES (SDC)

A SDC is sanctioned by state law to provide financial and managerial assistance to all businesses located within the state it serves. These development companies receive their capital from traditional funding outlets such as banks, pension funds, insurance companies, etc. In addition, SDCs can borrow from the U.S. Small Business Administration to provide loans to qualified small firms located in the state.

STATE GOVERNMENTS

Most state governments maintain programs to promote the economic well being of small businesses located within their jurisdiction. In many cases, assistance is also provided to individuals wishing to start a new business or purchase an existing operation. Appendices J and L contain a listing of state agencies, including the assistance each provides.

LOCAL GOVERNMENTS

Some local governments are actively involved in providing managerial and/or financial assistance to prospective entrepreneurs and existing small firms located within the municipality. Contact the city or county administrator's office to determine which agencies are responsible for this function.

Many local governments are providing help to firms of all sizes through the use of a relatively new financing mechanism referred to as industrial revenue bonds. A business may get approval from a local government to raise funds through the sale of tax-exempt bonds if the project provides direct benefits to the locality in the form of increased revenues, taxes, and employment. The project must also fit into the overall growth plan of the municipality. The principal advantage to this form of financing is its low cost. Generally, interest rates on the bonds sold run one to two percentage points below other conventional funding sources. Investors like these bonds because the interest income paid to them is free from federal, state, and local income taxes. There are two major drawbacks with industrial revenue bonds. Start-up firms are normally discouraged from pursuing this funding alternative due to the lack of operating history. It may be difficult to convince local officials and investors that a new business just starting out deserves consideration. In addition, using industrial revenue bonds may disqualify a business from utilizing other attractive government funding programs.

Some states allow their local municipalities to use this funding technique more than others. Check with the municipal manager to determine what projects may be funded. It is also wise to talk with officials of any state or federal government agency from which assistance may be forthcoming. See if the bonds will disturb anticipated help from this direction.

CERTIFIED DEVELOPMENT COMPANIES (CDC)
LOCAL DEVELOPMENT COMPANIES (LDC)

Local development companies (LDC) and certified development companies (CDC) are profit or non-profit corporations started by local business people with the intention of stimulating economic development within their immediate community. They are a little-known source of small business funding and assistance and are often overlooked by many existing businesses and prospective entrepreneurs. LDCs/CDCs do not see profit as their motivating objective. Primary consideration is given to positive economic impact on the community they serve. Like state development companies, LDCs/CDCs receive a large portion of their funding capability from the U.S. Small Business Administration for relending purposes to qualified small firms and entrepreneurs. SBA money passing through LDCs/CDCs may be loaned for up to 25 years at prevailing interest rates.

These organizations can provide valuable help because of their local nature. Many have established contacts within the immediate area allowing opportunity seekers access to conventional funding and managerial assistance.

Application Procedures

All private and government financial outlets require initial application forms to be completed. Appendix T contains the forms required by the U.S. Small Business Administration. The forms are elementary and easy to answer. But don't be fooled. The real work is just beginning. Additional documentation will be required. Most lenders and investors will request a detailed report outlining all particulars of a prospective business proposal. It's used in the funding decision to evaluate the soundness of the project and is called a business plan. Its construction can be a long, difficult, and tedious process. Some exceed 100 pages in duration. Length and detail depend on the amount of money requested, use of funds, type of business or industry, and whether the funding is used for a start-up or existing operation. Generally the more capital requested, the greater amount of information needed. Likewise, start-ups will require more data than firms already conducting business because of the increased uncertainty involved.

There are some exceptions to the above rules. For example, a business that has an established relationship with lenders may not have to go through the pains of constructing a business plan every time capital needs arise. Many lenders, acquainted with their clients, will request only a completed application form, business and personal financial statements, tax returns, and owner guarantees.

The business plan is discussed in the next chapter. The information provided is appropriate for most private and government funding requests.

Chapter VII

THE BUSINESS PLAN
Roadmap to Success

Design

Most individuals seeking capital to finance a business proposition fail to realize the importance of a properly structured business plan. One entrepreneur recently asked, "Why do I need to spend the time developing a business plan when it's the greatest idea in the world— everybody will invest." Because of this kind of thinking, over 90 percent of all plans requesting funds are rejected by financial outlets.

A business plan is essentially a sales tool used to stimulate investor interest. It must be packaged correctly in order to attract the necessary money sources. The design and construction can be a major undertaking challenging the most astute. An adequate business plan should run between 40 and 60 pages (typed and double spaced) with an adequate number of appendices for purposes of illustrations and detail. Hundreds of hours and many months will be consumed putting it together and perfecting the final document. In some cases, it may be costly. Entrepreneurs who lack business experience and expertise in one or more areas may have to pay professionals to research and/or write part or all of the plan. Its importance in the funding decision cannot be overstated. Prospective capital sources use it as an instrument to evaluate the merits of a proposal before risking their money. In addition, the plan lets potential investors know that the entrepreneur/ managing team has given deep and serious consideration to the business proposition and that they are capable of managing profitably. A well documented and convincing business plan portraying the potential for future profits is what capital sources are seeking. It should touch on all pertinent areas without being detailed to the point where investors get bored reading it.

The business plan should never be viewed as solely for the use of financial outlets. Indeed, it can be utilized by businesses as a guide pointing to the most profitable and least hazardous way to carry out an idea. It allows for a careful consideration of different objectives, alternatives, strategies and tactics, and analyzes available resources before committing funds. These initial evaluations will prevent many costly mistakes from becoming reality. In fact, the plan gives a five year path to follow by forcing entrepreneurs to set realistic goals, predict resource allocation, and project future earnings. Also, problems concerning competitive conditions, promotional opportunities, industry trends, etc., are addressed. Such a practice over a period of time will enhance the decision making ability of the entrepreneur and others involved in the enterprise.

In the final analysis, the business plan is the roadmap directing energies in a coherent fashion. It outlines what must be accomplished and how to carry it out. Developing a plan that can stand up to critical evaluation and the extreme scrutiny of investors is the initial hurdle which must be cleared.

The next major section of this chapter deals with the proper construction of an appropriate business plan. It should be reviewed and studied very carefully. The following is reprinted by permission of the copyright holder, Institute for New Enterprise Development, Cambridge, Massachusetts. This material, which begins with the sub heading "Table of Contents" and ends with "Proposed Company Offering," is a most useful guide when preparing a business plan.

TABLE OF CONTENTS

3. MARKETING PLAN
   A. Overall Marketing Strategy
   B. Pricing
   C. Sales Tactics
   D. Service and Warranty Policies
   E. Advertising and Promotion

4. DESIGN AND DEVELOPMENT PLANS
   A. Development Status and Tasks
   B. Difficulties and Risks
   C. Product Improvement and New Products
   D. Costs

5. MANUFACTURING AND OPERATIONS PLAN
   A. Geographic Location
   B. Facilities and Improvements
   C. Strategy and Plans
   D. Labor Force

6. MANAGEMENT TEAM
   A. Organization
   B. Key Management Personnel
   C. Managemennt Compensation and Ownership
   D. Board of Directors
   E. Management Assistance and Training Needs
   F. Supporting Professional Services

7. OVERALL SCHEDULE

8. CRITICAL RISKS AND PROBLEMS

9. COMMUNITY BENEFITS
   A. Economic Development
   B. Human Development
   C. Community Development

10. THE FINANCIAL PLAN
    A. Profit and Loss Forecast
    B. Pro Forma Cash Flows Analysis
    C. Pro Forma Balance Sheets
    D. Breakeven Chart
    E. Cost Control

    PRO FORMA INCOME STATEMENTS
    PRO FORMA CASH FLOWS STATEMENTS
    PRO FORMA BALANCE SHEETS
    BREAKEVEN CHART

11. PROPOSED COMPANY OFFERING
    A. Desired Financing
    B. Securities Offering
    C. Capitalization
    D. Use of Funds

THE SUMMARY

Many investors like to read through a one or two page summary of a business plan that highlights its important features and opportunities, and allows them to determine quickly whether or not the venture described is of interest.

Do not write your summary until you have written your plan. As you draft each section, circle one or two sentences that you think are important enough to be included in a summary.

Allow plenty of time to write an appealing and convincing summary, remembering that the summary is the first thing about you and your venture that the would-be investor is going to read. Unless it is appealing and convincing, it will also be the last. You may have spent many weeks on the rest of your plan and it may be very good. However, if that quality does not come through in your summary, you may not get a chance to make a presentation at which you can convincingly rebut criticism and clear up misunderstandings.

It is recommended that, as a minimum, your summary should contain brief statements about the following features of your venture.

The Company and Its Founders: You should indicate when the company was formed, what it will do, and what is special or unique about its product or technology. Also indicate what in the backgrounds of the entrepreneurs makes them particularly qualified to pursue the business opportunity.

If your company has been in business for a few years, indicate what its sales and profits were in its most recent fiscal year and the trend of sales and profits.

Market Opportunity: Identify and briefly explain the market opportunity. This explanation should include information on the size and growth rate of the market for your company's product or service, and a statement indicating the percentage of that market that will be captured. A brief statement about industry-wide trends is useful. You might also indicate any plans for expanding the initial product line.

Products and Technology: Identify any proprietary technology, trade secrets or unique skills that give you a competitive edge in the market place.

Financial Projections: State your sales and profit projections for the first and second year of operation after obtaining the necessary financing.

Proposed Financing: Briefly indicate how much equity financing you want, how much of your company you are prepared to offer for that financing, and what use will be made of the capital raised.

1. *THE INDUSTRY, THE COMPANY AND ITS PRODUCTS*

The purpose of this section is to give the investor some context in which to fit all that you are about to say concerning your product and its market. This section should clearly present the business that you are in, the product you will offer, the nature of your industry and the opportunities available to market your product.

The Industry

Present the current status and prospects for the industry in which the proposed business will operate. Discuss any new products or developments, new markets and customers, new requirements, new companies, and any other national or economic trends and factors that could affect the venture's business positively or negatively. Identify the source of all information used to describe industry trends.

The Company

Describe briefly what business area your company is in, or intends to enter; what products or services it will offer; and who are or will be its principal customers.

As background give the date your venture was incorporated and describe the identification and development of its products and the involvement of the company's principals in that development.

If your company has been in business for several years and is seeking expansion financing, review its history and cite its prior sales and profit performance. If your company has had set-backs or losses in prior years, discuss these and emphasize what has and will be done to prevent a recurrence of these difficulties and to improve your company's performance.

The Products or Services

The potential investor will be vitally interested in exactly what you are going to sell, what kind of product protection you have, and the opportunities and possible drawbacks to your product or service.

A. *Description:* Describe in detail the products or services to be sold. Discuss the application of your product or service. Describe the primary end-use as well as any significant secondary applications. Emphasize any unique features of your product or service, and highlight any differences between what is currently on the market and what you will offer that will account for your market penetration.

Define the present state of development of the product or service. For products, provide a summary of the functional specifications. Include photographs when available.

B. *Proprietary Position:* Describe any patents, trade secrets or other proprietary features. Discuss any head start that you might have that would enable you to achieve a favored or entrenched position in your industry.

C. *Potential:* Describe any features of your product or service that give it an advantage over the competition. Discuss any opportunities for the expansion of the product line or the development of related products or services. Emphasize your opportunities and explain how you will take advantage of them.

Discuss any product disadvantage or the possibilities of rapid obsolescence because of technological or styling changes, or marketing fads.

2. *MARKET RESEARCH AND ANALYSIS*

The purpose of this section of the plan is to present enough facts to convince the investor that your venture's product or service has a substantial market in a growing industry and can achieve sales despite the competition. The discussion and the guidlines given below should help you do this.

This section of the plan is one of the most difficult to prepare and also one of the most important. Almost all subsequent sections of the business plan depend on the sales estimates that are developed in this section. The sales levels you project based on the market research and analysis directly influence the size of the manufacturing operation, the marketing plan, and the amount of debt and equity capital you will require. Yet most entrepreneurs seem to have great difficulty preparing and presenting market research and analyses that will convince potential investors that the venture's sales estimates are sound and attainable.

Because of the importance of market analysis and the dependence of other parts of the plan on the sales projections, we generally advise entrepreneurs to prepare this section of the business plan before they do any other. We also advise entrepreneurs to take enough time to do this section very well and to check alternate sources of market data for key numbers such as "market size" and "market growth rates".

A. *Customers:* Discuss who the customers are for the anticipated application of the product or service. Classify potential customers into relatively homogeneous groups (major market segment) having common, identifiable characteristics. For example, an automotive part might be sold to automotive manufacturers or to parts distributors supplying the replacement market.

Who and where are the major purchasers for the product or service in each market segment? What is the basis for their purchase decisions: price, quality, service, personal contacts, political pressures or some combination of these factors?

List any potential customers who have expressed an interest in the product or service and indicate why. List any potential customers who have shown no interest in the proposed product or service and explain why this is so. Explain what you will do to overcome negative customer reaction. If you have an existing business, list your current principal customers and discuss the trend in your sales to them.

B. *Market Size and Trends:* What is the total size of the current market for the product or service offered? This market size should be determined from available market data sources and from a knowledge of the purchases of competing products by potential customers in each major market segment. Discussions with potential distributors, dealers, sales representatives and customers can be particularly useful in establishing the market size and trends. Describe the size of the total market in both units and dollars. If you intend to sell regionally, show the regional market size. Indicate the sources of data and methods used to establish current market size. Also state the credentials of people doing market research.

Describe the potential annual growth of the total market for your product or service for each major customer group. Total market projections should be made for at least three future years. Discuss the major factors affecting market growth (industry trends, socio-economic trends, government policy, population shifts). Also review previous trends in the market. Any differences between past and projected annual growth rates should be explained. Indicate the sources of all data and methods used to make projections.

C. *Competition:* Make a realistic assessment of the strengths and weaknesses of competitive products and services and name the companies that supply them. State the data sources used to determine which products are competitive and the strengths of the competition.

Compare competing products or services on the basis of price, performance, service, warranties and other pertinent features. A table can be an effective way of presenting these data. Present a short discussion of the current advantages and disadvantages of competing products and services and say why they are not meeting customer needs. Indicate any knowledge of competitors' actions that could lead you to new or improved products and an advantageous position.

Review the strengths and weaknesses of the competing companies. Determine and discuss each competitor's share of the market, sales, distribution and production capabilities. Also review the profitability of the competition and their profit trend. Who is the pricing leader; quality leader? Discuss why any companies have entered or dropped out of the market in recent years.

Discuss your three or four key competitors and why the customer buys from them. From what you know about their operations, explain why you think you can capture a share of their business. Discuss what makes you think it will be easy or difficult to compete with them.

D. *Estimated Market Share and Sales:* Summarize what it is about your product or service that will make it saleable in the face of current and potential competition.

Identify any major customers who are willing to make purchase commitments. Indicate the extent of those commitments and why they were made. Discuss which customers could be major purchasers in future years and why.

Based upon your assessment of the advantages of your product or service; the market size and trends; customers; the competition and their products, and the sales trends in prior years; estimate your share of the market, and your sales in units and dollars for each of the next three years. The growth of the company's sales and its estimated market share should be related to the growth of its industry, the customers and the strengths and weaknesses of competitors. This data can be presented in a table, as shown below.

The assumptions used to estimate market share and sales should be clearly stated. If yours is an existing business indicate the total market, and your market share and sales for two prior years.

Sales and Market Share Data

		1st Year				Year	
		1Q	2Q	3Q	4Q	2	3
Estimated Total	Units						
Market	Dollars						
Estimated Sales	Units						
	Dollars						
Estimated Market	Units						
Share, %	Dollars						

E. *Ongoing Market Evaluation:* Explain how you will evaluate your target markets on a continuing basis to assess customer needs; to guide product improvement and new product programs; to plan for expansions of your production facility; and to guide product/service pricing.

3. MARKETING PLAN

The marketing plan describes how the sales projections will be attained. It should detail the overall marketing strategy, sales and service policies, pricing, distribution and advertising strategies that will be used to achieve the estimated market share and sales projections. It should describe specifically *what* is to be done, *how* it will be done, and *who* will do it.

A. *Overall Marketing Strategy:* Describe the general marketing philosophy and strategy of the company. This should be derived partly from the market research and evaluation. It should include a discussion of: What kinds of customer groups will be targeted for initial intensive selling effort? What customer groups for later selling efforts? How will specific potential customers in these groups be identified and how will they be contacted? What features of the product or service—e.g., quality, price, delivery, warranty—will be emphasized to generate sales? Are there any innovative or unusual marketing concepts that will enhance customer acceptance—e.g., leasing where only sales were previously attempted?

Indicate whether the product or service will be introduced initially, nationally or on a regional level. If on a regional level, explain why and indicate if and when you plan to extend sales to other sections of the country.

Discuss any seasonal trends and what can be done to promote sales out of season.

Describe any plans to obtain government contracts to support product development costs and overhead.

B. *Pricing:* Many entrepreneurs have told us that they have a superior product that they plan to sell for a lower price than their competitors' product. This makes a bad impression for two reasons. First, if their product is as good as they say it is, they must think they are very poor sales people to have to offer it at a lower price than the competition. Second, costs tend to be underestimated. If you start out with low costs and prices, there is little room to maneuver; and price hikes will be tougher to implement than price cuts.

The pricing policy is one of the more important decisions you will have to make. The "price must be right" to penetrate the market, maintain a market position and produce profits. Devote ample time to considering a number of pricing strategies and convincingly present the one you select.

Discuss the prices to be charged for your products or services and compare your pricing policy with those of your major competitors. Discuss the gross profit margin between manufacturing and ultimate sales costs. Indicate whether this margin is large enough to allow you a profit and also allow for distribution and sales; warranty; service; amortization of development and equipment costs; and price competition.

Explain how the price you set will enable you to:

• Get the product or service accepted

• Maintain and profitably increase your market share in the face of competition

• Produce profits.

Justify any price increases over competitive items on the basis of newness, quality, warranty, and service.

If your product is to be priced lower than your competition's, explain how you will do this and maintain profitability—e.g., greater effectiveness in manufacturing and distributing the product, lower labor costs, lower overhead, or lower material costs.

Discuss the relationship of price, market share and profits. For example, a higher price may reduce volume but result in a higher gross profit. Describe any discount allowance for prompt payment of volume purchases.

C. *Sales Tactics:* Describe the methods that will be used to make sales and distribute the product or service. Will the company use its own sales force; sales representatives; distributors? Can you use manufacturers' sales organizations already selling related products? Describe both the initial plans and longer range plans for a sales force. Discuss the margins to be given to retailers, wholesalers, and salesmen and compare them to those given by your competition.

If distributors or sales representatives are to be used, describe how they have been selected, when they will start to represent you and the areas they will cover. Show a table that indicates the build-up of dealers and representatives by month and the expected sales to be made by each dealer. Describe any special policies regarding discounts, exclusive distribution rights, etc.

If a direct sales force is to be used, indicate how it will be structured and at what rate it will be built up. If it is to replace a dealer or representative organization, indicate when and how. Show the sales expected per salesperson per year, what commission incentive and/or salary they are slated to receive, and compare these figures to the average for your industry.

Present as an exhibit a selling schedule and a sales budget that includes all marketing, promotion and service costs. This sales expense exhibit should also indicate when sales will commence and the lapse between a sale and a delivery.

D. *Service and Warranty Policies:* If your company will offer a product that will require service and warranties, indicate the importance of these to the customers' purchasing decision and discuss your method of handling service problems. Describe the kind and term of any warranties to be offered, whether service will be handled by a company service organization, agencies, dealers and distributors, or factory return. Indicate the proposed charge for service calls and whether service will be a profitable or breakeven operation. Compare your service and warranty policies and practices to those of your principal competitors.

E. *Advertising and Promotion:* Describe the approaches the company will use to bring its product to the attention of prospective pruchasers. For OEM and industrial products indicate the plans for trade show participation, trade magazine advertisements, direct mailings, the preparation of product sheets and promotional literature, and the use of advertising agencies. For consumer products indicate what kind of advertising and promotional campaign is contemplated to introduce the product and what kind of sales aids will be provided to dealers. The schedule and cost of promotion and advertising should be presented. If advertising will be a significant part of company expenses, an exhibit showing how and when these costs will be incurred should be included.

4. DESIGN AND DEVELOPMENT PLANS

If the product, process or service of the proposed venture requires any design and development before it is ready to be placed on the market, the nature and extent of this work should be fully discussed. The investor will want to know the extent and nature of any design and development and the costs and time required to achieve a marketable product. Such design and development might be the engineering work necessary to convert a laboratory prototype to a finished product; or the design of special tooling; or the work of an industrial designer to make a product more attractive and saleable; or the identification and organization of manpower, equipment and special techniques to implement a service business—e.g., the equipment, new computer software and skills required for computerized credit checking.

A. *Development Status and Tasks:* Describe the current status of the product or service and explain what remains to be done to make it marketable. Describe briefly the competence or expertise that your company has or will acquire to complete this development. Indicate the type and extent of technical assistance that will be required, state who will supervise this activity within your organization and his experience in related development work.

B. *Difficulties and Risks:* Identify any major anticipated design and development problems and approaches to their solution. Discuss their possible effect on the schedule, cost of design and development, and time of market introduction.

C. *Product Improvement and New Products:* In addition to describing the development of the initial products, discuss any on-going design and development work that is planned to keep your product or service competitive and to develop new related products that can be sold to the same group of customers.

D. *Costs:* Present and discuss a design and development budget. The costs should include labor, materials, consulting fees, etc. Design and development costs are often underestimated. This can seriously impact cash flow projections. Accordingly, consider and perhaps show a 10%-20% cost contingency. These cost data will become an integral part of the financial plan.

5. MANUFACTURING AND OPERATIONS PLAN

The manufacturing and operations plan should describe the kind of facilities, plant location, space requirements, capital equipment and labor force (part- and full-time) that are required to provide the company's product or service. For a manufacturing business, discuss your policies regarding inventory control, purchasing, production control, and "make or buy decisions" (i.e., which parts of the product will be purchased and which operations will be performed by your work force). A service business may require particular attention and focus on an appropriate location, an ability to minimize overhead, lease the required equipment, and obtain competitive productivity from a highly skilled or a trained labor force.

The discussion guidelines given below are general enough to cover both product and service businesses. Only those that are relevant to your venture— be it product or service—should be addressed in the business plan.

A. *Geographic Location:* Describe the planned location of the business and discuss any advantages or disadvantages of the site in terms of wage rates, labor unions, labor availability, closeness to customers or suppliers, access to transportation, state and local taxes and laws, utilities and zoning. For a service business, proximity to customers is generally a "must."

B. *Facilities and Improvements:* If yours is an existing business, describe the facilities currently used to conduct the company's business. This should include plant and office space; storage and land areas; machinery, special tooling and other capital equipment.

If your venture is a start-up, describe how and when the necessary facilities to *start* production will be acquired. Discuss whether equipment and space will be leased or acquired (new or used) and indicate the costs and timing of such actions. Indicate how much of the proposed financing will be devoted to plant and equipment. (These cost data will become part of the financial plan.)

Discuss how and when plant space and equipment will be expanded to the capacities required for future sales projections. Discuss any plans to improve or add to existing plant space or move the facility. Explain future equipment needs and indicate the timing and cost of such acquisitions. A three year planning period should be used for these projections.

C. *Strategy and Plans:* Describe the manufacturing processes involved in your product's production and any decisions with respect to subcontracting component parts rather than manufacturing in-house. The "make or buy" strategy adopted should consider inventory financing, available labor skills and other non-technical questions as well as purely production, cost, and capability issues. Justify your proposed "make or buy" policy. Discuss any surveys you have completed of potential subcontractors and suppliers, and who these are likely to be.

Present a production plan that shows cost-volume information at various sales levels of operation with breakdowns of applicable material, labor, purchased components and factory overhead. Discuss the inventory required at various sales levels. These data will be incorporated into cash flow projections. Explain how any seasonal production loads will be handled without severe dislocation—e.g., by building inventory or using part-time help in peak periods.

Briefly, describe your approach to quality control, production control, inventory control. Explain what quality control and inspection procedures the company will use to minimize service problems and associated customer dissatisfaction.

Discuss how you will organize and operate your purchasing function to ensure that adequate materials are on hand for production, the best price has been obtained, and that raw materials and in-process inventory, and hence, working capital, have been minimized.

D. *Labor Force:* Exclusive of management functions (discussed later), does the local labor force have the necessary skills in sufficient quantity and quality (lack of absenteeism, productivity), to manufacture the products or supply the services of your company. If the skills of the labor force are inadequate to the needs of the company, describe the kinds of training that you will use to upgrade their skills. Discuss whether the business can provide training and still offer a competitive product both in the short-term (first year) and longer-term (2-5 years).

6. MANAGEMENT TEAM

The management team is the key to turning a good idea into a successful business. Investors look for a committed management team with a balance of technical, managerial and business skills, and experience in doing what is proposed.

Accordingly, this section of the business plan will be of primary interest to potential investors and will significantly influence their investment decisions. It should include a description of the key management personnel and their primary duties; the organizational structure; and the board of directors.

A. *Organization:* In a table, present the key management roles in the company and the invidual who will fill each position

Discuss any current or past situations where the key management people have worked together that indicate how their skills complement each other and result in an effective management team. If any key individuals will not be on hand at the start of the venture, indicate when they will join the company.

In a new business, it may not be possible to fill each executive role with a full-time person without excessively burdening the overhead of the venture. One solution is to use part-time specialists or consultants to perform some functions. If this is your plan, discuss it and indicate who will be used and when they will be replaced by a full-time staff member.

If the company is established and of sufficient size, an organization chart can be appended as an exhibit.

B. *Key Management Personnel:* Describe the exact duties and responsibilities of each of the key members of the management team. Include a brief (three or four sentence) statement of the career highlights of each individual that focuses on accomplishments that demonstrate his or her ability to perform the assigned role.

Complete resumes for each key management member should be included here or as an exhibit to the business plan. These resumes should stress training, experience and accomplishments of each person in performing functions similar to that person's role in the venture. Accomplishments should be discussed in such concrete terms as profit and sales improvement; labor management; manufacturing or technical achievements; and ability to meet budgets and schedules. Where possible it should be noted who can attest to accomplishments and what recognition or rewards were received—e.g., pay increases, promotions, etc.

C. *Management Compensation and Ownership:* The likelihood of obtaining financing for a start-up is small when the founding management team is not prepared to accept initial modest salaries. If the founders demand substantial salaries in excess of what they received at their prior employment, the potential investor will conclude that their psychological commitment to the venture is a good deal less than it should be.

State the salary that is to be paid to each key person and compare it to the salary received at his/her last independent job. Set forth the stock ownership planned for the key personnel, the amount of their equity investment (if any), and any performance-dependent stock option or bonus plans that are contemplated.

D. *Board of Directors:* Discuss the company's philosophy as to the size and composition of the board. Identify any proposed board members and include a one or two sentence statement of the member's background that shows how he or she can benefit the company.

E. *Management Assistance and Training Needs:* Describe, candidly, the strengths and weaknesses of your management team and Board of Directors. Discuss the kind, extent and timing of any management training that will be required to overcome the weaknesses and obtain effective venture operation. Also discuss the need for technical and management assistance during the first three years of your venture. Be as specific as you can as to the kind, extent and cost of such assistance and how it will be obtained.

F. *Supporting Professional Services:* State the legal (including patent), accounting, advertising and banking organizations that you have selected for your venture. Capable, reputable and well known supporting service organizations can not only provide significant direct, professional assistance, but can also add to the credibility of your venture. In addition, properly selected professional organizations can help you establish good contacts in the business community, identify potential investors and help you secure financing.

7. OVERALL SCHEDULE

A schedule that shows the timing and interrelationship of the major events necessary to launch the venture and realize its objectives is an essential part of a business plan. In addition to being a planning aid and showing deadlines critical to a venture's success, a well-prepared schedule can be an extremely effective sales tool in raising money from potential investors. A well-prepared and realistic schedule demonstrates the ability of the management team to plan for venture growth in a way that recognizes obstacles and minimizes risk.

Prepare, as a part of this section, a month-by-month schedule that shows the timing of activities such as product development, market planning, sales programs, and production and operations. Sufficient detail should be included to show the timing of the primary tasks required to accomplish an activity.

Show on the schedule the deadlines or milestones critical to the venture's success. This should include events such as:

- Incorporation of the venture (for a new business)

- Completion of design and development

- Completion of prototypes (a key date; its achievement is a tangible measure of the company's ability to perform)

- When sales representatives are obtained

- Displays at trade shows

- When distributors and dealers are signed up

- Order of materials in production quantities

- Start of production or operation (another key date because it is related to the production of income)

- Receipt of first orders

- First sales and deliveries (a date of maximum interest because it relates directly to the company's credibility and need for capital)

- Payment of first accounts receivable (cash in)

The schedule should also show the following and their relation to the development of the business:

- Number of management personnel

- Number of production and operations personnel

- Additions to plant or equipment

Discuss in a general way the activities most likely to cause a schedule slippage, and what steps you would take to correct such slippages. Discuss the impact of schedule slippages on the venture's operation, especially its potential viability and capital needs. Keep in mind that the time to do things tends to be underestimated—even more than financing requirements. So be realistic about your schedule.

8. CRITICAL RISKS AND PROBLEMS

The development of a business has risks and problems, and the business plan invariably contains some implicit assumptions about them. The discovery of any unstated negative factors by potential investors can undermine the credibility of the venture and endanger its financing.

On the other hand, identifying and discussing the risks in your venture demonstrates your skills as a manager and increases your credibility with a venture capital investor. Taking the initiative to identify and discuss risks helps you demonstrate to the investor that you have thought about them and can handle them. Risks then tend not to loom as large black clouds in the investor's thinking about your venture.

Accordingly, identify and discuss the major problems and risks that you think you will have to deal with to develop the venture. This should include a description of the risks relating to your industry, your company and its personnel, your product's market appeal and the timing and financing of your start-up. Among the risks that might require discussion are:

- Price cutting by competitors

- Any potentially unfavorable industry-wide trends

- Design or manufacturing costs in excess of estimates

- Sales projections not achieved

- Product development schedule not met

- Difficulties or long lead times encountered in the procurement of parts or raw materials

- Difficulties encountered in obtaining bank credit lines because of tight money

- Larger than expected innovation and development costs to stay competitive

- Availability of trained labor

This list is not meant to be complete but only indicative of the kinds of risks and assumptions that might be discussed.

Indicate which of your assumptions or potential problems are most critical to the success of the venture. Describe your plans for minimizing the impact of unfavorable developments in each risk area on the success of your venture.

9. COMMUNITY BENEFITS

The proposed venture should be an instrument of community and human development as well as economic development, and it should be responsive to the expressed desires of the community.

Describe and discuss the potential economic and non-economic benefits to members of the community that could result from your venture.

Among the potential benefits that may merit discussion are:

Economic Development

- number of jobs generated in each of the first three years of the venture

- number and kind of new employment opportunities for previously unemployed or underemployed individuals

- number of skilled and higher paying jobs
- ownership and control of venture assets by community residents
- purchase of goods and services from local suppliers

Human Development

- new technical skills development and associated career opportunities for community residents
- management development and training
- employment of unique skills within the community that are not unused

Community Development

- development of community's physical assets
- improved perception of CDC responsiveness and their role in the community
- provision of needed, but unsupplied, services or products to the community
- improvements in the living environment
- community support, participation and pride in the venture
- development of community-owned economic structure and decreased absentee business ownership

Describe any compromises or time lags in venture profitability that may result from trying to achieve some or all of the kinds of benefits cited above. Any such compromises or lags in profitability should be justified in the context of all the benefits achieved and the role of the venture in a total, planned program of economic, human and community development.

10. THE FINANCIAL PLAN

The financial plan is basic to the evaluation of an investment opportunity and should represent the entrepreneur's best estimates of future operations. Its purpose is to indicate the venture's potential and the timetable for financial viability. It can also serve as an operating plan for financial management of the venture.

In developing the financial plan, three basic forecasts must be prepared:

a. Profit and Loss Forecasts for three years

b. Cash Flows Projections for three years

c. Pro Forma Balance Sheets at start-up, semi-annually in the first year and at the end of each of the first three years of operation

In the case of an existing venture seeking expansion capital, balance sheets and income statements for the current and two prior years should be presented in addition to these financial projections.

Sample forms for preparing financial projections have been provided as Tables 18-20.[1] It is recommended that the venture's financial and marketing personnel prepare them, with assistance from an accountant if required. In addition to these three basic financial exhibits, a breakeven chart (Table 21) should be presented that shows the level of sales required to cover all operating costs.

After you have completed the preparation of the financial exhibits, briefly highlight in writing the important conclusions that can be drawn. This might include the maximum cash requirement, the amount to be supplied by equity and debt; the level of profits as a percent of sales; how fast any debts are repaid; etc.

A. *Profit and Loss Forecast (Table 18)*

The preparation of pro forma income statements is the profit planning part of financial management. Crucial to the earnings forecasts—as well as other projections—is the sales forecast. You have already developed sales forecasts while completing your Market Research and Analysis section. The sales data projected should be used here.

Once the sales forecasts are in hand, production costs (or operations costs for a service business) should be budgeted. The level of production or operation that is required to meet the sales forecasts and also to fulfill inventory requirements must be determined. The material, labor, service and manufacturing overhead requirements must be developed and translated into cost data. A separation of the fixed and variable elements of these costs is desirable, and the effect of sales volume on inventory, equipment acquisitions and manufacturing costs should be taken into account.

Sales expense should include the costs of selling the distribution, storage, discounts, advertising and promotion. General and administrative expense should include management salaries, secretarial costs, and legal and accounting expenses. Manufacturing or operations overhead includes rent, utilities, fringe benefits, telephone, etc.

[1]Robert Morris Associates (The National Association of Bank Loan Officers and Credit Men) also publishes forms for preparing financial projections as well as instructions for preparing supporting worksheets for Accounts Payable Disbursements, Accounts Receivables Collections, Material Flow and Purchases, etc. These instructions and forms are: Charles G. Zimmerman, "Projection of Financial Statements— And the Preparatory Use of Work Sheet Schedules for Budgets" and RMA Form C-117, "Projection of Financial Statements," (Philadelphia, Pennsylvania: Robert Morris Associates, 1961).

TABLE 18

PRO FORMA INCOME STATEMENTS

	1st Year – Months												2nd Year Quarters				3rd Year Quarters			
	1	2	3	4	5	6	7	8	9	10	11	12	1Q	2Q	3Q	4Q	1Q	2Q	3Q	4Q
Sales																				
Less: Discounts																				
Less: Bad Debt Provision																				
Less: Materials Used																				
Direct Labor																				
Manufacturing Overhead(1)																				
Other Manufacturing Expense (Leased Equipment)																				
Total Cost of Goods Sold																				
Gross Profit (or Loss)																				
Less: Sales Expense																				
Engineering Expense																				
General and Administrative Expense(2)																				
Operating Profit (or Loss)																				
Less: Other Expense (e.g., interest, depreciation)																				
Profit (Loss) Before Taxes																				
Income Tax Provision																				
Profit (Loss) After Taxes																				

(1) Includes rent, utilities, fringe benefits, telephone.
(2) Includes office supplies, accounting and legal services, management, etc.

Earnings projections should be prepared monthly in the first year of operation and quarterly for the second and third years.

If these earnings projections are to be useful they must represent management's realistic, best estimates of probable operating results. Sales or operating cost projections that are either too conservative or too optimistic have little value as aids to policy formulation and decision-making.

Discussion of Assumptions: Because of the importance of profit and loss projections as an indication of the potential financial feasibility of a new venture to potential investors, it is extremely important that any assumptions made in its preparation be fully explained and documented. Such assumptions could include the amount allowed for bad debts and discounts, and any assumptions made with respect to sales expenses or general and administrative costs which are fixed percentages of costs or sales.

Risks and Sensitivity: Once the income statements have been prepared, draw on Section 8 of these guidelines to highlight any major risks that could prevent the venture's sales and profit goals from being attained, and the sensitivity of profits to these risks.

This discussion should reflect the entrepreneur's thinking about the risks that might be encountered in the firm itself, the industry, and the environment. This could include such things as the effect of a 20% reduction in sales projections, or the impact over time of a learning curve on the level of productivity.

B. *Pro Forma Cash Flows Analysis (Table 19)*

For a new venture the cash flows forecast can be more important than the forecasts of profits because it details the amount and timing of expected cash inflows and outflows. Usually the level of profits, particularly during the start-up years of a venture, will not be sufficient to finance operating asset needs. Moreover, cash inflows do not match the outflows on a short-term basis. The cash flows forecast will indicate these conditions and allow management to plan cash needs.

Given a level of projected sales and capital expenditures over a specific period, the cash forecast will highlight the need for and timing of additional financing and indicate peak requirements for working capital. Management must decide how this additional financing is to be obtained, on what terms, and how it is to be repaid. Part of the needed financing will be supplied by the equity financing (that is sought by this business plan), part by bank loans for one to five years, and the balance by short-term lines of credit from banks. This information becomes part of the final cash flows forecast.

If the venture is in a seasonal or cyclical industry, or is in an industry in which suppliers require a new firm to pay cash, or if an inventory build-up occurs before the product can be sold and produce revenues, the cash flows forecast is crucial to the continuing solvency of the business. A detailed cash flows forecast which is understood and used by management can help them

TABLE 19

PRO FORMA CASH FLOWS

	1st Year – Months												2nd Year Quarters				3rd Year Quarters			
	1	2	3	4	5	6	7	8	9	10	11	12	1Q	2Q	3Q	4Q	1Q	2Q	3Q	4Q
Cash Balance: Opening																				
Add: Cash Receipts																				
Collection of Accounts Receivable																				
Miscellaneous Receipts																				
Bank Loan Proceeds																				
Sale of Stock																				
Total Receipts																				
Less: Disbursements																				
Trade Payables																				
Direct Labor																				
Manufacturing Overhead																				
Leased Equipment																				
Sales Expense																				
Warranty Expense																				
General and Administrative Expense																				
Fixed Asset Additions																				
Income Tax																				
Loan Interest @ ___ %																				
Loan Repayments																				
Other Payments																				
Total Disbursements																				
Cash Increase (Decrease)																				
Cash Balance: Closing																				

direct their attention to operating problems without distractions caused by periodic cash crises that should have been anticipated. Cash flows projections should be made for each month of the first year of operation and quarterly for the second and third years.

Discussion of Assumptions: This should include assumptions made about the timing of collections receivables, trade discounts given, terms of payments to vendors, planned salary and wage increases, anticipated increases in any operating expenses, seasonality of the business as it affects inventory requirements, inventory turnovers per year, and capital equipment purchases. Thinking about such assumptions when planning your venture is useful for identifying issues which may later require attention if they are not to become significant problems.

Cash Flow Sensitivity: Once the cash flow has been completed, discuss the impact on cash needs that possible changes in some of the crucial assumptions would have; e.g., slower receivables collection or scales below forecasts. This will enable you to test the sensitivity of the cash budget based on differing assumptions about business factors, and to view several possible outcomes. Investors are vitally interested in this because it helps them estimate the possibility that you will need more cash sooner than planned.

C. *Pro Forma Balance Sheets (Table 20)*

The balance sheets detail the assets required to support the projected level of operations and show how these assets are to be financed (liabilities and equity). Investors and bankers look at the projected balance sheets to determine if debt to equity ratios, working capital, current ratios, inventory turnover, etc., are within the acceptable limits required to justify future financings projected for the venture.

Pro forma balance sheets should be prepared at start-up, semi-annually for the first year, and at the end of each of the first three years of operation.

D. *Breakeven Chart (Table 21)*

A breakeven chart shows the level of sales (and hence, production) needed to cover all your costs. This includes those costs that vary with the production level (manufacturing labor, material, sales costs) and those that do not change with production (rent, interest charges, executive salaries, etc.). The sales level that exactly equals all costs is the breakeven level for your venture.

It is very useful for the investor and the management to know what the breakeven point is and whether it will be easy or difficult to attain. It is very desirable for your projected sales to be sufficiently larger than the breakeven sales so that small changes in your performance do not produce losses. You should prepare a breakeven chart and discuss how your breakeven point might be lowered in case you start to fall short of your sales projections. You should also discuss the effect on your breakeven point of lower production capacity requirements.

TABLE 20

PRO FORMA BALANCE SHEETS

	Start-up	End of 6 Months	End of First Year	End of Second Year	End of Third Year
ASSETS					
Current					
Cash					
Marketable Securities					
Accounts Receivable					
Inventories					
Raw Materials and Supplies					
Work in Process					
Finished Goods					
Total Inventory					
Prepaid Items					
Total Current Assets					
Plant and Equipment					
Less: Accumulated Depreciation					
Net Plant and Equipment					
Deferred Charges					
Other Assets (Identify)					
TOTAL ASSETS					
LIABILITIES AND STOCKHOLDERS' EQUITY					
Notes Payable to Banks					
Accounts Payable					
Accruals					
Federal and State Taxes					
Other					
TOTAL CURRENT LIABILITIES					
Long Term Notes					
Other Liabilities					
Common Stock					
Capital Surplus					
Retained Earnings					
TOTAL LIABILITIES AND STOCKHOLDERS' EQUITY					

TABLE 21

SAMPLE BREAKEVEN CHART

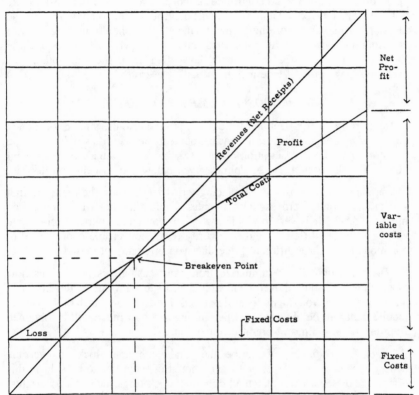

Units Produced

E. *Cost Control*

Your ability to meet your income and cash flows projections will depend on your ability to monitor and control costs. For this reason many investors like to know what type of accounting and cost control system you have or will use in your business. Accordingly, the financial plan should include a brief description of how you will obtain and report costs, who will be responsible for controlling various cost elements, how often he or she will obtain cost data, and how you will take action on budget overruns.

11. *PROPOSED COMPANY OFFERING*

The purpose of this section of the plan is to indicate the amount of money that is being sought, the nature and amount of the securities offered to the investor, and a brief description of the uses that will be made of the capital raised. The discussion and guidelines given below should help you do this.

You should realize that the financing terms you propose here are the first step in a negotiation process with a venture capital investor who is interested in your "deal." It is very possible that when you close your financing, you will be selling a different kind of security (e.g., convertible debt instead of common stock) for a different price than you originally proposed.

A. *Desired Financing:* Summarize from your cash flows projections how much money is required over the next three years to carry out the development and expansion of your business as described. Indicate how much of the capital requirement will be obtained by this offering and how much will be obtained from term loans, lines of credit or other sources.

B. *Securities Offering:* Describe the kind (common stock, convertible debenture, etc.), unit price, and total amount of securities to be sold in this offering. For securities other than common stock (e.g., debt with warrants, debt plus stock) indicate interest, maturity, and conversion conditions. Also show the percentage of the company that the investors of this offering will hold after it is completed, or after exercise of any stock conversion or purchase rights in the case of convertible debentures or warrants.

If the securities are being sold as a "private placement" (that is, exempt from SEC registration), you should include the following statement in this part of the plan:

"The shares being sold pursuant to this offering are restricted securities and may not be resold readily. The prospective investor should recognize that such securities might be restricted as to resale for an indefinite period of time. Each purchaser will be required to execute a Non-Distribution Agreement satisfactory in form to corporate counsel."

C. *Capitalization:* Present in tabular form the current and proposed (post-offering) number of outstanding shares of common stock. Indicate any shares offered by key management people and show the number of shares that they will hold after completion of the proposed financing.

Indicate how many shares of your company's common stock will remain authorized but unissued after the offering and how many of these will be reserved for stock options for future key employees.

D. *Use of Funds:* Investors like to know how their money is going to be spent. Provide a description of how the capital raised will be used. Summarize, as specifically as possible, what amount will be used for such things as product design and development; capital equipment; marketing; and general working capital needs.

The main body of the business plan ends here. Appendices begin at this point.

Final Note

All projections within a business plan must be based on realism. Accurate planning and performance measurement is dependent on realistic projections of future outcomes. In addition, projections will be the basis for critical decisions relating to all aspects of the firm's operation. Unreasonable expectations can cause resources to be spent unwisely and create suspicion among potential lenders and investors.

Every projection stated must be firmly documented, giving reasonable evidence that it can be achieved. A plan of action must be detailed, discussing strategy and tactics. For example, in a market forecast a firm must undertake an analysis of market opportunities and the capability of the firm to exploit those potentials. Once the sales projection is made, it should be backed by reasonable assurances of an expanding market. After this is accomplished, specific marketing steps to achieve the stated objective must be discussed. These endeavors might include the opening of new offices; introduction of new or modified products/services; addition of new sales personnel; new customer identification; expanding needs of existing customers; and/or enhanced promotion effort.

Whether it is sales projections, profit and loss estimates, cash-flow forecasts, or other financial predictions, realistic appraisals and approaches are mandatory in order to prevent unwise application of resources and disappointment among managers, creditors, and investors.

An entrepreneur should also consider and evaluate internal and external forces that affect the business in question and report their impact in the business plan under the section entitled "Critical Risks and Problems." These forces are listed in Tables 22 and 23.

TABLE 22

INTERNAL FACTORS

Expansion Plans
Pricing Structure
Operational Limitations
Financial Limitations
Research and Development
Introduction of New Product/Services
Marketing Dynamics
Revenue and Earnings Projections
Market Expansion

TABLE 23

ENVIRONMENTAL (EXTERNAL) FACTORS

Economic Cycles
Business Trends
Government Regulations
State of Technology
Competitive Conditions
Changing Demand Patterns
Industry Trends
Unions
Inflation
Changes in Population Profile
International Events

It is the opinion of many small business experts that entrepreneurs/ managing teams should not attempt to construct statements or attempt forecasting. Most simply lack the marketing, financial, and accounting expertise to accomplish these feats adequately and to the satisfaction of funding outlets. Therefore, competent business consultants and/or accountants should be sought out to complete this laborious and tedious task. Chapter III and Table 24 provide information on individuals and/or organizations that may provide assistance.

TABLE 24

OUTSIDE SOURCES OF INFORMATION

ECONOMIC

General
Chamber of Commerce
Business friends
Social friends
Advisory board
Local service clubs
Customers
Advertising, sales
Board of Directors
Newspapers
Competition—unknown

↑

TECHNOLOGICAL	COMPANY	POLITICAL
Professional		*Educational and*
Services		*Governmental*
Accountants		Universities
Lawyers	*Internal*	Private and public libraries
Technical consultants		Small Business Administration
Management consultants ←	Owner-manager	→ U.S. Department of
Advertising agency	Key subordinates	Commerce
Insurance	Employees	Department of Agriculture
Bankers		Other Federal, State,
Investment bankers		and local agencies

SOCIAL ↓

Trade

Trade associations
Suppliers
Professional journals
Competition—known

Chapter VIII

APPROACHING THE INVESTOR
What Is Expected

Beefing Up the Business Plan

The success of any business endeavor will hinge on the decisions made by the entrepreneur and managers involved. A comprehensive business plan will assist in the decision-making function by allocating the firm's limited resources and evaluating managerial decisions. In addition, it forces the business to establish reasonable objectives and make logical choices. The plan should be viewed and conveyed as a path to follow. It allows the business to guide itself through anticipated and unexpected economic environments by forcing the entrepreneur to identify and deal with real and potential problems before they threaten the business.

In reference to what was mentioned earlier, the business plan should run between 40 and 60 pages (typed and double spaced), with an adequate number of appendices for purposes of illustration and detail. There are exceptions to this rule. Some plans can get by with fewer pages and others take more. It depends on many factors, some of which include product/service being marketed, age of the firm, type of industry, nature of funding, etc. Whatever the case, the business plan must be detailed enough to tell the whole story without being so long and drawn out as to bore the reader. Copies of the finished plan will need to be made for prospective investors. All reproductions should have nice-looking protective covers so as to project a professional image. Do an adequate job, but don't go overboard. Too much attention to cosmetics will give investors the immediate impression that substance is being compromised for image purposes, even though this may not be the case. If it is apparent that lots of time and money was spent to produce an "attention getter" cover, investors will feel that extravagance is the name of the game. Recently, an entrepreneur and managing team of a small wholesale business submitted a business plan with an expensive gold-embossed cover to a New York venture capital firm. To make matters worse, the first page of the business plan contained a smiling photograph of the entrepreneur. Well, it was good for a couple of laughs before being returned with a rejection letter.

Keep in mind that certain aspects of the business plan are more important than others. Quality and capability of management is generally given the highest consideration and must be emphasized accordingly. "Good managers can sell anything. Look at the pet rock, it was really nothing, but they made it sell," quoted an investor. He went on to say that "management is given approximately 60 percent weight in a funding decision, with the rest divided among the various components of the business plan." In addition, the marketing research segment of the plan is of great importance because it attempts to convey the marketability of the firm's product or service. Therefore, this section should be given added emphasis.

Initial Contacts with Money Sources

Most financial outlets have specific investment preferences. Many will invest only in selected geographic areas and in certain types of businesses. Also, they limit themselves as to the amount invested. Many will entertain proposals only for existing firms while others welcome start-up situations. Some do both. Studying these particulars will save countless hours pursuing the wrong funding sources. Most of the investors mentioned in Chapter XI have been listed with their preferences. After matching proposition with correct source, the next step involves contact.

Financial outlets generally don't like phone calls. They prefer that entrepreneurs mail them a cover letter and a two- or three-page summary of the business plan for initial consideration. The summary section of the completed plan can be used for this purpose. Make sure a competent business consultant, attorney, or accountant has reviewed the summary before sending it to the investors. In fact, several people should evaluate the summation to determine its merits. Their recommendation should be carefully considered. Any changes that strengthen the document should be made without reservation. Just remember that the summary must never exceed three pages. It is strictly an attention getter designed to spark investors' interest in reading the entire business plan. If they are pleased with what they see, the whole plan will be requested for additional consideration. Don't get discouraged if this process takes some time. An excellent way to determine an investor's interest in the proposition is the amount of time he spends looking over the plan. Extensive evaluation is a positive signal, without question.

While the business plan is being examined, the entrepreneur should be making a background investigation of the investor. This must be done to protect the business from hooking up with an unethical or otherwise difficult capital source. Ask for references. Contacting firms that have received funds from the prospective funding outlet is an ideal way to get valuable insight into the nature of the investor. In addition, checking with the U.S. Small Business Administration in Washington might prove to be helpful. Also, speaking with the local chamber of commerce in the city where the investor resides should yield some information. Some investors belong to professional trade organizations (listed in appendices P and Q). Give them a call to check the credentials of the funding source. Potential investors should be carefully reviewed in reference to their relationships with affiliated entrepreneurs and to the degree in which they provide initial and ongoing managerial assistance. Taking these inexpensive and cautious measures in the beginning may eliminate costly headaches down the road.

After the investors have critically evaluated and scrutinized the business plan, the entrepreneur will be informed of the decision by letter or phone. If the response is negative, ask why and what can be done to improve chances of successful funding. Maybe they know another source that may be interested. A positive answer will invoke an invitation to meet the money source personally.

The aforementioned procedure just outlined applies to most financial outlets. The exceptions are banks and governmental sources of funding. These outlets will normally meet with entrepreneurs beforehand to discuss the proposal. They may even request that a simple application form be completed. Ultimately, these sources will also demand a comprehensive business plan.

Presentation of the Business Plan

When a financial outlet requests a verbal presentation of the business plan, respond at once to set an appointment. Go to the meeting dressed appropriately. Appear mildly confident and poised. Avoid excessive zeal. In addition, conducting oneself in a polite, professional and dignified manner is a must. Many entrepreneurs with good business plans have failed to obtain capital because they didn't project a solid character image to investors.

The presentation is used to evaluate the entrepreneur and/or management team more than the business plan. After all, the investors have already read the plan at this point. The entrepreneur and others involved must be prepared to discuss all facets of the proposal in an intelligent and convincing manner, with a command of the facts. Below are some observations that will probably be made during the presentation stage:

— Does the entrepreneur and/or managing team appear structured and systematic?
— Is there enough business and technical expertise involved in the proposition? Can it be obtained if lacking?
— Is the entrepreneur and others involved realistic in their estimates of projections, risks, time, resources, etc.?
— How is criticism handled? Can helpful comments be accepted?
— Is forthrightness displayed? Are inconsistencies admitted frankly or evaded?
— Does the entrepreneur and/or managing team communicate effectively?

Specific questions will be asked. Even though most have been covered extensively in the business plan, a verbal response will be expected. Remember, the investors are searching for weaknesses. They will attempt to detect contradictions between the verbal presentation and what is stated in the plan. The most common questions put to entrepreneurs during the presentation are as follows:

— How much capital is requested?
— For what purposes will it be used?
— How will it be repaid?

— What security is being offered?
— Describe the product or service to be marketed.
— Who are the customers?
— Why will they buy?
— Who are the competitors?
— Why is this product/service better than the competition?
— By how much is the total market for the product/service growing?
— How long will it take to gear up for marketing?
— When will marketing endeavors begin?
— What are the background and track record of the company's management relative to the product/service and industry?
— What are their relevant management and business skills?
— What are the risks involved in this venture?
— What are the strengths of the proposal?
— What are the weaknesses of the proposal?
— What is the credit history of the principals involved in the project?
— How much capital do the principals intend on investing in the project?
— Has all the appropriate personal and business insurance been considered?
— Does the business have a competent attorney? Accountant? Who are they?

The responses received from the aforementioned questions will determine to a great extent whether funding is approved. A good presentation will substantially enhance the chances of getting funds.

Give and Take in Final Funding Negotiations

If the entrepreneur and business plan live up to investor expectations, the next barrier to overcome regards funding terms. This is a major bone of contention between investor and management which demands careful consideration. Many good deals have fallen apart during this stage of discussion. In a lending situation, the point of confrontation centers around the interest rate to be charged. Most businesses feel that financial outlets are demanding too much while the lenders contend it's not enough. When equity (ownership) is involved in the discussions, the argument rages over how much ownership the entrepreneur and others involved must forfeit to investors in exchange for their capital. The question of who controls what takes center stage.

It all boils down to perceived risks by the investors. Greater risks will force the entrepreneur to give up a larger portion of ownership in an equity deal or pay higher interest rates if lending is the financing vehicle. There is no steadfast rule used by investors to determine the pitfalls in prospective business propositions. Each financial outlet sees things differently and will act accordingly, although there are some general guidelines used in analyzing risks. Knowing these before going into negotiations will reduce frustration from the outset. They are:

— The less capital invested by the entrepreneur and others involved in the business, the more ownership demanded by investors in an equity arrangement. If loans are contemplated, higher rates of interest will be required. Most investors prefer that management invest in the business proposition to the maximum degree possible. One venture capitalist recently commented that he sleeps better knowing individuals running the business have invested money. "If their money is on the line, you can bet they will try harder to make things work."

— A start-up company will need to give up more ownership and/or pay higher interest rates than a going operation. This reasoning is quite obvious. An existing concern has a greater chance of survival.

— A business that operates in a high growth industry (computers, medical technology, alternative energy, information transfer, etc.) will be able to negotiate better equity terms or lower interest rates on loans than a firm that finds itself in a less promising sector of the economy.

— The general economic climate will affect investor attitude. Periods of recession and stagnation will find financial outlets wary and extremely cautious, probably demanding more equity or higher interest rates than would be the case in an expanding economy.

— Anticipated earnings growth will also affect investor reactions. If the prospects for continued profits are good, a better equity or lending deal can be arranged with the funding outlets.

Before entering into negotiations with investors, do some homework. Study similar funding arrangements. Know what to expect. Consult attorneys, accountants, and consultants in reference to the business proposition. Being well informed will impress the investors and help insure a fair funding agreement. When negotiating, keep in mind that both parties must give and take. Try to establish a relationship with the investor by establishing a candid and friendly rapport. Disagreements will happen, but it is critically important to maintain a positive and professional posture at all times. Communication is an absolute necessity during the negotiation process. Each party must clearly state their goals and let the other know if changes in position occur. Without this interreaction, negotiation will eventually come to a halt.

The entrepreneur/managing team should be keen negotiators. Investors will respect shrewdness. If a loan is being discussed, tell the lender that a high interest rate will retard earnings and adversely affect the firm's rate of growth. Attempt to prove this with hard figures. In an equity situation, mention that giving up too much ownership will have a negative impact on managerial incentive. Throw the investors a "high ball." Tell them that a high percentage of ownership must be retained by management. Use this as a starting point in the discussions.

Always appear willing to negotiate. Investors expect to give and take. Above all, don't get greedy. It's a turn-off to serious funding sources. Recently, an inventor created a number of ingenious energy efficient products and several investors expressed interest in providing capital to finance marketing endeavors. The inventor refused to give up more than 75 percent ownership in the business for what he called "control purposes." Because the products were new and unproven the investors refused to provide funding under his conditions. They made a counter-offer to hold 60 percent of ownership and would further reduce it to 40 percent once earnings were generated, thereby giving the inventor control later down the road. He still declined the offer and the deal broke apart. Realizing his mistake, the inventor decided to accept the offer, but it was too late. The investors wouldn't have anything to do with the proposition.

Too much emphasis on the idea of control can kill a good deal as it did in the case mentioned above. Remember, it's better to have 20 percent of a watermelon than 80 percent of a raisin. A properly structured deal can insure the entrepreneur and others involved eventual control of the business. Many investors will negotiate incentive/equity deals. This is where the entrepreneurs are given a smaller percentage of ownership in the beginning, which will increase as the business grows.

Whatever the case, don't get desperate and accept anything that comes along, even though the money is desperately needed. Most businesses would be wise not to accept poor or inadequate funding offers. The ideal scenario would be teaming up with reputable investors who are willing to assist in making the proposition operate and function successfully. Investors willing to help rather than hinder should be sought out. Appendix S provides an outline of a typical investment agreement.

Twenty-four Reasons Why Funds Requests Are Rejected

Listed below are some of the more common reasons why financial outlets refuse funding requests. The problems stem from deficiencies within the business and/or because of difficulties with the entrepreneur/managing team.

— Lack of Continuity—The business plan must demonstrate that the firm will continue uninterrupted if key employees of the firm leave or die.

— Unwillingness to Part with Equity—Too many entrepreneurs are unduly concerned over giving up ownership and/or control of the business. Overemphasis on this issue can kill a good deal in short order.

— Inability to Take Criticism—Many investors will make helpful suggestions concerning the proposal. Defensive reactions on the part of the entrepreneur/managing team will leave a bad impression. It denotes immaturity.

— Underestimating Capital Needs—Many entrepreneurs tend to underestimate capital requirements for the business. In some cases, it is a deliberate attempt to impress investors that something can be accomplished with less. Well, it doesn't. In fact, it displays a lack of good business sense. One of the major reasons for business failure is lack of adequate capitalization.

— Lack of a Total Plan—Most business plans that are submitted to funding outlets are strictly financial in nature. They fail to consider non-financial aspects such as production considerations.

— Unrealistic, Low Expense Forecasts—Reasonable expense projections must be made in order to accurately predict earnings flow. Overstated profit expectations based on erroneous expense data will only give investors the impression that numbers are being "churned" in order to create an attractive picture.

— Overstated Revenue Projections—If revenues fail in living up to expectation, the chances are that profits will do the same. Since the technical aspects of funding deals rely heavily on projected revenues and profits, realistic projections need to be made. In fact, investors will not allow overstated forecasts. They will use their financial expertise to adjust the figures appearing in the business plan. It's nice to have it done right the first time around. It shows that the entrepreneur/managing team know what they are doing.

— Little or No Experience in the Area of Operation—Investors will feel uncomfortable knowing that the firm's management is weak in the product/service area. The firm can compensate for this by hiring a consultant and/or managers with experience and knowledge in the product/service and industry.

— Self-centered—Many entrepreneurs don't like delegating authority to others when it needs to be done. they tend to be egocentric and think everything must evolve around them. Most fear losing control. "Ego in itself is not bad," stated one investor. "It's the unrestrained ego that causes problems, and we steer clear of that type of individual."

— Too Much Show—Trying to impress investors with fancy offices and cars will have only a negative impact. They will feel that too much is being spent on cosmetics and not enough on substance. Normally it gives the impression of extravagance.

— Seeking More Than Is Needed—This is called "Fudging" and is considered a no-no. It is easy to detect, and invokes the question, why is the extra money needed? The entrepreneur will find that it's an embarrassing situation and could weaken the relationship with the investor.

— Using Investors Against Each Other—Don't try to pit money sources against each other to enhance the bargaining position. It's a turn-off to investors and will not work. Many will refuse to talk after being exposed to this tactic. Now don't get the wrong idea. It is okay to have other funding alternatives. Just don't use them as bait to squeeze out what might be considered a better deal. It shows lack of tact.

— Lack of Appreciation for the Learning Process—The ability to learn rapidly is essential in today's business environment. Entrepreneurs must convince investors that they are capable of catching on quickly. Formal and informal discussion between investor and entrepreneur will reveal this quality. Learn from what the investor has to say. If learning ability is not shown to investors, funding may not be forthcoming.

— Sweet Talk—Don't butter up the investors. It's obvious and they do not like it one bit. Being too sweet and nice could kill a deal in short order. The investors know something is up and it creates suspicion from the very beginning, and that is "strike one" against the entrepreneur.

— Lack of Managerial Wholeness—Management is the most important consideration in the funding decision. Without the proper breadth of management and business experience to run the operation with a good chance of success, the probability of securing funds is nil.

— Wrong Timing—The product or service may not be ready for the market at this time, or the right time has already passed and there are too many existing competitors.

— Lack of Pragmatism—Entrepreneurs must remember that funding negotiations are a give and take situation requiring compromise on both sides. Unreasonable demands denote lack of practicality and will result in an invitation out the door. "One entrepreneur demanded to keep 65 percent of the business and invest only $10,000," says a New York venture capitalist. "Hell, he wanted us to foot $500,000 and retain only 35 percent of the business, and it was a start-up situation with no track record." The entrepreneur refused to compromise and the deal fell apart quickly.

— Inability to Communicate—Entrepreneurs who can't convey their ideas clearly and concisely in written or verbal form stand little chance of being funded. A banker for Chase Manhattan Bank recently stated that "if the entrepreneur and managing team can't explain and answer questions about the proposal in a clear and logical fashion, how are they going to market their service or product?"

— Lack of Trust—Many entrepreneurs feel that funding outlets can't be trusted and are cheats. It becomes obvious very quickly.

Information is withheld, former relationships are criticized, and complaints are made about rotten terms they got from other funding sources. One investor recently remarked that "When a paranoid entrepreneur comes down the pike, we run for the hills. It's trouble from the start."

— Lack of Appreciation for the Team Approach— "The entrepreneur who thinks he/she can do it all is a danger signal," stated an investor recently. He went on to say that "entrepreneurs who fail to recognize the need for a unified effort are being naïve. Today's business environment demands it."

— Intolerance—Information about personality and background will be sought by the prospective investors. Entrepreneurs who get insulted and upset when probing questions are asked leave a bad impression.

— Lack of Appreciation for a Buck—If the entrepreneur/managing team fail to show investors that their money is going to be treated with a lot of consideration and prudence, the deal will come apart. One of the biggest fears on the part of investors is that once their money is given to the entrepreneurs, it will be spent indiscriminately and recklessly. Entrepreneurs need to dispel this fear by showing the investor exactly how funds will be employed.

— Lack of Testing—A product or service should be tested on a small scale to evaluate results before attempting large distribution efforts. Testing reveals potentially costly faults that can be corrected before large efforts are executed. Telling investors that the product/service is ready to be marketed on a large scale without appropriate testing because "it's the greatest thing ever developed" is giving the wrong impression and will scare off serious investors. The business plan should make reference to testing procedures. If testing has already taken place, the results should be revealed.

— Lack of Caution—Studies have shown that most successful entrepreneurs are moderate risk takers and not the "high stakes rollers" they are publicized to be.

Chapter IX

MAKE IT SUCCESSFUL
Sweat and Money Are at Stake

Aim Toward the Future

Setting long-term goals and objectives can prove to be a roadmap guiding the business along a path to future profits and success. One of the foremost reasons for America's lack of competitive success in the international marketplace is the unwillingness of domestic business leaders to plan for the future. U.S. managers have been criticized throughout the industrial world for being "short termers," exploiting only immediate opportunities and, therefore, compromising long-term considerations that could prove to be more profitable. In reality, it is not the fault of the managers, but of society at large. American business leaders are rewarded by shareholders for their yearly performance. Consequently, they will do their best to look good on a short-term basis in order to enhance their immediate compensation and position. This problem is cultural and needs to be addressed by the country's political, business, and academic leadership.

Whatever the case, when looking to the future, an entrepreneur must also consider the past and present. By analyzing past and current business performance, insight can be gained into the forecasting function. Evaluating the firm's strengths and weaknesses, relative to financial performance, will set the stage for accurate projections. In addition, knowing the environmental conditions besetting the marketplace should play a significant role in the process of establishing forecasts.

Always plan at least five years into the future. Be flexible enough to allow for emergency situations that may or may not be anticipated (this is called "crisis planning"). For example, prior to the predicted gasoline crunch of 1979, Mayor Kelley of Ocean City, Maryland, which is a large eastern summer resort, stockpiled gas supplies and promised every visitor that he would have enough gas to get them home. He saved the resort from financial disaster that year.

Failure to plan for the long haul will result in short-term adventurism, thereby mis-allocating the firm's limited resources and compromising greater profit potentials.

Intimate Knowledge Is Critical for Success

It is important to know every aspect of the business inside and out. Knowledge of what makes the firm tick and move can be valuable in successfully overcoming present and future problems. Good information resources and personal experiences can be used to gain this valuable insight.

Managing for Success

Management is a broad topic covering many different disciplines. It is impossible to discuss all facets of the subject in the confines of this book. However, the important managerial elements of running a small business must be highlighted, and they are broadly reviewed here.

MANAGING CASH AND CREDIT

Always remember that money is a commodity that is bought and sold for a price (interest rates). It is one of the most precious resources available to a business and requires effective management if the firm is to survive and prosper.

Send out invoices consistently and promptly at about the same time each month. The bills should contain all relevant information about the sale (date purchased, cost, account balance, terms, etc.). When income is received from receivables or cash sales, deposit it promptly in interest bearing checking accounts or other insured accounts that can be drawn on readily. After paying obligations due, put the remaining cash back into the operation immediately so as to generate additional sales and profits. Idle cash or money sitting in low yielding accounts is not an example of effective money management.

Make sure that accounts receivable are current and take steps to keep them that way. Past dues can be costly if money must be borrowed or existing funds used to finance operations until accounts are collected. Therefore, credit and collection control procedures are critical to successful operation. Grant credit based upon certain conditions that may vary depending on the customer. This can be accomplished by evaluating potential accounts relative to their ability to pay. After that, payment terms and credit limits can be established. Also, existing accounts should be reviewed periodically in order to determine if changes in credit arrangements are necessary.

All prospective and existing accounts must be required to fill out a credit application form. The form should include a promise to pay according to the terms of the credit agreement and it can be used to investigate customers' credit history. Make sure the application has a release statement allowing permission to conduct a credit investigation.

If accounts are offered to customers, expect some problems to surface, especially during periods of economic recession. Normally, it is advisable and advantageous to work with slow payers instead of being overly rigid and maybe losing business as a result. Set up procedures for dealing with slow or delinquent accounts. Degrees of slowness should be established with the objective of applying increasing measures of pressure the longer the overdue remains unpaid. Extreme cases may have to be pursued legally. Many of these delinquent situations can be avoided if standards are developed and instituted to disallow existing or prospective customers from billing beyond their ability to repay.

When the business decides to use credit, always exercise conservatism and precedence. Pay bills on or before due dates so as to maintain a healthy credit history. A bad payment record can be expensive in terms of loss of credit privilege and higher interest charged by worried lenders. Take advantage of early payment discounts if they are economically favorable from a cash float standpoint (savings generated from the payment discount must be greater than the income that could be created by using the money in another way before the invoice is due).

In addition, maintaining good relations with all creditors, including bankers, can prove to be beneficial in the long run. Keep them informed as to what is happening with the business. Below are some tips that may help to accomplish this information function.

— Be candid about positive and negative situations. Many creditors will work with a business in a difficult environment if they are aware of the problems besetting the enterprise and its industry.
— Help the creditors to understand the business and industry. Sometimes ignorance is the biggest stumbling block to effective relationships.
— Provide some insight into management and control functions. This will gain the creditor's confidence and faith in that it shows a willingness to make things operate smoothly and efficiently.
— Be specific about short-term, intermediate-term, long-term, and crisis planning. Creditors dislike unanticipated disruptions. Tell them when things are going to take place.

It is not necessary to incorporate the aforementioned tips into creditor relationships, but they will help relieve some of the natural and obvious tensions that exist between borrowers and creditors. An atmosphere of mutual trust and respect will also be fostered leading to a lasting and growing relationship.

MANAGING OTHER FINANCES

Existing and prospective small business owners should attempt to understand the financial complexities involved in business operations. A thorough understanding of financial statements (balance sheet, profit and loss statement, cash flow statement) will provide a solid foundation for making good business decisions. These statements, showing all revenue, expense, asset, and liability accounts, should be prepared and examined once a month by a competent accountant and reviewed by the firm's owner(s). Each account within the statements should be shown for the current period and the same period for last year. In addition, current year-to-date totals can be given for financial control purposes.

Good financial statements will also serve to contain costs. Studying past and present information concerning cost accounts may provide valuable insight into the conditions affecting expense figures. Also, an examination of revenue accounts may indicate the degree of product/ service mark-up or mark-down required to maintain adequate levels of sales and profits. It may show a need to alter existing lines through modification, new introductions, and/or phase-out.

Financial statements are discussed extensively in Chapter VII.

Managing Growth

Growing too fast can be as hazardous as a no-growth situation, if not more so. Growth must be implemented and managed carefully to insure that the business does not expand beyond its ability to control and/or finance operation. Many firms have met with demise because of uncontrollable expansion. The giant, W. T. Grant, failed because it grew beyond its capability to finance expansion internally and externally. The result was bankruptcy.

Growth should be mapped out well in advance. Within these plans a reasonable estimation of resources necessary in carrying out objectives must be evaluated and scrutinized to determine the feasibility of expansion. If resources will be lacking because of internal constraints and/or environmental factors, expansion objectives should be altered to meet with the realities of the situation.

Managing Inventory

Proper inventory management can mean the difference between profit or loss, and in some cases survival. Excessive inventories will lock up needed cash that would otherwise be used to generate sales and profits.

If an inventory system is to be effective, its main objectives should be cost containment and efficient delivery. A study of purchase activity relative to finished goods and raw materials will need to be performed in order to accomplish these goals. Once the study and evaluation is completed, a minimum amount of inventory within each item and raw material classification can be stored to satisfy short-term customer orders. In addition, production can be maintained.

Below are some additional tips for addressing the inventory problem.

— Compare prices among suppliers.
— Purchasing should be controlled by one individual or department. Duplication of effort is a waste of time and money.
— All finished goods or raw material orders should be confirmed in writing, outlining every cost and condition, to avoid misunderstandings which do occur at times.
— When goods are delivered, check to make sure that everything is received in proper condition.
— Cross-reference the supplier's invoice with the written quotation. This will avoid overcharges which occasionally happen.

Whatever inventory procedure is implemented, the cost of the endeavor must be less than its potential savings. Excessive inventory control can inflict the same harm as too little. A balance must be struck. The optimum solution is hard to find, but it is imperative if the business is to manage resources correctly.

There are complex statistical methods used to determine optimum inventory levels. Discussion of these are beyond the scope of this book. Therefore, seek out a competent business consultant when faced with inventory problems. Talking with other business owners who have faced similar difficulties may provide a wealth of helpful information. Also, seeking out college professors with specialties in the field of information sciences may prove to be useful in solving problems related to inventory control.

MANAGING MARKETS

All businesses survive based upon their ability to react to changes in market conditions and consumer tastes. If a business expects to prosper, it should be constantly on guard for future trends that may provide opportunities if exploited or even help avoid costly disasters. Expanding markets must be carefully evaluated against available resources to determine the possibility of further penetration or introduction. Stagnating markets require serious review if the business is involved. Can existing sales be maintained profitably? Is there any room for new sales? If so, why and how can they be achieved? Does the firm possess unique advantages allowing it to beat competition in stagnant markets? Declining markets are equally important to understand, especially when existing sales are at stake. Are sales holding firm or declining slower than the total market? Can further profits be squeezed out? When should market exit take place?

Addressing the reality of changing markets will help insure continual existence and profitable operation. Constantly be aware of trends and try to determine how the business may be affected.

MANAGING PEOPLE

Many business experts contend that people are a firm's most important resource. This reasoning revolves around the fact that labor is generally the largest expenditure faced by most businesses. Therefore, it would make economic sense to manage labor resources efficiently.

Periodically analyze and evaluate personnel requirements. Make sure there are enough people to get the job done. Failure to operate at demand capacity will result in lost opportunities and increased costs. If too many workers are employed, expenses will increase faster than sales or profits on a percentage basis, thereby suggesting a reduction in force. In addition, all positions within the business should be reviewed regularly to determine their relative importance and worth to the business. Time will constantly change perceptions. This job analysis may reveal such things as redundant effort, reduced work load, down time, etc., that would justify employment cuts. It may be discovered that full-time positions should be reduced to part-time status. Generally, it is less costly to maintain two part-timers than one full-timer doing the same job, although there are hazards to this approach. Small businesses have enough problems attracting good help because of financial constraints. Emphasizing part-time positions too heavily may turn good employees or prospective candidates away.

Employment cutback decisions are difficult to make because of the human element involved. But remember, "It is better to rule from the head than to be dominated by the heart in a business situation." Employees singled out for cuts should be given ample warning. Try to assist them in finding new jobs. In addition, explaining the reasons for cuts to terminated and remaining employees will lessen the negative impact on morale.

It is also wise to develop a plan for absenteeism, which can be costly in terms of lost efficiency and the paying of overtime to someone else to perform the necessary work. For example, most absenteeism occurs on Monday which, of course, follows the weekend. One large company adopted a policy of distributing paychecks on Monday, and no-shows were reduced by 50 percent within two weeks of the decision. Another illustration explaining the effectiveness of a policy directed toward controlling absenteeism can be found in the Small Business Administration's management aid number 206, written by Jack H. Feller. It states that an "owner/manager of one small company eliminated vacations and sick leave. Instead, this owner/manager gave each employee thirty days' annual leave to use as the employee saw fit. At the end of the year, the employees were paid at regular rates for the leave they didn't use. To qualify for the year-end pay, the employee had to prove that sick leave was taken only for that purpose. Nonsick leave had to be applied for in advance. As a result, unscheduled absences and overtime pay were reduced significantly. In addition, employees were happier and more productive than they were under the old system."

When approaching worker incentives, always recognize and compensate exceptional work and effort. Both monetary (money and fringes) and psychological (non-monetary benefits) rewards should be used to stimulate interest, productivity, and satisfaction. In addition, always try to involve employees in the management of the business. Seek out their advice and counsel. Many employees have ideas that may not be apparent to the owners and/or managers. Giving them a feeling of worth and allowing their input into the decision-making function will usually provide positive reinforcement for all concerned.

Keeping good records is also an important part of people management. It can also protect the business from unwarranted legal actions taken by disgruntled employees or governmental bodies. The firm should make all employees fill out application forms that conform to federal government standards. Asking the wrong questions on the form can bring legal suit, but the procedure is necessary to insure accurate information on employees. In addition, records concerning work history (absenteeism, sick leave, vacation time, promotion, demotion, salary/wage increases or decreases) should be verified by appropriate documentation. For example, use written appraisal forms when evaluating employees. Review the contents of the forms with workers and then ask them to sign the final appraisal documents. This will protect the firm in the event that certain employees pursue legal action because of the firm's reactions due to the results appearing on the appraisal form. Also, interviewing and asking exiting employees to sign an exit document outlining their reason for leaving can save the firm expenses incurred because of unjust unemployment insurance claims.

Businesses employing workers must have an in-depth knowledge of every job within the firm. First, a job analysis needs to be completed which attempts to identify the specific tasks within each position and how the particular jobs relate to their immediate environment. Table 25 contains a checklist for conducting a job analysis. Second, after the job analysis is performed, a description of each position must be written detailing the responsibilities and conditions of each position in the business. This job description, as it is called, is utilized for purposes of promoting, demoting, selecting, transferring, and training existing or prospective employees. An outline of a job description appears in Table 26. Third, job specifications must be developed and used to identify and describe the physical and mental qualifications needed to perform the tasks in question. Generally, this document will also outline the

TABLE 25

SUMMARY/REVIEW CHECKLIST FOR CONDUCTING
A JOB ANALYSIS

_____ 1. Gather data concerning the duties and qualifications of the job:

   _____a. think about the various duties, responsibilities and qualifications of the job and write them down.

   _____b. utilize the job analysis outline form to help you organize your thoughts.

   _____c. ask an employee who now holds the job to list the duties and responsibilities of the job as well as the qualifications which he or she believes are needed.

   _____d. review the duties, responsibilities and qualifications for the job with the person who supervises the job, if you are not doing that yourself directly.

   _____e. combine all job analysis notes to create a clear picture of the job.

_____ 2. Keep in mind the ultimate goals of the analysis: to simplify and improve employee recruitment, training and development; to evaluate jobs so that appropriate salary and wage rates can be set.

SOURCE: U.S. Small Business Administration.

TABLE 26

OUTLINE FOR WRITING A JOB DESCRIPTION

INSTRUCTIONS: Determine the positions for which you would like to write job descriptions. Remember that job descriptions are particularly useful in areas where job turnover is high, since they aid in recruitment, selection, and training of new employees. Now, complete the information below.

JOB DESCRIPTION

Date: _____

JOB TITLE:

STATEMENT OF THE JOB
(A brief summary of the job, stating its general nature)

MAJOR DUTIES
(including responsibilities for quantity and quality of work, safety of others, equipment, decisions to be made, and schedules to be met. Most jobs can be described in outline form with three to eight duties)

1.

MINOR DUTIES
(include those duties only performed occasionally)

RELATIONSHIPS
(whom does a person in this position supervise? report to? work with?)

SOURCE: U.S. Small Business Administration.

hazards inherent in these positions. Test requirements may also be included in order to evaluate the capabilities of existing or potential employees. The job specification procedure will protect the firm against legitimate discrimination decision. For example, the specification document might state that individuals over six feet tall are unsuitable for a particular task. Therefore, people exceeding six feet in height will probably be hard-pressed to bring suit unless they can prove that the job specification itself is flawed. An outline for writing a job specification is shown in Table 27. Fourth, a job classification is needed to evaluate the value of particular positions to a business. This is determined by examining job complexities, duties, and contribution to the firm. Once this procedure is completed, pay scales are developed.

TABLE 27

OUTLINE FOR WRITING A JOB SPECIFICATION

INSTRUCTIONS: Determine the positions for which you would like to write job specifications. (Remember that job specifications are particularly useful in areas where job turnover is high, since they aid recruitment, selection, and training of new employees.) Now, complete the information below.

JOB SPECIFICATION

JOB TITLE: *Date:* _____

Education (List only that which is really necessary for the job, e.g., high school, college, trade schools, or other special training.)

Experience (The amount of previous and related experience which a new employee should have.)

Knowledge/Skills (List the specific knowledge and skills which the job may require.)

Physical and Mental Requirements (Mention any special physical or mental abilities required for the job, e.g., 20/20 eyesight, ability to lift 80 lb. bags, availability for irregular work hours, ability to work under time pressure, etc.)

SOURCE: U.S. Small Business Administration.

Many employers are learning the benefits of conducting orientation programs for new employees. Their purpose should be to familiarize new workers with the firm and their work environment. The objective is to reduce early turnovers, which can be a costly business expense. Generally, most firms do not begin to recover their cost of maintaining new inexperienced employees until after the first six months of employment. Unfortunately, this is when the greatest amount of turnover takes place. Most is due to misunderstandings or lack of communication between the firm and new workers. It may result in employees feeling out of place and/or overwhelmed. Involuntary termination or voluntary departure normally follows suit. Table 28 contains a checklist for establishing a job orientation program.

TABLE 28

JOB ORIENTATION CHECKLIST

_____Explain:

    _____company purpose
    _____company image
    _____kind of clients catered to

_____Introduce to other employees and positions

_____Explain relationship between new employee's position and other positions

_____Tour the building:

    _____working areas
    _____management office
    _____rest facilities
    _____records
    _____employee locker room or closet
    _____other relevant areas

_____Explain facilities and equipment

_____Review the duties and responsibilities of the job from the job description

_____Introduce to emergency equipment and safety procedures

_____Questions and answers

SOURCE: U.S. Small Business Administration.

MANAGING PRODUCTS/SERVICES

Those products or services offering the greatest potential for sales and/or profits should be given highest priority in the marketing effort. Individual items or services being sold should have enough mark-up to cover all costs associated with it, including handling, warranties, and servicing arrangements, plus an adequate profit margin.

Products and services travel through "life cycles" and most will become less appealing to the marketplace as time passes on. Therefore, it is essential that business owners be constantly aware of changing conditions and customer tastes. Modify existing lines when necessary and move into new product or service areas when market forces demand to shift. Look at insurance companies today. A decade ago "whole-life" policies were in style and now they won't sell. Inflation made them obsolete because of their low dividend yields on the cash values built into the policies. Consequently, the insurance industry has replaced the "whole-life" concept with what is called "universal-life" which pays higher yields on the cash values. Incidentally, "whole-life" policies can still be purchased, but the primary marketing thrust, on the part of many insurance companies, has been directed to "universal-life."

Managing Risk

Understanding risk is an important aspect of running any business. Some experts contend that an adequate insurance program designed to reduce risk is just as vital to the success of a firm as are other business functions. Without question, assets left unprotected could compromise the future existence of the business if loss occurred. Therefore, a sound risk reduction plan should be implemented and carefully managed to insure economic viability in the event of loss due to unanticipated events.

The items listed below should be considered by all existing business owners and prospective entrepreneurs thinking about purchasing a small enterprise.

— Determine how loss may occur—Recognizing the probability of loss is the initial step in understanding risk. Realistic appraisal is a must in order to protect the firm's assets and livelihood.
— Seek professional advice—Talk to agents employed by insurance companies and independent agents representing different companies. Ask for their assistance in determining insurance needs. To insure the credibility of the agents, request references and check them out. In addition, talking to other business owners may provide reliable agent contacts.
— Shop around for the best buy—Insurance products are subject to competitive forces; therefore, prices will differ among companies. Following a few simple rules will help to reduce the cost of carrying insurance coverage.

  • Identify risks and the potential for loss.

- Insure the largest risk factor initially.

- Try to use deductibles. High deductibles will reduce insurance costs.

- Eliminate all overlapping insurance coverage. It is a waste of money, since most companies share the burden of loss as opposed to the owner getting extra coverage.

- Purchase insurance in large units, if possible. Avoid many small policies, since they tend to be more expensive for the same coverage.

- Some insurance companies sell consolidated policies incorporating all coverage into one central agreement. In addition, many professional and trade associations have insurance products at discount group rates. For example, the National Small Business Association located at 1604 K. Street, N.W., in Washington, DC 20006, provides some attractive insurance programs at reasonable prices.

- Always evaluate the firm's risk exposure on a timely and regular basis for purposes of upgrading or downgrading. This will insure adequate coverage at reasonable cost, and, in some cases, the phase out of protection that has become necessary.

— Structure an insurance program—A formalized plan outlining all aspects of the insurance program should be set forth for management purposes. The plan may include, but is not limited to, the following procedures:

- State the objective of the insurance plan.

- Try to deal with only one agent, if possible. Dealing with several may create confusion and disinformation.

- Assign responsibility for the program to one individual.

- Prevent or minimize losses through safety and inspection procedures.

• State the potential for loss candidly. Failure to acquire needed coverage because of disinformation can be a threat to the viability of the firm.

• No matter how small the chance for loss, all risks should be covered. Avoid underestimation of asset value to save money. If loss does occur, the firm may not recover its investment.

• Periodically, evaluate the insurance program to determine the need for modification. Some risk programs have automatic cost-of-living increases built in to protect against loss caused by increasing asset value due to inflation. All assets should be appraised occasionally to determine insurance requirement.

• Always maintain adequate records concerning the risk reduction program. This information may be helpful later when attempting to change or modify coverage.

The following insurance checklist is provided courtesy of the U.S. Small Business Administration; it was written by Professor Mark R. Greene. It is designed to provide insight into the insurance needs of small businesses.

Points reviewed in the checklist are classified into three groups. They are as follows: essential coverage, desirable but non-essential coverage, and employee coverage. After reading each statement, place a check under the column entitled "No action needed" if the statement and how it affects the insurance plan is understood. If it isn't, check the column entitled "Look into this." After completing the study, evaluate existing and/or prospective insurance coverage, keeping in mind the points covered in the checklist. Discuss any problems or concerns with an agent.

Essential Coverage

Four kinds of insurance are essential: fire insurance, liability insurance, automobile insurance, and workers' compensation insurance. In some areas and in some kinds of businesses, crime insurance, which is discussed under "Desirable Coverages," is also essential.

Are you certain that all the following points have been given full consideration in your insurance program?

Fire Insurance

1. You can add other perils—such as windstorm, hail, smoke, explosion, vandalism, and malicious mischief—to your basic fire insurance at a relatively small additional cost.

2. If you need comprehensive coverage, your best buy may be one of the all-risk contracts that offer the broadest available protection for the money.

3. The insurance company may indemnify you—that is, compensate you for your losses—in any one of several ways: (1) It may pay actual cash value of the property at the time of loss. (2) It may repair or replace the property with material of like kind and quality. (3) It may take all the property at the agreed or appraised value and reimburse you for your loss.

4. You can insure property you don't own. You must have an insurable interest—a financial interest—in the property when a loss occurs but not necessarily at the time the insurance contract is made. For instance, a repair shop or drycleaning plant may carry insurance on customers' property in the shop, or a person holding a mortgage on a building may insure the building although he doesn't own it.

5. When you sell property, you cannot assign the insurance policy along with the property unless you have permission from the insurance company.

6. Even if you have several policies on your property, you can still collect only the amount of your actual cash loss. All the insurers share the payment proportionately. Suppose, for example, that you are carrying two policies—one for $20,000 and one for $30,000—on a $40,000 building, and fire causes damage to the building amounting to $12,000. The $20,000 policy will pay $4,800; that is,

$\frac{20,000}{50,000}$, or $\frac{2}{5}$, of $12,000. The $30,000 policy will pay

$7,200; which is $\frac{30,000}{50,000}$, or $\frac{3}{5}$, of $12,000.

7. Special protection other than the standard fire policy is needed to cover the loss by fire of accounts, bills, currency, deeds, evidences of debt, and money and securities.

8. If an insured building is vacant or unoccupied for more than 60 consecutive days, coverage is suspended unless you have a special endorsement to your policy cancelling this provision.

		No Action Needed	Look Into This

Fire Insurance

9. If, either before or after a loss, you conceal or misrepresent to the insurer any material fact or circumstance concerning your insurance or the interest of the insured, the policy may be voided. ____ ____

10. If you increase the hazard of fire, the insurance company may suspend your coverage even for losses not originating from the increased hazard. (An example of such a hazard might be renting part of your building to a drycleaning plant.) ____ ____

11. After a loss, you must use all reasonable means to protect the property from further loss or run the risk of having your coverage cancelled. ____ ____

12. To recover your loss, you must furnish within 60 days (unless an extension is granted by the insurance company) a complete inventory of the damaged, destroyed, and undamaged property, showing in detail quantities, costs, actual cash value, and amount of loss claimed. ____ ____

13. If you and the insurer disagree on the amount of loss, the question may be resolved through special appraisal procedures provided for in the fire-insurance policy. ____ ____

14. You may cancel your policy without notice at any time and get part of the premium returned. The insurance company also may cancel at any time with a 5-day written notice to you. ____ ____

15. By accepting a co-insurance clause in your policy, you get a substantial reduction in premiums. A co-insurance clause states that you must carry insurance equal to 80 or 90 percent of the value of the insured property. If you carry less than this, you cannot collect the full amount of your loss, even if the loss is small. What percent of your loss you can collect will depend on what percent of the full value of the property you have insured it for. ____ ____

16. If your loss is caused by someone else's negligence, the insurer has the right to sue this negligent third party for the amount it has paid you under the policy. This is known as the insurer's right of subrogation. However, the insurer will usually waive this right upon request. For example, if you have leased your insured building to someone and have waived your right to recover from the tenant for any insured damages to your property, you should have your agent request the insurer to waive the subrogation clause in the fire policy on your leased building. ____ ____

	No Action Needed	Look Into This

Fire Insurance

17. A building under construction can be insured for fire, lightning, extended coverage, vandalism and malicious mischief. ____ ____

Liability Insurance

1. Legal liability limits of $1 million are no longer considered high or unreasonable even for a small business. ____ ____

2. Most liability policies require you to notify the insurer immediately after an incident on your property that might cause a future claim. This holds true no matter how unimportant the incident may seem at the time it happens. ____ ____

3. Most liability policies, in addition to covering bodily injuries, may now cover personal injuries (libel, slander, and so on), if these are specifically insured. ____ ____

4. Under certain conditions, your business may be subject to damage claims even from trespassers. ____ ____

5. You may be legally liable for damages even in cases where you used "reasonable care." ____ ____

6. Even if the suit against you is false or fraudulent, the liability insurer pays court costs, legal fees, and interest on judgments in addition to the liability judgments themselves. ____ ____

7. You can be liable for the acts of others under contracts you have signed with them. This liability is insurable. ____ ____

8. In some cases you may be held liable for fire loss to property of others in your care. Yet, this property would normally not be covered by your fire or general liability insurance. This risk can be covered by fire legal liability insurance or through requesting subrogation waivers from insurers of owners of the property. ____ ____

Automobile Insurance

1. When an employee or a subcontractor uses his own car on your behalf, you can be legally liable even if you don't own a car or truck yourself. ____ ____

2. Five or more automobiles or motorcycles under one ownership and operated as a fleet for business purposes can generally be insured under a low-cost fleet policy against both material damage to your vehicle and liability to others for property damage or personal injury. ____ ____

	No Action Needed	Look Into This

Automobile Insurance

3. You can often get deductibles of almost any amount—say $250 or $500—and thereby reduce your premiums. ____ ____

4. Automobile medical-payments insurance pays for medical claims, including your own, arising from automobile accidents regardless of the question of negligence. ____ ____

5. In most states, you must carry liability insurance or be prepared to provide other proof (surety bond) of financial responsibility when you are involved in an accident. ____ ____

6. You can purchase uninsured-motorist protection to cover your own bodily-injury claims from someone who has no insurance. ____ ____

7. Personal property stored in an automobile and not attached to it (for example, merchandise being delivered) is not covered under an automobile policy. ____ ____

Workers' Compensation

1. Common law requires that an employer (1) provide his employees a safe place to work, (2) hire competent fellow employees, (3) provide safe tools, and (4) warn his employees of an existing danger. ____ ____

2. If an employer fails to provide the above, under both common law and workers' compensation laws he is liable for damage suits brought by an employee. ____ ____

3. State law determines the level or type of benefits payable under workers' compensation policies. ____ ____

4. Not all employees are covered by workers' compensation laws. The exceptions are determined by state law and therefore vary from state to state. ____ ____

5. In nearly all states, you are not legally required to cover your workers under workers' compensation. ____ ____

6. You can save money on workers' compensation insurance by seeing that your employees are properly classified. ____ ____

7. Rates for workers' compensation insurance vary from 0.1 percent of the payroll for "safe" occupations to about 25 percent or more of the payroll for very hazardous occupations. ____ ____

8. Most employers in most states can reduce their workers' compensation premium cost by reducing their accident rates

below the average. They do this by using safety and loss-prevention measures.   ____ ____

DESIRABLE COVERAGES

Some types of insurance coverage, while not absolutely essential, will add greatly to the security of your business. These coverages include business interruption insurance, crime insurance, glass insurance, and rent insurance.

Business Interruption Insurance

1. You can purchase insurance to cover fixed expenses that would continue if a fire shut down your business—such as salaries to key employees, taxes, interest, depreciation, and utilities—as well as the profits you would lose.   ____ ____

2. Under properly written contingent business interruption insurance, you can also collect if fire or other peril closes down the business of a supplier or customer and this interrupts your business.   ____ ____

3. The business interruption policy provides payments for amounts you spend to hasten the reopening of your business after a fire or other insured peril.   ____ ____

4. You can get coverage for the extra expenses you suffer if an insured peril, while not actually closing your business down, seriously disrupts it.   ____ ____

5. When the policy is properly endorsed, you can get business interruption insurance to indemnify you if your operations are suspended because of failure or interruption of the supply of power, light, heat, gas, or water furnished by a public utility company.   ____ ____

Crime Insurance

1. Burglary insurance excludes such property as accounts, articles in a showcase window, and manuscripts.   ____ ____

2. Coverage is granted under burglary insurance only if there are visible marks of the burglar's forced entry.   ____ ____

3. Burglary insurance can be written to cover, in addition to money in a safe, inventoried merchandise and damage incurred in the course of a burglary.   ____ ____

	No Action Needed	*Look Into This*

Crime Insurance

4. Robbery insurance protects you from loss of property, money, and securities by force, trickery, or threat of violence on or off your premises.

5. A comprehensive crime policy written just for small businessmen is available. In addition to burglary and robbery, it covers other types of loss by theft, destruction, and disappearance of money and securities. It also covers thefts by your employees.

6. If you are in a high-risk area and cannot get insurance through normal channels without paying excessive rates, you may be able to get help through the federal crime insurance plan. Your agent or State Insurance Commissioner can tell you where to get information about these plans.

Glass Insurance
1. You can purchase a special glass insurance policy that covers all risk to plate-glass windows, glass signs, motion-picture screens, glass brick, glass doors, showcases, countertops, and insulated glass panels.

2. The glass insurance policy covers not only the glass itself, but also its lettering and ornamentation, if these are specifically insured, and the costs of temporary plates or boarding up when necessary.

3. After the glass has been replaced, full coverage is continued without any additional premium for the period covered.

Rent Insurance
1. You can buy rent insurance that will pay your rent if the property you lease becomes unusable because of fire or other insured perils and your lease calls for continued payments in such a situation.

2. If you own property and lease it to others, you can insure against loss if the lease is cancelled because of fire and you have to rent the property again at a reduced rental.

EMPLOYEE BENEFIT COVERAGES

Insurance coverages that can be used to provide employee benefits include group life insurance, group health insurance, disability insurance, and retirement income. Key-man insurance protects the company

Group Life Insurance

against financial loss caused by the death of a valuable employee or partner.

Group Life Insurance
1. If you pay group-insurance premiums and cover all employees up to $50,000, the cost to you is deductible for Federal income-tax purposes, and yet the value of the benefit is not taxable income to your employees. ___ ___

2. Most insurers will provide group coverages at low rates even if there are 10 or fewer employees in your group. ___ ___

3. If the employees pay part of the cost of the group insurance, state laws require that 75 percent of them must elect coverage for the plan to qualify as group insurance. ___ ___

4. Group plans permit an employee leaving the company to convert his group-insurance coverage to a private plan, at the rate for his age, without a medical exam if he does so within 30 days after leaving his job. ___ ___

Group Health Insurance
1. Group health insurance costs much less and provides more generous benefits for the worker than individual contracts would. ___ ___

2. If you pay the entire cost, individual employees cannot be dropped from a group plan unless the entire group policy is cancelled. ___ ___

3. Generous programs of employee benefits, such as group health insurance, tend to reduce labor turnover. ___ ___

Disability Insurance
1. Workers' compensation insurance pays an employee only for time lost because of work injuries and work-related sickness, not for time lost because of disabilities incurred off the job. But you can purchase, at a low premium, insurance to replace the lost income of workers who suffer short-term or long-term disability not related to their work. ___ ___

2. You can get coverage that provides employees with an income for life in case of permanent disability resulting from work-related sickness or accident. ___ ___

	No Action Needed	Look Into This

Retirement Income

1. If you are self-employed, you can get an income tax deduction for funds used for retirement for you and your employees through plans of insurance or annuities approved for use under the Employees Retirement Income Security Act of 1974 (ERISA).

2. Annuity contracts may provide for variable payments in the hope of giving the annuitants some protection against the effects of inflation. Whether fixed or variable, an annuity can provide retirement income that is guaranteed for life.

Key-Man Insurance

1. One of the most serious setbacks that can come to a small company is the loss of a key man. But your key man can be insured with life insurance and disability insurance owned by and payable to your company.

2. Proceeds of a key-man policy are not subject to income tax, but premiums are not a deductible business expense.

3. The cash value of key-man insurance, which accumulates as an asset of the business, can be borrowed against, and the interest and dividends are not subject to income tax as long as the policy remains in force.

MANAGING TAXES

Prospective entrepreneurs and existing business owners must realize the importance of paying and managing their tax liabilities. Improper use of taxes due can be costly in terms of penalties imposed by state, local and federal revenue agencies, not to mention the time involved in audits that will surely ensue. Effective management of tax obligations entails the following major points.

— Know the degree of tax liability in reference to the taxes imposed, their dollar amounts, and when they are due.
— Make sure that funds are available to pay the tax obligations.
— Always pay on or before the due date to avoid costly late payment charges which can exceed 25 percent of the amount due in some cases.
— Seek competent tax advice from an expert in the field (CPA and/ or Tax Attorney).

Below is a list of taxes that a business owner may expect to face when running an operation. Types and amounts of taxes will vary depending upon many factors such as line of business, state residency, and profitability, to mention but a few. For example, five state governments do not have income taxes imposed on business profits.

— Federal Income Tax
— State Income Tax
— Local Income Tax
— Social Security Tax
— Federal Unemployment Tax
— State Unemployment Tax
— Excise Taxes
— State Sales Tax
— Local Sales Tax

Taxes are normally paid on a periodic basis to the various government agencies. Payments are accompanied with a form supplied by the governing body. Check with the appropriate agency responsible for the collection of taxes to determine payment procedures. Table 29 contains a worksheet that can be used by a business when analyzing and computing tax obligations.

Managing Problems

A good manager has been defined as an individual with the ability to solve potential problems before they become real problems and threaten the business. Most management experts agree that solving difficulties should be a sequential process involving a number of specific procedures. They are listed below.

— Problem Definition: The problem must be clearly stated and understood. An evaluation concerning the direct and indirect effects of the difficulty must be made. Problem identification is the single largest stumbling block to effective decision making. Also, the unwillingness or inability to deal with difficulties once apparent will greatly impede progress toward goal attainment.

— Initial Investigation: This stage attempts to obtain a concise definition of the problem and its potential ramifications.

TABLE 29

Kind of Tax	Due Date	Amount Due	Pay to	Date For Writing The Check
FEDERAL TAXES				
Employee Income Tax and Social Security Tax				
Excise Tax				
Owner-Manager's and/or corporation's income tax				
Unemployment Tax				
STATE TAXES				
Unemployment Taxes				
Income Taxes				
Sales Taxes				
Franchise Tax				
Other				
LOCAL TAXES				
Sales Tax				
Real Estate Tax				
Personal Property Tax				
Licenses (retail, vending machine, etc.)				
Other				

— Identify and Select Alternative Courses of Action: Several plans should be developed with the objective of defusing the problem or minimizing its impact.

— Collection of Relevant Data: Information in relation to each course of action must be collected, organized, and evaluated to determine which one is the suitable solution. Statistical analysis is often used in this stage.

— Selection of the Alternative: Once the optimum alternative is identified it should be officially adopted as the solution to the problem.

— Implement the Course of Action: Put the solution into effect.

— Evaluate the Course of Action Taken: Periodic examination of the action implemented is needed in order to determine its effectiveness. Evaluation may reveal a need for modification of the existing alternative or the employment of a new course of action.

The experiences gained and recorded by using problem solving procedures and solutions will help to develop and refine the decision-making abilities of owners/managers.

Decision Making Is Necessary

When the time comes for decision making, business owners and managers should not procrastinate. Hesitation is one of the foremost reasons for missed opportunities and the assumption of unreasonable costs. This is not to say that an owner should react without due consideration. On the contrary, when lacking appropriate information, it may be a good idea to delay a decision, but dangers and opportunities may still present themselves. The delayed decision must be weighed against the potential losses due to inaction.

The optimum solution is to have reliable and accurate information available at all times. This will help to avoid the unpleasant situation of making decisions using inadequate data or taking no action at all.

Knowing When to Seek Advice

When the need for outside assistance becomes apparent, get it immediately without hesitation. Delay can be costly, especially if problems grow to the point of unmanageability. Also, avoid being egotistical and trying to solve insurmountable problems without assistance or by utilizing limited in-house staff. Businesses that are both large and small occasionally need the help of outside expertise when facing environmental or internal problems. Sources of professional assistance were discussed earlier in Chapter III.

Chapter X

IMPORTANT CONSIDERATIONS
Before Venturing

Cover the Bases

Every prospective or practicing entrepreneur must consider and evaluate certain critical elements before starting or, in some cases, relocating operations. Failure to do so could lead to disastrous consequences. It is impossible to discuss all the different small businesses relative to these important features within the confines of this book. Therefore, the four major categories of business classification (retail, wholesale, service, and manufacturing) will be used as a means of broad comparison.

Table 30 shows which elements should be considered by the various business categories. An asterisk (*) means evaluation is definitely necessary while an (X) means some critical analysis is needed. Blanks indicate little or no relationship.

Consider These Carefully

CAPITAL

All businesses must be concerned that an adequate amount of capital is available to begin and support operations. Service firms, by their very nature, are generally less capital intensive than other types of businesses. Therefore, they can operate on the proverbial shoestring.

Capital needs are discussed extensively in Chapter V.

Channels of Distribution

Most manufacturers must worry about getting their products in the hands of the ultimate consumer. In many cases, this is accomplished through the use of intermediaries which are commonly referred to as "middlemen." These intermediaries are links in a channel of distribution and help move the product to its destination. Wholesalers must also be concerned with this matter because many employ middlemen known as agents and brokers to facilitate the flow of their products to retailers. Service businesses should not be overly concerned with channels of distribution since most services are performed by the originator. Some businesses franchise their operations to achieve growth. In these cases, the franchisee would serve as the distributor for the franchisor.

TABLE 30
ELEMENTS TO CONSIDER BEFORE VENTURING

	Retail	Wholesale	Service	Manufacturing
1. Capital	*	*	X	*
2. Channels of Distribution		X		*
3. Climate	X			*
4. Competition	*	*	*	*
5. Credit Policies	*	*	*	*
6. Delivery	X	*		*
7. Demographics	*	*	*	*
8. Economic Climate	*	*	*	*
9. Financial Control	*	*	*	*
10. Government Regulation	X	*	X	*
11. Industry Trends	*	*	*	*
12. Inflation	*	*	*	*
13. International Events	X	X		*
14. Labor	*	*	*	*
15. Licenses	X	*	X	*
16. Location	*	*		*
17. Market Research	*	*	*	*
18. Operations Policy	*	*	*	*
19. Pricing	*	*	*	*
20. Product/Service	*	*	*	*
21. Raw Materials				*
22. Research & Development				*
23. Service	*	*	X	*
24. State of Technology	X	X	X	*
25. Storage	X	*		*
26. Topography	X	*	X	*
27. Trade Credit	*	*		*
28. Vendors (Suppliers)	*	*	X	*
29. Warranties	*	*	*	*

Below are listed the more common channels of distribution:

Manufacturer-Wholesaler-Retailer-Customer
Manufacturer-Broker-Wholesaler-Retailer-Customer
Manufacturer-Broker-Agent-Wholesaler-Retailer-Customer
Manufacturer-Broker-Jobber-Wholesaler-Retailer-Customer
Manufacturer-Broker-Retailer-Customer
Manufacturer-Jobber-Retailer-Customer
Service Originator-Customer
Service Originator-Agent-Customer

Many products and industries have standardized channels of distribution that have been used for years. Some companies mistakenly think they can reduce costs and increase profits by eliminating middlemen. Most firms that attempt to do this fail in their efforts. Always remember that intermediaries are specialists in their fields and they know the ropes. Consequently, they are cost effective to use even though they charge commissions and represent an added link in the channel. The only way a company can make money by eliminating these organizations is to gain the necessary expertise and apply it better than the middlemen being replaced. A few large discount chains have accomplished this feat.

CLIMATE

Some manufacturing and retailing establishments must consider the effects of climatic conditions on their business. Failure to do so could be detrimental to profitable operations. For example, some years ago the Del Monte Corporation built a large pineapple cannery in Mexico on a river. The fruit groves were located up-river. During picking season the fruit was to be barged down-river to the cannery for processing and shipment. Management failed to consider one very important point and it was a costly mistake. The river's flood stage and picking season just so happened at the same time. Consequently, the river could not support barge movement and the factory was never used. Millions were lost due to failure in considering the climate's effect on operations.

Retail firms can also be affected by climate. Stores and shops located along coastal resorts can be adversely affected if unseasonably cold weather grips their areas for a season or two. Likewise, retail businesses in winter resorts can experience the same fate if a warmer than normal winter occurs.

Wholesaling and servicing enterprises are not affected by weather as compared to the aforementioned. Wholesalers sell to retailers and, therefore, it is the retailer's responsibility to get the product to the ultimate customer. Service firms normally take the product directly to the customer, thereby minimizing the impact of weather on a potential customer. For example, an electrician or plumber will work rain or shine. Of course, extreme weather conditions can stymie any operation.

COMPETITION

The impact of competition is important to any business operation. The degree and strength of competitive forces within a particular market should be considered and evaluated very carefully to determine the effects on existing or prospective endeavors. Is there room for another seller? If the market is crowded with competitors, can an enterprise with exceptional management skills survive or prosper, forcing other less efficient firms to concede market share.

More details concerning competitive factors can be found in Chapter VII.

CREDIT POLICIES

Most businesses are forced to give customers credit privileges because of competitive forces within most markets. A standardized credit policy is a must in order to establish uniformity and minimize the possibility of credit discrimination. In addition, it will establish procedures for granting credit and collecting past dues. A good policy will facilitate the entire credit function. More insight about credit can be gained by referring to Chapter IX.

DELIVERY

Product delivery is a primary concern for wholesale and manufacturing operations. These organizations must deliver their products to the appropriate link in the channel of distribution in order to ultimately sell the goods. Some retail firms, such as mail order companies, are also involved in the process of delivery, although to a much lesser extent than the previously mentioned types of business. Service companies normally do not worry about delivery, since services are delivered when performed. There are exceptions. For example, consulting firms, research firms, photo-copy centers, etc., may be involved in the delivery of various papers and reports.

DEMOGRAPHICS

All businesses must be concerned with the characteristics of the marketplace they are trying to exploit. An understanding of demographics will help accomplish this by classifying the total market into various segments. This is called market segmentation. The most common classifications are listed below:

Age
Income
Geographic Area
Marital Status
Religion
Sex
Occupation

ECONOMIC CLIMATE

The systematic risk inherent in the overall economy will affect all businesses. Having an idea when recessions will occur can help insure proper preparation and thus defense against the impact of economic downturns. It is interesting to note the number of companies who fail to take heed of a recession's warning signals and fall victim. Businesses that are on guard normally weather the storm and some even prosper.

Below are listed the more common recession signals:

— Steady increase in the general level of interest rates. (When short-term rates exceed long-term rates it is called an "inversion" and a recession will generally follow suit.)
— Falling economic output
— Falling corporate profits
— Leading economic indicators constantly down
— Consumer and business confidence constantly negative
— Consistently rising levels of business inventories

Most of these statistics are reported monthly in a government publication known as *The Survey of Current Business,* available at many libraries or directly from The Superintendent of Documents, U.S. Government Printing Office, Washington, D.C. 20402. The cost is $30 per year.

FINANCIAL CONTROL

Maintaining financial control of a business is contingent upon managing resources so as to generate adequate profit levels. The management of physical, financial, and intangible assets would fall in this category. Chapter IX deals heavily with this subject.

GOVERNMENT REGULATION

Local, state, and federal government regulations affect all businesses, both large and small, costing the American business community approximately 175 billion dollars per year. Even though the larger firms tend to be watched more closely, small firms are expected to abide by all codes and statutes. Writing to government agencies and requesting information on laws affecting a particular line of business would be wise.

INDUSTRY TRENDS

All businesses must be concerned with events taking place within their industries. Even though the overall economy is recovering from the recession, many industries are failing to respond. Some will never regain their former strength and a few will slowly die. The service industries have, for the most part, been unaffected by economic downturns. In fact, services which now account for 60 percent of the nation's output will climb to 80 percent of economic activity by the end of this decade.

Checking activities within a particular industry in question will help gain insight into the dynamic forces working to strengthen, stagnate, or weaken performance in that area.

INFLATION

Inflation affects all businesses. Initially, the results of rising inflation are quite positive, with sales and profits increasing, although much of the increase is artificial. For example, if a business achieves a ten percent return on investment (ROI) one year and inflation for that same period runs at eight percent, the firm has only realized a two percent gain on its investment, although most companies would report a ten percent increase. Many establishments actually base expansion plans on inflated figures and later down the pike experience a capital squeeze because (inflation adjusted) accounting records were not used to make the decision.

All financial and accounting records should reflect the damage caused by inflation. Failure to do so could lead to disaster. In addition, high levels of inflation (exceeding ten percent per year) generally cause recessions. So inflation can be viewed as an indicator of future economic vitality. Conversely, lower levels of inflation (two to four percent) are considered good for the economy. An economic system experiencing either no inflation or deflation (declining price levels) is thought to be in serious trouble.

INTERNATIONAL EVENTS

Whether or not it is a popular nation, the United States has joined the world economic community out of necessity because of resource dependency. Consequently, the American economy is subject to forces beyond the immediate control of domestic leaders. Some lines of businesses are more affected than others. A knowledge of international forces that may do harm to particular industries and firms will help to insure survivability if negative events occur. For example, what should petroleum retailers and wholesalers do if OPEC imposes another embargo? How can American automobile manufacturers and dealers respond to the ever-increasing tide of foreign competition?

Much has been said about the inability of American manufacturers to compete with the more efficient and productive foreign counterparts. This is largely true, and domestic producers will have to respond in order to survive. On the other hand, retailers and wholesalers may be affected only temporarily due to overseas competition, because they can always change to more marketable foreign products. Service firms are generally insulated from foreign competition since most nations haven't concentrated upon exporting services as of this date. In fact, the service sector is considered an area where American firms could compete successfully in the international marketplace.

LABOR

All firms must insure that adequate human resources are available to support operations. A manufacturing firm should be concerned that a particular location has enough skilled, semi-skilled, and managerial talent. Businesses offering technical services may be interested in the number of qualified technical personnel who could be hired in a given location.

Firms failing to consider the implications of inadequate labor supply before starting or relocating operations will suffer the additional cost of attracting needed individuals located outside the immediate area of operation.

LICENSES

Most local and state agencies require business establishments to apply for any number of licenses. In addition, many want payment of a flat and/or percentage of estimated sales fee before granting permits. Requirements vary from one area to another. Larger concerns may need federal permits. For example, a license must be acquired from the U.S. Department of Commerce before a firm may engage in export activities.

Small firms should check with the local Clerk of the Court. He/she will have information concerning any local, state, or federal licensing requirements for particular types of businesses.

LOCATION

It is important for manufacturing businesses to be located near their markets. Transportation costs can be minimized. Some manufacturers may also decide to locate in the proximity of its needed raw materials. For example, steel mills in Pennsylvania are located near large coal deposits which are critical to the steel-making process. Transportation charges for coal are astronomical, thereby necessitating a location near the source of the raw material. Wholesaling firms normally attempt to optimize their distribution facilities between the many retail customers they serve. Retail establishments want to locate where traffic flow is adequate enough to support operations. Specialty retail stores need not worry to the same degree because customers will make special efforts to obtain items of specific characteristics and quality. Finally, only those service firms that provide in-house services need not worry about location. When the customer must come to the place of business, location can be of prime importance.

MARKET RESEARCH

Market research is necessary to determine whether a product or service can be successfully sold. This research, if conducted properly, will reveal the threats inherent in the marketplace as well as any opportunities that may exist. Many small businesses fail because of not considering the impact of competitive forces and overestimating customer base. Market research will address these weaknesses.

Chapter VII addresses the topic of market research extensively.

OPERATIONS POLICY

An operations policy explains the procedures to follow in maintaining effective operations. Generally, the need for operations policy increases as a firm grows. It is not surprising to find many small retail or service businesses operating efficiently without an operations policy, although they probably maintain at least an employee policy to insure compliance with employment laws.

The standard operations policy should include a description of key functions within the business and who is in charge of each. An organizational chart would normally be part of the policy manual, along with a description of responsibilities and spans of control to reduce administrative overlap. Standard operating procedures (SOPs) would be established for each function. A statement relating to events not covered by SOPs is generally incorporated with policy to reduce confusion if an exceptional situation were to occur.

PRICING

All businesses must worry about pricing their products and services. After all, the prices chosen will affect a firm's ability to successfully compete. Price setting can be a complicated task. Many things need to be considered carefully. For example, if the product/service is new, a higher price can normally be set. Conversely, strong competitive forces within the market would force a lower price. Pricing strategy should also be integrated with long-term goals. A "skimming" price policy means that a firm is setting a high price in order to achieve large profit margins. However, a lower market share is achieved. Consequently, when competitors enter the field, the ability to survive will be in question due to a thin customer base. On the other hand, a "penetration" policy sets a lower price to achieve a wider market acceptance, which helps to fight off competitive threats.

An interesting illustration of these two pricing policies can be found in analyzing the battle between Texas Instruments and Bowmar Corporation. Bowmar introduced one of the first hand-held calculators and chose a skimming price policy. Therefore, only a small market share was gained. Texas Instruments came out with their calculator (basically the same product), but adopted a penetration policy to achieve a wider market share. The rest is history. Bowmar went out of business because its market share was too small to support operations after competition set in.

Pricing is discussed in Chapter VII.

PRODUCT/SERVICE

The product or service offered will determine business success. Obviously, many products and services are widely available today from many different sources. Some will continue to be in demand while others will stagnate or die. New ones will come and go. The trick is to find a line that has achieved some degree of success in the marketplace with a lot of growth potential left and yet only a few competitors. Chapter VII contains information about product development.

Franchising is staged to make a comeback, but a franchise is only as good as the product or service it represents. Details concerning franchise ownership are discussed in Chapter II.

Below are listed some good and bad business prospects that exist today. Keep in mind that changing economic conditions could alter what constitutes a positive or negative proposition.

Good Prospects:
— Information Services
— Computer Software and Hardware
— Medical Instruments, Services, and Supplies
— Aerospace and Defense-Related Products and Services
— Entertainment Products and Services
— Sports Products and Services
— Educational Products and Services
— Specialty Retailing
— Financial and Tax Services
— Convenience Stores
— Fast-Food Outlets
— Precision Instruments
— Do-It-Yourself Stores
— Consulting Services

Bad Prospects:
— Domestic Car Dealers
— Gasoline Service Stations
— Conventional Grocery Stores
— General Department Stores
— Residential Construction
— Steel Related Businesses
— Textile Related Businesses

RAW MATERIALS

The location of raw materials is of primary concern to manufacturing outfits. Some will locate their operations near sources of raw materials in order to minimize the cost of transportation that is usually passed on to the manufacturer. This is usually the case where raw materials are extremely heavy and bulky. For example, many steel mills will locate near coal mines. In addition, availability is a major consideration. Manufacturers must insure that adequate raw materials and/or components are available to keep production flowing. Failure to deliver finished goods to customers on time may result in a loss of goodwill.

Some manufacturers may attempt to optimize their location between major customers and sources of materials needed for production. In some cases, it may be more advantageous to locate near markets as opposed to suppliers. It could be that both market and raw material locations are minimized in favor of a location that is more favorable because of wages, taxes, and/or climate.

RESEARCH AND DEVELOPMENT (R&D)

Research and Development is a primary concern for manufacturing firms for survival reasons. Without the new products or processes initially created through R&D efforts, a company's ability to compete effectively would be compromised. In fact, many economists feel that the United States manufacturers are becoming less competitive than foreign firms because industry as a whole is spending much less on R&D in real terms (inflation adjusted) than it did a decade ago. At the same time foreign manufacturers have been increasing their R&D emphasis. This situation underscores the necessity in maintaining an adequate R&D program if the future is to be met with success.

Retail, wholesale, and service businesses should concern themselves with research and development to the extent that trends affect their marketing endeavors. Obviously, existing products and services will give way to new ones. The trick is to know when these events will happen and how they can be exploited. Research will tell how.

SERVICE

Some products need periodic servicing. The work can be done either by the retailer, wholesaler, or manufacturer. Generally, there exist cooperative agreements between the aforementioned to decide who will handle what and when. In any case, the need to service products sold must be taken into account. Making sure the proper service capability is available can be of primary importance to potential customers. Even a service business should be concerned. For example, let's say a management consultant performs a market study for a firm. Six or seven weeks after the study is finished the consultant should call or visit the firm to determine if the study has indeed been of assistance. This is called "servicing the service." If everybody is happy with the previous work, it would be an ideal time to push additional services.

STATE OF TECHNOLOGY

Technology is changing the way all firms conduct themselves in the marketplace. Failure to acknowledge and use the latest in technical innovations will insure demise. To illustrate, many American manufacturers have failed to innovate to the same degree as their foreign counterparts. Consequently, international markets have been losing to the more productive foreign producers. Even on a smaller scale, those retailers and service firms failing to consider the impact of technology on their existing lines will fall victim to changing demand patterns.

Determine which emerging technologies will affect existing and/or prospective lines and to what degree. Outline how these changes may be exploited profitably.

STORAGE

A retail business must store inventory in order to fulfill customer wants when immediate demand occurs. Some retail outlets succeed or fail based on their ability to provide a quick and adequate supply of their product, especially in a competitive market. Wholesalers and manufacturers generally need larger storage facilities to accommodate the enormous volume of finished and unfinished material that must be stored until production or shipment is made. Storage is not a big problem for service firms, since services are intangibles and cannot be warehoused.

The right amount of storage space is important. Too little might cause production and delivery delays, thereby resulting in a loss of customer goodwill. On the other hand, under-utilized space is wasteful and is an overhead expense not covered by revenues.

TOPOGRAPHY

Many areas are not conducive to manufacturing facilities because of land contour. There is one county in the state of Virginia where 85 percent of the land has an incline exceeding 15 degrees, which is considered restrictive for manufacturing and large wholesaling purposes. Normally, this situation would not affect retail or service establishments which tend to be smaller by nature, although any area that is largely inaccessible would be bad for businesses dependent on traffic flow. Another thing to be considered is the impact of no industrial growth. Opportunities for any type of business may be restricted if growth is stymied. To illustrate, the seat of the aforementioned county is a town of 8,000 people. It has one of the highest failure rates for small businesses in the state. Main Street is littered with empty storefronts and many existing operations are barely afloat.

TRADE CREDIT

It is wise to check with prospective suppliers about their credit arrangements. If the business is new it can expect to pay cash on delivery for merchandise and supplies during the first few months of operation. This obstacle can be overcome if the owner has a good credit rating and is willing to personally guarantee payment. Then immediate credit terms are normally available.

Many businesses fail to follow through in getting better terms with a supplier after a relationship has been established. One small motorcycle and repair shop in Virginia was dealing with four different suppliers for 18 months and all were demanding cash on delivery. A consultant advised the owners to write and demand favorable credit terms or other vendors would be found. Three graciously gave credit while one refused. Luckily, the one that resisted was the smallest and least important of the four. In addition, ask suppliers for a discount upon making early payments. Many will grant a one or two percent reduction for paying bills within ten days. Evaluate the cost of paying cash, taking into consideration the discount against the advantage of using the float (suppliers' credit). The answer will be determined by analyzing the rate of return on utilized dollars. For example, if the average annual rate of return on invested capital exceeds the annual adjusted rate of the suppliers' discount, it would not be wise to make early payments because the business can make more return by using the suppliers' float. If the rate is less, early payments may be appropriate.

Also, playing one supplier against the other for purposes of securing better credit terms might be a good idea at times. Many businesses have found that some vendors will extend payment terms from the traditional net 30 days to 45 or 60 days. In some industries, terms of 90 to 180 days have been achieved.

Vendors (Suppliers)

Most small retailers purchase from wholesalers who in turn buy from manufacturers and/or jobbers. Manufacturing firms must buy their raw materials and components from other sources. The point to remember is that all businesses should have several sources of supplies readily available. Relying on a single vendor can be risky. What happens if the vendor goes out of business or changes marketing approaches so as not to include particular types of businesses?

In addition, it may be wise to let suppliers know that several vendors are being used. It will keep them on their toes. Again, it may be useful to play them against each other to negotiate better prices.

Warranties

For competitive reasons, most businesses must give warranties that guarantee the successful performance of their products or services. Warranties, whether implied or expressed, are contracts that must be taken seriously. Broken warranties can lead to costly legal battles with disenfranchised customers, not to mention governmental agencies. In addition, the possibility of bad press must be taken into account, and the loss of goodwill it will cause. When considering warranties, try to estimate the cost of making such guarantees and what means will be used to deliver what is promised.

When projecting warranties, try to do it in a novel and unique way. A new slant can do wonders to stimulate sales. For example, a couple of years ago a mail order firm decided to incorporate a unique approach to making a guarantee. The company in question told potential buyers that their checks or money orders would not be cashed for 30 days and if they were not satisfied with the product it could be returned within a month. Upon the return of the merchandise, the uncashed monies would be sent back. The favorable result of this new twist was tremendous.

Basic Business Start-up*

Starting a new business is at best a dubious adventure in itself. It is of utmost importance to be organized from the beginning, to have a plan, to know what information is already in hand and what remains to be discovered. The value of being organized cannot be over-emphasized. Certain tasks must be completed, some in a definite sequence; without organization, something is likely to be overlooked.

In the next four sections, we will examine the most basic steps to starting up four different businesses: one retail, one wholesale, one manufacturing and one service business. Some basic steps are common to all businesses from the point where market research is completed, the type of business has been established and the financing for the venture is in hand. Following these basic steps will make the new business expedition somewhat less dubious and increase the potential for success.

THE RETAIL BUSINESS: "PENNY'S HOT SHOP"

Penny Reynolds, a private caterer, decided to open a sandwich shop for business people in the downtown district of her community. Several restaurants were already established, but they were either geared for full meal and high atmosphere, or they were small specialty shops serving limited ethnic cuisine. Penny determined there was a market for a restaurant which would serve only sandwiches of a traditional sort, with a minimum of side dishes, and emphasis on fast service.

With business plan and financing in hand, the steps Penny took to open her shop were:

1. She looked at available rental property in the area she wanted to service. She talked with several realtors to find the best location for the best price and made a tentative agreement to rent a space which had been an ice-cream parlor under previous renters.

*This section is provided by Alicelee Riley, who is a small business consultant located in Winchester, Virginia. She is owner of Riley Management Services.

2. She met with the building and fire inspectors from the city to determine what must be done to bring the building in line with regulations for her type of business. In addition, she needed to find out restrictions, limits on seating capacity, and other regulations that might apply.

3. Penny then met with the sanitation inspector to determine what regulations for food preparation and storage would apply.

4. Once she was sure she could afford to make the necessary improvements to the space (after consulting her business counsellor and checking with local contractors), she signed a lease and arranged for utilities and telephone.

5. Penny went to city hall and applied for her business license and obtained other information she needed regarding local taxes and regulations.

6. The state government had a sales tax, so she applied for the necessary reporting forms, tax tables, and book of regulations.

7. Knowing she would have employees, Penny applied to the Internal Revenue Service for a federal employer identification number. (The federal government supplies a book of instructions and forms when the number is assigned).

8. While work was being completed on the space, Penny began negotiating with restaurant equipment dealers to provide the necessary equipment and fixtures for her shop. She ordered what was needed.

9. Next, she located food distributors and gathered information from them.

10. The actual menu was selected and she worked closely with her business counsellor to plan mark-ups on the menu items and initial stock levels.

11. Her record-keeping system (as a sole proprietorship) and other important files were established.

12. After meeting with several agents, Penny purchased a comprehensive business insurance plan which suited her needs.

13. Penny decided initially to hire one full-time and one part-time employee. She placed a request with the local state employment office and interviewed prospects. By the time her space was completed and equipment began arriving, she had her employees and they were helping with the final stages.

14. The menu and advertising handbills were designed and printed.

15. Penny and her employees did the interior decorating to create a pleasing atmosphere in the shop.

16. All food items were ordered, along with serving, storage and cleaning supplies.

17. Penny paid for advertising on radio and in the local newspaper to announce the opening of her shop. Handbills were distributed.

18. The staff was trained and a couple of warm-up exercises were given so that opening day could go smoothly.

19. Finally, the sanitation inspector was called in one final time, after all was ready, to make sure the shop was in compliance with local codes.

Always remember, however, that extensive decision-making was necessary at every step. Items such as employee compensation, advertising, budgeting, etc., required close attention. But by following this basic sequence, Penny was able to open on schedule with a minimum of difficulty.

THE WHOLESALE BUSINESS: "POTTERY CENTRAL"

Fred Jenkins was a plant nursery specialist. On a vacation trip to Mexico, he encountered a number of pottery makers who were producing decorative pots which were much less costly than undecorated domestic ones. He determined there would be a market for such pottery in the U.S. and decided to start a wholesale pottery business. After Fred obtained the necessary financing and developed a plan of action, he went to work.

1. Since Fred's concept involved importing, he contacted the U.S. Commerce Department and Customs Service for information regarding importing, licensing, etc.

2. He met with his accountant and attorney to wade through the information because of the tax implications and the complexities of both importing and engaging in interstate trade.

3. He met with representatives of various trucking firms to learn about shipping rates and regulations.

4. Fred went shopping for warehouse-office space. As a wholesaler, Fred did not need a fancy building, but adequate space with easy access for shipping was necessary. He made a tentative agreement for renting a small warehouse with an attached office just outside of town.

5. He checked with the zoning, building and fire authorities about regulations and needed improvements.

6. Once he had consulted with local contractors, he signed a lease for the building and arranged for the improvements, utilities, and telephone.

7. He then applied for a business license, a federal employer identification number, and requested information on state and local taxes applicable to wholesaling.

8. He contacted Chambers of Commerce, advertising agencies, friends, and business associates for names of nurseries and florists in the region.

9. He worked closely with his business advisors to determine initial stock levels, mark-ups, and equipment requirements. Also, he contacted the Mexican potters and placed his first orders, including packing supplies. Fred also negotiated orders with domestic potters for some of their pottery pieces to complement his imported products.

10. Next, Fred decided to hire a secretary-bookkeeper, shipping clerk, and warehouseman because he planned to spend a good deal of his time on the road visiting potential customers. He placed want ads in the newspaper and with the local employment office. It wasn't long before he interviewed prospects and chose his employees.

11. Working with his accountant, Fred set up his sole proprietor record-keeping system and inventory system, and developed invoicing forms, billing policies, and other necessary items and procedures.

12. He met with various agents and purchased a sound business insurance plan.

13. With the help of a small advertising agency, business cards, sales literature, and company stationery were developed and printed. Other advertising approaches were explored and decisions made.

14. Once the space was ready, Fred and his employees organized the storage areas. Office equipment and furniture were then purchased.

15. The staff received training about business operation and Fred spent some of his time pre-selling several customers.

16. When the first shipments arrived, Fred sent a mass mailing to all the potential customers on his list and opened the doors for business.

Obviously, there are major differences between this wholesale business and the retail approach. Space requirements and marketing emphases differ widely. Once again, many details have been excluded, particularly regarding importing and shipping. Nevertheless, this scenario contains the basic start-up logic.

The Service Business: "Clean Sweepers"

Jim Black and John Simmons were servicemen for a woodstove firm. They observed a need for chimney sweep services in their community and decided to form a partnership to open a chimney sweep business. Together they met with an accountant and attorney to develop a business plan and a viable partnership agreement. Shortly thereafter, they met with their banker to arrange financing. Once these major preliminaries were concluded, they got down to the start-up details:

1. Jim owned several acres of property on the outskirts of town. On the property was a small barn in fairly good condition. The two men decided to use this building for their business. However, the area was zoned as residential. It was necessary for them to obtain a zoning variance through the city zoning board in order to locate their business in the barn.

2. Along with obtaining the variance, they met with the building and fire inspectors to determine what work was needed to bring the building in compliance with local codes. Arrangements were made with local contractors for the work to be completed.

3. The two men then applied for local business licenses and obtained other necessary information on state and local taxes applicable to their business.

4. They arranged for utilities and telephone service for their building.

5. Anticipating they would need to hire at least one employee, they filed for a federal employer identification number and accompanying forms and information.

6. They obtained information prices from various distributors regarding equipment and supplies. Orders were soon placed.

7. Since they would be traveling to their customers, a large van was purchased to accommodate all their equipment.

8. With the help of their business advisors, they set up a partnership record-keeping system, developed billing forms and procedures, and established a pricing structure for their services.

9. They consulted with several insurance agents and purchased a comprehensive business insurance plan.

10. They contacted the local employment agency, interviewed prospects, and hired a secretary-bookkeeper, their only other employee.

11. Working with a local ad agency, they developed business cards, stationery, and an advertising plan, which was executed right away.

12. After their equipment arrived and the final building inspections were made, they opened for business.

A service business is often one of the easiest to start, but frequently takes more intense marketing to convince the consumer that he needs the service, since it is an intangible. Depending on the cost of equipment and supplies, a service business, especially if it can be run from home, may have less overhead expense than other types of businesses. Pricing for services, however, is critical, since many people tend to undervalue their time, and therefore do not have enough income to keep the business operating. Sound advice is very important.

THE MANUFACTURING BUSINESS: "NATURALURES, INC."

George McDonald, Ed Frye and Paul Smith were fishing buddies. For years they had fished the waters of the region and the problem of inexpensive and realistic lures was a frequent topic of discussion. Ed was a chemist for a gasket company. Paul was a machinist and George was a salesman. They tinkered with making their own plastic lures in Ed's workshop. Finally, they developed some fine products and decided to manufacture these lures to sell to tackle wholesalers.

After pooling their financial resources and developing a plan with the aid of their accountant, they began to build their business:

1. Before going further, they met with their attorney and accountant to prepare and file their articles of incorporation with the state. A board of directors was appointed and stock apportioned among the three stockholders.

2. Ed's workshop was too small to produce lures in quantity, so they sought a basic warehouse building which could be set up for manufacturing. They found a small location in the county industrial park and made a tentative agreement to rent.

3. They then contacted the building and fire inspectors and determined what improvements were needed to the site to bring it up to code for their type of business. The OSHA representative was contacted to determine what federal regulations affected their operation.

4. Contractors were hired to do the work. Also, a lease was signed for the building and utilities were arranged.

5. Meanwhile, since the men felt they had developed a new concept in manufacturing plastic lures, it was necessary to find out if their method could be patented and if the name, "Naturalures," could qualify for trademark. Their local attorney referred them to a lawyer who specialized in patents and trademarks. He handled those transactions for them.

6. They applied for local business licenses and obtained other information on taxes and regulations affecting a manufacturing business.

7. They filed for a federal employer identification number for the corporation in anticipation of hiring several employees.

8. Working closely with their board of directors and accountant, pricing and start-up production levels were developed.

9. Suppliers for needed machinery and raw materials were found, and queried for their best prices and terms. Orders were then placed.

10. Meetings with various shippers were held and packaging decisions were made as part of nailing down the details on shipping.

11. They contacted the local employment agency and hired a secretary-bookkeeper, shipping-inventory clerk, and two other individuals to assist with production.

12. They purchased a business insurance plan through a reputable agent after thorough study of various alternatives.

13. Their accountant helped them set up a corporate record-keeping system, inventory system, production system, and billing systems. All special forms were designed and printed.

14. Office equipment and furniture were ordered and installed.

15. With the help of an advertising agency, business cards, stationery, and a marketing plan were designed and developed to target the wholesale market.

16. Through local sporting goods stores, they gathered the names of major wholesalers of fishing gear, contacted them and sent samples of their lures.

17. Employees were trained and special safety instruction was provided to all production workers, based on OSHA regulations.

18. Following a final building inspection, the production of "Naturalures" began.

Manufacturing requires certain technical knowledge very different from retailing and wholesaling. Generally, establishing a manufacturing business is more costly because of the equipment involved.

Likewise, a manufacturing business can be more risky, especially if it involves developing new markets. Marketing effectiveness and quality control are critical factors in this field.

There are many factors to consider in any business venture. All these considerations may seem overwhelming to the person starting a business for the first time. Keeping overhead down, purchasing wisely, pricing competitively, and marketing effectively are important to early success. Investigating licensing regulations, building codes, and taxing regulations are critical. But as much as any of these, it is absolutely necessary for the novice entrepreneur to have a clear objective, to be motivated, to know as much about the pitfalls as he or she does about the potentials, and to stay organized. Following a logical plan and understanding the basic steps will help make the business adventure a more pleasant, fulfilling and profitable experience.

Chapter XI

DIRECTORY OF CAPITAL SOURCES
Something for Everyone

Private Sources

PRIVATE CAPITAL COMPANIES

This section contains a list of venture capital firms, small business investment companies (SBICs), minority enterprise small business investment companies (MESBICs), and consulting firms specializing in small business funding. These organizations have provided detailed information concerning their investment preferences. Chapter VI describes the differences between these funding outlets and how they operate.

ARIZONA

Dineh Cooperatives, Incorporated
P. O. Box 569
Chinle, Navaho Nation, AZ 86503
602 674 3411

CONTACT: Jon D. Colvin
TYPE OF FIRM: Venture Capital Firm
FUNDING PREFERENCE:
  Seed Funding
  Start-Up Funding
INDUSTRY PREFERENCE: Diversified
GEOGRAPHIC PREFERENCE: Business within, or benefitting the
  Navaho Nation

TYPES OF FUNDS:
   Equity (stock purchases)
   Loans
INVESTMENT AMOUNTS PREFERRED:
   Minimum: Flexible
   Maximum: Flexible

FBS Venture Capital Company
6900 E. Camelback Rd., Suite 452
Scottsdale, AZ 85251
602 941 2160

CONTACT: William B. McKee
TYPE OF FIRM: SBIC
FUNDING PREFERENCE:
   Start-Up Funding
   First-Round Funding
   Second-Round Funding
   Leveraged Buyouts
INDUSTRY PREFERENCE:
   Communications Technology
   Computer Hardware
   Computer Software
   Manufacturing
   Medical Technology
   Other High Technologies Not Mentioned
GEOGRAPHIC PREFERENCE:
   Arizona
   Minnesota
TYPES OF FUNDS:
   Equity (stock purchases)
   Loans With Equity Kickers
INVESTMENT AMOUNTS PREFERRED:
   Minimum: $100,000
   Maximum: $500,000

CALIFORNIA

Arscott, Norton & Associates
369 Pine Street, Suite 506
San Francisco, CA 94104
415 956 3386

CONTACT: Leal Norton
TYPE OF FIRM: Venture Capital Firm

FUNDING PREFERENCE:
  Seed Funding
  Start-Up Funding
  First-Round Funding
INDUSTRY PREFERENCE:
  Diversified
  Communications Technology
  Computer Hardware
  Computer Software
  Manufacturing
  Medical Technology
  Other High Technologies Not Mentioned
GEOGRAPHIC PREFERENCE: No Preference
TYPES OF FUNDS:
  Equity (stock purchases)
INVESTMENT AMOUNTS PREFERRED:
  Minimum: Open
  Maximum: Open

Asset Management Company
1417 Edgewood Drive
Palo Alto, CA 94301
415 321 3131

CONTACT: Craig Taylor
TYPE OF FIRM: Venture Capital Firm
FUNDING PREFERENCE:
  Seed Funding
  Start-Up Funding
INDUSTRY PREFERENCE:
  Communications Technology
  Computer Hardware
  Computer Software
  Medical Technology
  Other High Technologies Not Mentioned
GEOGRAPHIC PREFERENCE:
  Northwest
  Far West
  Southwest
TYPES OF FUNDS:
  Equity (stock purchases)
INVESTMENT AMOUNTS PREFERRED:
  Minimum: $200,000
  Maximum: $750,000

Associates Venture Capital Corporation
425 California Street, Suite 2203
San Francisco, CA 94108
415 956 1444

CONTACT: Walter P. Strycker
TYPE OF FIRM: Venture Capital Firm
FUNDING PREFERENCE:
  Seed Funding
  Start-Up Funding
  Leveraged Buyouts
INDUSTRY PREFERENCE:
  Alternative Energy
  Communications Technology
  Computer Hardware
  Medical Technology
GEOGRAPHIC PREFERENCE: No Preference
TYPES OF FUNDS:
  Loans With Equity Kickers
INVESTMENT AMOUNTS PREFERRED:
  Minimum: $100,000
  Maximum: $3,000,000

Bay Partners
1927 Landings Drive, Suite B
Mountain View, CA 94043
415 961 5800

CONTACT: W. Charles Hazel
TYPE OF FIRM: Venture Capital Firm
FUNDING PREFERENCE:
  Start-Up Funding
  First-Round Funding
  Second-Round Funding
INDUSTRY PREFERENCE:
  Communications Technology
  Computer Hardware
  Computer Software
GEOGRAPHIC PREFERENCE:
  Far West
TYPES OF FUNDS:
  Equity (stock purchases)
INVESTMENT AMOUNTS PREFERRED:
  Minimum: $300,000
  Maximum: $600,000

Bay Venture Group
One Embarcadero Center, Suite 3303
San Francisco, CA 94111
415 989 7680

CONTACT: William Chandler
TYPE OF FIRM: Venture Capital Firm
FUNDING PREFERENCE:
  Seed Funding
  Start-Up Funding
INDUSTRY PREFERENCE:
  Computer Hardware
  Computer Software
  Manufacturing
  Medical Technology
  Other High Technologies Not Mentioned
GEOGRAPHIC PREFERENCE:
  Immediate Area
TYPES OF FUNDS:
  Equity (stock purchases)
  Loans With Equity Kickers
INVESTMENT AMOUNTS PREFERRED:
  Minimum: N/A
  Maximum: $200,000

Cal Fed Venture Capital Corporation
5670 Wilshire Boulevard
Los Angeles, CA 90036
213 932 4077

CONTACT: Anna Henry
TYPE OF FIRM: SBIC
FUNDING PREFERENCE:
  Start-Up Funding
  Later-Stage Funding
  Leveraged Buyouts
INDUSTRY PREFERENCE:
  Diversified
GEOGRAPHIC PREFERENCE: No Preference
TYPES OF FUNDS:
  Equity (stock purchases)
  Loans With Equity Kickers
INVESTMENT AMOUNTS PREFERRED:
  Minimum: $500,000
  Maximum: N/A

CDB Inc./Irvine Technology Fund
4600 Campus Drive
Newport Beach, CA
714 540 0900

CONTACT: Walter Cruttenden
TYPE OF FIRM: Venture Capital Firm
FUNDING PREFERENCE:
    Seed Funding
    Start-Up Funding
    First-Round Funding
INDUSTRY PREFERENCE:
    Computer Hardware
    Computer Software
    Medical Technology
    Retail
    Wholesale Distribution
GEOGRAPHIC PREFERENCE:
    California
    Within Two Two Hours of Office
TYPES OF FUNDS:
    Equity (stock purchases)
    Subordinate Debt With Equity Kickers
INVESTMENT AMOUNTS PREFERRED:
    Minimum: $500,000
    Maximum: $5,000,000

Charter Venture Capital
525 University Avenue #1500
Palo Alto, CA 94301
415 321 6953

CONTACT: A. Barr Dolan
TYPE OF FIRM: Venture Capital Firm
FUNDING PREFERENCE:
    Seed Funding
    Start-Up Funding
    First-Round Funding
    Second-Round Funding
INDUSTRY PREFERENCE:
    Alternative Energy
    Communications Technology
    Computer Hardware
    Computer Software
    Medical Technology
    Other High Technologies Not Mentioned

GEOGRAPHIC PREFERENCE:
  No Preference
TYPES OF FUNDS:
  Equity (stock purchases)
INVESTMENT AMOUNTS PREFERRED:
  Minimum: $300,000
  Maximum: $600,000

Chester W. Troudy, President
San Joaquin Capital Corporation
P. O. Box 2538
Bakersfield, CA 93303
805 323 7581

CONTACT: Chester W. Troudy
TYPE OF FIRM: SBIC
FUNDING PREFERENCE:
  Second-Round Funding
  Leveraged Buyouts
INDUSTRY PREFERENCE:
  Diversified
GEOGRAPHIC PREFERENCE:
  Far West
TYPES OF FUNDS:
  Loans With Equity Kickers
INVESTMENT AMOUNTS PREFERRED:
  Minimum: $100,000
  Maximum: $200,000

Churchill International
545 Middlefield Road, #160
Menlo Park, CA 94025
415 328 4401

CONTACT: Robert C. Weeks
TYPE OF FIRM:
  Venture Capital Firm
  SBIC
FUNDING PREFERENCE:
  Start-Up Funding
  First-Round Funding
  Second-Round Funding
  Third-Round Funding
  Fourth-Round Funding
  Later-Stage Funding

Leveraged Buyouts
Acquisitions
INDUSTRY PREFERENCE:
Communications Technology
Computer Hardware
Computer Software
Medical Technology
Other High Technologies Not Mentioned
GEOGRAPHIC PREFERENCE:
No Preference
TYPES OF FUNDS:
Equity (stock purchases)
Loans With Equity Kickers
INVESTMENT AMOUNTS PREFERRED:
Minimum: $200,000
Maximum: $1,000,000

City Ventures, Incorporated
404 N. Roxbury Drive, Suite 800
Beverly Hills, CA 90210
213 858 5314
212 550 0416

CONTACT: Mimi Shepard
TYPE OF FIRM:
Venture Capital Firm
SBIC
FUNDING PREFERENCE:
Second-Round Funding
Leveraged Buyouts
INDUSTRY PREFERENCE:
Diversified
Manufacturing
GEOGRAPHIC PREFERENCE:
No Preference
TYPES OF FUNDS:
Loans With Equity Kickers
INVESTMENT AMOUNTS PREFERRED:
Minimum: $100,000
Maximum: $500,000 & larger amounts syndicated

Continental Capital Ventures
555 California Street, #5070
San Francisco, CA 94104
415 989 2020

CONTACT: William Bolger
TYPE OF FIRM: Venture Capital Firm
FUNDING PREFERENCE:
    Start-Up Funding
    First-Round Funding
INDUSTRY PREFERENCE:
    Computer Hardware
    Computer Software
    Medical Technology
    Other High Technologies Not Mentioned
GEOGRAPHIC PREFERENCE:
    Far West
TYPES OF FUNDS:
    Equity (stock purchases)
    Loans
INVESTMENT AMOUNTS PREFERRED:
    Minimum: $250,000
    Maximum: $1,000,000

Early Stages Company
244 California Street
San Francisco, CA 94111
415 986 5700

CONTACT: Woody Kuehn
TYPE OF FIRM: Venture Capital Firm
FUNDING PREFERENCE:
    Start-Up Funding
    First-Round Funding
    Second-Round Funding
INDUSTRY PREFERENCE:
    Diversified
    Computer Software
    Medical Technology
    Retail
    Services
GEOGRAPHIC PREFERENCE:
    No Preference
TYPES OF FUNDS:
    Equity (stock purchases)
INVESTMENT AMOUNTS PREFERRED:
    Minimum: $250,000
    Maximum: $750,000

Bryan Edwards
3000 Sand Hill Road
Building 2, Suite 260
Menlo Park, CA 94025
415 854 1555

CONTACT: William C. Edwards
TYPE OF FIRM:
    Venture Capital Firm
    SBIC
    Individual Investor
FUNDING PREFERENCE:
    Seed Funding
    Start-Up Funding
    First-Round Funding
    Second-Round Funding
INDUSTRY PREFERENCE:
    Diversified
    Retail
    Conventional Energy
    Communications Technology
    Computer Hardware
    Computer Software
    Manufacturing
    Medical Technology
    Other High Technologies Not Mentioned
GEOGRAPHIC PREFERENCE:
    Northwest
    Far West
    Southwest
TYPES OF FUNDS:
    Equity (stock purchases)
    Loans With Equity Kickers
INVESTMENT AMOUNTS PREFERRED:
    Minimum: $50,000
    Maximum: $750,000

First Interstate Capital, Inc.
515 S. Figueroa Street
Suite 1900
Los Angeles, CA 90071
213 622 1922

CONTACT: Jonathan E. Funk
TYPE OF FIRM: Venture Capital Firm
    SBIC

FUNDING PREFERENCE:
   Seed Funding
   Start-Up Funding
   First-Round Funding
   Leveraged Buyouts
INDUSTRY PREFERENCE:
   Communications Technology
   Computer Hardware
   Computer Software
   Medical Technology
   Other High Technologies Not Mentioned
GEOGRAPHIC PREFERENCE:
   Rocky Mountain States
   Northwest
   Far West
   No Preference if not the lead investor
TYPES OF FUNDS:
   Equity
   Loans with Equity Kickers
   Bonds with Equity Kickers
INVESTMENT AMOUNTS PREFERRED:
   Minimum: $500,000
   Maximum: $1,800,000

First Interstate Capital Incorporated
515 S. Figueroa Street
Los Angeles, CA 90071
213 622 1922

CONTACT: William Ingram
TYPE OF FIRM: Venture Capital Firm
   SBIC
FUNDING PREFERENCE:
   Start-Up Funding
   First-Round Funding
   Leveraged Buyouts
INDUSTRY PREFERENCE:
   Communications Technology
   Computer Hardware
   Computer Software
   Manufacturing
   Medical Technology
   Other High Technologies Not Mentioned
GEOGRAPHIC PREFERENCE:
   Northwest
   Far West
   Southwest

TYPES OF FUNDS:
  Equity (stock purchases)
INVESTMENT AMOUNTS PREFERRED:
  Minimum: $500,000
  Maximum: $2,000,000

First Interstate Equities Corporation
515 S. Figueroa Street
Suite 1900
Los Angeles, CA 90071
213 662 1922

CONTACT: Jonathan E. Funk
TYPE OF FIRM: Venture Capital Firm
FUNDING PREFERENCE:
  Seed Funding
  Start-Up Funding
  Later-Stage Funding
  Leveraged Buyouts
INDUSTRY PREFERENCE:
  Communications Technology
  Computer Hardware
  Computer Software
  Medical Technology
  Other High Technologies Not Mentioned
GEOGRAPHIC PREFERENCE:
  Rocky Mountain States
  Northwest
  Far West
  No preference if not the lead investor
TYPES OF FUNDS:
  Equity
  Loans with Equity Kickers
  Bonds with Equity Kickers
INVESTMENT AMOUNTS PREFERRED:
  Minimum: $500,000
  Maximum: $2,000,000

First Small Business Investment Company of California
Security Pacific Capital Corporation
4000 MacArthur Boulevard, Suite 950
Newport Beach, CA 92660
714 754 4780

CONTACT: Brian Jones
TYPE OF FIRM: Venture Capital Firm
   SBIC
FUNDING PREFERENCE:
   First-Round Funding
   Second-Round Funding
   Leveraged Buyouts
   Acquisitions
INDUSTRY PREFERENCE:
   Diversified
   Manufacturing
GEOGRAPHIC PREFERENCE:
   No Preference
TYPES OF FUNDS:
   Equity (stock purchases)
   Loans With Equity Kickers
INVESTMENT AMOUNTS PREFERRED:
   Minimum: $100,000
   Maximum: $10,000,000

Bruce Glaspell
57 Post Street, Suite 513
San Francisco, CA 94104
415 781 1313

CONTACT: Bruce Glaspell
TYPE OF FIRM: Venture Capital Firm
   Investment Banking Firm
FUNDING PREFERENCE:
   Seed Funding
   Start-Up Funding
   First-Round Funding
   Second-Round Funding
   Third-Round Funding
   Fourth-Round Funding
   Later-Stage Funding
   Leveraged Buyouts
   Acquisitions
INDUSTRY PREFERENCE:
   Diversified
GEOGRAPHIC PREFERENCE:
   No Preference
TYPES OF FUNDS:
   Equity (stock purchases)

INVESTMENT AMOUNTS PREFERRED:
Minimum: $250,000
Maximum: $1,000,000

Grosspoint Investment Corporation
1015 Corporation Way
Palo Alto, CA 94303
415 964 3545

TYPE OF FIRM: SBIC
FUNDING PREFERENCE:
Second-Round Funding
Leveraged Buyouts
INDUSTRY PREFERENCE:
Diversified
Communications Technology
Medical Technology
GEOGRAPHIC PREFERENCE:
Far West
Southwest
TYPES OF FUNDS:
Bonds With Equity Kickers
INVESTMENT AMOUNTS PREFERRED:
Minimum: $100,000
Maximum: $150,000

Harvest Ventures Incorporated
1333 Lawrence Expressway, Suite 150
Santa Clara, CA 95051
408 985 5800

CONTACT: Cloyd Marvin
TYPE OF FIRM: Venture Capital Firm
SBIC
FUNDING PREFERENCE:
Seed Funding
Start-Up Funding
First-Round Funding
Second-Round Funding
INDUSTRY PREFERENCE:
Communications Technology
Computer Software
Medical Technology
Other High Technologies Not Mentioned

GEOGRAPHIC PREFERENCE:
No Preference (U.S. Only)
TYPES OF FUNDS:
Equity (stock purchases)
INVESTMENT AMOUNTS PREFERRED:
Minimum: $600,000
Maximum: $1,200,000

Hub Enterprises, Ltd.
5878 Doyle Street
Emeryville, CA 94608
415 428 2181

CONTACT: Jack M. Atkin
TYPE OF FIRM: MESBIC
FUNDING PREFERENCE:
Seed Funding
Start-Up Funding
First-Round Funding
INDUSTRY PREFERENCE:
Diversified
GEOGRAPHIC PREFERENCE:
Northern California
TYPES OF FUNDS:
Equity (stock purchases)
Loans
Loans With Equity Kickers
INVESTMENT AMOUNTS PREFERRED:
Minimum: $25,000
Maximum: $100,000

Idanta Partners
3344 North Torrey Pines Court
Suiute 200
La Jolla, CA 92037
619 455 5280

CONTACT: Harry Lange
TYPE OF FIRM: Venture Capital Firm
FUNDING PREFERENCE:
Seed Funding
Start-Up Funding
First-Round Funding
Leveraged Buyouts

INDUSTRY PREFERENCE:
  Diversified
  Communications Technology
  Computer Hardware
  Computer Software
  Manufacturing
  Medical Technology
  Other High Technologies Not Mentioned
  Retail
  Service
  Wholesale Distribution
GEOGRAPHIC PREFERENCE:
  No Preference
TYPES OF FUNDS:
  Equity
INVESTMENT AMOUNTS PREFERRED:
  Minimum: $300,000
  Maximum: None

International Business Sponsors, Inc.
765 Bridgeway Boulevard
Sausalito, CA 94965
415 331 2262

CONTACT: Mel L. Bacharach
TYPE OF FIRM: Venture Capital Firm
FUNDING PREFERENCE:
  Second-Round Funding
  Later-Stage Funding
INDUSTRY PREFERENCE:
  Diversified
GEOGRAPHIC PREFERENCE:
  Far West
TYPES OF FUNDS:
  Equity (stock purchases)
  Loans With Equity Kickers
  Bonds With Equity Kickers
INVESTMENT AMOUNTS PREFERRED:
  Minimum: $50,000
  Maximum: $500,000

Ivanhoe Venture Capital, Ltd.
737 Pearl Street, Suite 201
La Jolla, CA 92037
619 454 8882

CONTACT: Alan R. Toffler
TYPE OF FIRM: Venture Capital Firm
  SBIC
FUNDING PREFERENCE:
  Second-Round Funding
  Third-Round Funding
  Leveraged Buyouts
INDUSTRY PREFERENCE:
  Diversified
GEOGRAPHIC PREFERENCE:
  Southwest
TYPES OF FUNDS:
  Equity (stock purchases)
  Loans
  Loans With Equity Kickers
INVESTMENT AMOUNTS PREFERRED:
  Minimum: $100,000
  Maximum: $2,000,000

Lasung Investment & Finance Company
36000 Wilshire Boulevard, #1410
Los Angeles, CA 90010
213 384 7548

CONTACT: Yoon C. Na
TYPE OF FIRM: MESBIC
FUNDING PREFERENCE:
  Start-Up Funding
  First-Round Funding
INDUSTRY PREFERENCE:
  Diversified
GEOGRAPHIC PREFERENCE:
  Far West
TYPES OF FUNDS:
  Equity (stock purchases)
  Loans
INVESTMENT AMOUNTS PREFERRED:
  Minimum: $30,000
  Maximum: $300,000

MCA New Ventures, Incorporated
100 Universal City Plaza, 500/3
Universal City, CA 91608
213 508 1808

CONTACT: Deborah Smith-Pegues
TYPE OF FIRM: MESBIC
FUNDING PREFERENCE:
  Seed Funding
  Later-Stage Funding
INDUSTRY PREFERENCE:
  Communications Technology
  Other High Technologies Not Mentioned
GEOGRAPHIC PREFERENCE:
  Far West
TYPES OF FUNDS:
  Loans With Equity Kickers
INVESTMENT AMOUNTS PREFERRED:
  Minimum: $100,000
  Maximum: $250,000

Metropolitan Venture Company
8383 Wilshire Boulevard
Beverly Hills, CA 90211
213 651 2173

CONTACT: Esther Lowy
TYPE OF FIRM: SBIC
FUNDING PREFERENCE:
  Second-Round Funding
  Acquisitions
INDUSTRY PREFERENCE:
  Diversified
  Medical Technology
  Real Estate
GEOGRAPHIC PREFERENCE:
  Southwest (California)
TYPES OF FUNDS:
  Equity (stock purchases)
  Bonds With Equity Kickers
INVESTMENT AMOUNTS PREFERRED:
  Minimum: $100,000
  Maximum: $200,000

Miller & LaHaye/Peregrine Associates
606 Wilshire Boulevard, #602
Santa Monica, CA 90401
213 458 1441

CONTACT: Gene Miller
TYPE OF FIRM: Venture Capital Firm

FUNDING PREFERENCE:
  Start-Up Funding
  First-Round Funding
INDUSTRY PREFERENCE:
  Diversified
  Communications Technology
  Computer Hardware
  Computer Software
  Manufacturing
  Medical Technology
  Other High Technologies Not Mentioned
  Services
GEOGRAPHIC PREFERENCE:
  No Preference
TYPES OF FUNDS:
  Equity (stock purchases)
INVESTMENT AMOUNTS PREFERRED:
  Minimum: $100,000
  Maximum: $1,500,000

Myriad Capital, Inc.
8820 Sepulveda Blvd., Suite 204
Los Angeles, CA 90045
213 641 7936

CONTACT: Kuo-Hung Chen
TYPE OF FIRM: MESBIC
FUNDING PREFERENCE:
  Second-Round Funding
INDUSTRY PREFERENCE:
  Diversified
GEOGRAPHIC PREFERENCE:
  No Preference
TYPES OF FUNDS:
  Equity (stock purchases)
  Loans
  Loans With Equity Kickers
INVESTMENT AMOUNTS PREFERRED:
  Minimum: $50,000
  Maximum: $400,000

National Investment Management, Inc.
3838 Carson Street, #302
Torrance, CA 90503
213 540 1227

CONTACT: Richard D. Robins
TYPE OF FIRM: Venture Capital Firm
FUNDING PREFERENCE:
  Third-Round Funding
  Fourth-Round Funding
  Later-Stage Funding
  Leveraged Buyouts
  Acquisitions
INDUSTRY PREFERENCE:
  Diversified
  Manufacturing
  Wholesale Distribution
GEOGRAPHIC PREFERENCE:
  No Preference
TYPES OF FUNDS:
  Equity (stock purchases)
  Bonds With Equity Kickers
INVESTMENT AMOUNTS PREFERRED:
  Minimum: $200,000
  Maximum: $1,000,000

New West Partners
180 Newport Center Drive, #200
Newport Beach, CA 92660
714 759 0884

CONTACT: Timothy Haldinger
TYPE OF FIRM: SBIC
FUNDING PREFERENCE:
  First-Round Funding
  Second-Round Funding
  Third-Round Funding
  Fourth-Round Funding
  Later-Stage Funding
  Leveraged Buyouts
  Acquisitions
INDUSTRY PREFERENCE:
  Diversified
  Conventional Energy
  Media
  Natural Resources
  Real Estate
GEOGRAPHIC PREFERENCE:
  Rocky Mountain States
  Northwest
  Far West
  Southwest

TYPES OF FUNDS:
  Equity (stock purchases)
  Loans With Equity Kickers
  Bonds With Equity Kickers
INVESTMENT AMOUNTS PREFERRED:
  Minimum: $250,000
  Maximum: N/A

Oscco Ventures
3000 Sand Hill Road, 3-120
Menlo Park, CA 94025-7117
415 854 2222

CONTACT: F. Ward Paine
TYPE OF FIRM: Venture Capital Firm
FUNDING PREFERENCE:
  Seed Funding
  Start-Up Funding
  First-Round Funding
INDUSTRY PREFERENCE:
  Diversified
  Communications Technology
  Computer Hardware
  Computer Software
  Medical Technology
  Other High Technologies Not Mentioned
GEOGRAPHIC PREFERENCE:
  Far West
  Southwest
  Home State
  Immediate Area
TYPES OF FUNDS:
  Equity (stock purchases)
INVESTMENT AMOUNTS PREFERRED:
  Minimum: $200,000
  Maximum: $1,000,000

San Jose Capital Corporation
100 Park Central Plaza, Suite 427
San Jose, CA 95113
408 293 7708

CONTACT: Robert T. Murphy
TYPE OF FIRM: Venture Capital Firm
FUNDING PREFERENCE:
  Start-Up Funding

First-Round Funding
Leveraged Buyouts
INDUSTRY PREFERENCE:
Communications Technology
Computer Hardware
Computer Software
Manufacturing
Medical Technology
Other High Technologies Not Mentioned
GEOGRAPHIC PREFERENCE:
No Preference
TYPES OF FUNDS:
Equity (stock purchases)
Loans With Equity Kickers
INVESTMENT AMOUNTS PREFERRED:
Minimum: $200,000
Maximum $500,000

Seaport Ventures, Inc.
770 B Street, Suite 420
San Diego, CA 92101
619 232 4069

CONTACT: Michael Stolper
TYPE OF FIRM: SBIC
FUNDING PREFERENCE:
Second-Round Funding
Third-Round Funding
Leveraged Buyouts
INDUSTRY PREFERENCE:
Diversified
GEOGRAPHIC PREFERENCE:
No Preference
TYPES OF FUNDS:
Loans With Equity Kickers
INVESTMENT AMOUNTS PREFERRED:
Minimum: $50,000
Maximum: $300,000

Space Ventures, Inc.
3931 MacArthur Blvd., Suite 212
Newport Beach, CA 92660
714 851 0855

CONTACT: Thomas Trigg or Leslie Brewer
TYPE OF FIRM: MESBIC
FUNDING PREFERENCE:
  Second-Round Funding
  Third-Round Funding
  Fourth-Round Funding
  Later-Stage Funding
  Leveraged Buyouts
  Acquisitions
INDUSTRY PREFERENCE:
  Diversified
GEOGRAPHIC PREFERENCE:
  Far West
  Southwest
  Home State—California
  Immediate Area—Southern California
TYPES OF FUNDS:
  Loans With Equity Kickers
INVESTMENT AMOUNTS PREFERRED:
  Minimum: $100,000
  Maximum: $300,000

Sutter Hill Ventures
Two Palo Alto Square, Suite 700
Palo Alto, CA 94306
415 493 5600

CONTACT: G. Leonard Baker, Jr.
TYPE OF FIRM: Venture Capital Firm
FUNDING PREFERENCE:
  Seed Funding
  Start-Up Funding
  First-Round Funding
  Second-Round Funding
INDUSTRY PREFERENCE:
  Communications Technology
  Computer Hardware
  Computer Software
  Medical Technology
GEOGRAPHIC PREFERENCE:
  Far West
TYPES OF FUNDS:
  Equity (stock purchases)
INVESTMENT AMOUNTS PREFERRED:
  Minimum: $200,000
  Maximum: $2,000,000

238   DIRECTORY OF CAPITAL SOURCES

Technology Venture Investors
3000 Sand Hill Road
Bldg. 4, Suite 210
Menlo Park, CA 94025
415 854 7472

CONTACT: Burton J. McMurtry
TYPE OF FIRM: Venture Capital Firm
FUNDING PREFERENCE:
    Start-Up Funding
    First-Round Funding
    Second-Round Funding
INDUSTRY PREFERENCE:
    Communications Technology
    Computer Hardware
    Computer Software
    Medical Technology
    Other High Technologies Not Mentioned
GEOGRAPHIC PREFERENCE:
    California
TYPES OF FUNDS:
    Equity (stock purchases)
INVESTMENT AMOUNTS PREFERRED:
    Minimum: $500,000
    Maximum: N/A

Union Venture Corporation
445 S. Figueroa Street
Los Angeles, CA 90071
213 236 6292

CONTACT: Jeffrey A. Watts
TYPE OF FIRM: Venture Capital Firm
    SBIC
FUNDING PREFERENCE:
    Start-Up Funding
    First-Round Funding
    Second-Round Funding
INDUSTRY PREFERENCE:
    Diversified
    Communications Technology
    Computer Hardware
    Computer Software
    Manufacturing
    Medical Technology
    Other High Technologies Not Mentioned

GEOGRAPHIC PREFERENCE:
No Preference
Far West
California
TYPES OF FUNDS:
Equity (stock purchases)
INVESTMENT AMOUNTS PREFERRED:
Minimum: $300,000
Maximum: $1,500,000

Vanguard Associates
3000 Sand Hill Road
Bldg. 1 Suite 190
Menlo Park, CA 94024
415 854 8709

CONTACT: Jack Gill
TYPE OF FIRM: Venture Capital Firm
FUNDING PREFERENCE:
Start-Up Funding
First-Round Funding
INDUSTRY PREFERENCE:
Communications Technology
Computer Hardware
Computer Software
Medical Technology
GEOGRAPHIC PREFERENCE:
California
TYPES OF FUNDS:
Equity (stock purchases)
INVESTMENT AMOUNTS PREFERRED:
Minimum: $350,000–500,000
Maximum: $1,000,000 +

Walden Capital
303 Sacramento Street
San Francisco, CA 94111
415 391 7225

CONTACT: George Sarlo
TYPE OF FIRM: Venture Capital Firm
SBIC
FUNDING PREFERENCE:
First-Round Funding
Second-Round Funding

INDUSTRY PREFERENCE:
  Diversified
  Communications Technology
  Computer Hardware
  Computer Software
  Manufacturing
  Medical Technology
  Other High Technologies Not Mentioned
GEOGRAPHIC PREFERENCE: No Preference
TYPES OF FUNDS:
  Equity (stock purchases)
  Loans With Equity Kickers
  Bonds With Equity Kickers
INVESTMENT AMOUNTS PREFERRED:
  Minimum: $200,000
  Maximum: $1,500,000

Xerox Venture Capital
2029 Century Park East
Suite 740
Los Angeles, CA 90067
213 278 7940

CONTACT: Alvin Talbot
TYPE OF FIRM: Venture Capital Firm
FUNDING PREFERENCE:
  Open
INDUSTRY PREFERENCE:
  Communications Technology
  Computer Hardware
  Computer Software
GEOGRAPHIC PREFERENCE:
  No Preference
TYPES OF FUNDS:
  Equity
INVESTMENT AMOUNTS PREFERRED:
  Minimum: $500,000
  Maximum: $1,000,000

COLORADO

Colorado Growth Capital, Inc.
1600 Broadway, Suite 2125
Denver, CO 80202
303 629 0205

CONTACT: Debra Chavez
TYPE OF FIRM: SBIC

FUNDING PREFERENCE:
  Second-Round Funding
  Leveraged Buyouts
INDUSTRY PREFERENCE:
  Manufacturing
GEOGRAPHIC PREFERENCE:
  Rocky Mountain States
TYPES OF FUNDS:
  Equity (stock purchases)
  Loans
  Loans With Equity Kickers
INVESTMENT AMOUNTS PREFERRED:
  Minimum: $50,000
  Maximum: $200,000

Electro-Service Management Corp.
Suite 100, 5370 Manhattan Circle
Boulder, CO 80303
303 494 7119

CONTACT: Robert Keeley
TYPE OF FIRM: Venture Capital Firm
FUNDING PREFERENCE:
  Start-Up Funding
  First-Round Funding
  Second-Round Funding
INDUSTRY PREFERENCE:
  Communications Technology
  Computer Hardware
  Computer Software
  Manufacturing
  Medical Technology
GEOGRAPHIC PREFERENCE:
  No Preference
TYPES OF FUNDS:
  Equity (stock purchases)
  Loans With Equity Kickers
INVESTMENT AMOUNTS PREFERRED:
  Minimum: $100,000
  Maximum: $400,000

Investment Securities of Colorado, Inc.
4605 Denice Drive
Englewood, CO 80111
303 781 7813

CONTACT: Vern D. Kornelsen
TYPE OF FIRM: Venture Capital Firm

FUNDING PREFERENCE:
  Seed Funding
  Start-Up Funding
INDUSTRY PREFERENCE:
  Computer Hardware
  Computer Software
  Manufacturing
  Medical Technology
  Other High Technologies Not Mentioned
GEOGRAPHIC PREFERENCE:
  Rocky Mountain States
TYPES OF FUNDS:
  Equity (stock purchases)
INVESTMENT AMOUNTS PREFERRED:
  Minimum: None
  Maximum: $300,000

Norwest Venture Capital Management, Inc.
1801 California Street, Suite 585
City Center Four Building
Denver, CO 80202
303 297 0537

CONTACT: Larry Wonnacott
TYPE OF FIRM: Venture Capital Firm
  SBIC
FUNDING PREFERENCE:
  Seed Funding
  Start-Up Funding
  First-Round Funding
  Second-Round Funding
  Leveraged Buyouts
INDUSTRY PREFERENCE:
  Communications Technology
  Computer Hardware
  Computer Software
  Manufacturing
  Medical Technology
  Other High Technologies Not Mentioned
GEOGRAPHIC PREFERENCE:
  No Preference
TYPES OF FUNDS:
  Equity
INVESTMENT AMOUNTS PREFERRED:
  Minimum: $750,000
  Maximum: Several Million

Stephenson Merchant Banking
899 Logan Street
Denver, CO 80203
303 837 1700

CONTACT: N/A
TYPE OF FIRM: Venture Capital Firm
FUNDING PREFERENCE:
  Second-Round Funding
  Third-Round Funding
  Leveraged Buyouts
  Acquisitions
INDUSTRY PREFERENCE:
  Conventional Energy
  Communications Technology
  Computer Hardware
  Computer Software
  Manufacturing
  Media
  Medical Technology
  Other High Technologies Not Mentioned
  Retail
  Services
  Wholesale Dist.
GEOGRAPHIC PREFERENCE:
  Mid-West
  Rocky Mountain States
  Northwest
  Far West
  Southwest
TYPES OF FUNDS:
  Equity
  Loans with Equity Kickers
  Bonds with Equity Kickers
INVESTMENT AMOUNTS PREFERRED:
  Minimum: $50,000
  Maximum: $500,000

CONNECTICUT

A B Small Business Investment Co., Inc.
275 Schoolhouse Road
Cheshire, CT 06410
203 272 3511

CONTACT: Malcolm Ball
TYPE OF FIRM: SBIC

FUNDING PREFERENCE:
  First-Round Funding
INDUSTRY PREFERENCE:
  Retail
GEOGRAPHIC PREFERENCE:
  Connecticut
  New York
  New Jersey
TYPES OF FUNDS:
  CD's
INVESTMENT AMOUNTS PREFERRED:
  Minimum: $10,000
  Maximum: $100,000

Beacon Partners
111 Hubbard Avenue
Stamford, CT 06905
203 348 8858

CONTACT: Leonard Vignola
TYPE OF FIRM: Consulting Firm
FUNDING PREFERENCE:
  First-Round Funding
INDUSTRY PREFERENCE:
  Diversified
  Communications Technology
  Computer Software
  Manufacturing
  Medical Technology
  Services
GEOGRAPHIC PREFERENCE:
  Northeast
  Mid-West
TYPES OF FUNDS:
  N/A
INVESTMENT AMOUNTS PREFERRED:
  Minimum: N/A
  Maximum: N/A

Hawley & Associates
999 Summer Street
Stamford, CT 06905
203 348 6669

CONTACT: F. J. Hawley, Jr.
TYPE OF FIRM: Venture Capital Firm

FUNDING PREFERENCE:
  Second-Round Funding
  Third-Round Funding
  Fourth-Round Funding
  Leveraged Buyouts
  Acquisitions
INDUSTRY PREFERENCE:
  Diversified
  Conventional Energy
  Communications Technology
  Manufacturing
  Services
  Wholesale Distribution
GEOGRAPHIC PREFERENCE:
  No Preference
TYPES OF FUNDS:
  Equity (stock purchases)
  Loans With Equity Kickers
INVESTMENT AMOUNTS PREFERRED:
  Minimum: $300,000
  Maximum: $3,000,000

James B. Kobak & Company
774 Hollow Tree Ridge Road
Darien, CT 06820
203 655 8764

CONTACT: Jim Kobak
TYPE OF FIRM: Consulting Firm
FUNDING PREFERENCE:
  N/A
INDUSTRY PREFERENCE:
  Media
GEOGRAPHIC PREFERENCE:
  No Preference
TYPES OF FUNDS:
  Other, rarely
INVESTMENT AMOUNTS PREFERRED:
  Minimum: N/A
  Maximum: $100,000

Oxford Partners
72 Cummings Pt. Road
Stamford, CT 06902
203 964 0592

CONTACT: Kenneth W. Rind
TYPE OF FIRM: Venture Capital Firm
FUNDING PREFERENCE:
  Start-Up Funding
  First-Round Funding
  Second-Round Funding
  Leveraged Buyouts
INDUSTRY PREFERENCE:
  Other High Technologies Not Mentioned
  Alternative Energy
  Communications Technology
  Computer Hardware
  Computer Software
  Manufacturing
  Media
  Medical Technology
GEOGRAPHIC PREFERENCE:
  No Preference
TYPES OF FUNDS:
  Equity (stock purchases)
INVESTMENT AMOUNTS PREFERRED:
  Minimum: $250,000
  Maximum: $1,000,000

Prime Capital L. P.
One Landmark Square, Suite 800
Stamford, CT 06901
203 964 0642

CONTACT: Dean E. Fenton
TYPE OF FIRM: Venture Capital Firm
FUNDING PREFERENCE:
  Start-Up Funding
  First-Round Funding
  Second-Round Funding
INDUSTRY PREFERENCE:
  Alternative Energy
  Communications Technology
  Computer Hardware
  Computer Software
  Medical Technology
  Other High Technologies Not Mentioned
GEOGRAPHIC PREFERENCE:
  No Preference (U.S.)
TYPES OF FUNDS:
  Equity (stock purchases)

INVESTMENT AMOUNTS PREFERRED:
  Minimum: $300,000–$600,000
  Maximum: $1,000,000–$2,000,000

Vista Technology Ventures, Inc.
2410 Long Ridge Road
Stamford, CT 06903
203 322 0091

CONTACT: Irwin Rudich
TYPE OF FIRM:
  Venture Capital Firm/Investment Banking Firm
  Individual Investor/Consulting Firm
FUNDING PREFERENCE:
  Seed Funding
  Start-Up Funding
  First-Round Funding
INDUSTRY PREFERENCE:
  Diversified
  Alternative Energy
  Communications Technology
  Computer Hardware
  Computer Software
  Manufacturing
  Magazines
  Medical Technology
  Other High Technology
GEOGRAPHIC PREFERENCE:
  Northeast
  Middle Atlantic
TYPES OF FUNDS:
  Loans with Equity Kickers
  Equity (stock purchases)
  Bonds With Equity Kickers
INVESTMENT AMOUNTS PREFERRED:
  Minimum: $500,000
  Maximum: $2,000,000

Vista Ventures
1600 Summer Street
Stamford, CT 06905
203 359 3500

CONTACT: Gerald B. Bay
TYPE OF FIRM: Venture Capital Firm

FUNDING PREFERENCE:
  Seed Funding
  Start-Up Funding
  First-Round Funding
  Second-Round Funding
  Third-Round Funding
INDUSTRY PREFERENCE:
  Diversified
  Alternative Energy
  Communications Technology
  Computer Hardware
  Computer Software
  Manufacturing
  Medical Technology
  Other High Technologies Not Mentioned
  Services
GEOGRAPHIC PREFERENCE:
  No Preference
TYPES OF FUNDS:
  Equity (stock purchases)
  Loans With Equity Kickers
INVESTMENT AMOUNTS PREFERRED:
  Minimum: $250,000
  Maximum: $2,500,000

Whitehead Associates
15 Valley Drive
Greenwich, CT 06830
203 629 4633

CONTACT: William E. Engbers
TYPE OF FIRM: Venture Capital Firm
FUNDING PREFERENCE:
  No Preference
INDUSTRY PREFERENCE:
  Diversified
GEOGRAPHIC PREFERENCE:
  No Preference
TYPES OF FUNDS:
  Equity (stock purchases)
INVESTMENT AMOUNTS PREFERRED:
  Minimum: $100,000
  Maximum: $1,000,000

DELAWARE

Kiernan Petroleum Corporation
P.O. Box 4636
Newark, DEL 19715
302 386 7910

CONTACT: George H. Kiernan
TYPE OF FIRM: Venture Capital Firm and
   Integrated energy firm—V.C.O.
FUNDING PREFERENCE:
   Any except
   Later-Stage Funding
   Leveraged Buyouts
   Acquisitions
INDUSTRY PREFERENCE:
   Any
GEOGRAPHIC PREFERENCE:
   I.E.F. (hereof)
   especially not:
      Northeast
      Middle Atlantic
TYPES OF FUNDS:
   Equity
   Bonds
INVESTMENT AMOUNTS PREFERRED:
   Minimum: $5,000
   Maximum: open (depending upon particular situation)

FLORIDA

Electro-Science Management Corp.
600 Courtland St., Suite 490
Orlando, FL 32804
305 645 1188

CONTACT: G. A. Herbert
TYPE OF FIRM: Venture Capital Firm
FUNDING PREFERENCE:
   Start-Up Funding
   First-Round Funding
INDUSTRY PREFERENCE:
   Communications Technology
   Computer Hardware
   Computer Software

Medical Technology
Other High Technologies Not Mentioned
GEOGRAPHIC PREFERENCE:
Southeast
Rocky Mountain States
TYPES OF FUNDS:
Equity
Loans with Equity Kickers
Bonds with Equity Kickers
INVESTMENT AMOUNTS PREFERRED:
Minimum: $100,000
Maximum: $300,000

First American Advisory Corporation
Advisor to Massachusetts Capital
Corporation and First American Invest. Co.
325 Mary St., Suite 308
Coconut Grove, FL 33133
305 441 0924

CONTACT: Mary Helen Blakeslee
TYPE OF FIRM: SBIC
FUNDING PREFERENCE:
Start-Up Funding
First-Round Funding
Second-round Funding
Leveraged Buyouts
INDUSTRY PREFERENCE:
Communications Technology
Computer Hardware
Computer Software
Medical Technology
Other High Technologies Not Mentioned
Diversified
GEOGRAPHIC PREFERENCE:
Southeast
TYPES OF FUNDS:
Equity
INVESTMENT AMOUNTS PREFERRED:
Minimum: $100,000
Maximum: $500,000 initial investment

First Miami SBIC
250 South Ocean Blvd., Suite 18-D
Boca Raton, FL 33432
305 392 4424

CONTACT: I.L. Libby
TYPE OF FIRM: SBIC
FUNDING PREFERENCE:
Start-Up Funding
Leveraged Buyouts
Acquisitions
INDUSTRY PREFERENCE:
Communications Technology
Media
Real Estate
Services
GEOGRAPHIC PREFERENCE:
Southeast
Southwest
TYPES OF FUNDS:
Loans with Equity Kickers
Convertibles
Bonds with Equity Kickers
INVESTMENT AMOUNTS PREFERRED:
Minimum: $100,000
Maximum: $500,000

Gold Coast Capital Corp.
3550 Biscayne Blvd., Suite 601
Miami, FL 33137
305 576 2012

CONTACT: William I. Gold
TYPE OF FIRM: SBIC
FUNDING PREFERENCE:
First-Round Funding
Second-Round Funding
Third-Round Funding
Fourth-Round Funding
Later-Stage Funding
INDUSTRY PREFERENCE:
Diversified
Manufacturing
Real Estate
Retail
Services
Wholesale Distribution
GEOGRAPHIC PREFERENCE:
Southeast
Home State—Florida
TYPES OF FUNDS:
Loans

INVESTMENT AMOUNTS PREFERRED:
   Minimum: $25,000
   Maximum: $500,000

Interstate Capital Corporation
701 E. Caminor Real
Suite 9A
Boca Raton, FL 33432
305 395 8466

CONTACT: William C. McConnell, Jr.
TYPE OF FIRM:
   Venture Capital Firm
   Individual Investor
   Consulting Firm
FUNDING PREFERENCE:
   Start-Up Funding
   First-Round Funding
INDUSTRY PREFERENCE:
   Communications Technology
   Manufacturing
   Medical Technology
   Other High Technologies Not Mentioned
   Services
GEOGRAPHIC PREFERENCE:
   Northeast
   Southeast
   Mid-West
TYPES OF FUNDS:
   Equity
   Loans with Equity Kickers
INVESTMENT AMOUNTS PREFERRED:
   Minimum: $50,000
   Maximum: $500,000

Jets Venture Capital Corporation
615 Park Street
Jacksonville, FL 32204
904 356 2032

CONTACT: James L. Morrell
TYPE OF FIRM: MESBIC
FUNDING PREFERENCE:
   Start-Up Funding
   First-Round Funding

INDUSTRY PREFERENCE:
  Diversified
GEOGRAPHIC PREFERENCE:
  Southeast
TYPES OF FUNDS:
  Equity
  Loans
  Loans with Equity Kickers
INVESTMENT AMOUNTS PREFERRED:
  Minimum: $20,000
  Maximum: $300,000

JRR Investments Inc.
4747 N. Ocean Blvd., #215
Fort Lauderdale, FL 33308
305 781 0308

CONTACT: John Rhodes
TYPE OF FIRM: Venture Capital Firm
  Investment Banking Firm
FUNDING PREFERENCE:
  Start-up Funding
  Acquisitions
INDUSTRY PREFERENCE:
  Diversified
  Real Estate
GEOGRAPHIC PREFERENCE:
  Southeast
  Home State—Florida
  Immediate Area—S. Florida
TYPES OF FUNDS:
  Equity
  Loans with Equity Kickers
INVESTMENT AMOUNTS PREFERRED:
  Minimum: $250,000
  Maximum: N/A

South Atlantic Capital Corporation
201 East Kennedy Boulevard, Suite 911
Tampa, FL 33602
813 229 7400

CONTACT: Donald W. Burton
TYPE OF FIRM: Venture Capital Firm

FUNDING PREFERENCE:
  First-Round Funding
  Second-Round Funding
INDUSTRY PREFERENCE:
  All except:
  Wholesale Distribution
  Alternative Energy
  Conventional Energy
  Media
  Natural Resources
GEOGRAPHIC PREFERENCE:
  Southeast
TYPES OF FUNDS:
  Equity
INVESTMENT AMOUNTS PREFERRED:
  Minimum: $300,000
  Maximum: $750,000

Venture Opportunities Corporation
444 Brickell Avenue, Suite 930
Miami, FL 33131
305 358 0359

CONTACT: Fred March
TYPE OF FIRM: Consulting Firm
  Venture Capital Firm
  MESBIC
FUNDING PREFERENCE:
  Second-Round Funding
  Leveraged Buyouts
  Acquisitions
INDUSTRY PREFERENCE:
  Diversified
GEOGRAPHIC PREFERENCE:
  Northeast
  Middle Atlantic
  Southeast
TYPES OF FUNDS:
  Equity
  Loans
  Loans with Equity Kickers
  Bonds with Equity Kickers
INVESTMENT AMOUNTS PREFERRED:
  Minimum: $100,000
  Maximum: $175,000

Western Financial Capital Corp.
12550 Biscayne Blvd.
Suite 400
North Miami, FL 33181
305 891 0823

CONTACT: F. M. Rosemore
TYPE OF FIRM: SBIC
   SBLC
   Consulting Firm
FUNDING PREFERENCE:
   Second-Round Funding
   Third-Round Funding
   Fourth-Round Funding
   Later-Stage Funding
INDUSTRY PREFERENCE:
   Diversified
   Manufacturing
   Medical Technology
   Real Estate
   Services
GEOGRAPHIC PREFERENCE:
   Home State
TYPES OF FUNDS:
   Loans
   Loans with Equity Kickers
INVESTMENT AMOUNTS PREFERRED:
   Minimum: $50,000
   Maximum: $550,000

GEORGIA

Philipps J. Hook & Assoc. Inc.
5600 Roswell Rd., Suite. 300 N.
Atlanta, GA 30342
404 252 1994

CONTACT: Phil Hook
TYPE OF FIRM: Investment Banking Firm
FUNDING PREFERENCE:
   Leveraged Buyouts
   Acquisitions
INDUSTRY PREFERENCE:
   Diversified
GEOGRAPHIC PREFERENCE:
   No Preference

TYPES OF FUNDS:
   Equity
   Loans
INVESTMENT AMOUNTS PREFERRED:
   Minimum: $1,000,000
   Maximum: N/A

HAWAII

Capital Formation Consultants, Inc.
P.O. Box 798, Diablo CA 94828
& 1720 Ala Moana Blvd., #1506 B
Honolulu, HI 96815
415 820 8030 & 808 949 0544

CONTACT: John H. Rohan
TYPE OF FIRM: Venture Capital Firm
FUNDING PREFERENCE:
   Start-up Funding
INDUSTRY PREFERENCE:
   Diversified
GEOGRAPHIC PREFERENCE:
   Home State
TYPES OF FUNDS:
   Equity
   R&D Partnerships
INVESTMENT AMOUNTS PREFERRED:
   Minimum: $250,000
   Maximum: $1,000,000

ILLINOIS

Chicago Community Ventures, Inc.
108 North State Street, Suite 902
Chicago, IL 60602
312 726 6084

CONTACT: Phyllis George
TYPE OF FIRM: MESBIC
FUNDING PREFERENCE:
   Second-Round Funding
   Later-Stage Funding
   Leveraged Buyouts
   Acquisitions
INDUSTRY PREFERENCE:
   Diversified
   Manufacturing
   Retail

GEOGRAPHIC PREFERENCE:
  Mid-West
  Metropolitan Chicagoland Area
TYPES OF FUNDS:
  Loans
  Loans with Equity Kickers
INVESTMENT AMOUNTS PREFERRED:
  Minimum: $50,000
  Maximum: $300,000

First Capital Corporation of Chicago
Suite 2628
One First National Plaza
Chicago, IL 60670
312 732 5400

CONTACT: John A. Canning—Chicago
TYPE OF FIRM: Venture Capital Firm
FUNDING PREFERENCE:
  All except:
  Seed Funding
  Acquisitions
INDUSTRY PREFERENCE:
  All except:
  Alternative Energy
  Conventional Energy
  Media
  Natural Resources
  Services
  Wholesale Distribution
GEOGRAPHIC PREFERENCE:
  No Preference
TYPES OF FUNDS:
  Equity
INVESTMENT AMOUNTS PREFERRED:
  Minimum: $500,000
  Maximum: $10,000,000

Heizer Corporation
20 North Wacker Drive
Chicago, IL 60606
312 641 2200

CONTACT: E. F. Heizer, Jr.
  M. Mead Montgomery
TYPE OF FIRM: Publicly held Business Development Co.

FUNDING PREFERENCE:
  Will consider any stage
INDUSTRY PREFERENCE:
  Communications Technology
  Computer Hardware
  Computer Software
GEOGRAPHIC PREFERENCE:
  No Preference
TYPES OF FUNDS:
  Equity
INVESTMENT AMOUNTS PREFERRED:
  Minimum: $100,000
  Maximum: $3,000,000

IEG Venture Partners
Three First National Plaza
Chicago, IL 60602
312 899 0185

CONTACT: Frank Blair
TYPE OF FIRM: Venture Capital Firm
FUNDING PREFERENCE:
  Seed Funding
  Start-Up Funding
  First-Round Funding
INDUSTRY PREFERENCE:
  Diversified
GEOGRAPHIC PREFERENCE:
  Mid-West
TYPES OF FUNDS:
  Equity
INVESTMENT AMOUNTS PREFERRED:
  Minimum: $250,000
  Maximum: $1,500,000

The Institutional Venture Capital Fund
The First National Bank of Chicago
Suite 0140
Three First National Plaza
Chicago, IL 60670
312 732 7974

CONTACT: Daniel W. O'Connell
TYPE OF FIRM:
  Commercial Bank with Trust Investment
  Venture Capital Activity

FUNDING PREFERENCE:
  First-Round Funding
  Second-Round Funding
  Third-Round Funding
  Fourth-Round Funding
  Later-State Funding
  Leveraged Buyouts
  Acquisitions
INDUSTRY PREFERENCE:
  Alternative Energy
  Communications Technology
  Computer Software
  Medical Technology
  Other High Technologies Not Mentioned
GEOGRAPHIC PREFERENCE:
  No Preference
TYPES OF FUNDS:
  Equity
  Loans with Equity Kickers
INVESTMENT AMOUNTS PREFERRED:
  Minimum: $300,000
  Maximum: $900,000

Mesirow Financial Services, Inc.
135 S. LaSalle
Chicago, IL 60603
312 443 5757

CONTACT: James C. Tyree
TYPE OF FIRM: Investment Banking Firm
  Venture Capital Firm
  SBIC
FUNDING PREFERENCE:
  All except:
  Seed Funding
  Start-Up-Funding
INDUSTRY PREFERENCE:
  Diversified
  Communications Technology
  Manufacturing
  Media
  Retail
  Services
  Wholesale Distribution
GEOGRAPHIC PREFERENCE:
  No Preference

TYPES OF FUNDS:
  Equity
  Loans with Equity Kickers
  Bonds with Equity Kickers
INVESTMENT AMOUNTS PREFERRED:
  Minimum: $250,000
  Maximum: $5,000,000

North American Capital Group
449 North Wells Street, Suite 1E
Chicago, IL 60610
312 645 0831

CONTACT: Gregory Krovitt
TYPE OF FIRM: Venture Capital Firm
FUNDING PREFERENCE:
  Later-Stage Funding
  Leveraged Buyouts
  Acquisitions
INDUSTRY PREFERENCE:
  Communications Technology
  Manufacturing
  Media
  Medical Technology
  Real Estate
  Retail
  Services
  Wholesale Distribution
GEOGRAPHIC PREFERENCE:
  Mid-West
TYPES OF FUNDS:
  Loans with Equity Kickers
INVESTMENT AMOUNTS PREFERRED:
  Minimum: $100,000
  Maximum: $1,000,000

INDIANA

First Indiana Equity Group, Inc.
20 North Meridian St.
Indianapolis, IN 46204
317 636 7242

CONTACT: Sam B. Sutphin
TYPE OF FIRM: Venture Capital Firm
  SBIC affiliated with Investment Banking Firm

FUNDING PREFERENCE:
  Second-Round Funding
  Leveraged Buyouts
INDUSTRY PREFERENCE:
  Diversified
  Medical Technology
GEOGRAPHIC PREFERENCE:
  Home State—Indiana
TYPES OF FUNDS:
  Bonds with Equity Kickers
INVESTMENT AMOUNTS PREFERRED:
  Minimum: $50,000
  Maximum: $200,000

White Ruier Capital Corp.
500 Washington Street
Columbus, IN 47201
812 376 1759

CONTACT: David J. Blair
TYPE OF FIRM: SBIC
FUNDING PREFERENCE:
  Second-Round Funding
  Third-Round Funding
  Fourth-Round Funding
  Later-Stage Funding
  Leveraged Buyouts
INDUSTRY PREFERENCE:
  Diversified
GEOGRAPHIC PREFERENCE:
  Mid-West
  Home State
TYPES OF FUNDS:
  Loans with Equity Kickers
INVESTMENT AMOUNTS PREFERRED:
  Minimum: $100,000
  Maximum: $200,000

IOWA

North America Capital Corporation
300 American Bldg.
Cedar Rapids, IA 52401
319 363 8249

CONTACT: Jerry M. Burrows
TYPE OF FIRM: SBIC

FUNDING PREFERENCE:
  First-Round Funding
  Second-Round Funding
  Third-Round Funding
  Leveraged Buyouts
  Acquisitions
INDUSTRY PREFERENCE:
  Diversified
  Communications Technology
  Computer Hardware
  Computer Software
  Manufacturing
  Medical Technology
  Other High Technologies Not Mentioned
GEOGRAPHIC PREFERENCE:
  Mid-West
TYPES OF FUNDS:
  Equity
  Loans with Equity Kickers
INVESTMENT AMOUNTS PREFERRED:
  Minimum: $200,000
  Maximum: $1,000,000

KENTUCKY

Financial Opportunities, Inc.
981 South 3rd St.
Louisville, KY 40203
502 584 1281

CONTACT: Gary F. Duerr
TYPE OF FIRM: SBIC
FUNDING PREFERENCE:
  First-Round Funding
  Second-Round Funding
INDUSTRY PREFERENCE:
  Diversified
  Retail
GEOGRAPHIC PREFERENCE:
  Northeast
  Southeast
  Home State—Kentucky
TYPES OF FUNDS:
  Loans
  Loans with Equity Kickers
INVESTMENT AMOUNTS PREFERRED:
  Minimum: $50,000
  Maximum: $180,000

LOUISIANA

Capital For Terrebonne, Inc.
P.O. Box 1868, 1613 Barrow St.
Houma, LA 70361
504 868 3933

CONTACT: Hartwell A. Lewis
TYPE OF FIRM: SBIC
FUNDING PREFERENCE:
  Second-Round Funding
INDUSTRY PREFERENCE:
  Diversified
GEOGRAPHIC PREFERENCE:
  Immediate Area—Terrebonne Parish, Louisiana
TYPES OF FUNDS:
  Loans
INVESTMENT AMOUNTS PREFERRED:
  Minimum: $50,000
  Maximum: $200,000

S.C.D.F. Investment Corporation
P.O. Box 3885L, 1006 Surrey St.
Lafayette, LA 90502
318 292 3769

CONTACT: Howard Boulte', Jr.
TYPE OF FIRM: MESBIC
FUNDING PREFERENCE:
  Start-Up Funding
  Later-Stage Funding
INDUSTRY PREFERENCE:
  Diversified
GEOGRAPHIC PREFERENCE:
  Southeast
TYPES OF FUNDS:
  Loans with Equity Kickers
INVESTMENT AMOUNTS PREFERRED:
  Minimum: $50,000
  Maximum: $400,000

MAINE

Maine Capital Corporation
One Monument Square
Portland, ME 04101
207 772 1001

CONTACT: David Coit
TYPE OF FIRM: SBIC
FUNDING PREFERENCE:
  Start-Up Funding
  First-Round Funding
  Second-Round Funding
  Third-Round Funding
  Fourth-Round Funding
  Later-Stage Funding
  Leveraged Buyouts
INDUSTRY PREFERENCE:
  Diversified
GEOGRAPHIC PREFERENCE:
  Home State—Maine
TYPES OF FUNDS:
  Equity
  Loans with Equity Kickers
INVESTMENT AMOUNTS PREFERRED:
  Minimum: $50,000
  Maximum: $150,000

MARYLAND

Albright Venture Capital, Inc.
8005 Rappahannock Avenue
Jessup, MD 20794
301 799 7935

CONTACT: William A. Albright
TYPE OF FIRM: MESBIC
FUNDING PREFERENCE:
  Start-Up Funding
  Later-Stage Funding
INDUSTRY PREFERENCE:
  Diversified
GEOGRAPHIC PREFERENCE:
  Northeast
  Middle Atlantic
  Southeast
TYPES OF FUNDS:
  Equity
  Loans
INVESTMENT AMOUNTS PREFERRED:
  Minimum: $10,000
  Maximum: $150,000

Broventure Capital Management
16 West Madison Street
Baltimore, MD 21201
301 727 4520

CONTACT: William Gust/Harvey Branch
TYPE OF FIRM: Venture Capital Firm
FUNDING PREFERENCE:
   Start-Up Funding
   First-Round Funding
INDUSTRY PREFERENCE:
   Communications Technology
   Computer Hardware
   Computer Software
   Manufacturing
   Medical Technology
   Other High Technologies Not Mentioned
GEOGRAPHIC PREFERENCE:
   Middle Atlantic
   Southeast
TYPES OF FUNDS:
   Equity
INVESTMENT AMOUNTS PREFERRED:
   Minimum: $300,000
   Maximum: $1,000,000

Development Credit Corporation of Md.
40 W. Chesapeake Avenue, Suite 211
P.O. Box 10629
Towson, MD 21204
301 828 4711

CONTACT: W. G. Brooks Thomas
TYPE OF FIRM:
   Privately financed statewide
   long term loan development bank
FUNDING PREFERENCE:
   Prefer term loans with equity kickers to smaller
   companies with some evidence
   of an ability to operate profitably
INDUSTRY PREFERENCE:
   Consider them all
GEOGRAPHIC PREFERENCE:
   Home State—Md. (by law)

TYPES OF FUNDS:
  Loans
  Loans with Equity Kickers
INVESTMENT AMOUNTS PREFERRED:
  Minimum: $50,000
  Maximum: $650,000

First Financial Management Services, Inc.
7316 Wisconsin Ave., Suite 215
Bethesda, MD 20814
301 951 9670

CONTACT: Kendall Wilson
TYPE OF FIRM: Consulting Firm
FUNDING PREFERENCE:
  Seed Funding
  Start-Up Funding
  First-Round Funding
INDUSTRY PREFERENCE:
  Diversified
GEOGRAPHIC PREFERENCE:
  Middle Atlantic
TYPES OF FUNDS:
  Other as appropriate
INVESTMENT AMOUNTS PREFERRED:
  Minimum: N/A
  Maximum: N/A

New Enterprise Associates
300 Cathedral Pl., Suite 100
Baltimore, MD 21201
301 244 0715

CONTACT: Charles Dowhall III
TYPE OF FIRM: Venture Capital Firm
FUNDING PREFERENCE:
  Seed Funding
  Start-Up Funding
  First-Round Funding
INDUSTRY PREFERENCE:
  Communications Technology
  Computer Hardware
  Computer Software
  Medical Technology
  Other High Technologies Not Mentioned

GEOGRAPHIC PREFERENCE:
  Northeast
  Middle Atlantic
  Southeast
  Far West
  Southwest
TYPES OF FUNDS:
  Equity
INVESTMENT AMOUNTS PREFERRED:
  Minimum: $250,000
  Maximum: $1,500,000

New Enterprise Associates
300 Cathedral St., Suite 110
Baltimore, MD 21201
301 244 0115

CONTACT: Nancy Dorman
TYPE OF FIRM: Venture Capital Firm
FUNDING PREFERENCE:
  Seed Funding
  Start-Up Funding
  First-Round Funding
  Second-Round Funding
INDUSTRY PREFERENCE:
  Alternative Energy
  Communications Technology
  Computer Hardware
  Computer Software
  Medical Technology
  Other High Technologies Not Mentioned
  Natural Resources
  Retail—specialty
GEOGRAPHIC PREFERENCE:
  No Preference
TYPES OF FUNDS:
  Equity
INVESTMENT AMOUNTS PREFERRED:
  Minimum: $450,000
  Maximum: $1.5 million   for initial investment

MASSACHUSETTS

The Charles River Partnerships
133 Federal St.
Boston, MA 02110
617 482 9370

CONTACT:
  Robert F. Higgins, Richard M. Burnes
  Patrick R. Liles, John T. Nersis
TYPE OF FIRM: Venture Capital Firm
FUNDING PREFERENCE:
  Seed-Funding
  Start-Up Funding
  First-Round Funding
  Second-Round Funding
  Third-Round Funding
INDUSTRY PREFERENCE:
  Communications Technology
  Computer Hardware
  Computer Software
  Media
  Medical Technology
  Other High Technologies Not Mentioned
GEOGRAPHIC PREFERENCE:
  No Preference
TYPES OF FUNDS:
  Equity
INVESTMENT AMOUNTS PREFERRED:
  Minimum: $250,000
  Maximum: $2,000,000

Eastech Management Company, Inc.
One Liberty Square
Boston, MA 02109
617 338 0200

CONTACT: Michael H. Shanahan
TYPE OF FIRM: Venture Capital Firm
FUNDING PREFERENCE:
  Start-Up Funding
  First-Round Funding
INDUSTRY PREFERENCE:
  Computer Hardware
  Computer Software
GEOGRAPHIC PREFERENCE:
  Northeast
TYPES OF FUNDS:
  Equity
INVESTMENT AMOUNTS PREFERRED:
  Minimum: $250,000
  Maximum: $500,000

First Capital Corporation of Boston
100 Federal Street
Boston, MA 02110
617 434 2442

CONTACT: Bruce G. Rossiter
TYPE OF FIRM: Venture Capital Firm
    SBIC
    Subsidiary of a national bank
FUNDING PREFERENCE:
    Start-Up Funding
    First-Round Funding
    Second-Round Funding
INDUSTRY PREFERENCE:
    Diversified
    Communications Technology
    Computer Hardware
    Computer Software
    Manufacturing
    Other High Technologies Not Mentioned
GEOGRAPHIC PREFERENCE:
    Northeast
    Northwest
    Far West
TYPES OF FUNDS:
    Equity (stock purchases)
    Loans with Equity Kickers
INVESTMENT AMOUNTS PREFERRED:
    Minimum: $500,000
    Maximum: $1,000,000

Fowler Anthony & Co.
20 Walnut St.
Wellesley, MA 02181
617 237 4201

CONTACT: John Quag Liaroli
TYPE OF FIRM: Venture Capital Firm
    Investment Banking Firm
FUNDING PREFERENCE:
    Seed Funding
    Start-Up Funding
    First-Round Funding
    Second-Round Funding
    Acquisitions

INDUSTRY PREFERENCE:
  Diversified
  Communications Technology
  Computer Hardware
  Computer Software
  Manufacturing
  Medical Technology
  Other High Technologies Not Mentioned
  Services
GEOGRAPHIC PREFERENCE:
  Northeast
TYPES OF FUNDS:
  Equity (stock purchases)
  Loans
  Loans with Equity Kickers
INVESTMENT AMOUNTS PREFERRED:
  Minimum: N/A
  Maximum: N/A

Investments Orange Nassau, Inc.
One Post Office Square
Boston, MA 02109
617 451 6220

CONTACT: Joost E. Tiaden
TYPE OF FIRM: Venture Capital Firm
FUNDING PREFERENCE:
  Second-Round Funding
  Later-Stage Funding
  Leveraged Buyouts
  Acquisitions
INDUSTRY PREFERENCE:
  Communications Technology
  Computer Hardware
  Computer Software
  Manufacturing
  Medical Technology
  Services
  Wholesale Distribution
GEOGRAPHIC PREFERENCE:
  No Preference
TYPES OF FUNDS:
  Equity
  Loans
  Loans with Equity Kickers

INVESTMENT AMOUNTS PREFERRED:
    Minimum: $1,000,000
    Maximum: N/A

Massachusetts Venture Capital Corp.
59 Temple Place
Boston, MA 02111
617 426 0208

CONTACT: Beth Sax
TYPE OF FIRM: Venture Capital Firm
FUNDING PREFERENCE:
    Second-Round Funding
    Leveraged Buyouts
    Acquisitions
INDUSTRY PREFERENCE:
    Diversified
GEOGRAPHIC PREFERENCE:
    Northeast
TYPES OF FUNDS:
    Loans with Equity Kickers
INVESTMENT AMOUNTS PREFERRED:
    Minimum: $50,000
    Maximum: $200,000

New England Capital Corporation
One Washington Mall
Boston, MA 02108
617 722 6400

CONTACT: E. David Patterson
Melvin W. Ellis
TYPE OF FIRM: SBIC
FUNDING PREFERENCE:
    First-Round Funding
    Second-Round Funding
    Third-Round Funding
    Fourth-Round Funding
    Later-Stage Funding
    Leveraged Buyouts
INDUSTRY PREFERENCE:
    Communications Technology
    Computer Hardware
    Manufacturing

Medical Technology
Other High Technologies Not Mentioned
GEOGRAPHIC PREFERENCE:
No Preference
TYPES OF FUNDS:
Equity
Loans with Equity Kickers
INVESTMENT AMOUNTS PREFERRED:
Minimum: $100,000 to $300,000
Maximum: $200,000 to $500,000

New England MESBIC, Inc.
50 Kearney Rd., Suite 3
Needham, MA 02194
617 449 2066

CONTACT: Dr. E. Chen
TYPE OF FIRM: MESBIC
FUNDING PREFERENCE:
Seed Funding
Start-Up Funding
First-Round Funding
INDUSTRY PREFERENCE:
Diversified
Communications Technology
Computer Hardware
Computer Software
Manufacturing
Medical Technology
Other High Technologies Not Mentioned
Retail
Services
Wholesale Distribution
GEOGRAPHIC PREFERENCE:
No Preference
TYPES OF FUNDS:
Equity (stock preference)
Loans
Loans with Equity Kickers
INVESTMENT AMOUNTS PREFERRED:
Minimum: $50,000
Maximum: $150,000

Plant Resources Venture Fund
175 Federal Street
Boston, MA 02110
617 542-5005

CONTACT: John R. Hesse
TYPE OF FIRM: Venture Capital Firm
FUNDING PREFERENCE:
  First-Round Funding
  Second-Round Funding
INDUSTRY PREFERENCE:
  Agriculture and Food Technology
  Genetic Improvement of Crops
  Biotechnology
  Water and Toxic Waste Technology
  Horticulture
  Natural Resources
GEOGRAPHIC PREFERENCE:
  No Preference
  U.S. and International
TYPES OF FUNDS:
  Equity (stock purchases)
INVESTMENT AMOUNTS PREFERRED:
  Minimum: $100,000—$300,000
  Maximum: $2,500,000 (in stages)

Transatlantic Capital Corporation
24 Federal Street
Boston, MA 02110
617 482 0015

CONTACT: Bayard Henry
  John O. Flender
TYPE OF FIRM: Venture Capital Firm
  SBIC
FUNDING PREFERENCE:
  Start-Up Funding
  First-Round Funding
  Second-Round Funding
INDUSTRY PREFERENCE:
  Communications Technology
  Computer Hardware
  Manufacturing
  Medical Technology

Other High Technologies Not Mentioned
Services
GEOGRAPHIC PREFERENCE:
  Northeast
  Middle Atlantic
  Mid-West
TYPES OF FUNDS:
  Equity (stock purchases)
  Loans with Equity Kickers
INVESTMENT AMOUNTS PREFERRED:
  Minimum: $150,000
  Maximum: $600,000

UST Capital Corp.
30 Court Street
Boston, MA 02108
617 726 7137

CONTACT: Richard W. Kohn
TYPE OF FIRM: SBIC
FUNDING PREFERENCE:
  First-Round Funding
  Second-Round Funding
INDUSTRY PREFERENCE:
  Diversified
  Communications Technology
  Computer Hardware
  Computer Software
  Medical Technology
  Other High Technologies Not Mentioned
GEOGRAPHIC PREFERENCE:
  Northeast
TYPES OF FUNDS:
  Equity
  Loans with Equity Kickers
INVESTMENT AMOUNTS PREFERRED:
  Minimum: $100,000
  Maximum: N/A

The Venture Capital Fund of New England
100 Franklin Street
Boston, MA 02110
617 451 2575

CONTACT: Richard A. Farrell
TYPE OF FIRM:
  Venture Capital Firm
FUNDING PREFERENCE:
  Start-Up Funding
  First-Round Funding
INDUSTRY PREFERENCE:
  Diversified
  Computer Software
  Media
  Medical Technology
  Other High Technologies Not Mentioned
GEOGRAPHIC PREFERENCE:
  Northeast
  Home State—New England
TYPES OF FUNDS:
  Equit (stock purchases)
  Loans with Equity Kickers
  Bonds with Equity Kickers
INVESTMENT AMOUNTS PREFERRED:
  Minimum: $100,000
  Maximum: $1,000,000

Venture Founders Corporation
100 5th Avenue
Waltham, MA 02154
617 890 1000

CONTACT: Ross Yeiter
TYPE OF FIRM: Venture Capital Firm
FUNDING PREFERENCE:
  Seed Funding
  Start-Up Funding
  First-Round Funding
INDUSTRY PREFERENCE:
  Diversified
  Communications Technology
  Computer Hardware
  Computer Software
  Manufacturing
  Medical Technology
GEOGRAPHIC PREFERENCE:
  Northeast
  Mid-West
  Far West

TYPES OF FUNDS:
  Equity (stock purchases)
INVESTMENT AMOUNTS PREFERRED:
  Minimum: open
  Maximum: $750,000

WCCI Capital Corporation
791 Main Street
Worcester, MA 01610
617 791 0941

CONTACT: Gerald A. Garrity
TYPE OF FIRM: Venture Capital Firm
FUNDING PREFERENCE:
  Seed Funding
INDUSTRY PREFERENCE:
  Communications Technology
  Computer Hardware
  Computer Software
  Medical Technology
GEOGRAPHIC PREFERENCE:
  Northeast
  Immediate Area—Worcester
TYPES OF FUNDS:
  Loans with Equity Kickers
INVESTMENT AMOUNTS PREFERRED:
  Minimum: $50,000
  Maximum: $100,000

Zero State Capital Equity Fund, Limited Partnership
156 Sixth Street
Cambridge, MA 02142
617 876 5355

CONTACT: Paul M. Kelley
TYPE OF FIRM: Venture Capital Firm
FUNDING PREFERENCE:
  Seed Funding
  Start-Up Funding
INDUSTRY PREFERENCE:
  Diversified
GEOGRAPHIC PREFERENCE:
  Northeast
TYPES OF FUNDS:
  Equity

TYPES OF FUNDS:

INVESTMENT AMOUNTS PREFERRED:
Minimum: $50,000
Maximum: $150,000

MICHIGAN

Dearborn Capital Corporation
P.O. Box 1729
Dearborn, MI 48121
313 337 8577

CONTACT: Stephen M. Aronson
TYPE OF FIRM: MESBIC
FUNDING PREFERENCE:
First-Round Funding
Second-Round Funding
INDUSTRY PREFERENCE:
Manufacturing
Diversified (tied to automotive industry)
GEOGRAPHIC PREFERENCE:
No Preference
TYPES OF FUNDS:
Loans
INVESTMENT AMOUNTS PREFERRED:
Minimum: $50,000
Maximum: $300,000

Doan Resources Corporation
P.O. Box 1431
Midland, MI 48640
517 631 2471

CONTACT: Ian R. N. Bund, Pres.
TYPE OF FIRM: SBIC
FUNDING PREFERENCE:
Start-Up Funding
First-Round Funding
Second-Round Funding
Later-Stage Funding
Leveraged Buyouts
INDUSTRY PREFERENCE:
Communications Technology
Computer Hardware
Computer Software
Manufacturing (automation equip.)
Medical Technology

GEOGRAPHIC PREFERENCE:
  Mid-West
  Far West
  Home State—Michigan
TYPES OF FUNDS:
  Equity (stock purchases)
  Loans
  Loans With Equity Kickers
INVESTMENT AMOUNTS PREFERRED:
  Minimum: $100,000—300,000
  Maximum: $100,000—300,000

Inner-City Capital Access Center, Inc.
1505 Woodward Avenue
Suite 700
Detroit, MI 48226-2059
313 961 2470

CONTACT: Calvin C. Cupidore, Jr.
TYPE OF FIRM: MESBIC
FUNDING PREFERENCE:
  First-Round Funding
  Second-Round Funding
  Leveraged Buyouts
  Acquisitions
INDUSTRY PREFERENCE:
  Diversified
GEOGRAPHIC PREFERENCE:
  Mid-West
TYPES OF FUNDS:
  Loans with Equity Kickers
INVESTMENT AMOUNTS PREFERRED:
  Minimum: $75,000
  Maximum: $150,000

Michigan Capital and Service, Inc.
440 City Center Building
Ann Arbor, MI 48104
313 663 0702

CONTACT: James A. Parsons
TYPE OF FIRM: Venture Capital Firm
  SBIC
FUNDING PREFERENCE:
  First-Round Funding
  Second-Round Funding

Third-Round Funding
Fourth-Round Funding
Later-Stage Funding
Leveraged Buyouts
INDUSTRY PREFERENCE:
Communications Technology
Computer Hardware
Computer Software
Manufacturing
Medical Technology
Other High Technologies Not Mentioned
GEOGRAPHIC PREFERENCE:
Mid-West
TYPES OF FUNDS:
Equity
Loans with Equity Kickers
INVESTMENT AMOUNTS PREFERRED:
Minimum: $250,000
Maximum: $800,000

Michigan Investment Fund L.P.
P.O. Box 1431
Midland, MI 48640
517 631 2471

CONTACT: Ian R. N. Bund, Pres.
TYPE OF FIRM: Venture Capital Firm
FUNDING PREFERENCE:
Start-Up Funding
First-Round Funding
Later-Stage Funding
Leveraged Buyouts
INDUSTRY PREFERENCE:
Communications Technology
Computer Hardware
Computer Software
Manufacturing
Medical Technology
GEOGRAPHIC PREFERENCE:
Northeast
Mid-West
Far West
Southwest
TYPES OF FUNDS:
Equity (stock purchases)
Loans
Loans with Equity Kickers

INVESTMENT AMOUNTS PREFERRED:
  Minimum: N/A
  Maximum: $500,000—$750,000

MINNESOTA

Control Data Capital Corp.
8100 34th Ave. S.
Bloomington, MN 55420
612 853 4389

CONTACT: W. S. Anderson
TYPE OF FIRM: Venture Capital Firm
  SBIC
  MESBIC
FUNDING PREFERENCE:
  Start-Up Funding
  First-Round Funding
INDUSTRY PREFERENCE:
  Alternative Energy
  Communications Technology
  Computer Hardware
  Computer Software
  Manufacturing
GEOGRAPHIC PREFERENCE:
  Home State—Minnesota
TYPES OF FUNDS:
  Equity (stock purchases)
  Loans With Equity Kickers
INVESTMENT AMOUNTS PREFERRED:
  Minimum: $100,000
  Maximum: $700,000

Entre Source
1300 First Bank Place West
Minneapolis, MN 55402
612 375 4655

CONTACT: Charles H. Lucas
TYPE OF FIRM: Venture Capital Firm
FUNDING PREFERENCE:
  Second-Round Funding
  Third-Round Funding
  Fourth-Round Funding
INDUSTRY PREFERENCE:
  Diversified

GEOGRAPHIC PREFERENCE:
  Mid-West
TYPES OF FUNDS:
  Equity (stock purchases)
INVESTMENT AMOUNTS PREFERRED:
  Minimum: Open
  Maximum: Open

First Midwest Capital Corporation
1010 Plymouth Building
12 S. Sixth Street
Minneapolis, MN 55402
612 339 9303

CONTACT: Thomas M. Neitge
TYPE OF FIRM: SBIC
FUNDING PREFERENCE:
  Start-up Funding
  First-Round Funding
  Second-Round Funding
  Third-Round Funding
  Leveraged Buyouts
INDUSTRY PREFERENCE:
  Communications Technology
  Computer Hardware
  Computer Software
  Manufacturing
  Do some low-tech projects
  Medical Technology
  Other High Technologies Not Mentioned
  Retail
GEOGRAPHIC PREFERENCE:
  Mid-West but participate throughout USA
TYPES OF FUNDS:
  Equity (stock purchases)
  Loans with Equity Kickers
INVESTMENT AMOUNTS PREFERRED:
  Minimum: $300,000
  Maximum: $1,000,000 plus through syndication

Pathfinder Venture Capital Fund
7300 Metro Blvd., Suite 585
Minneapolis, MN 55435
612 835 1121

CONTACT: Mr. A. J. Greenshields
TYPE OF FIRM: Venture Capital Firm
FUNDING PREFERENCE:
  Start-Up Funding
  First-Round Funding
  Second-Round Funding
  Third-Round Funding
  Leveraged Buyouts
INDUSTRY PREFERENCE:
  Communications Technology
  Computer Hardware
  Computer Software
  Manufacturing
  Medical Technology
  Other High Technologies Not Mentioned
GEOGRAPHIC PREFERENCE:
  No Preference
TYPES OF FUNDS:
  Equity (stock purchases)
INVESTMENT AMOUNTS PREFERRED:
  Minimum: $200,000
  Maximum: $1,500,000—$2,000,000

Retailers Growth Fund, Inc.
5100 Gamble Drive
Minneapolis, MN 55416
612 546 8989

CONTACT: Carnell L. Moore
TYPE OF FIRM: SBIC
FUNDING PREFERENCE:
  Second-Round Funding
  Acquisitions
INDUSTRY PREFERENCE:
  Retail
GEOGRAPHIC PREFERENCE:
  Mid-West
TYPES OF FUNDS:
  Loans
INVESTMENT AMOUNTS PREFERRED:
  Minimum: $100,000
  Maximum: $150,000

MISSISSIPPI

Delta Capital Corp.
P.O. Box 588
Greenville, MS 38701
601 335 5291

CONTACT: Chester B. Smith
TYPE OF FIRM: MESBIC
FUNDING PREFERENCE:
  Seed Funding
  Start-Up Funding
  First-Round Funding
  Second-Round Funding
INDUSTRY PREFERENCE:
  Diversified
  Communications Technology
  Computer Software
  Media
  Real Estate
GEOGRAPHIC PREFERENCE:
  Southeast
  Southwest
TYPES OF FUNDS:
  Equity (stock purchases)
  Loans
INVESTMENT AMOUNTS PREFERRED:
  Minimum: N/A
  Maximum: $250,000

NEW HAMPSHIRE

Hampshire Capital Corp.
One Wipple St.
Portsmouth, NH 03801
603 431 1415

CONTACT: Philip G. Baker
TYPE OF FIRM: SBIC
FUNDING PREFERENCE:
  Start-Up Funding
  First-Round Funding
  Second-Round Funding
  Leveraged Buyouts
  Acquisitions

INDUSTRY PREFERENCE:
   Diversified
GEOGRAPHIC PREFERENCE:
   Northeast
   Middle Atlantic
   Southeast
TYPES OF FUNDS:
   Loans With Equity Kickers
INVESTMENT AMOUNTS PREFERRED:
   Minimum: $50,000
   Maximum: $100,000

NEW JERSEY

Broad Arrow Investment Corp.
P.O. Box 2231 R
Moorestown, NJ 07960
201 766 8255

CONTACT: N/A
TYPE OF FIRM: MESBIC
FUNDING PREFERENCE:
   Start-Up Funding
INDUSTRY PREFERENCE:
   Diversified
GEOGRAPHIC PREFERENCE:
   No Preference
TYPES OF FUNDS:
   Loans With Equity Kickers
INVESTMENT AMOUNTS PREFERRED:
   Minimum: $25,000
   Maximum: $50,000

DSV Partners III
221 Nassau St.
Princeton, NJ 08542
609 924 6420

CONTACT: James Bergman
   Mort Collins
   Robert Hillas
TYPE OF FIRM: Venture Capital Firm
FUNDING PREFERENCE:
   Start-Up Funding
INDUSTRY PREFERENCE:
   Communications Technology
   Computer Hardware

Computer Software
Manufacturing
Medical Technology
Other High Technologies Not Mentioned
GEOGRAPHIC PREFERENCE:
No Preference
TYPES OF FUNDS:
Equity (stock purchases)
INVESTMENT AMOUNTS PREFERRED:
Minimum: $500,000
Maximum: $1,500,000

Innoven
Park 80 Plaza West-One
Saddle Brook, NJ 07662
201 845 4900

CONTACT: Bart Holaday
John Martinson
TYPE OF FIRM: Venture Capital Firm
FUNDING PREFERENCE:
Seed Funding
Start-Up Funding
First-Round Funding
Second-Round Funding
INDUSTRY PREFERENCE:
Communications Technology
Computer Hardware
Computer Software
Medical Technology
Other High Technologies Not Mentioned
GEOGRAPHIC PREFERENCE: No Preference
TYPES OF FUNDS:
Equity (stock purchases)
INVESTMENT AMOUNTS PREFERRED:
Minimum: $200,000
Maximum: $1,500,000

Raybar Small Business Investment Corp.
255 W. Spring Valley Avenue
Maywood, NJ 07607
201 368 2280

CONTACT: Patrick F. McCort
TYPE OF FIRM: SBIC

FUNDING PREFERENCE:
  Later-Stage Funding
INDUSTRY PREFERENCE:
  Diversified
GEOGRAPHIC PREFERENCE:
  Northeast
  Immediate Area—New York Metropolitan
TYPES OF FUNDS:
  Loans
  Leasing
INVESTMENT AMOUNTS PREFERRED:
  Minimum: $20,000
  Maximum: $100,000

Rutgers Minority Investment Co.
180 University Avenue
Newark, NJ 07102
201 648 5627

CONTACT: Oscar Figueroa
TYPE OF FIRM: MESBIC
FUNDING PREFERENCE:
  No specific preference
INDUSTRY PREFERENCE:
  Diversified
GEOGRAPHIC PREFERENCE:
  Northeast
TYPES OF FUNDS:
  Loans with Equity Kickers
INVESTMENT AMOUNTS PREFERRED:
  Minimum: $25,000
  Maximum: $100,000

Unicorn Ventures, Ltd.
14 Commerce Drive
Cranford, NJ 07016
201 276 7880

CONTACT: Frank P. Diassi
TYPE OF FIRM: SBIC
FUNDING PREFERENCE:
  Seed Funding
  Start-Up Funding
  First-Round Funding
  Second-Round Funding

Third-Round Funding
Fourth-Round Funding
Leveraged Buyouts
Acquisitions
INDUSTRY PREFERENCE:
  Diversified
GEOGRAPHIC PREFERENCE:
  No Preference
TYPES OF FUNDS:
  Equity (stock purchases)
INVESTMENT AMOUNTS PREFERRED:
  Minimum: $200,000
  Maximum: $500,000

NEW MEXICO

Albuquerque SBIC
P.O. Box 487
Albuquerque, NM 87103
505 247 0145

CONTACT: Albert T. Ussery
TYPE OF FIRM: SBIC
FUNDING PREFERENCE:
  First-Round Funding
INDUSTRY PREFERENCE:
  Diversified
GEOGRAPHIC PREFERENCE:
  Southwest
TYPES OF FUNDS:
  Loans With Equity Kickers
INVESTMENT AMOUNTS PREFERRED:
  Minimum: $75,000
  Maximum: $100,000

Associated Southwest Investors, Inc.
2425 Alamo S.E.
Albuquerque, NM 87106
505 842 5955

CONTACT: John R. Rice, President
TYPE OF FIRM: MESBIC
FUNDING PREFERENCE:
  Seed Funding
  Start-Up Funding
  First-Round Funding

Second-Round Funding
Leveraged Buyouts
INDUSTRY PREFERENCE:
Diversified
GEOGRAPHIC PREFERENCE:
Rocky Mountain States
Southwest
TYPES OF FUNDS:
Equity (stock purchases)
Loans
Loans with Equity Kickers
INVESTMENT AMOUNTS PREFERRED:
Minimum: $75,000
Maximum: $750,000

Fluid Capital Corporation
8421 B. Montgomery Bl.
Albuquerque, NM 87111
505 292 4747

CONTACT: George T. Slaughter
TYPE OF FIRM: SBIC
  MESBIC
FUNDING PREFERENCE:
Second-Round Funding
Leveraged Buyouts
INDUSTRY PREFERENCE:
Communications Technology
Manufacturing
Real Estate
GEOGRAPHIC PREFERENCE:
Mid-West
Southwest
TYPES OF FUNDS:
Loans with Equity Kickers
INVESTMENT AMOUNTS PREFERRED:
Minimum: $100,000
Maximum: $460,000

NEW YORK

Adler & Company
280 Park Avenue
New York, NY 10017
212 986 3010

CONTACT: N/A
TYPE OF FIRM: Venture Capital Firm
FUNDING PREFERENCE:
   Start-Up Funding
INDUSTRY PREFERENCE:
   Communications Technology
   Computer Hardware
   Computer Software
   Medical Technology
   Other High Technologies Not Mentioned
GEOGRAPHIC PREFERENCE: No Preference
TYPES OF FUNDS:
   Equity (stock purchases)
INVESTMENT AMOUNTS PREFERRED:
   Minimum: $100,000
   Maximum: $1,000,000

Aleph Null Corp.
One Old Country Road
Carle Place, NY 11514
516 742 9527

CONTACT: Herman Fialkov
TYPE OF FIRM: Venture Capital Firm
FUNDING PREFERENCE:
   Seed Funding
   Start-Up Funding
INDUSTRY PREFERENCE:
   Communications Technology
   Computer Hardware
   Medical Technology
GEOGRAPHIC PREFERENCE:
   Northeast
TYPES OF FUNDS:
   Equity (stock purchases)
INVESTMENT AMOUNTS PREFERRED:
   Minimum: $100,000 Average
   Maximum: N/A

Atalanta Investment Company, Inc.
450 Park Ave.
New York, NY 10022
212 832 1104

CONTACT: Robert Vitale
  L. Mark Newman
TYPE OF FIRM: SBIC
FUNDING PREFERENCE:
  First-Round Funding
  Second-Round Funding
INDUSTRY PREFERENCE:
  Diversified
GEOGRAPHIC PREFERENCE:
  No Preference
TYPES OF FUNDS:
  Loans With Equity Kickers
  Bonds With Equity Kickers
INVESTMENT AMOUNTS PREFERRED:
  Minimum: $100,000
  Maximum: $1,500,000

Biotech Capital Corp.
600 Madison Ave.
New York, NY 10022
212 758 7722

CONTACT: John E. Koonce
TYPE OF FIRM: Venture Capital Firm
FUNDING PREFERENCE:
  First-Round Funding
  Later-Stage Funding
  Acquisitions
INDUSTRY PREFERENCE:
  Communications Technology
  Computer Hardware
  Medical Technology
  Other High Technologies Not Mentioned
GEOGRAPHIC PREFERENCE:
  No Preference
TYPES OF FUNDS:
  Equity (stock purchases)
  Loans
  Loans With Equity Kickers
INVESTMENT AMOUNTS PREFERRED:
  Minimum: $500,000
  Maximum: $1,000,000

D. H. Blair Flo., Inc.
44 Wall St.
New York, NY 10005
212 747 0066

CONTACT: J. Morton Davis, President
TYPE OF FIRM: Venture Capital Firm
  Investment Banking Firm
FUNDING PREFERENCE:
  Start-Up Funding
  First-Round Funding
  Second-Round Funding
INDUSTRY PREFERENCE:
  Communications Technology
  Computer Software
  Medical Technology
  Other High Technologies Not Mentioned
GEOGRAPHIC PREFERENCE:
  No Preference
TYPES OF FUNDS:
  Equity (stock purchases)
INVESTMENT AMOUNTS PREFERRED:
  Minimum: $250,000
  Maximum: $12,000,000

Citicorp Venture Capital, Ltd.
399 Park Avenue
New York, NY 10005
212 559 1113

CONTACT: N/A
TYPE OF FIRM: Venture Capital Firm
FUNDING PREFERENCE:
  Start-Up Funding
  First-Round Funding
  Second-Round Funding
  Third-Round Funding
  Fourth Round Funding
  Later-Stage Funding
  Leveraged Buyouts
INDUSTRY PREFERENCE:
  Diversified
GEOGRAPHIC PREFERENCE:
  No Preference

TYPES OF FUNDS:
  Equity (stock purchases)
  Loans With Equity Kickers
INVESTMENT AMOUNTS PREFERRED:
  Minimum: $500,000
  Maximum: $3,000,000

CMNY Capital Company, Inc.
77 Water Street
New York, NY 10005
212 437 7078

CONTACT: Robert Davidoff
TYPE OF FIRM: SBIC
FUNDING PREFERENCE:
  Start-Up Funding
  Later-Stage Funding
  Leveraged Buyouts
INDUSTRY PREFERENCE:
  Diversified
GEOGRAPHIC PREFERENCE:
  No Preference
TYPES OF FUNDS:
  Loans with Equity Kickers
INVESTMENT AMOUNTS PREFERRED:
  Minimum: $100,000
  Maximum: $400,000

Coleman Ventures, Inc.
5909 Northern Blvd.
East Norwich, NY 11732
516 626 3642

CONTACT: Gregory S. Coleman
TYPE OF FIRM: Venture Capital Firm
  Individual Investor
  Consulting Firm
FUNDING PREFERENCE:
  Seed Funding
  Start-Up Funding
  Leveraged Buyouts
  Acquisitions
INDUSTRY PREFERENCE:
  Alternative Energy
  Communications Technology

Computer Hardware
Computer Software
Medical Technology
Other High Technologies Not Mentioned
Natural Resources
Real Estate
GEOGRAPHIC PREFERENCE:
Northeast
Middle Atlantic
Home State—New York
TYPES OF FUNDS:
Equity
INVESTMENT AMOUNTS PREFERRED:
Minimum: $50,000
Maximum: $500,000

CVC Capital Corporation
666 Fifth Avenue
New York, NY 10103
212 246 1980

CONTACT: Mr. J. Klebe
TYPE OF FIRM: MESBIC
FUNDING PREFERENCE:
Start-Up Funding
Acquisitions
INDUSTRY PREFERENCE:
Media
Real Estate
GEOGRAPHIC PREFERENCE:
Northeast
Middle Atlantic
TYPES OF FUNDS:
Loans With Equity Kickers
INVESTMENT AMOUNTS PREFERRED:
Minimum: $350,000
Maximum: $600,000

Drexel Burnham Lambert Inc.
60 Broad St.
New York, NY 10004
212 480 5161

CONTACT: Brad Yoneoka
TYPE OF FIRM: Investment Banking Firm

FUNDING PREFERENCE:
  First-Round Funding
  Second-Round Funding
  Third-Round Funding
  Leveraged Buyouts
INDUSTRY PREFERENCE:
  Communications Technology
  Computer Hardware
  Computer Software
  Medical Technology
  Other High Technologies Not Mentioned
  Services
GEOGRAPHIC PREFERENCE:
  No Preference
TYPES OF FUNDS:
  Equity (stock purchases)
  Loans With Equity Kickers
INVESTMENT AMOUNTS PREFERRED:
  Minimum: $500
  Maximum: $1,000

Equico Capital Corporation
1290 Avenue of the Americas, Suite 3400
New York, NY 10019
212 554 8413

CONTACT: Duane E. Hill, President & CEO
TYPE OF FIRM: MESBIC
FUNDING PREFERENCE:
  Start-Up Funding
  First-Round Funding
  Second-Round Funding
  Third-Round Funding
  Fourth-Round Funding
  Later-Stage Funding
  Leveraged Buyouts
  Acquisitions
INDUSTRY PREFERENCE:
  Diversified
  Manufacturing
GEOGRAPHIC PREFERENCE:
  No Preference
TYPES OF FUNDS:
  Equity (stock purchases)
  Loans
  Loans With Equity Kickers

INVESTMENT AMOUNTS PREFERRED:
  Minimum: $100,000
  Maximum: $500,000

Euclid Partners
50 Rockefeller Plaza, Room 840
New York, NY 10020
212 489 1770

CONTACT: Jeffery T. Hamilton
TYPE OF FIRM: Venture Capital Firm
FUNDING PREFERENCE:
  Start-Up Funding
  First-Round Funding
  Second-Round Funding
  Third-Round Funding
INDUSTRY PREFERENCE:
  Diversified (High Technology)
GEOGRAPHIC PREFERENCE:
  No Preference
TYPES OF FUNDS:
  Equity (stock purchases)
INVESTMENT AMOUNTS PREFERRED:
  Minimum: $350,000
  Maximum: $750,000

Founders Ventures, Inc.
477 Madison Ave.
New York, NY 10022
212 752 7409

CONTACT: John L. Teeger
TYPE OF FIRM: Venture Capital Firm
  Investment Banking Firm
FUNDING PREFERENCE:
  Leveraged Buyouts
  Acquisitions
INDUSTRY PREFERENCE:
  Manufacturing
  Media
  Real Estate
  Retail
  Services
GEOGRAPHIC PREFERENCE:
  No Preference

TYPES OF FUNDS:
   Equity (stock purchases)
   Bonds With Equity Kickers
INVESTMENT AMOUNTS PREFERRED:
   Minimum: $4,000,000
   Maximum: $20,000,000

The Franklin Corp.
1185 Avenue of the Americas, 10036
New York, NY 10022
212 919 4844

CONTACT: H. E. Gardman
TYPE OF FIRM: Venture Capital Firm
   SBIC
   MESBIC
FUNDING PREFERENCE:
   First-Round Funding
   Second-Round Funding
   Leveraged Buyouts
INDUSTRY PREFERENCE:
   Diversified
   Manufacturing
   Other High Technologies Not Mentioned
   Retail
GEOGRAPHIC PREFERENCE:
   Southwest
   Alaska
TYPES OF FUNDS:
   Equity (stock purchases)
   Loans
   Loans With Equity Kickers
INVESTMENT AMOUNTS PREFERRED:
   Minimum: $250,000
   Maximum: $2,000,000

The Greenhouse Investment Fund
4 Cedar Swamp Road
Glen Cove, NY 11542
516 759 1982

CONTACT: Evelyn Berezn
TYPE OF FIRM: Venture Capital Firm
FUNDING PREFERENCE:
   Start-Up Funding

INDUSTRY PREFERENCE:
  Communications Technology
  Computer Hardware
  Computer Software
  Medical Technology
  Beotedinology
GEOGRAPHIC PREFERENCE:
  Northeast
TYPES OF FUNDS:
  R & D Investment
INVESTMENT AMOUNTS PREFERRED:
  Minimum: $200
  Maximum: $1000

Hambro International Venture Fund
17 E. 71 St.
New York, NY 10021
212 288 7778

CONTACT: Frances N. Janis
TYPE OF FIRM: Venture Capital Firm
FUNDING PREFERENCE:
  Seed Funding
  Start-Up Funding
  First-Round Funding
INDUSTRY PREFERENCE:
  Diversified
  Communications Technology
  Computer Hardware
  Computer Software
  Media
  Medical Technology
  Services
GEOGRAPHIC PREFERENCE:
  No Preference
TYPES OF FUNDS:
  Equity (stock purchases)
INVESTMENT AMOUNTS PREFERRED:
  Minimum: $500,000
  Maximum: $1,000,000

Harrison Capital Inc.
2000 Westchester Ave.
White Plains, NY 10650
914 253 7992

CONTACT: W. T. Corl, President
TYPE OF FIRM: Venture Capital Firm
FUNDING PREFERENCE:
   Start-Up Funding
   First-Round Funding
INDUSTRY PREFERENCE:
   Diversified
   Communications Technology
   Computer Hardware
   Computer Software
   Medical Technology
   Other High Technologies Not Mentioned
GEOGRAPHIC PREFERENCE:
   No Preference
TYPES OF FUNDS:
   Equity (stock purchases)
INVESTMENT AMOUNTS PREFERRED:
   Minimum: $250,000
   Maximum: $2,000,000

Walter E. Heller & Co.
Heller Capital Services Inc.
101 Park Ave.
New York, NY 10022
212 880 7047

CONTACT: J. A. Prizzi, EVP
TYPE OF FIRM: Venture Capital Firm
   SBIC
FUNDING PREFERENCE:
   Start-Up Funding
   First-Round Funding
INDUSTRY PREFERENCE:
   Diversified Expect*
   *Conventional Energy (oil, natural gas, and coal)
   *Natural Resources
   *Real Estate
   *Retail
GEOGRAPHIC PREFERENCE:
   No Preference
TYPES OF FUNDS:
   Equity (stock purchases)
   Bonds With Equity Kickers
INVESTMENT AMOUNTS PREFERRED:
   Minimum: $300,000
   Maximum: $750,000

Investech, L.P.
515 Madison Avenue, Suite 2400
New York, NY 10022
212 308 5811

CONTACT: Carl S. Hutman, General Partner
TYPE OF FIRM: Venture Capital Firm
FUNDING PREFERENCE:
  Seed Funding
  Start-Up Funding
  First-Round Funding
  Second-Round Funding
  Later-Stage Funding
INDUSTRY PREFERENCE:
  Communications Technology
  Computer Hardware
  Computer Software
  Manufacturing
  Medical Technology
  Other High Technologies Not Mentioned
GEOGRAPHIC PREFERENCE:
  No Preference
TYPES OF FUNDS:
  Equity (stock purchases)
INVESTMENT AMOUNTS PREFERRED:
  Minimum: $100,000
  Maximum: $1,000,000

Irving Capital Corporation
1290 Avenue of the Americas, Third Floor
New York, NY 10019
212 922 8790

CONTACT: Kathleen Snyder
TYPE OF FIRM: SBIC
FUNDING PREFERENCE:
  Later-Stage Funding
  Leveraged Buyouts
  Acquisitions
INDUSTRY PREFERENCE:
  Manufacturing
  Wholesale Distribution
GEOGRAPHIC PREFERENCE:
  No Preference
TYPES OF FUNDS:
  Loans With Equity Kickers
  Bonds With Equity Kickers

INVESTMENT AMOUNTS PREFERRED:
  Minimum: $300,000
  Maximum: $3,000,000

ITC Capital Corporation
1290 Avenue of the Americas, Third Floor
New York, NY 10019
212 922 8790

CONTACT: Kathleen Snyder
TYPE OF FIRM: Bank Holding Co.
FUNDING PREFERENCE:
  Later-Stage Funding
  Leveraged Buyouts
  Acquisitions
INDUSTRY PREFERENCE:
  Manufacturing
  Wholesale Distribution
GEOGRAPHIC PREFERENCE:
  No Preference
TYPES OF FUNDS:
  Loans With Equity Kickers
  Bonds With Equity Kickers
INVESTMENT AMOUNTS PREFERRED:
  Minimum: $300,000
  Maximum: $3,000,000

Carl Marks & Co., Inc.
77 Water Street
New York, NY 10005
212 437 7078

CONTACT: Robert Davidoff
TYPE OF FIRM: Investment Banking Firm
FUNDING PREFERENCE:
  Later-Stage Funding
  Leveraged Buyouts
  Acquisitions
INDUSTRY PREFERENCE:
  Diversified
GEOGRAPHIC PREFERENCE:
  No Preference
TYPES OF FUNDS:
  Loans with Equity Kickers

INVESTMENT AMOUNTS PREFERRED:
  Minimum: $250,000
  Maximum: NONE

Merrill Lynch Venture Capital Inc.
One Liberty Plaza, 165 Broadway
New York, NY 10080
212 766 6215

CONTACT: George Kokkinakis
TYPE OF FIRM: Venture Capital Firm
FUNDING PREFERENCE:
  Start-Up Funding
  First-Round Funding
  Second-Round Funding
  Leveraged Buyouts
INDUSTRY PREFERENCE:
  Communications Technology
  Computer Hardware
  Computer Software
  Medical Technology
  Other High Technologies Not Mentioned
GEOGRAPHIC PREFERENCE:
  No Preference
TYPES OF FUNDS:
  Equity
INVESTMENT AMOUNTS PREFERRED:
  Minimum: $500,000
  Maximum: $2,000,000

Minority Equity Capital Company Inc.
275 Madison Avenue
New York, NY 10016
212 686 9710

CONTACT: Donald F. Greene, Sr. Investment Officer
TYPE OF FIRM: MESBIC
FUNDING PREFERENCE:
  Start-Up Funding
  First-Round Funding
  Second-Round Funding
  Leveraged Buyouts
  Acquisitions
INDUSTRY PREFERENCE:
  Diversified

GEOGRAPHIC PREFERENCE:
No Preference
TYPES OF FUNDS:
Equity (stock purchases)
Loans
Loans With Equity Kickers
INVESTMENT AMOUNTS PREFERRED:
Minimum: $150,000
Maximum: $800,000

Nelson Capital Corp.
591 Stewart Avenue
Garden City, NY 11530
516 222 2555

CONTACT: Irwin B. Nelson, President
TYPE OF FIRM: SBIC
FUNDING PREFERENCE:
Third-Round Funding
Leveraged Buyouts
Acquisitions
INDUSTRY PREFERENCE:
Diversified
GEOGRAPHIC PREFERENCE:
Northeast
Middle Atlantic
Southeast
Mid-West
Far West
TYPES OF FUNDS:
Loans
Loans With Equity Kickers
INVESTMENT AMOUNTS PREFERRED:
Minimum: $75,000
Maximum: $3,000,000

New Oasis Capital Corp.
114 Liberty St., Suite #304
New York, NY 10006
212 349 2804

CONTACT: James Huang
TYPE OF FIRM: MESBIC
FUNDING PREFERENCE:
Seed Funding
Start-Up Funding

INDUSTRY PREFERENCE:
  Diversified
GEOGRAPHIC PREFERENCE:
  Northeast
TYPES OF FUNDS:
  Equity (stock purchases)
  Loans
INVESTMENT AMOUNTS PREFERRED:
  Minimum: N/A
  Maximum: $150,000

North Street Capital Corp.
250 North Street
White Plains, NY 10625
914 335 0901

CONTACT: Mr. Ralph L. McNeal, Sr.
TYPE OF FIRM: MESBIC
FUNDING PREFERENCE:
  First-Round Funding
  Second-Round Funding
  Third-Round Funding
  Fourth-Round Funding
  Later-Stage Funding
  Leveraged Buyouts
  Acquisitions
INDUSTRY PREFERENCE:
  Diversified
GEOGRAPHIC PREFERENCE:
  No Preference
TYPES OF FUNDS:
  Loans With Equity Kickers
INVESTMENT AMOUNTS PREFERRED:
  Minimum: $150,000
  Maximum: $300,000

Alan Patricof Associates, Inc.
545 Madison Avenue
New York, NY 10022
212 753 6300

CONTACT: Alan J. Patricof, Chairman
Robert G. Faris, President
TYPE OF FIRM: Venture Capital Firm
FUNDING PREFERENCE:
  Start-Up Funding

INDUSTRY PREFERENCE:
  Diversified
GEOGRAPHIC PREFERENCE:
  No Preference
TYPES OF FUNDS:
  Equity (stock purchases)
INVESTMENT AMOUNTS PREFERRED:
  Minimum: $500,000
  Maximum: $3,000,000

Allan E. Skora Associates
500 Fifth Avenue, Suite 2305
New York, NY 10036
212 691 9895

CONTACT: Allan E. Skora, President
TYPE OF FIRM: Venture Capital Firm
  Investment Banking Firm
FUNDING PREFERENCE:
  Seed Funding
  Start-Up Funding
  First-Round Funding
  Second-Round Funding
  Third-Round Funding
  Fourth-Round Funding
  Later-Stage Funding
  Leveraged Buyouts
  Acquisitions
INDUSTRY PREFERENCE:
  Diversified
  Alternative Energy
  Conventional Energy (oil, natural gas, coal)
  Communications Technology
  Computer Hardware
  Computer Software
  Manufacturing
  Media
  Medical Technology
  Other High Technology Not Mentioned
  Retail
  Services
  Wholesale Distribution
  Films & Video Projects
  Natural Resources
GEOGRAPHIC PREFERENCE:
  No Preference

TYPES OF FUNDS:
  Equity (stock purchases)
  R & D Ltd. Partnerships
INVESTMENT AMOUNTS PREFERRED:
  Minimum: $100,000
  Maximum: $5,000,000

Smith Barney Venture Corp./First Century Partnership
1345 Avenue of the Americas
New York, NY 10104
212 399 6000

CONTACT: David S. Lobfel (NY)
  Walter C. Johnsen (CA)
TYPE OF FIRM: Venture Capital Firm
  Investment Banking Firm
FUNDING PREFERENCE:
  Seed Funding
  Start-Up Funding
  First-Round Funding
  Leveraged Buyouts
INDUSTRY PREFERENCE:
  Conventional Energy (oil, natural gas, and coal)
  Communications Technology
  Computer Hardware
  Computer Software
  Medical Technology
  Other High Technologies Not Mentioned
  Wholesale Distribution
GEOGRAPHIC PREFERENCE:
  No Preference
TYPES OF FUNDS:
  Equity (stock purchases)
INVESTMENT AMOUNTS PREFERRED:
  Minimum: $500,000
  Maximum: $1,500,000

Taroco Capital Corp.
19 Rector St., 35th Floor
New York, NY 10006
212 344 6690

CONTACT: Thomas Lee
TYPE OF FIRM: MESBIC
FUNDING PREFERENCE:
  Second-Round Funding

INDUSTRY PREFERENCE:
  Retail
  Services
GEOGRAPHIC PREFERENCE:
  Immediate Area—NYC
TYPES OF FUNDS:
  Equity (stock purchases)
  Loans
INVESTMENT AMOUNTS PREFERRED:
  Minimum: $10,000
  Maximum: $150,000

Transportation SBIC, Inc.
122 East 42nd Street
New York, NY 10168
212 986 6050

CONTACT: Melvin L. Hirsch
TYPE OF FIRM: MESBIC
FUNDING PREFERENCE:
  Start-Up Funding
INDUSTRY PREFERENCE:
  N/A
GEOGRAPHIC PREFERENCE:
  Immediate Area—New York City
TYPES OF FUNDS:
  Loans
INVESTMENT AMOUNTS PREFERRED:
  Minimum: $50,000
  Maximum: $350,000

Warburg, Pincus Capital Partners
277 Park Ave.
New York, NY 10172
212 593 0300

CONTACT: Christopher W. Brody
TYPE OF FIRM: Venture Capital Firm
FUNDING PREFERENCE:
  Seed Funding
  Start-Up Funding
  First-Round Funding
  Second-Round Funding
  Third-Round Funding
  Fourth-Round Funding

Later-Stage Funding
Leveraged Buyouts
INDUSTRY PREFERENCE:
Diversified
GEOGRAPHIC PREFERENCE:
Continental United States
TYPES OF FUNDS:
Equity (stock purchases)
INVESTMENT AMOUNTS PREFERRED:
Minimum: $350,000
Maximum: $20,000,000

J. H. Whitney & Co.
630 Fifth Ave., Rm. 3200
New York, NY 10111
212 757 0500

CONTACT: E. Ryan, General Partner
TYPE OF FIRM: Venture Capital Firm
FUNDING PREFERENCE:
Start-Up Funding
First-Round Funding
Second-Round Funding
Leveraged Buyouts
INDUSTRY PREFERENCE:
Diversified
GEOGRAPHIC PREFERENCE:
No Preference
TYPES OF FUNDS:
Equity (stock purchases)
INVESTMENT AMOUNTS PREFERRED:
Minimum: $1,000
Maximum: open

Vega Capital Corp.
10 East 40th Street
New York, NY 10016
212 685 8222

CONTACT: Ronald Linden
TYPE OF FIRM: SBIC
FUNDING PREFERENCE:
First-Round Funding
Second-Round Funding
Third-Round Funding

Fourth-Round Funding
Later-Stage Funding
Leveraged Buyouts
Acquisitions
INDUSTRY PREFERENCE:
Diversified
Manufacturing
GEOGRAPHIC PREFERENCE:
Northeast
Middle Atlantic
Southeast
Home State—New York
Immediate Area—Metropolitan NY
TYPES OF FUNDS:
Loans
Loans With Equity Kickers
INVESTMENT AMOUNTS PREFERRED:
Minimum: $100,000
Maximum: $1,000,000

Vencon Management, Inc.
301 West 53rd Street
New York, NY 10019
212 581 8787

CONTACT: I. Barash
TYPE OF FIRM: Venture Capital Firm
FUNDING PREFERENCE:
Leveraged Buyouts
Acquisitions
INDUSTRY PREFERENCE:
Manufacturing
Medical Technology
Other High Technologies Not Mentioned
GEOGRAPHIC PREFERENCE:
No Preference
TYPES OF FUNDS:
Equity (stock purchases)
INVESTMENT AMOUNTS PREFERRED:
Minimum: $500,000
Maximum: $10 million

NORTH CAROLINA

Falcon Capital Corporation
311 So. Evans St.
Greenville, NC 27834
919 752 5918

CONTACT: Dr. P. S. Prasad, President
TYPE OF FIRM: SBIC
FUNDING PREFERENCE:
  No Preference—Depends on individual case
INDUSTRY PREFERENCE:
  Diversified
GEOGRAPHIC PREFERENCE:
  No Preference
TYPES OF FUNDS:
  Loans With Equity Kickers
INVESTMENT AMOUNTS PREFERRED:
  Minimum: N/A
  Maximum: Up to $100,000 to $150,000

Heritage Capital Corporation
2290 First Union Plaza
Charlotte, NC 28282
704 334 2867

CONTACT: J. Randolph Gregory
TYPE OF FIRM: SBIC
FUNDING PREFERENCE:
  First-Round Funding
  Second-Round Funding
  Leveraged Buyouts
INDUSTRY PREFERENCE:
  Diversified
GEOGRAPHIC PREFERENCE:
  Southeast
TYPES OF FUNDS:
  Loans With Equity Kickers
INVESTMENT AMOUNTS PREFERRED:
  Minimum: $150,000
  Maximum: $1,000,000 in syndicates

Vanguard Investment Co., Inc.
4517 Bragg Blvd., Suite 3
Fayerreville, NC 28303
919 864 4447

CONTACT: Marion "Rex" Harris
TYPE OF FIRM: MESBIC
  Venture Capital
FUNDING PREFERENCE:
  First-Round Funding
  Later-Stage Funding
  Acquisitions

INDUSTRY PREFERENCE:
  Diversified
  Communications Technology
  Media
  Other High Technologies Not Mentioned
GEOGRAPHIC PREFERENCE:
  No Preference
TYPES OF FUNDS:
  Equity (stock purchases)
  Loans
  Loans With Equity Kickers
INVESTMENT AMOUNTS PREFERRED:
  Minimum: $100,000
  Maximum: $200,000

OHIO

Cardinal Development Capital Fund
155 E. Broad St.
Columbus, OH 43215
614 464 5552

CONTACT: Richard F. Bannon
TYPE OF FIRM: Venture Capital Firm
FUNDING PREFERENCE:
  N/A
INDUSTRY PREFERENCE:
  Communications Technology
  Computer Hardware
  Computer Software
  Manufacturing
  Medical Technology
  Other High Technologies Not Mentioned
GEOGRAPHIC PREFERENCE:
  Mid-West
TYPES OF FUNDS:
  Equity (stock purchases)
INVESTMENT AMOUNTS PREFERRED:
  Minimum: $500,000
  Maximum: Open

Scientific Advances, Inc., Subsidiary
  of Battelle Memorial Institute
601 West Fifth Avenue
Columbus, OH 43201
614 294 5541

CONTACT: Thomas W. Harvey, Paul F. Purcell and Daniel J. Shea, all Vice Presidents
TYPE OF FIRM: Venture Capital Firm
FUNDING PREFERENCE:
  Start-Up Funding
  First-Round Funding
  Second-Round Funding
INDUSTRY PREFERENCE:
  Diversified-Technical only
  Alternative Energy
  Communications Technology
  Computer Hardware
  Computer Software
  Medical Technology
  Other High Technologies Not Mentioned
GEOGRAPHIC PREFERENCE:
  No Preference
TYPES OF FUNDS:
  Equity (stock purchases)
INVESTMENT AMOUNTS PREFERRED:
  Minimum: $500,000
  Maximum: $1,000,000

OKLAHOMA

Alliance Business Investment Company
One Williams Center, Suite 2000
Tulsa, OK 74172
918 742 8685

CONTACT: Barry M. Davis, President
TYPE OF FIRM: Venture Capital Firm
  SBIC
FUNDING PREFERENCE:
  Later-Stage Funding
  Leveraged Buyouts
  Acquisitions
INDUSTRY PREFERENCE:
  Conventional Energy (oil, natural gas, and coal)
  Communications Technology
  Manufacturing
  Media
  Medical Technology
GEOGRAPHIC PREFERENCE:
  Mid-West
  Southwest

TYPES OF FUNDS:
  Loans With Equity Kickers
  Bonds With Equity Kickers
INVESTMENT AMOUNTS PREFERRED:
  Minimum: $300,000
  Maximum: $600,000

Southwest Venture Capital, Inc.
4120 #51st., Suite E
Tulsa, OK 74135
918 742 3177

CONTACT: Donald M. Wetzler
TYPE OF FIRM: SBIC
FUNDING PREFERENCE:
  First-Round Funding
  Leveraged Buyouts
INDUSTRY PREFERENCE:
  Diversified
GEOGRAPHIC PREFERENCE:
  Home State Oklahoma
TYPES OF FUNDS:
  Loans With Equity Kickers
INVESTMENT AMOUNTS PREFERRED:
  Minimum: N/A
  Maximum: $100,000

Western Venture Capital Corporation
4880 S. Lewis, P.O. Box 7727
Tulsa, OK 74105
918 749 7981

CONTACT: Gary L. Smith
TYPE OF FIRM: SBIC
FUNDING PREFERENCE:
  First-Round Funding
  Second-Round Funding
  Third-Round Funding
  Leveraged Buyouts
INDUSTRY PREFERENCE:
  Diversified
  Alternative Energy
  Conventional Energy
  Manufacturing
  Medical Technology

Other High Technologies Not Mentioned
Natural Resources
Real Estate
Retail
Wholesale Dist.
GEOGRAPHIC PREFERENCE:
  Southwest
  Home State
  Immediate Area
TYPES OF FUNDS:
  Loans with Equity Kickers
INVESTMENT AMOUNTS PREFERRED:
  Minimum: $250,000
  Maximum: $400,000

OREGON

Norwest Venture Capital
1300 SW 5th Ave., #3018
Portland, OR 97201
503 223 6622

CONTACT: N/A
TYPE OF FIRM: Venture Capital Firm
  SBIC
FUNDING PREFERENCE:
  N/A
INDUSTRY PREFERENCE:
  Diversified
GEOGRAPHIC PREFERENCE:
  No Preference
TYPES OF FUNDS:
  Equity (stock purchases)
INVESTMENT AMOUNTS PREFERRED:
  Minimum: $1,000,000
  Maximum: $5,000,000

PENNSYLVANIA

Alliance Enterprise Corporation
1801 Market Street
Philadelphia, PA 19103
215 972 4230

CONTACT: Duane C. McKnight
TYPE OF FIRM: MESBIC

FUNDING PREFERENCE:
  Start-Up Funding
  First-Round Funding
  Second-Round Funding
  Third-Round Funding
  Fourth-Round Funding
  Later-Stage Funding
INDUSTRY PREFERENCE:
  Diversified
  Manufacturing
  Medical Technology
GEOGRAPHIC PREFERENCE:
  Northeast
  Southeast
  Southwest
TYPES OF FUNDS:
  Equity
  Loans
  Loans with Equity Kickers
  Bonds
  Bonds with Equity Kickers
INVESTMENT AMOUNTS PREFERRED:
  Minimum: $75,000—100,000
  Maximum: $250,000

Capital Corporation of America
225 S. 15th Street
Philadelphia, PA 19102
215 732 1666

CONTACT: Martin M. Newman
TYPE OF FIRM: SBIC
FUNDING PREFERENCE:
  First-Round Funding
  Second-Round Funding
  Leveraged Buyouts
  Acquisitions
INDUSTRY PREFERENCE:
  Diversified
  Computer Hardware
  Computer Software
  Manufacturing
  Medical Technology
GEOGRAPHIC PREFERENCE:
  No Preference
TYPES OF FUNDS:
  Loans with Equity Kickers

INVESTMENT AMOUNTS PREFERRED:
  Minimum: $50,000
  Maximum: $1,000,000

Fostin Capital Corporation
P.O. Box 67
Pittsburgh, PA 15230
412 928 8900

CONTACT: William F. Woods
TYPE OF FIRM: Venture Capital Firm
FUNDING PREFERENCE:
  First-Round Funding
  Second-Round Funding
  Leveraged Buyouts
INDUSTRY PREFERENCE:
  Communications Technology
  Computer Hardware
  Computer Software
  Medical Technology
  Other High Technologies Not Mentioned
GEOGRAPHIC PREFERENCE:
  No Preference
TYPES OF FUNDS:
  Equity
  Loans with Equity Kickers
  Bonds with Equity Kickers
INVESTMENT AMOUNTS PREFERRED:
  Minimum: $250,000
  Maximum: $2,000,000

Howard & Company
1528 Walnut Street
Philadelphia, PA 19102
215 735 2815

CONTACT: T. Patrick Hurley, Jr.
TYPE OF FIRM: Consulting Firm
FUNDING PREFERENCE:
  First-Round Funding
  Second-Round Funding
  Third-Round Funding
  Fourth-Round Funding
  Later-Stage Funding
  Leveraged Buyouts

Acquisitions
Initial Public Offering
INDUSTRY PREFERENCE:
  Diversified
GEOGRAPHIC PREFERENCE:
  Northeast
  Middle Atlantic
  Southeast
TYPES OF FUNDS:
  N/A
INVESTMENT AMOUNTS PREFERRED:
  Minimum: N/A
  Maximum: N/A

Pennsylvania Growth Investment Corp.
1000 RIDC Plaza, Suite 311
Pittsburgh, PA 15238
412 963 9339

CONTACT: M. G. Dell
TYPE OF FIRM: Venture Capital Firm
  SBIC
FUNDING PREFERENCE:
  First-Round Funding
  Second-Round Funding
  Leveraged Buyouts
  Acquisitions
INDUSTRY PREFERENCE:
  Diversified
GEOGRAPHIC PREFERENCE:
  Middle Atlantic
TYPES OF FUNDS:
  Equity
  Loans
  Loans with Equity Kickers
INVESTMENT AMOUNTS PREFERRED:
  Minimum: $200,000
  Maximum: $500,000

PNC Venture Group
PNB Building, 18th Floor
Fifth Avenue & Wood Street
Pittsburgh, PA 15222
412 355 2245

CONTACT: Jeffrey H. Schutz
TYPE OF FIRM: Venture Capital Firm
  SBIC
FUNDING PREFERENCE:
  First-Round Funding
  Second-Round Funding
  Third-Round Funding
  Fourth-Round Funding
  Later-Stage Funding
  Leveraged Buyouts
INDUSTRY PREFERENCE:
  Diversified
GEOGRAPHIC PREFERENCE:
  No Preference
TYPES OF FUNDS:
  Equity
INVESTMENT AMOUNTS PREFERRED:
  Minimum: $150,000
  Maximum: $500,000

Southeastern PA Development Fund
3 Penn Center Plaza, Suite 604
Philadelphia, PA 19102
215 568 4677

CONTACT: Paul A. Mitchell
TYPE OF FIRM: N/A
FUNDING PREFERENCE:
  Second-Round Funding
  Third-Round Funding
  Fourth-Round Funding
  Later-Stage Funding
  Leveraged Buyouts
INDUSTRY PREFERENCE:
  Diversified
  Manufacturing
GEOGRAPHIC PREFERENCE:
  Immediate Area—Philadelphia
TYPES OF FUNDS:
  Loans
  Loans with Equity Kickers
INVESTMENT AMOUNTS PREFERRED:
  Minimum: $150,000
  Maximum: $500,000

Venture Associates
1528 Walnut Street
Philadelphia, PA 19102
215 735 2815

CONTACT: Donald A. Bailey
TYPE OF FIRM: Investment Banking Firm
  Venture Financing Organization
FUNDING PREFERENCE:
  Seed Funding
  Start-Up Funding
  First-Round Funding
INDUSTRY PREFERENCE:
  Alternative Energy
  Communications Technology
  Computer Hardware
  Computer Software
  Manufacturing
  Medical Technology
  Other High Technologies Not Mentioned
GEOGRAPHIC PREFERENCE:
  No Preference
TYPES OF FUNDS:
  Equity
  Wide Flexibility on Structuring
INVESTMENT AMOUNTS PREFERRED:
  Minimum: $100,000
  Maximum: N/A

PUERTO RICO

Manuel L. Prats
PancedeLeon #623
Banco Corporation, Plaza Suite #604
HavRey, PR
809 751 8040

CONTACT: Manuel L. Prats
TYPE OF FIRM: MESBIC
FUNDING PREFERENCE:
  First-Round Funding
INDUSTRY PREFERENCE:
  Diversified
GEOGRAPHIC PREFERENCE:
  No Preference
TYPES OF FUNDS:
  Loans

INVESTMENT AMOUNTS PREFERRED:
  Minimum: N/A
  Maximum: N/A

Santiago Ruiz Betancourt
P.O. Box 992
Caguas, PR 00625
809 743 4213

CONTACT: Santiago Ruiz Betancourt
TYPE OF FIRM: MESBIC
FUNDING PREFERENCE:
  Later-Stage Funding
INDUSTRY PREFERENCE:
  Diversified
  Manufacturing
  Real Estate
  Retail
  Services
  Wholesale Distribution
GEOGRAPHIC PREFERENCE:
  Home State—Puerto Rico
TYPES OF FUNDS:
  Loans
  Loans with Equity Kickers
INVESTMENT AMOUNTS PREFERRED:
  Minimum: $50,000
  Maximum: $250,000

RHODE ISLAND

Fleet Growth Resources, Inc.
111 Westminster Street
Providence, RI 02903
401 278 5597

CONTACT: Robert M. Van Degna
TYPE OF FIRM: Venture Capital Firm
FUNDING PREFERENCE:
  Leveraged Buyouts
INDUSTRY PREFERENCE:
  Diversified
GEOGRAPHIC PREFERENCE:
  Northeast
  Middle Atlantic
  Southeast
  Mid-West

TYPES OF FUNDS:
  Equity
INVESTMENT AMOUNTS PREFERRED:
  Minimum: $1,000,000
  Maximum: $2,000,000

Fleet Venture Resources, Inc.
111 Westminster Street
Providence, RI 02903
401 278 5597

CONTACT: Robert M. Van Degna
TYPE OF FIRM: SBIC
FUNDING PREFERENCE:
  Start-Up Funding
  First-Round Funding
  Second-Round Funding
  Leveraged Buyouts
  Acquisitions
INDUSTRY PREFERENCE:
  Diversified
  Communications Technology
  Computer Hardware
  Medical Technology
GEOGRAPHIC PREFERENCE:
  Northeast
  Middle Atlantic
  Southeast
  Mid-West
TYPES OF FUNDS:
  Equity
INVESTMENT AMOUNTS PREFERRED:
  Minimum: $250,000
  Maximum: $500,000

Narragansett Capital Corporation
40 Westminster Street
Providence, RI 02903
401 751 1000

CONTACT: Gregory Barber
TYPE OF FIRM: Venture Capital Firm
FUNDING PREFERENCE:
  Second-Round Funding
  Leveraged Buyouts
  Acquisitions

INDUSTRY PREFERENCE:
  Diversified
GEOGRAPHIC PREFERENCE:
  No Preference
TYPES OF FUNDS:
  Equity
  Loans
  Loans with Equity Kickers
INVESTMENT AMOUNTS PREFERRED:
  Minimum: $100,000
  Maximum: $750,000

RIHT Capital Corporation
One Hospital Trust Plaza
Providence, RI 02903
401 278 8819

CONTACT: Peter Van Oosterhout
TYPE OF FIRM: SBIC
FUNDING PREFERENCE:
  Second-Round Funding
  Third-Round Funding
  Fourth-Round Funding
  Later-Stage Funding
  Leveraged Buyouts
INDUSTRY PREFERENCE:
  Diversified
  Communications Technology
  Computer Hardware
  Computer Software
  Manufacturing
  Medical Technology
  Real Estate
  Services
GEOGRAPHIC PREFERENCE:
  Northeast
  Middle Atlantic
  Southeast
  Mid-West
TYPES OF FUNDS:
  Loans with Equity Kickers
INVESTMENT AMOUNTS PREFERRED:
  Minimum: $200,000
  Maximum: $750,000

SOUTH CAROLINA

Carolina Venture Capital Corporation
P.O. Box 3110
Hilton Head Island, SC 29928
803 842 3101

CONTACT: Thomas H. Harvey, III
TYPE OF FIRM: SBIC
FUNDING PREFERENCE:
  Second-Round Funding
INDUSTRY PREFERENCE:
  Diversified
  Communications Technology
  Media
  Real Estate
GEOGRAPHIC PREFERENCE:
  Southeast
TYPES OF FUNDS:
  Equity
  Loans with Equity Kickers
INVESTMENT AMOUNTS PREFERRED:
  Minimum: $50,000
  Maximum: $200,000

Charleston Capital Corporation
111 Church Street
P.O. Box 328
Charleston, SC 29402
803 723 6464

CONTACT: Henry Yaschik
TYPE OF FIRM: SBIC
  Individual Investor
FUNDING PREFERENCE:
  First-Round Funding
  Second-Round Funding
INDUSTRY PREFERENCE:
  Diversified
  Real Estate
  Retail
  Wholesale Distribution
GEOGRAPHIC PREFERENCE:
  Southeast

TYPES OF FUNDS:
  Equity
  Loans
  Loans with Equity Kickers
INVESTMENT AMOUNTS PREFERRED:
  Minimum: None
  Maximum: $250,000 +

TENNESSEE

Capital Services & Resources, Inc.
5159 Wheelis
Suite 104
Memphis, TN 38117
901 761 2156

CONTACT: C. Y. Bancroft
TYPE OF FIRM: Other—Pvt. Investment Firm
FUNDING PREFERENCE:
  Third-Round Funding
  Leveraged Buyouts
  Acquisitions
INDUSTRY PREFERENCE:
  Diversified
  Manufacturing
  Medical Technology
GEOGRAPHIC PREFERENCE:
  Southeast
TYPES OF FUNDS:
  Leasing
INVESTMENT AMOUNTS PREFERRED:
  Minimum: $50,000
  Maximum: $1,750,000

Tennessee Equity Capital Corporation
1102 Stonewall Jackson
Nashville, TN 37220
615 373 4502

CONTACT: Walter S. Cohen
TYPE OF FIRM: MESBIC
FUNDING PREFERENCE:
  First-Round Funding
  Leveraged Buyouts
  Acquisitions

INDUSTRY PREFERENCE:
  Diversified
  Real Estate
  Services
  Wholesale Distribution
GEOGRAPHIC PREFERENCE:
  No Preference
TYPES OF FUNDS:
  Equity
INVESTMENT AMOUNTS PREFERRED:
  Minimum: $100,000
  Maximum: $1,000,000

West Tennessee Venture Capital Corporation
Suite 1718, Sterick Building
8 N. third Street
Memphis, TN 38107
901 527 6091

CONTACT: Bennie L. Marshall
TYPE OF FIRM: MESBIC
FUNDING PREFERENCE:
  Second-round Funding
  Leveraged Buyouts
INDUSTRY PREFERENCE:
  Diversified
GEOGRAPHIC PREFERENCE:
  Southeast
TYPES OF FUNDS:
  Loans with Equity Kickers
INVESTMENT AMOUNTS PREFERRED:
  Minimum: $50,000
  Maximum: $300,000

TEXAS

American Energy Investment Corporation
1010 Lamar Street
Suite 1680
Houston, TX 77002
713 651 0220

CONTACT: Robert J. Moses
TYPE OF FIRM: SBIC
FUNDING PREFERENCE:
  Second-Round Funding

INDUSTRY PREFERENCE:
  Conventional Energy
GEOGRAPHIC PREFERENCE:
  No Preference
TYPES OF FUNDS:
  Loans with Equity Kickers
INVESTMENT AMOUNTS PREFERRED:
  Minimum: $300,000
  Maximum: $500,000

BancTEXAS Capital, Inc.
P.O. Box 2249
1601 Elm
Dallas, TX 75221
214 969 6382

CONTACT: Ronald B. Gordon
TYPE OF FIRM: SBIC
FUNDING PREFERENCE:
  Second-Round Funding
  Third-Round Funding
  Leveraged Buyouts
  Acquisitions
INDUSTRY PREFERENCE:
  Diversified
GEOGRAPHIC PREFERENCE:
  Immediate Area—Texas Only
TYPES OF FUNDS:
  Loans with Equity Kickers
INVESTMENT AMOUNTS PREFERRED:
  Minimum: $50,000
  Maximum: $150,000

Bow Lane Capital
2401 Fountainview
Suite 950
Houston, TX 77057
713 977 7421

CONTACT: Stuart Schube
TYPE OF FIRM: SBIC
FUNDING PREFERENCE:
  First-Round Funding
  Second-Round Funding
  Third-Round Funding

INDUSTRY PREFERENCE:
  Diversified
  Communications Technology
  Computer Hardware
  Computer Software
  Medical Technology
  Other High Technologies Not Mentioned
GEOGRAPHIC PREFERENCE:
  No Preference
TYPES OF FUNDS:
  Equity
  Loans with Equity Kickers
INVESTMENT AMOUNTS PREFERRED:
  Minimum: $250,000
  Maximum: $3,000,000

Business Capital Corporation of Arlington
1112 Copeland Road
Suite 100
Arlington, TX 76011
817 261 4936

CONTACT: Keith Martin
TYPE OF FIRM: SBIC
FUNDING PREFERENCE:
  Second-Round Funding
  Leveraged Buyouts
INDUSTRY PREFERENCE:
  Diversified
  Manufacturing
GEOG RAPHIC PREFERENCE:
  Southwest
TYPES OF FUNDS:
  Loans with Equity Kickers
INVESTMENT AMOUNTS PREFERRED:
  Minimum: $200,000
  Maximum: $400,000

Charter Venture Group, Inc.
5150 N. Shepherd
Suite 218
Houston, TX 77018
713 699 3588

CONTACT: Kent E. Smith
TYPE OF FIRM: SBIC

FUNDING PREFERENCE:
  First-Round Funding
  Second-Round Funding
  Third-Round Funding
  Fourth-Round Funding
  Later-Stage Funding
  Leveraged Buyouts
INDUSTRY PREFERENCE:
  Diversified
GEOGRAPHIC PREFERENCE:
  Southwest
TYPES OF FUNDS:
  Equity
  Loans with Equity Kickers
INVESTMENT AMOUNTS PREFERRED:
  Minimum: $100,000
  Maximum: $200,000

DASBIC, Inc.
333 Meadows Building
Dallas, TX 75206
214 691 0711

CONTACT: Joseph Sullivan
TYPE OF FIRM: Other—Diversified Investment & Operating Group
FUNDING PREFERENCE:
  Second-Round Funding
  Later-Stage Funding
  Leveraged Buyouts
  Acquisitions
INDUSTRY PREFERENCE:
  Diversified
GEOGRAPHIC PREFERENCE:
  Home State
TYPES OF FUNDS:
  Equity
  Loans with Equity Kickers
INVESTMENT AMOUNTS PREFERRED:
  Minimum: $250,000
  Maximum: None

Enterprise Capital Corporation
3401 Allen Parkway
Suite 108
Houston, TX 77019
713 524 5170

CONTACT: Deborah A. Frost
TYPE OF FIRM: SBIC
FUNDING PREFERENCE:
  First-Round Funding
  Second-Round Funding
INDUSTRY PREFERENCE:
  Diversified
GEOGRAPHIC PREFERENCE:
  Southwest
TYPES OF FUNDS:
  Equity
  Loans
  Loans with Equity Kickers
INVESTMENT AMOUNTS PREFERRED:
  Minimum: $100,000
  Maximum: $500,000

JVIG U.S. Management, Inc.
1008 N. Bowen Road
Arlington, TX 76012
817 860 5222

CONTACT: John Ross
TYPE OF FIRM: Other—Merchant Banking
  Investment Banking Firm
  Consulting Firm
FUNDING PREFERENCE:
  First-Round Funding
  Second-Round Funding
  Third-Round Funding
  Fourth-Round Funding
  Later-Stage Funding
  Leveraged Buyouts
  Acquisitions
INDUSTRY PREFERENCE:
  Diversified
GEOGRAPHIC PREFERENCE:
  No Preference
TYPES OF FUNDS:
  Loans
  Bonds
INVESTMENT AMOUNTS PREFERRED:
  Minimum: $250,000
  Maximum: $10,000,000

Mercantile Dallas Corporation
P.O. Box 222090
Dallas, TX 75222
214 741 1469

CONTACT: Tom Mitchell
TYPE OF FIRM: SBIC
FUNDING PREFERENCE:
  Third-Round Funding
  Fourth-Round Funding
  Leveraged Buyouts
INDUSTRY PREFERENCE:
  Diversified
GEOGRAPHIC PREFERENCE:
  Southwest
TYPES OF FUNDS:
  Equity
  Loans
  Loans with Equity Kickers
INVESTMENT AMOUNTS PREFERRED:
  Minimum: $250,000
  Maximum: $2,000,000

MESBIC Financial Corporation of Houston
1801 Main
Suite 320
Houston, TX 77002
713 228 8321

CONTACT: Richard Rothfeld
TYPE OF FIRM: MESBIC
FUNDING PREFERENCE:
  Second-Round Funding
INDUSTRY PREFERENCE:
  Diversified
  Manufacturing
  Services
  Wholesale Distribution
GEOGRAPHIC PREFERENCE:
  Immediate Area—Houston, Galveston
TYPES OF FUNDS:
  Loans
  Loans with Equity Kickers
INVESTMENT AMOUNTS PREFERRED:
  Minimum: $25,000
  Maximum: $250,000

MESBIC of San Antonio, Inc.
2300 W. Commerce
San Antonio, TX 78201
512 224 0909

CONTACT: Ruben M. Saenz
TYPE OF FIRM: MESBIC
FUNDING PREFERENCE:
   Later-Stage Funding
INDUSTRY PREFERENCE:
   Diversified
GEOGRAPHIC PREFERENCE:
   Home State—Texas
TYPES OF FUNDS:
   Loans with Equity Kickers
INVESTMENT AMOUNTS PREFERRED:
   Minimum: $50,000
   Maximum: $200,000

MSI Capital Corporation
6510 Abrams Road
Suite 650
Dallas, TX 75231
214 341 1553

CONTACT: Nich Stanfield
TYPE OF FIRM: Venture Capital Firm
   Investment Banking Firm
FUNDING PREFERENCE:
   Seed Funding
   Start-Up Funding
   First-Round Funding
   Leveraged Buyouts
INDUSTRY PREFERENCE:
   Diversified
   Communications Technology
   Computer Hardware
   Computer Software
   Manufacturing
   Services
   Wholesale Distribution
GEOGRAPHIC PREFERENCE:
   Southwest
TYPES OF FUNDS:
   Equity
   Bonds with Equity Kickers

INVESTMENT AMOUNTS PREFERRED:
  Minimum: $100,000 or less
  Maximum: $500,000

New Business Resources
P.O. Box 796
Addison, TX 75001
214 235 6631

CONTACT: Richard J. Hanschen
TYPE OF FIRM: Venture Capital Firm
FUNDING PREFERENCE:
  Start-Up Funding
  Leveraged Buyouts
  Acquisitions
INDUSTRY PREFERENCE:
  Communications Technology
  Computer Hardware
  Computer Software
  Medical Technology
GEOGRAPHIC PREFERENCE:
  No Preference
TYPES OF FUNDS:
  Equity
INVESTMENT AMOUNTS PREFERRED:
  Minimum: $100,000
  Maximum: $500,000

San Antonio Venture Group, Inc.
2300 W. Commerce
San Antonio, TX 78201
512 224 0909

CONTACT: Ruben M. Saenz
TYPE OF FIRM: SBIC
FUNDING PREFERENCE:
  Later-Stage Funding
INDUSTRY PREFERENCE:
  Diversified
GEOGRAPHIC PREFERENCE:
  Home State—Texas
TYPES OF FUNDS:
  Loans with Equity Kickers
INVESTMENT AMOUNTS PREFERRED:
  Minimum: $50,000
  Maximum: $200,000

SBI Capital Corporation
P.O. Box 771668
Houston, TX 77215
713 975 1188

CONTACT: W. E. Wright
TYPE OF FIRM: Venture Capital Firm
    SBIC
FUNDING PREFERENCE:
    First-Round Funding
    Second-Round Funding
    Leveraged Buyouts
INDUSTRY PREFERENCE:
    Diversified
    Conventional Energy
    Computer Hardware
    Computer Software
    Manufacturing
    Medical Technology
    Other High Technologies Not Mentioned
GEOGRAPHIC PREFERENCE:
    Southwest
    Home State—Texas
TYPES OF FUNDS:
    Loans with Equity Kickers
    Bonds with Equity Kickers
INVESTMENT AMOUNTS PREFERRED:
    Minimum: $125,000
    Maximum: $200,000

Sunwestern Management, Inc.
2720 Stemmons Freeway
#816 South Tower
Dallas, TX 75207
214 638 2100

CONTACT: Floyd W. Collins
TYPE OF FIRM: Venture Capital Firm
    SBIC
FUNDING PREFERENCE:
    Start-Up Funding
    First-Round Funding
    Second-Round Funding
    Leveraged Buyouts
INDUSTRY PREFERENCE:
    Diversified
    Conventional Energy

Communications Technology
Computer Software
Medical Technology
GEOGRAPHIC PREFERENCE:
Southwest
TYPES OF FUNDS:
Equity
Loans with Equity Kickers
INVESTMENT AMOUNTS PREFERRED:
Minimum: $250,000
Maximum: $500,000

Texas Capital Corporation
333 Clay Street
Suite 2100
Houston, TX 77002

CONTACT: David G. Franklin
TYPE OF FIRM: Venture Capital Firm
SBIC
FUNDING PREFERENCE:
First-Round Funding
Second-Round Funding
Leveraged Buyouts
INDUSTRY PREFERENCE:
Communications Technology
Manufacturing
Media
Medical Technology
GEOGRAPHIC PREFERENCE:
Southeast
Mid-West
Rocky Mountain States
Southwest
TYPES OF FUNDS:
Equity
Loans with Equity Kickers
Bonds with Equity Kickers
INVESTMENT AMOUNTS PREFERRED:
Minimum: $300,000
Maximum: $600,000

VIRGINIA

Atlantic Venture Partners
P.O. Box 1493
Richmond, VA 23212
804 644 5496

CONTACT: Robert Pratt
TYPE OF FIRM: Venture Capital Firm
FUNDING PREFERENCE:
  Start-Up Funding
  First-Round Funding
  Second-Round Funding
  Later-Stage Funding
  Leveraged Buyouts
  Acquisitions
INDUSTRY PREFERENCE:
  Diversified
GEOGRAPHIC PREFERENCE:
  Northeast
  Middle Atlantic
  Southeast
TYPES OF FUNDS:
  Equity
  Loans with Equity Kickers
INVESTMENT AMOUNTS PREFERRED:
  Minimum: $300,000
  Maximum: $700,000

James River Capital Associates
9 S. 12th Street
Richmond, VA 23219
804 643 7358

CONTACT: Hugh Ewing
TYPE OF FIRM: SBIC
FUNDING PREFERENCE:
  Second-Round Funding
  Third-Round Funding
  Fourth-Round Funding
  Later-Stage Funding
  Leveraged Buyouts
  Acquisitions
INDUSTRY PREFERENCE:
  Diversified
GEOGRAPHIC PREFERENCE:
  Middle Atlantic
  Southeast
  Home State—Virginia
TYPES OF FUNDS:
  Loans with Equity Kickers
  Bonds with Equity Kickers

INVESTMENT AMOUNTS PREFERRED:
  Minimum: $100,000
  Maximum: $200,000

Metropolitan Capital Corporation
2550 Huntington Avenue
Alexandria, VA 22303
703 960 4698

CONTACT: M. A. Riebe
TYPE OF FIRM: SBIC
FUNDING PREFERENCE:
  First-Round Funding
  Second-Round Funding
INDUSTRY PREFERENCE:
  Diversified
GEOGRAPHIC PREFERENCE:
  Immediate Area
TYPES OF FUNDS:
  Equity
  Loans with Equity Kickers
INVESTMENT AMOUNTS PREFERRED:
  Minimum: $70,000
  Maximum: $200,000

Venture Capital Group
401 First Street N.W.
Roanoke, VA 24016
703 344 6624

CONTACT: David Erickson
TYPE OF FIRM: Venture Capital Firm
FUNDING PREFERENCE:
  Second-Round Funding
INDUSTRY PREFERENCE:
  Diversified
GEOGRAPHIC PREFERENCE:
  Home State—Virginia
TYPES OF FUNDS:
  Loans with Equity Kickers
  Leasing
INVESTMENT AMOUNTS PREFERRED:
  Minimum: $25,000
  Maximum: $500,000

WASHINGTON

Walden Investors/Capital Resource Corporation
1001 Logan Building
Seattle, WA 98101
206 623 6550

CONTACT: Theodore M. Wright
TYPE OF FIRM: Venture Capital Firm
  SBIC
FUNDING PREFERENCE:
  Start-Up Funding
  First-Round Funding
  Second-Round Funding
INDUSTRY PREFERENCE:
  Communications Technology
  Computer Software
  Manufacturing
  Medical Technology
  Other High Technologies Not Mentioned
GEOGRAPHIC PREFERENCE:
  No Preference
TYPES OF FUNDS:
  Equity
INVESTMENT AMOUNTS PREFERRED:
  Minimum: $500,000
  Maximum: $1,000,000

WASHINGTON, D.C.

Allied Capital Corporation
1625 Eye Street, N.W.
Washington, DC 20006
202 331 1112

CONTACT: David Gladstone
TYPE OF FIRM: Venture Capital Firm
FUNDING PREFERENCE:
  All except:
  Seed Funding
  Start-Up Funding
INDUSTRY PREFERENCE:
  All except:
  Alternative Energy
  Conventional Energy (oil, natural gas, and coal)
  Natural Resources
  Real Estate

GEOGRAPHIC PREFERENCE:
  Northeast
  Middle Atlantic
  Southeast
  Mid-West
TYPES OF FUNDS:
  Loans with Equity Kickers
INVESTMENT AMOUNTS PREFERRED:
  Minimum: $100,000
  Maximum: $500,000

Malcolm Bund & Associates
Suite 600
1225 Nineteenth St., N.W.
Washington, DC 20036
202 293 2910

CONTACT: Malcolm Bund
TYPE OF FIRM: Consulting Firm
FUNDING PREFERENCE:
  First-Round Funding
  Leveraged Buyouts
  Acquisitions
INDUSTRY PREFERENCE:
  Diversified
  Manufacturing
  Medical Technology
  Other High Technologies Not Mentioned
  Real Estate
  Wholesale Distribution
GEOGRAPHIC PREFERENCE:
  No Preference
TYPES OF FUNDS:
  Arrange investments and sometimes co-invest
INVESTMENT AMOUNTS PREFERRED:
  Minimum: N/A
  Maximum: N/A

Fulcrum Venture Capital Corporation
2021 K Street, N.W., Suite 301
Washington, DC 20006
202 833 9590

CONTACT: Divakar Kamath
TYPE OF FIRM: MESBIC

FUNDING PREFERENCE:
  First-Round Funding
  Second-Round Funding
INDUSTRY PREFERENCE:
  All except:
  Conventional Energy
  Computer Software
  Natural Resources
  Real Estate
  Retail
  Services (exceptional companies only)
GEOGRAPHIC PREFERENCE:
  U.S. only
TYPES OF FUNDS:
  Equity
  Loans
  Loans with Equity Kickers
INVESTMENT AMOUNTS PREFERRED:
  Minimum: $100,000
  Maximum: $400,000

Blake Ordway & Co.
1101 30th Street, N.W.
Suite 101
Washington, DC 20007
202 833 9031

CONTACT: N/A
TYPE OF FIRM: Venture Capital Firm
FUNDING PREFERENCE:
  Start-Up Funding
  First-Round Funding
  Acquisitions
INDUSTRY PREFERENCE:
  Alternate Energy
  Communications Technology
  Manufacturing
  Medical Technology
GEOGRAPHIC PREFERENCE:
  No Preference
TYPES OF FUNDS:
  Equity
INVESTMENT AMOUNTS PREFERRED:
  Minimum: N/A
  Maximum: N/A

WISCONSIN

Lubar & Co., Inc.
Suite 3060
First Wisconsin Center
Milwaukee, WI 53202
414 291 9000

CONTACT: William T. Donovan
TYPE OF FIRM: Venture Capital Firm
  Investment Banking Firm
FUNDING PREFERENCE:
  Second-Round Funding
  Leveraged Buyouts
  Acquisitions
INDUSTRY PREFERENCE:
  Diversified
  Conventional Energy
  Manufacturing
  Medical Technology
GEOGRAPHIC PREFERENCE:
  Mid-West
  Rocky Mountain States
TYPES OF FUNDS:
  Equity
  Loans with Equity Kickers
INVESTMENT AMOUNTS PREFERRED:
  Minimum: $350,000
  Maximum: $10,000,000

SC Opportunities, Inc.
1112 7th Avenue
Monroe, WI 53566
608 328 8409

CONTACT: Richard E. Becker
TYPE OF FIRM: MESBIC
FUNDING PREFERENCE:
  Start-Up Funding
INDUSTRY PREFERENCE:
  Retail
GEOGRAPHIC PREFERENCE:
  Mid-West
TYPES OF FUNDS:
  Equity

Loans
Loans with Equity Kickers
INVESTMENT AMOUNTS PREFERRED:
Minimum: $30,000
Maximum: $90,000

WYOMING

Capital Corporation of Wyoming, Inc.
P.O. Box 612
145 S. Durbin, Suite 201
Casper, WY 82602
307 234 5351

CONTACT: Larry McDonald
TYPE OF FIRM: Venture Capital Firm
  SBIC
  Other—Real Estate Investor
FUNDING PREFERENCE:
  Second-Round Funding
  Third-Round Funding
  Fourth-Round Funding
  Later-Stage Funding
  Leveraged Buyouts
  Acquisitions
INDUSTRY PREFERENCE:
  Other High Technologies Not Mentioned
  Diversified
  Alternative Energy
  Conventional Energy
  Communications Technology
  Manufacturing
  Media
  Medical Technology
  Natural Resources
  Real Estate
  Services
  Wholesale Distribution
GEOGRAPHIC PREFERENCE:
  Home State—Wyoming
TYPES OF FUNDS:
  Leasing
  Equity
  Loans
  Loans with Equity Kickers
  Other-Build to suit/leasebacks purchase leasebacks

INVESTMENT AMOUNTS PREFERRED:
 Minimum: $25,000
 Maximum: $650,000

CANADA

Canadian Enterprise Development Corporation, Ltd.
199 Bay Street
Suite 1103
Toronto, Ontario M5J 1L4
416 366 7607

CONTACT: Gerald D. Sutton
TYPE OF FIRM: Venture Capital Firm
FUNDING PREFERENCE:
 Start-Up Funding
 First-Round Funding
INDUSTRY PREFERENCE:
 Communications Technology
 Computer Hardware
 Computer Software
 Manufacturing
 Medical Technology
 Other High Technologies Not Mentioned
GEOGRAPHIC PREFERENCE:
 Southeast
 Mid-West
TYPES OF FUNDS:
 Equity
 Loans
 Loans with Equity Kickers
INVESTMENT AMOUNTS PREFERRED:
 Minimum: $150,000
 Maximum: $800,000

UNDERWRITING FIRMS

Underwriting firms assist growth-oriented companies that seek funds for expansion purposes or start-up. Some of these funding organizations specialize in small businesses and are listed here. They will help an enterprise sell equity ownership or debt in order to raise funds if the proposition in question has merit in their opinion. Underwriting companies were discussed in Chapter VI.

Colorado

Alta Investment
(303) 573:7244

Atlantis Securities
(303) 692-0965

Blinder, Robinson, and Co., Inc.
1860 Lincoln Street
Suite 1272
Denver, CO 80203

Centennial State Securities, Inc.
Orchard Place 4
5990 S. Syracuse Street
Suite 200
Englewood, CO 80111
(303) 779-8800

Chesley & Dunn, Inc.
1777 S. Harrison Street
Denver, CO 80210
(303) 753-9930

Columbine Securities, Inc.
1818 Prudential Plaza
Denver, CO 80202

S. W. Devanney & Co.
2455 1st Federal National Building
Denver, CO 80239
(303) 337-3223

N. Doland & Co.
Writer's Square
1512 Larimer
Denver, CO 80222

First Colorado Investment & Securities, Inc.
621 17th Street
Suite 1801
Denver, CO 80293
(303) 623-3361

First Financial Securities
2851 S. Parker Road
Aurora, CO 80014

Gattini & Co.
10200 E. Girard
Denver, CO 80231
(800) 821-4920
(303) 696-9410

T. Geimer Securities
2955 East First Avenue
Suite 400
Denver, CO 80206
(303) 388-4400

E. J. Pittock & Co.
5325 S. Valentia Way
Suite 220
Denver, CO 80111

Rigel Securities
1401 Potter Drive
Colorado Springs, CO 80909
(303) 597-4963

Securities Clearing of Colorado
700 Broadway
Denver, CO 80203
(800) 525-3562

Vantage Securities
Plaza 7000
Suite 307
E. Belleview
Englewood, CO 80111

Walford, DeMaret & Co.
1512 Larimer Street
Denver, CO 80222
(303) 629-7800

Wall Street West, Inc.
5340 S. Quebec
Suite 100
Englewood, CO 80111
(303) 740-8444

Florida

First Equity Corporation
100 N. Biscayne Boulevard
Suite 2708
Miami, FL 33132
(305) 379-0731

RLR Securities Group, Inc.
7539 W. Oakland Park Boulevard
Laudehill, FL 33319
(800) 327-9193

Minnesota

Engles & Budd Co.
801 Nicollett Mall
Minneapolis, MN 55402
(612) 333-1161

New Jersey

Friedman Manger & Co.
30 Howe Avenue
Passaic, NJ 07055
(201) 778-7377

Kobrin Securities
(201) 238-4800

Marvest Securities
(201) 530-7200

M. H. Meyerson & Co.
15 Exchange Place
Jersey City, NJ 07302
(800) 526-3166

Patten Securities Corporation
308 Main Street
P.O. Box 741
Millburn, NJ 07041

Southeast Securities
5 Marine View Plaza
Hoboken, NJ 07030
(800) 526-6057

J. W. Weller & Co.
230 Broad Street
Bloomfield, NJ 07003

New York

American Ventures Securities, Inc.
115 Broadway
Suite 1200
New York, NY 10006
(212) 587-6120
(800) 221-3411

Brodis, Glant Securities
1 Great Neck Road
Great Neck, NY 11021

Brooks, Hamburger, Satnick, Inc.
80 Broad Street
New York, NY 10004
(212) 344-9515

Citiwide Securities
111 Broadway
New York, NY 10006
(800) 242-2484

S. D. Cohn & Co.
55 Broad Street
New York, NY 10004

Constantino & De Felice, Inc.
40 Exchange Place
New York, NY

First Philadelphia Corporation
80 Wall Street
New York, NY 10005

A. L. Havens Securities
26 Broadway
New York, NY 10004
(212) 422-8882

Jay W. Kaufmann & Co.
111 Broadway
New York, NY 10006
(212) 349-3030

Marsan Securities
(212) 709-0800

Monarch Funding Corporation
79 Wall Street
New York, NY 10005
(212) 943-3880

Norbay Securities, Inc.
39-02 Bell Boulevard
Bayside, NY 11361

North Hills Investors
(516) 482-5370

M. Rimson & Co.
150 Broadway
New York, NY 10038
(800) 221-4934

Sunrise Capital Corporation
381 Sunrise Highway
Lynbrook, NY 11563
(212) 343-7900

Tower Securities
(212) 355-5915

Unified Securities Corporation
120 Broadway
New York, NY
(800) 221-8584

Unified Securities, Inc.
55 Broad Street
New York, NY 10004
(212) 825-8000

Oklahoma

Fitzgerald, Dearman & Roberts, Inc.
30005 E. Skeely Drive
Tulsa, OK 74105

Houchin Adamson & Co.
604 Reunion Circle
9 E. 4th Street
Tulsa, OK 74103

Oregon

Paulson Investment Company, Inc.
729 S. W. Alder Street
Portland, OR 97205
(800) 547-2828
(503) 243-6000

Utah

Cannon Securities
(801) 533-8000

Covey & Co.
29 E. 2nd South
Salt Lake City, UT 84111
(801) 521-3830

Main Street Securities, Inc.
50 Main Street
Suite 400
Crossroads Plaza
Salt Lake City, UT 84144
(800) 426-3076
(801) 531-7447

Olsen & Co.
405 S.. Main Street
Salt Lake City, UT
(801) 363-6771

Western Capital & Securities
P.O. Box 11268
Salt Lake City, UT 84147
(801) 532-5337

Washington

Dillon Securities
243 Peyton Building
N. 10 Post Street
Spokane, WA 99201
(800) 541-0857
(509) 838-6455
(509) 466-3419

Wyoming

First Western Securities of Wyoming
120 N. Center Street
Casper, WY 82601
(307) 265-8900
(800) 442-3913

Government Sources

STATE FUNDING PROGRAMS

State governments have realized the importance of a viable small business sector to their respective economies. Consequently, many states maintain funding programs, varying in depth and effectiveness, directed to the small business community. Other states are currently evaluating various funding alternatives with the idea of having financing vehicles in place soon. If a particular state of interest is not listed, it would be wise to write or call that state's Small Business Assistance Office to determine if new funding programs are now in operation or forthcoming. Those offices are listed in Appendix J. In addition, call or write the U.S. Small Business Administration field office in a particular state of interest to determine the state and local development companies operating and providing funds. SBA field offices are listed in Appendix E.

ALASKA
Division of Business Loans
Department of Commerce and Economic Development
Pouch D
Juneanu, AL 99811

CALIFORNIA
Office of Local Economic Development
Department of Economic and Business Development
1120 "N" Street
Sacramento, CA 95805
(916) 322-1398

CONNECTICUT
State of Connecticut
Department of Economic Development
Office of Small Business Affairs
Hartford, CT

HAWAII
Department of Planning and Economic Development
250 South King Street
Honolulu, HI 96813
(808) 548-4616

ILLINOIS
Illinois Industrial Development Authority
P.O. Box 397
400 East DeYoung
Marion, IL 62959
(618) 997-6318

INDIANA
Indiana Economic Development Authority
State House
Indianapolis, IN 46204

IOWA
Iowa Business Development Credit Corporation
Des Moines, IA
(515) 281-3592

KENTUCKY
Small Business Development Section
Small and Minority Business Development Division
Kentucky Department of Commerce
Capital Plaza Tower
Frankfort, KY 40601

Kentucky Development Finance Authority
Capital Plaza Tower, 24th Floor
Frankfort, KY 40601
(502) 564-4554

MAINE
Maine Small Business Loan Authority
Community Drive
Augusta, ME 04333
(207) 289-2094

MARYLAND
Maryland Small Business Investment Authority
The World Trade Center
Suite 2223
Baltimore, MD 21202
(301) 659-4270

MASSACHUSETTS
Massachusetts Technology Development Corporation (MTDC)
131 State Street
Boston, MA 02109
(617) 723-4920

Massachusetts Business Development Corporation
One Boston Place
Boston, MA 02108
(617) 723-7515

Mass Capital Resource Company
11 Beacon Street
Boston, MA 02108

MICHIGAN
Michigan Department of Commerce
4th Floor, Law Building
Box 30004
Lansing, MI 48909
(517) 373-1820

Small Business Development Division
Office of Economic Development
Michigan Department of Commerce
P.O. Box 30225
Lansing, MI 48909
(517) 373-0637

MINNESOTA

Department of Economic Development
480 Cedar Street
St. Paul, MN 55101
(612) 296-5011

MISSISSIPPI
State of Mississippi
Agricultural and Industrial Board
Small Business Assistance Division
Jackson, MS
(601) 359-3437

MISSOURI
Missouri Division of Community & Economic Development
P.O. Box 118
301 W. High 7 South
Jefferson City, MO 65102
(314) 751-4855

MONTANA
Office of Commerce and Small Business Development
Governor's Office, Room 212
Capital Station
Helena, MT 59601
(406) 449-3923

NEW JERSEY
New Jersey Department of Labor and Industry
Trenton, NJ 08625
(609) 292-9587

New Jersey Economic Development Authority
Trenton, NJ 08625

OHIO
Ohio Development Financing Commission
State Office Tower
Columbus, OH 43216

OKLAHOMA
Oklahoma Industrial Finance Authority
Oklahoma City, OK 73152

OREGON
Energy Related Loans
Oregon Department of Energy
(503) 378-4040

PENNSYLVANIA
Small Business Action Center
South Office Building, Dept. of Commerce
Harrisburg, PA 17120
(717) 783-5700

RHODE ISLAND
Department of Economic Development
One Weybosset Hill
Providence, RI 02903
(401) 277-2601

TENNESSEE
Tennessee Industrial Development Authority
1021 Andrew Jackson Building
Nashville, TN 37219
(615) 741-1381

TEXAS
Texas Industrial Commission
Sam Houston State Office Building
Capitol Station
Austin, TX 78711

VERMONT
Vermont Industrial Development Authority
Montpelier, VT 05602
(802) 828-2384

WEST VIRGINIA
Small Business Service Unit
Governor's Office of Economic and Community Development
1426 Kanawha Blvd., East
Charleston, WV 25301
(304) 348-2960

WYOMING
Wyoming Industrial Development Corporation
Casper, WY 82601

VIRGIN ISLANDS
Small Business Development Agency
Post Office Box 2058
St. Thomas, Virgin Islands 00801
(809) 774-1331

U.S. GOVERNMENT FUNDING PROGRAMS

This section contains information on U.S. Government funding programs directed to small businesses. These sources represent an expansion of programs mentioned in Chapter VI.

AGRICULTURAL STABILIZATION AND CONSERVATION SERVICE

COMMODITY LOANS AND PURCHASES
   OBJECTIVES: To improve and stabilize farm income, to assist in bringing about a better balance between supply and demand of the commodities, and to assist farmers in the orderly marketing of their crops.

TYPES OF ASSISTANCE: Direct payments with unrestricted use; direct loans.

FINANCIAL ASSISTANCE AND AVAILABILITY: Direct payments (purchases): Range not available. Loans: $50 to $2,000,000.

CONTACT: Agricultural Stabilization and Conservation Service, Department of Agriculture, P.O. Box 2415, Washington, D.C. 20013. (202) 447-5237.

DAIRY INDEMNITY PAYMENTS

OBJECTIVES: To indemnify dairy farmers and manufacturers of dairy products who are directed to remove their milk, milk cows or dairy products from commercial markets because of contamination with residues of pesticides resulting from no misaction on the part of the dairy farmer or the manufacturer of the dairy product. Dairy farmers can also be indemnified because of contamination with chemicals or toxic substances, nuclear radiation or fallout.

TYPES OF ASSISTANCE: Direct payments with unrestricted use.

FINANCIAL ASSISTANCE AND AVAILABILITY: $348 to $29,075.

CONTACT: Emergency and Indemnity Programs Division, Agricultural Stabilization and Conservation Service, Department of Agriculture, P.O. Box 2415, Washington, D.C. 20013. (202) 447-5237.

EMERGENCY CONSERVATION PROGRAM

OBJECTIVES: To enable farmers to perform emergency conservation measures to control wind erosion on farmlands, or to rehabilitate farmlands damaged by wind erosion, floods, hurricanes, or other natural disasters; and to carry out emergency water conservation or water enhancing measures during periods of severe drought.

TYPES OF ASSISTANCE: Project grants.

FINANCIAL ASSISTANCE AND AVAILABILITY: $400 to $10,000.

CONTACT: Conservation and Environmental Protection Division, Agricultural Stabilization and Conservation Service, Department of Agriculture, P.O. Box 2415, Washington, D.C. 20013. (202) 447-5237.

FEED GRAIN PRODUCTION STABILIZATION

OBJECTIVES: To attract the production needed to meet domestic and foreign demand, to protect income for farmers, and to assure adequate supplies at fair and reasonable prices.

TYPES OF ASSISTANCE: Direct payments with unrestricted use.

FINANCIAL ASSISTANCE AND AVAILABILITY: $3 to $45,000. (Feed grain wheat and cotton payments, in total, may not exceed $45,000 to any one person for the 1979 crop year. Disaster payments are excluded from any payment limitation beginning with the 1977 crop year.)

CONTACT: Production Adjustment Division, Agricultural Stabilization and Conservation Service, Department of Agriculture, P.O. Box 2415, Washington, D.C. 20013. (202) 447-5237.

STORAGE FACILITIES AND EQUIPMENT LOANS

OBJECTIVES: To complement the commodity loan and grain reserve programs by providing adequate financing for needed on-farm storage facilities, drying equipment, and operating equipment, thereby affording farmers the opportunity for orderly marketing of their crops.

TYPES OF ASSISTANCE: Direct loans.

FINANCIAL ASSISTANCE AND AVAILABILITY: $200 to $50,000.

CONTACT: Price Support and Loan Division, Agricultural Stabilization and Conservation Service, Department of Agriculture, P.O. Box 2415, Washington, D.C., 20013. (202) 447-5237.

WHEAT PRODUCTION STABILIZATION

OBJECTIVES: To attract the production that is needed to meet domestic and foreign demand for food, to protect income for farmers, and to assure adequate supplies at fair and reasonable prices.

TYPES OF ASSISTANCE: Direct payments with unrestricted use.

FINANCIAL ASSISTANCE AND AVAILABILITY: $3 to $45,000. (Wheat, feed grains, and cotton payments, in total may not exceed $45,000 to any one person for the 1979 crop year. Disaster payments are excluded from any payment limitation beginning with the 1977 crop year.)

CONTACT: Production Adjustment Division, Agricultural Stabilization and Conservation Service, Department of Agriculture, P.O. Box 2415, Washington, D.C. 20013. (202) 447-5357.

NATIONAL WOOL ACT PAYMENTS

OBJECTIVES: To encourage increased domestic production of wool at prices fair to both producers and consumers in a way that has the least adverse effect on domestic and foreign trade and to encourage producers to improve the quality and marketing of their wool and mohair.

TYPES OF ASSISTANCE: Direct payments with unrestricted use.

FINANCIAL ASSISTANCE AND AVAILABILITY: $5 to $179,000.

CONTACT: Emergency and Indemnity Programs Division, Agricultural Stabilization and Conservation Service, Department of Agriculture, P.O. Box 2415, Washington, D.C. 20013. (202) 447-5237.

BEEKEEPER INDEMNITY PAYMENTS

OBJECTIVES: To indemnify beekeepers who through no fault of their own have suffered losses of honey bees as a result of utilization of economic poisons near or adjacent to the property on which the bee hives were located.

TYPES OF ASSISTANCE: Direct payments with unrestricted use.

FINANCIAL ASSISTANCE AND AVAILABILITY: $7.50 to $125,000.

CONTACT: Emergency and Indemnity Programs Division, Agricultural Stabilization and Conservation Service, Department of Agriculture, P.O. Box 2415, Washington, D.C. 20013. (202) 447-5237.

WATER BANK PROGRAM
   OBJECTIVES: To conserve surface waters; preserve and improve migra-
      tory waterfowl habitat and wildlife resources; and secure other
      environmental benefits.
   TYPES OF ASSISTANCE: Project grants; advisory services and
      counseling.
   FINANCIAL ASSISTANCE AND AVAILABILITY: From $4 to $55 per
      acre.
   CONTACT: Conservation and Environmental Protection Division, Agri-
      cultural Stabilization and Conservation Service, Department of Agricul-
      ture, P.O. Box 2415, Washington, D.C. 20013. (202) 447-5237.

AGRICULTURAL CONSERVATION PROGRAM
   OBJECTIVES: Control of erosion and sedimentation, voluntary com-
      pliance with Federal and State requirements to solve point and non-point
      source pollution, priorities in the National Environmental Policy Act,
      improvement of water quality, and assurance of a continued supply of
      necessary food and fiber for a strong and healthy people and economy.
      The program will be directed toward the solution of critical soil, water,
      woodland and pollution abatement problems on farms and ranches.
   TYPES OF ASSISTANCE: Project grants.
   FINANCIAL ASSISTANCE AND AVAILABILITY: Individual agree-
      ment $3 to $3,500. Pooling agreement $3 to $10,000.
   CONTACT: Conservation and Environmental Protection Division, Agri-
      cultural Stabilization and Conservation Service, Department of Agricul-
      ture, P.O. Box 2415, Washington, D.C. 20013. (202) 447-5237.

FORESTRY INCENTIVES PROGRAM
   OBJECTIVES: To increase the supply of timber primarily to meet
      demands for construction materials through a combination of public and
      private investments on the most productive sites on eligible individual or
      consolidated ownerships of efficient size and operation.
   TYPES OF ASSISTANCE: Project grants.
   FINANCIAL ASSISTANCE AND AVAILABILITY: $1 to $10,000 per
      year.
   CONTACT: Conservation and Environmental Protection Division, Agri-
      cultural Stabilization and Conservation Service, Department of Agricul-
      ture, P.O. Box 2415, Washington, D.C. 20013. (202) 447-5237.

RICE PRODUCTION STABILIZATION
   OBJECTIVES: To provide the production needed to meet domestic and
      foreign demand, to protect income for farmers and to assure adequate
      supplies at fair and reasonable prices.
   TYPES OF ASSISTANCE: Direct payments with unrestricted use.
   FINANCIAL ASSISTANCE AND AVAILABILITY: $3 to $50,000 per
      person for 1979 crop excluding disaster payments.

CONTACT: Production Adjustment Division, Agricultural Stabilization and Conservation Service, Department of Agriculture, P.O. Box 2415, Washington, D.C. 20013. (202) 447-5237.

EMERGENCY FEED PROGRAM
OBJECTIVES: To assist in the preservation and maintenance of livestock in any area of the United States where because of flood, drought, fire, hurricane, earthquake, storm, or other natural disaster, it is determined that an emergency exists.
TYPES OF ASSISTANCE: Direct payments with unrestricted use.
FINANCIAL ASSISTANCE AND AVAILABILITY: $3 to $100,000.
CONTACT: Emergency and Indemnity Programs Division, Agricultural Stabilization and Conservation Service, Department of Agriculture, P.O. Box 2415, Washington, D.C. 20013. (202) 447-5237.

GRAIN RESERVE PROGRAM
OBJECTIVES: To insulate sufficient quantities of grain from the market to increase price to farmers. To improve and stabilize farm income and to assist farmers in the orderly marketing of their crops.
TYPES OF ASSISTANCE: Direct payments with unrestricted use.
FINANCIAL ASSISTANCE AND AVAILABILITY: $25 to $50,000.
CONTACT: Price Support and Loan Division, Agricultural Stabilization and Conservation Service, Department of Agriculture, P.O. Box 2415, Washington, D.C. 20013. (202) 447-5237.

BUREAU OF INDIAN AFFAIRS

INDIAN BUSINESS ENTERPRISE DEVELOPMENT
OBJECTIVES: To create both jobs and raise income levels for Indians; and to involve Indians more deeply in management and ownership of businesses.
TYPES OF ASSISTANCE: Direct payments for specified use; advisory services and counseling; dissemination of technical information.
FINANCIAL ASSISTANCE AND AVAILABILITY: Technical assistance program—feasibility studies, marketing surveys, management audits, planning assistance, etc.
CONTACT: Chief, Indian Business Enterprise Division, Bureau of Indian Affairs, Main Interior Building, 18th and E Sts., N.W., Room 4543, Washington, D.C. 20240. (202) 655-4000.

INDIAN LOANS—ECONOMIC DEVELOPMENT
OBJECTIVES: To provide assistance to Indians, Alaska natives, tribes, and Indian organizations to obtain financing from private and governmental sources which serve other citizens. When otherwise unavailable, financial assistance through the Bureau is provided eligible applicants for any purpose that will promote the economic development of a Federal Indian Reservation.

TYPES OF ASSISTANCE: Project grants, direct loans, guaranteed/insured loans; provision of specialized services.

FINANCIAL ASSISTANCE AND AVAILABILITY: $100 to over $1,000,000.

CONTACT: Director, Office of Tribal Resources Development, Bureau of Indian Affairs, 18th and C Streets, N.W., Rm. 4650, Washington, D.C. 20245. (202) 655-4000.

COMMODITY CREDIT CORPORATION

AGRICULTURAL FUNDING

OBJECTIVES: To provide non-recourse loans on commodities stored on the farm or in commercial warehouses in order to provide price support and enable farmers to carry out an orderly marketing program. In addition, funding is available to expand or build farm storage facilities, or to buy drying equipment for use with stored commodities.

TYPES OF ASSISTANCE: Direct loans.

CONTACT: Commodity Credit Corporation, U.S. Department of Agriculture, Independence Avenue between 12th & 14th Street, S.W., Washington, D.C. 20003. (202) 447-7583.

ECONOMIC DEVELOPMENT ADMINISTRATION

ECONOMIC DEVELOPMENT–BUSINESS DEVELOPMENT ASSISTANCE

OBJECTIVES: To sustain industrial and commercial viability in designated areas by providing financial assistance to businesses that create or retain permanent jobs, expand or establish plans in redevelopment areas for projects where financial assistance is not available from other sources, on terms and conditions that would permit accomplishment of the project and further economic development in the area.

TYPES OF ASSISTANCE: Direct loans, guaranteed/insured loans.

FINANCIAL ASSISTANCE AND AVAILABILITY: $260,000 to $5,200,000.

CONTACT: Office of Private Investment, Economic Development Administration, Department of Commerce, Washington, D.C. 20230. (202) 377-2000.

TRADE ADJUSTMENT ASSISTANCE

OBJECTIVES: To provide trade adjustment assistance to firms, business and industry associations and communities adversely affected by increased imports.

TYPES OF ASSISTANCE: Direct loans; guaranteed/insured loans.

FINANCIAL ASSISTANCE AND AVAILABILITY: Up to $3 million.

CONTACT: Office of Private Investment, Economic Development Administration, Department of Commerce, Washington, D.C. 20230. (202) 377-2000.

DEPARTMENT OF ENERGY

RESEARCH AND DEVELOPMENT IN ENERGY CONSERVATION
OBJECTIVES: To provide financial support for basic and applied research and development undertaken to enhance present technology and develop new knowledge and procedures in the field of energy conservation.
TYPES OF ASSISTANCE: Project grants (contracts).
FINANCIAL ASSISTANCE AND AVAILABILITY: No limitation.
CONTACT: Division of Procurement, Department of Energy, Washington, D.C. 20585. (202) 252-5000.

ENERGY-RELATED INVENTIONS
OBJECTIVES: To encourage innovation in developing non-nuclear energy technology by providing assistance to individual inventors and small business research and development companies in the development of promising energy-related inventions.
TYPES OF ASSISTANCE: Project grants; use of property, facilities and equipment; advisory services and counseling; dissemination of technical information.
FINANCIAL ASSISTANCE AND AVAILABILITY: Grant awards average $67,000.
CONTACT: Department of Energy, Inventors' Program, Division of Business Programs, Washington, D.C. 20585. (202) 252-6260.

RESEARCH AND DEVELOPMENT—FISSION, FOSSIL, SOLAR, GEOTHERMAL, ELECTRIC AND STORAGE SYSTEMS, MAGNETIC FUSION
OBJECTIVES: To assure the continued conduct of research and development in areas pertinent to the acquisition of an expanded fund of knowledge in Energy Technology matters.
TYPES OF ASSISTANCE: Project grants; direct payments for specified use; research contract.
FINANCIAL ASSISTANCE AND AVAILABILITY: No limitations.
CONTACT: U.S. Department of Energy, Washington, D.C. 20585. (202) 376-4916.

BASIC ENERGY SCIENCES, HIGH ENERGY AND NUCLEAR PHYSICS, AND ADVANCED TECHNOLOGY AND ASSESSMENT PROJECTS
OBJECTIVES: To provide financial support for fundamental research in the basic sciences and advanced technology projects and assessments in fields related to energy.
TYPES OF ASSISTANCE: Project grants (contracts).
FINANCIAL ASSISTANCE AND AVAILABILITY: No limitations.
CONTACT: U.S. Department of Energy, Washington, D.C. 20585. (202) 376-1699.

ELECTRIC AND HYBRID VEHICLE LOAN GUARANTEES

OBJECTIVES: To accelerate the development of electric and hybrid vehicles for introduction into the nation's transportation fleet by encouraging and assisting qualified borrowers; minimizing a lender's financial risk to encourage the flow of credit; and developing normal borrower-lender relationships.

TYPES OF ASSISTANCE: Guaranteed/insured loans.

FINANCIAL ASSISTANCE AND AVAILABILITY: Up to $3 million.

CONTACT: Electric and Hybrid Vehicles Division, Office of Transportation Programs, Department of Energy, Washington, D.C. 20585. (202) 252-5000.

AMERICAN INDIAN ENERGY PRODUCTION AND EFFICIENCY

OBJECTIVES: To stimulate energy production and efficiency among American Indians.

TYPES OF ASSISTANCE: Grants.

FINANCIAL ASSISTANCE AND AVAILABILITY: Up to $70,000.

CONTACT: Department of Energy, 1000 Independence Avenue, S.W., Washington, D.C. 20585. (202) 252-5000.

BIOMASS LOAN GUARANTEES

OBJECTIVES: To accelerate the commercialization of biomass energy systems for production and conversion of biomass to useable energy forms to reduce the dependence of the United States on imported petroleum and natural gas.

TYPES OF ASSISTANCE: Guaranteed loans.

FINANCIAL ASSISTANCE AND AVAILABILITY: N/A.

CONTACT: Biomass Energy Systems Division, Department of Energy, Washington, D.C. 20585. (202) 376-5000.

APPROPRIATE ENERGY TECHNOLOGY

OBJECTIVES: To encourage research and development of energy related small scale technologies.

TYPES OF ASSISTANCE: Grants.

FINANCIAL ASSISTANCE AND AVAILABILITY: Up to $50,000.

CONTACT: Inventions and Small Scale Technologies, Department of Energy, Washington, D.C. 20585. (202) 252-9104.

COAL LOAN GUARANTEES

OBJECTIVES: To encourage and provide assistance to small and medium sized coal producing companies so as to increase production of underground low sulfur coal and to promote competition within the coal industry.

TYPES OF ASSISTANCE: Guaranteed/insured loans.

FINANCIAL ASSISTANCE AND AVAILABILITY: Up to $30 million.

CONTACT: Office of Coal Loan Programs, Department of Energy, 1200 Washington, D.C. 20585. (202) 252-5000.

GEOTHERMAL LOAN GUARANTEES

OBJECTIVES: To accelerate the commercial development and utilization of geothermal energy by minimizing a lender's risk to assure the flow of credit for geothermal projects; enhance competition; encouraging new entrants into the geothermal marketplace; developing normal borrower-lender relationships; and demonstrating the commercial viability of several projects.

TYPES OF ASSISTANCE: Guaranteed/insured loans.

FINANCIAL ASSISTANCE AND AVAILABILITY: Up to $200 million.

CONTACT: Geothermal Loan Guaranty Program, Department of Energy, Washington, D.C. 20585. (202) 252-5000.

EXPORT-IMPORT BANK

INSURANCE PROGRAM

OBJECTIVES: To authorize the Foreign Credit Insurance Association (FCIA) to issue policies covering commercial and/or political risks on short and medium term credit extended by U.S. exporters to their overseas customers.

TYPES OF ASSISTANCE: Insurance.

CONTACT: Export-Import Bank, 811 Vermont Avenue, N.W., Washington, D.C. 20005. (202) 566-2117.

GUARANTEE PROGRAM

OBJECTIVES: Provides guarantees directly to U.S. firms covering commercial and political risks involved in consignment, or exhibition of U.S. goods in foreign markets.

TYPES OF ASSISTANCE: Guarantees.

CONTACT: Export-Import Bank, 811 Vermont Avenue, N.W., Washington, D.C. 20005. (202) 566-2117.

LOAN PROGRAM

OBJECTIVES: To provide direct loans to overseas buyers of U.S. goods and services, enabling them to pay cash to the U.S. exporters.

TYPES OF ASSISTANCE: Direct loans.

CONTACT: Export-Import Bank, 811 Vermont Avenue, N.W., Washington, D.C. 20005. (202) 566-2117.

FARM CREDIT ADMINISTRATION

This agency does not lend directly to farmers, but provides funds to federal land banks and production credit associations for relending purposes to the farm community. The objectives of this agency is to

provide long term mortgage credit to purchase, enlarge, or to improve
farms and to refinance debts. In addition, short and intermediate term
credit is made available for farm production purposes. For more
information contact:

Farm Credit Administration
490 L'Enfant Plaza West, S.W.
Washington, D.C. 20024
(202) 755-2195

FARMERS HOME ADMINISTRATION

EMERGENCY LOANS
OBJECTIVES: To assist farmers, ranchers and aquaculture operators with
loans to cover losses resulting from a major and/or natural disasters, for
annual farm operating expenses, and for other essential needs necessary
to return the disaster victims' farming operation(s) to a financially sound
basis in order that they will be able to return to local sources of credit as
soon as possible.
TYPES OF ASSISTANCE: Guaranteed/insured loans.
FINANCIAL ASSISTANCE AND AVAILABILITY: $500 to $6,400,000.
CONTACT: Administrator, Farmers Home Administration, Department of
Agriculture, Washington, D.C. 20250. (202) 447-4323.

FARM LABOR HOUSING LOANS AND GRANTS
OBJECTIVES: To provide decent, safe and sanitary low-rent housing and
related facilities for domestic farm laborers.
TYPES OF ASSISTANCE: Project grants; guaranteed/insured loans.
FINANCIAL ASSISTANCE AND AVAILABILITY: Initial grants
$22,750 to $1,760,000. Initial loans to individuals $3,000 to $50,000.
Initial loans to organizations $130,000 to $1,978,000.
CONTACT: Administrator, Farmers Home Administration, Department of
Agriculture, Washington, D.C. 20250. (202) 447-4323.

FARM OPERATING LOANS
OBJECTIVES: To enable operators of not larger than family farms
(primarily limited resource operators, new operators and low income
operators), through the extension of credit and supervisory assistance, to
make efficient use of their land, labor, and other resources. Youth loans
enable rural youths to establish and operate modest income-producing
farm or nonfarm projects. Projects are educational and practical and
provide the youth an opportunity to learn basic economic and credit
principles.
TYPES OF ASSISTANCE: guarantee/insured loans.
FINANCIAL ASSISTANCE AND AVAILABILITY: Insured loans up to
$100,000; guaranteed loans up to $200,000.

CONTACT: Director, Production Loan Division, Farmers Home Administration, Department of Agriculture, Washington, D.C. 20250. (202) 447-4323.

FARM OWNERSHIP LOANS

OBJECTIVES: To assist eligible farmers and ranchers, including cooperatives, partnerships and corporations, through the extension of credit and supervisory assistance, to become owner-operators of not larger than family farms; to make efficient use of the land, labor, and other resources; to carry on sound and successful operations on the farm, and afford the family, cooperative, partnership or corporation an opportunity to have a reasonable standard of living. Farm ownership loans are also available to eligible applicants, including individuals, corporations, cooperatives, or partnership, with limited incomes and resources who are unable to pay the regular interest rate and have special problems such as undeveloped managerial ability. Due to the complex nature of the problem, special help and supervisory assistance is needed.

TYPES OF ASSISTANCE: Guaranteed/insured loans.

FINANCIAL ASSISTANCE AND AVAILABILITY: $16,000 to $200,000.

CONTACT: Administrator, Farmers Home Administration, Department of Agriculture, Washington, D.C. 20250. (202) 447-4323.

GRAZING ASSOCIATION LOANS

OBJECTIVES: To increase the income of farm families and those who reside in rural areas and to readjust the use of land so that each acre is used for a purpose which will better serve the community.

TYPES OF ASSISTANCE: Guaranteed/insured loans.

FINANCIAL ASSISTANCE AND AVAILABILITY: $44,300 to $1,029,900.

CONTACT: Administrator, Farmers Home Administration, Department of Agriculture, Washington, D.C. 20250. (202) 447-4323.

IRRIGATION, DRAINAGE, AND OTHER SOIL AND WATER CONSERVATION LOANS

OBJECTIVES: To increase the income of farm families and other rural residents and to readjust the use of land so that each acre is used for a purpose which will better serve the community.

TYPES OF ASSISTANCE: Guaranteed/insured loans.

FINANCIAL ASSISTANCE AND AVAILABILITY: $32,000 to $612,000.

CONTACT: Administrator, Farmers Home Administration, Department of Agriculture, Washington, D.C. 20250. (202) 447-7967.

SOIL AND WATER LOANS

OBJECTIVES: To facilitate improvement, protection, and proper use of farmland by providing adequate financing and supervisory assistance for soil conservation; water development, conservation and use; forestation; drainage of farmland; the establishment and improvement of permanent pasture; develop pollution abatement and control facilities on farms; and related measures.

TYPES OF ASSISTANCE: Guaranteed/insured loans.

FINANCIAL ASSISTANCE AND AVAILABILITY: $3,300 to $100,000.

CONTACT: Administrator, Farmers Home Administration, Department of Agriculture, Washington, D.C. 20250. (202) 447-7967.

INDIAN TRIBES AND TRIBAL CORPORATION LOANS

OBJECTIVES: To enable tribes and tribal corporations to mortgage lands as security for loans from the Farmers Home Administration to buy additional land within the reservation.

TYPES OF ASSISTANCE: Guaranteed/insured loans.

FINANCIAL ASSISTANCE AND AVAILABILITY: $260,000 to $7,000,000.

CONTACT: Administrator, Farmers Home Administration, Department of Agriculture, Washington, D.C. 20250. (202) 447-7967.

BUSINESS AND INDUSTRIAL LOANS

OBJECTIVES: To assist public, private, or cooperative organizations organized for profit or nonprofit, Indian tribes or individuals in rural areas to obtain quality loans for the purpose of improving, developing or financing business, industry, and employment and improving the economic and environmental climate in rural communities including pollution abatement and control, and the conservation, development, and utilization of water for aquaculture purposes.

TYPES OF ASSISTANCE: Guaranteed/insured loans.

FINANCIAL ASSISTANCE AND AVAILABILITY: $11,000 to $33,000,000.

CONTACT: Administrator, Farmers Home Administration, Department of Agriculture, Washington, D.C. 20250. (202) 447-4323.

EMERGENCY LIVESTOCK LOANS

OBJECTIVES: To make more credit available during the period authorized by Public Law 93-357 as amended in the form of loans guaranteed by FmHA to bona fide farmers and ranchers who are primarily and directly engaged in agricultural production and who have substantial livestock operations, in order that they may continue their normal farming or ranching operations.

TYPES OF ASSISTANCE: Guaranteed/insured loans.

FINANCIAL ASSISTANCE AND AVAILABILITY: Up to $350,000.

CONTACT: Administrator, Farmers Home Administration, Department of Agriculture, Washington, D.C. 20250. (202) 447-4323.

ECONOMIC EMERGENCY LOANS

OBJECTIVES: To make adequate financial assistance available in the form of loans insured or guaranteed for bona fide farmers, ranchers and aquaculture operators who are primarily and directly engaged in agricultural production. This is done so that they may continue their normal farming or ranching operations during the economic emergency which has caused a lack of agricultural credit due to national or area wide economic stress. Examples of these are a general tightening of agricultural credit or an unfavorable relationship between production costs and prices received for agricultural commodities.

TYPES OF ASSISTANCE: Guaranteed/insured loans.

FINANCIAL ASSISTANCE AND AVAILABILITY: Up to $200,000.

CONTACT: Administrator, Farmers Home Administration, Department of Agriculture, Washington, D.C. 20250. (202) 447-4323.

FEDERAL RESERVE BOARD

DEFENSE PRODUCTION PROGRAM

OBJECTIVES: To facilitate and expedite the financing of persons or firms having contracts or engaged in operations deemed necessary for National Defense.

TYPES OF ASSISTANCE: Loan guarantees.

CONTACT: Federal Reserve Board, Constitution Avenue between 20th & 21st Street, N.W., Washington, D.C. 20001. (202) 452-3000.

U.S. GEOLOGICAL SURVEY

MINERALS DISCOVERY LOAN PROGRAM

OBJECTIVES: To encourage exploration for specified minerals within the United States, its territories, and possessions.

TYPES OF ASSISTANCE: Direct loans.

FINANCIAL ASSISTANCE AND AVAILABILITY: Up to $25,000.

CONTACT: Office of Minerals Exploration, Geological Survey, National Center, Mailstop 953, 12201 Sunrise Valley Drive, Reston, VA 22092. (703) 860-7000.

MARITIME ADMINISTRATION

CONSTRUCTION–DIFFERENTIAL SUBSIDIES

OBJECTIVES: To promote the development and maintenance of the U.S. Merchant Marine by granting financial aid to equalize cost of construction of a new ship in a U.S. shipyard with the cost of constructing the same ship in a foreign shipyard.

TYPES OF ASSISTANCE: Direct payments for specified use.

FINANCIAL ASSISTANCE AND AVAILABILITY: The average amount of subsidy per new ship in fiscal year 1977 was approximately $16,800,000. The subsidy ranged from under $5,000,000 to almost $40,000,000. The average subsidy per reconstruction in fiscal year 1977

was approximately $2,200,000; historically, subsidy for reconstruction has ranged from under $300,000 to almost $7,400,000.
CONTACT: Maritime Administration, Department of Transportation, 400 7th Street S.W., Washington, D.C. 20024. (202) 426-5812.

FEDERAL SHIP FINANCING GUARANTEES
OBJECTIVES: To promote construction and reconstruction of ships in the foreign and domestic commerce of the United States by providing government guarantees of obligations so as to make commercial credit more readily available.
TYPES OF ASSISTANCE: Guaranteed/insured loans.
FINANCIAL ASSISTANCE AND AVAILABILITY: $106,000 to $126,300,000.
CONTACT: Maritime Administration, Department of Transportation, 400 7th Street S.W., Washington, D.C. 20024. (202) 426-5812.

OPERATING–DIFFERENTIAL SUBSIDIES
OBJECTIVES: To promote development and maintenance of U.S. Merchant Marine by granting financial aid to equalize cost of operating a U.S. flag ship with cost of operating a competitive foreign flag ship.
TYPES OF ASSISTANCE: Direct payments for specified use.
FINANCIAL ASSISTANCE AND AVAILABILITY: Depending upon the type of service vessel and trade, the per day subsidy payments normally range from about $2,000 to $6,000 for general cargo and bulk services, exclusive of USSR bulk programs.
CONTACT: Maritime Administration, Department of Transportation, 400 7th Street S.W., Washington, D.C. 20024. (202) 426-5812.

CAPITAL CONSTRUCTION FUND
OBJECTIVES: To provide for replacement vessels, additional vessels or reconstructed vessels, built and documented under the laws of the United States for operation in the United States foreign, Great Lakes or noncontiguous domestic trades.
TYPES OF ASSISTANCE: Direct payments for specified use.
FINANCIAL ASSISTANCE AND AVAILABILITY: Applicant receives tax benefits for depositing assets in accordance with the program.
CONTACT: Maritime Administration, Department of Transportation, 400 7th Street S.W., Washington, D.C. 20240. (202) 426-5812.

NATIONAL OCEANIC AND ATMOSPHERIC ADMINISTRATION

FISHING VESSEL OBLIGATION GUARANTEES
OBJECTIVES: To provide government guarantees of private loans to upgrade the U.S. fishing fleet.
TYPES OF ASSISTANCE: Guaranteed/insured loans.
FINANCIAL ASSISTANCE AND AVAILABILITY: $15,000 to $1,500,000.

CONTACT: Chief, Financial Services Division, National Marine Fisheries Service, Department of Commerce, 3300 Whitehaven St. N.W., Washington, D.C. 20007. (202) 634-7295.

FISHERMEN'S CONTINGENCY FUND

OBJECTIVES: To compensate U.S. commercial fishermen for damage to or loss of fishing gear and resulting economic loss due to oil and gas related activities in any area of the Outer Continental Shelf.

TYPES OF ASSISTANCE: Direct payments.

FINANCIAL ASSISTANCE AND AVAILABILITY: Payments up to $3,500.

CONTACT: Chief, Financial Services Division, National Marine Fisheries Service, 3300 Whitehaven Street, N.W., Washington, D.C. 20007. (202) 634-7295.

FISHING VESSEL AND GEAR DAMAGE COMPENSATION FUND

OBJECTIVES: To compensate U.S. fishermen for the loss, damage, or destruction of their vessels by foreign or domestic fishing vessels and their gear, or by "acts of God."

TYPES OF ASSISTANCE: Direct payments.

FINANCIAL ASSISTANCE AND AVAILABILITY: Payments up to $7,000.

CONTACT: Chief, Financial Services Division, National Marine Fisheries Service, Department of Commerce, 3300 Whitehaven Street, N.W., Washington, D.C. 20007. (202) 634-7295.

FISHERIES DEVELOPMENT AND UTILIZATION RESEARCH AND DEVELOPMENT GRANTS AND COOPERATIVE AGREEMENTS PROGRAM

OBJECTIVES: To foster the development and strengthening of the fishing industry of the United States and increase the supply of wholesome, nutritious fish products available to consumers.

TYPES OF ASSISTANCE: Grants.

FINANCIAL ASSISTANCE AND AVAILABILITY: $5,000 to $2,500,000.

CONTACT: Office of Utilization And Development, National Marine Fisheries Service, National Oceanic and Atmospheric Administration, Department of Commerce, 3300 Whitehaven Street N.W., Washington, D.C. 20007. (202) 634-7259.

NATIONAL SCIENCE FOUNDATION

INTERGOVERNMENTAL PROGRAM

OBJECTIVES: To facilitate the integration of scientific and technical resources into the policy formulation, management support, and program operation activities in state and local governments.

TYPES OF ASSISTANCE: Project grants.

FINANCIAL ASSISTANCE AND AVAILABILITY: $10,000 to $250,000.

CONTACT: Director, Intergovernmental Program, Division of Intergovernmental Science and Public Technology, National Science Foundation, Washington, D.C. 20550. (202) 655-4000.

APPLIED SCIENCE AND RESEARCH APPLICATIONS

OBJECTIVES: To support research and related activities which contribute to the understanding and resolution of significant problems facing the nation. Areas of research include: integrated basic research; applied social and behavioral sciences; applied physical, mathematical, and biological sciences, and engineering; intergovernmental science and public technology; and problem-focused research applications (programs currently include earthquake hazards mitigation, alternative biological sources of materials, science and technology to aid the physically handicapped, and human nutrition.)

TYPES OF ASSISTANCE: Project grants; research contracts.

FINANCIAL ASSISTANCE AND AVAILABILITY: $1,000 to $800,000.

CONTACT: Programs and Resources Officer, National Science Foundation, 1800 G St., N.W., Washington, D.C. 20550. (202) 655-4000.

MATHEMATICAL AND PHYSICAL SCIENCES AND ENGINEERING

OBJECTIVES: To promote the progress of science and thereby insure the continued scientific strength of the nation; to increase the store of scientific knowledge and enhance understanding of major problems confronting the nation. Most of the research supported is basic in character, though work of an applied nature may be supported. The program includes support of research project grants in the following disciplines: physics, chemistry, mathematical sciences, engineering, materials research, and computer research. Support is also provided for research workshops, symposia and conferences, and for the purchase of scientific equipment. In addition, awards are made to encourage innovative engineering research by scientists recently awarded their Ph.D. degrees.

TYPES OF ASSISTANCE: Project grants.

FINANCIAL ASSISTANCE AND AVAILABILITY: $10,000 to $3,600,000.

CONTACT: Assistant Director, Directorate for Mathematical and Physical Sciences and Engineering, National Science Foundation, 1800 G St., N.W., Washington, D.C. 20550. (202) 357-7939.

ASTRONOMICAL, ATMOSPHERIC, EARTH AND OCEAN SCIENCES

OBJECTIVES: To promote the progress of science and thereby insure the continued scientific strength of the nation; to increase the store of scientific knowledge and enhance understanding of major problems confronting the nation. The program includes research project grants for the support of basic research in astronomical, atmospheric, earth and ocean sciences, and in appropriate disciplines in the Antarctic and Arctic, that will increase our knowledge of the physical environment, both on earth and in space. General objectives are to support basic research leading to new knowledge in astronomy and the atmospheric sciences over the entire spectrum of physical phenomena; a better understanding of the physical and chemical makeup of the earth and its geologic history; and to increase insight into the oceans, their composition, structure, behavior, and resources.

TYPES OF ASSISTANCE: Project grants, research contracts.

FINANCIAL ASSISTANCE AND AVAILABILITY: Undetermined.

CONTACT: Assistant Director, Directorate for Mathematical and Physical Sciences and Engineering, National Science Foundation, 1800 G St., N.W., Washington, D.C. 20550. (202) 357-9715.

NEW COMMUNITY DEVELOPMENT CORPORATION
DEPARTMENT OF HOUSING AND URBAN DEVELOPMENT

NEW COMMUNITIES—LOAN GUARANTEES

OBJECTIVES: To encourage the development of well-planned, diversified, and economically sound new communities, including major additions to existing communities.

TYPES OF ASSISTANCE: Guaranteed/insured loans.

FINANCIAL ASSISTANCE AND AVAILABILITY: $7,500,000 to $50,000,000.

CONTACT: General Manager, New Community Development Corporation, Department of Housing and Urban Development, 451 Seventh Street, S.W., Washington, D.C. 20410. (202) 755-7920.

OFFICE OF HUMAN DEVELOPMENT SERVICES
DEPARTMENT OF HEALTH, AND HUMAN SERVICES

NATIVE AMERICAN PROGRAMS

OBJECTIVES: To promote the goal of economic and social self-sufficiency for American Indians, Native Hawaiians, and Alaskan Natives.

TYPES OF ASSISTANCE: Project grants (contracts).

FINANCIAL ASSISTANCE AND AVAILABILITY: $40,000 to $5,000,000 for tribal grants, and from $40,000 to $200,000 for urban grants.

CONTACT: Administration for Native Americans, Department of Health, Education and Welfare, 300 Independence Avenue, S.W., Washington, D.C. 20201. (202) 245-7776.

OVERSEAS PRIVATE INVESTMENT CORPORATION

FOREIGN INVESTMENT GUARANTEES
OBJECTIVES: To guarantee loans and other investments made by eligible U.S. investors in developing friendly countries and areas.
TYPES OF ASSISTANCE: Guaranteed/insured loans.
FINANCIAL ASSISTANCE AND AVAILABILITY: Undetermined.
CONTACT: Information Officer, Overseas Private Investment Corporation, Washington, D.C. 20527. (202) 653-2920.

FOREIGN INVESTMENT INSURANCE
OBJECTIVES: To insure investments of eligible U.S. investors in developing friendly countries and areas, against the risks of inconvertibility, expropriation, and war, revolution and insurrection.
TYPES OF ASSISTANCE: Insurance.
FINANCIAL ASSISTANCE AND AVAILABILITY: $4,000 to $50,000,000.
CONTACT: Information Officer, Overseas Private Investment Corporation, Washington, D.C. 20527. (202) 653-2920.

PRE-INVESTMENT ASSISTANCE
OBJECTIVES: To initiate and support through financial participation, the identification, assessment, surveying and promotion of private investment opportunities.
TYPES OF ASSISTANCE: Direct payments for specified use.
FINANCIAL ASSISTANCE AND AVAILABILITY: $10,000 to $300,000.
CONTACT: Information Officer, Overseas Private Investment Corporation, Washington, D.C. 20527. (202) 653-2920.

DIRECT INVESTMENT LOANS
OBJECTIVES: To make loans for projects in developing countries.
TYPES OF ASSISTANCE: Direct loans.
FINANCIAL ASSISTANCE AND AVAILABILITY: $325,000 to $2,500,000.
CONTACT: Information Officer, Overseas Private Investment Corporation, Washington, D.C. 20527. (202) 653-2920.

SMALL BUSINESS ADMINISTRATION

DISPLACED BUSINESS LOANS
OBJECTIVES: To assist small businesses to continue in business, purchase a business, or establish a new business if substantial economic injury has been suffered as a result of displacement by, or location in or

near a program or project involving Federal government funds or a program or project by a State or local government or public service entity having authority to exercise the right of eminent domain on such program or project.

TYPES OF ASSISTANCE: Direct loans; guaranteed/insured loans.

FINANCIAL ASSISTANCE AND AVAILABILITY: Direct loans: $5,000 to $904,000. Guaranteed loans: Up to $86,000.

CONTACT: Director, Office of Financing, Small Business Administration, 1441 L Street, N.W., Washington, D.C. 20416. (202) 653-6570.

ECONOMIC INJURY DISASTER LOANS

OBJECTIVES: To assist business concerns suffering economic injury as a result of certain Presidential, SBA, and Department of Agriculture disaster designations.

TYPES OF ASSISTANCE: Direct loans; guaranteed/insured loans (immediate participation loans).

FINANCIAL ASSISTANCE AND AVAILABILITY: $250,000 to $1,083,200.

CONTACT: Office of Disaster Operations, Small Business Administration, 1441 L Street, N.W., Washington, D.C. 20416. (202) 653-6570.

ECONOMIC OPPORTUNITY LOANS FOR SMALL BUSINESS

OBJECTIVES: To provide loans up to $100,000, with maximum maturity of 15 years, to small businesses owned by low-income or economically disadvantaged persons.

TYPES OF ASSISTANCE: Direct loans; guaranteed/insured loans; advisory services and counseling.

FINANCIAL ASSISTANCE AND AVAILABILITY: Direct loans: $1,000 to $100,000; $30,019. Guaranteed loans: $2,250 to $315,600; $33,377.

CONTACT: Director, Office of Financing, Small Business Administration, 1441 L Street, N.W., Washington, D.C. 20416. (202) 653-6570.

PHYSICAL DISASTER LOANS

OBJECTIVES: To provide loans to restore, as nearly as possible, the victims of physical type disasters to predisaster condition.

TYPES OF ASSISTANCE: Direct loans; guaranteed, and immediate participation loans. Guaranteed/insured loans (immediate participation loans).

FINANCIAL ASSISTANCE AND AVAILABILITY: Direct home loans $55,000 limit plus $50,000 additional in some special cases to refinance existing liens. Direct business loans $500,000. Additional amounts are available as guaranteed loans made by financial institutions.

CONTACT: Office of Disaster Operations, Small Business Administration, 1441 L Street, N.W., Washington, D.C. 20416. (202) 653-6570.

PRODUCT DISASTER LOANS
OBJECTIVES: To assist small business concerns which have suffered economic injury as a result of inability to market a product for human consumption because of finding of toxicity in the product.
TYPES OF ASSISTANCE: Direct loans; guaranteed/insured loans (guaranteed and immediate participation loans).
FINANCIAL ASSISTANCE AND AVAILABILITY: $3,700 to $268,800; $43,630.
CONTACT: Office of Disaster Operations, Small Business Administration, 1441 L Street, N.W., Washington, D.C. 20416. (202) 653-6570.

SMALL BUSINESS LOANS
OBJECTIVES: To aid small businesses which are unable to obtain financing in the private credit marketplace, including agricultural enterprises.
TYPES OF ASSISTANCE: Direct loans; guaranteed/insured loans.
FINANCIAL ASSISTANCE AND AVAILABILITY: $1,000 to $350,000; $54,782. Guaranteed loans; $1,800 to $500,000; $113,589.
CONTACT: Director, Office of Financing, Small Business Administration, 1441 L Street, N.W., Washington, D.C. 20416. (202) 653-6570.

MINE SAFETY AND HEALTH LOANS
OBJECTIVES: To assist small coal mine operators in complying with Federal Safety and Health standards.
TYPES OF ASSISTANCE: Direct loans; guaranteed/insured loans.
FINANCIAL ASSISTANCE AND AVAILABILITY: Not applicable.
CONTACT: Director, Office of Financing, Small Business Administration, 1441 L Street, N.W., Washington, D.C. 20416. (202) 653-6570.

BOND GUARANTEES FOR SURETY COMPANIES
OBJECTIVES: To encourage the commercial surety market to make surety bonds more available to small contractors unable for various reasons to obtain a bond without a guarantee.
TYPES OF ASSISTANCE: Guaranteed/insured loans.
FINANCIAL ASSISTANCE AND AVAILABILITY: Size range of contracts awarded and bonded, $2,000 to $1,000,000; Approximately $71,000.
CONTACT: Director, Office of Special Guarantees, Small Business Administration, 1441 L St., N.W., 8th Floor, Washington, D.C. 20416. (202) 563-6570.

CONSUMER PROTECTION LOANS
OBJECTIVES: To assist small business concerns which suffer substantial economic injury caused by compliance with standards established under Egg Products Inspection Act of 1970, the Wholesome Poultry and

Poultry Products Act of 1968, or the Wholesome Meat Act of 1967, or any other regulation or order of a duly authorized Federal, State, Regional or local agency issued in conformity with such Federal law, designed to protect the consumer.
TYPES OF ASSISTANCE: Direct loans; guaranteed/insured loans.
FINANCIAL ASSISTANCE AND AVAILABILITY: $70,635 to $165,000; $117,067.
CONTACT: Director, Office of Financing, Small Business Administration, 1441 L Street, N.W., Washington, D.C. 20416. (202) 653-6570.

BASE CLOSING ECONOMIC INJURY LOANS
OBJECTIVES: To assist small business concerns subject to economic injury as the result of closing by the Federal Government of a major military installation under the Department of Defense, or as the result of a severe reduction in the scope and size of operation of such an installation.
TYPES OF ASSISTANCE: Direct loans; guaranteed/insured loans.
FINANCIAL ASSISTANCE AND AVAILABILITY: $6,000 to $500,000; $154,113.
CONTACT: Director, Office of Financing, Small Business Administration, 1441 L Street, N.W., Washington, D.C. 20416. (202) 653-6570.

HANDICAPPED ASSISTANCE LOANS
OBJECTIVES: To provide loans and loan guarantees for nonprofit sheltered workshops and other similar organizations to enable them to produce and provide marketable goods and services; and to assist in the establishment, acquisition, or operation of a small business owned by handicapped individuals.
TYPES OF ASSISTANCE: Direct loans; guaranteed/insured loans.
FINANCIAL ASSISTANCE AND AVAILABILITY: $500 to $350,000; $70,353, (direct); $15,000 to $346,500; $110,075, (guaranteed).
CONTACT: Director, Office of Financing, Small Business Administration, 1441 L Street, N.W., Washington, D.C. 20416. (202) 653-6570.

EMERGENCY ENERGY SHORTAGE ECONOMIC INJURY LOANS
OBJECTIVES: To assist small business concerns seriously and adversely affected by a shortage of fuel, electrical energy, energy-producing resources, or by a shortage of raw or processed materials resulting from such shortages.
TYPES OF ASSISTANCE: Direct loans; guaranteed/insured loans.
FINANCIAL ASSISTANCE AND AVAILABILITY: $1,000 to $500,000; $23,088.
CONTACT: Director, Office of Financing, Small Business Administration, 1441 L Street, N.W., Washington, D.C. 20416. (202) 653-6570.

STRATEGIC ARMS ECONOMIC INJURY LOANS
OBJECTIVES: To assist small businessmen subject to economic injury as a result of international strategic arms limitation treaties.

TYPES OF ASSISTANCE: Direct loans, guaranteed/insured loans.
FINANCIAL ASSISTANCE AND AVAILABILITY: Not calculated.
CONTACT: Director, Office of Financing, Small Business Administration,
1441 L Street, N.W., Washington, D.C. 20416. (202) 653-6570.

WATER POLLUTION CONTROL LOANS

OBJECTIVES: To assist small business concerns which are likely to suffer
substantial economic injury caused by adding to or altering their
equipment, facilities, or methods of operation to comply with standards
established by the Federal Water Pollution Control Act.
TYPES OF ASSISTANCE: Direct loans; guaranteed/insured loans.
FINANCIAL ASSISTANCE AND AVAILABILITY: $5,687 to $470,000;
$124,510.
CONTACT: Director, Office of Financing, Small Business Administration,
1441 L Street, N.W., Washington, D.C. 20416. (202) 653-6570.

AIR POLLUTION CONTROL LOANS

OBJECTIVES: To assist small business concerns subject to economic
injury as the result of meeting requirements of the Clean Air Act of
1970, or laws and regulations issued pursuant thereto.
TYPES OF ASSISTANCE: Direct loans; guaranteed/insured loans.
FINANCIAL ASSISTANCE AND AVAILABILITY: $35,000 to
$2,585,600; $408,608.
CONTACT: Director, Office of Financing, Small Business Administration,
1441 L Street, N.W., Washington, D.C. 20416. (202) 653-6570.

ECONOMIC DISLOCATION LOANS

OBJECTIVES: To assist those otherwise financially sound businesses in
the impacted regions or business sectors that will either become
insolvent or be unable to return quickly to their former level of
operations. Economic dislocation includes extraordinary, severe, and
temporary natural conditions or other economic dislocation as defined
by SBA.
TYPES OF ASSISTANCE: Direct loans; guaranteed/insured loans.
FINANCIAL ASSISTANCE AND AVAILABILITY: $3,900 to $100,000;
$55,403.
CONTACT: Director, Office of Financing, Small Business Administration,
1441 L Street, N.W., Washington, D.C. 20416. (202) 653-6570.

REGULATORY LOANS

OBJECTIVES: To assist any small business concern in effecting addition
to or alterations in its plant, facilities or methods of operation to meet
requirements imposed on such concern pursuant to any Federal law, any
State law enacted in conformity therewith, or any regulation or order of
a duly authorized Federal, State, regional or local agency issued in
conformity with such Federal law if substantial economic injury has
been suffered as a result of such order.
TYPES OF ASSISTANCE: Direct loans; guaranteed/insured loans (immediate or guaranty participation loans).

FINANCIAL ASSISTANCE AND AVAILABILITY: Information not yet available.

CONTACT: Director, Office of Disaster Loans, Small Business Administration, 1441 L Street, N.W., Washington, D.C. 20416. (202) 653-6570.

SMALL BUSINESS ENERGY LOANS

OBJECTIVES: To assist small business concerns to finance plant construction, expansion, conversion, or startup; and the acquisition of equipment facilities, machinery, supplies or materials to enable such concerns to manufacture, design, market, install or service specific energy measures.

TYPES OF ASSISTANCE: Direct loans; guaranteed/insured loans.

FINANCIAL ASSISTANCE AND AVAILABILITY: Information not yet available.

CONTACT: Office of Financing, Small Business Administration, 1441 L Street, N.W., Washington, D.C. 20416. (202) 653-6570.

SMALL BUSINESS POLLUTION CONTROL FINANCING GUARANTEE

OBJECTIVES: To help small businesses meet pollution control requirements and remain competitive.

TYPES OF ASSISTANCE: Guaranteed/insured loans (immediate and guaranty participation loans)

FINANCIAL ASSISTANCE AND AVAILABILITY: $5,000,000. Approximately $1,000,000.

CONTACT: Pollution Control Financing Division, Office of Special Guarantees, Small Business Administration, 1441 L Street, N.W., Washington, D.C. 20416. (202) 653-6570.

DISASTER ASSISTANCE TO NONAGRICULTURAL BUSINESSES (MAJOR SOURCE OF EMPLOYMENT)

OBJECTIVES: To enable a nonagricultural business that is a major source of employment in a major disaster area and which is no longer in substantial operation as a result of such disaster to resume operations in order to assist in restoring the economic viability of the disaster area.

TYPES OF ASSISTANCE: Direct loans; guaranteed/insured loans (immediate or guaranty participation loans).

FINANCIAL ASSISTANCE AND AVAILABILITY: No dollar limit. Amount of supportable damage and/or injury.

CONTACT: Office of Disaster Operations, Small Business Administration, 1441 L Street, N.W., Washington, D.C. 20416. (202) 653-6570.

OCCUPATIONAL SAFETY AND HEALTH LOANS

OBJECTIVES: To assist small firms that are likely to suffer substantial economic injury caused by compliance with standards established by the Occupational Safety and Health Act of 1970.

TYPES OF ASSISTANCE: Guaranteed/insured loans (immediate or guaranty participation loans).

FINANCIAL ASSISTANCE AND AVAILABILITY: $2,000 to $1,200,000.

CONTACT: Office of Disaster Operations, Small Business Administration, 1441 L Street, N.W., Washington, D.C. 20416. (202) 653-6570.

APPENDICES

APPENDIX A

Dun & Bradstreet
99 Church Street
New York, New York 10007

KEY BUSINESS RATIOS

Retailing
Auto and home supplies
Children's and infants' wear stores
Clothing and furnishings, men's and boys'
Department stores
Discount stores
Discount stores, leased departments
Family clothing stores
Furniture stores
Gasoline service stations
Grocery stores
Hardware stores
Household appliance stores
Jewelry stores
Lumber and other building materials dealers
Miscellaneous general merchandise stores
Motor vehicle dealers
Paint, glass and wallpaper stores
Radio and television stores
Retail nurseries, lawn and garden supply dealers
Shoe stores
Variety stores
Women's ready-to-wear stores

Wholesaling
Air conditioning and refrigeration equipment and supplies
Automotive equipment
Beer, wine and alcoholic beverages

Chemicals and allied products
Clothing and accessories, women's and children's
Clothing and furnishings, men's and boys'
Commercial machines and equipment
Confectionery
Dairy products
Drugs, drug proprietaries, and sundries
Electrical appliances, TV and radio sets
Electrical apparatus and equipment
Electronic parts and equipment
Farm machinery and equipment
Footwear
Fresh fruits and vegetables
Furniture and home furnishings
Groceries, general line
Hardware
Industrial machinery and equipment
Lumber and construction materials
Meats and meat products
Metals and minerals
Paints, varnishes, and supplies
Paper and its products
Petroleum and petroleum products
Piece goods
Plumbing and heating equipment and supplies
Poultry and poultry products
Scrap and waste materials
Tires and tubes
Tobacco and its products

Manufacturing and Construction
Agricultural chemicals
Airplane parts and accessories
Bakery products
Blast furnaces, steel works, and rolling mills
Blouses and waists
Books, publishing and printing
Broad woven fabrics, cotton
Canned and preserved fruits and vegetables
Commercial printing except lithographic
Communication equipment
Concrete, gypsum and plaster products
Confectionery and related products
Construction, mining and handling machinery and equipment
Converted paper and paperboard products
Cutlery, hand tools and general hardware
Dairy products
Dresses

Drugs
Electric lighting and wiring equipment
Electric transmission and distribution equipment
Electrical industrial apparatus
Electrical work
Electronic components and accessories
Engineering, laboratory and scientific instruments
Fabricated structural metal products
Farm machinery and equipment
Footwear
Fur goods
General building contractors
General industrial machinery and equipment
Grain mill products
Heating and plumbing equipment
Heavy construction, except highway and street
Hosiery
Household appliances
Industrial

COST OF DOING BUSINESS

Retailing
Apparel and accessories
Automotive dealers
Building materials, hardware, and farm equipment
Drug and proprietary stores
Eating and drinking places
Food stores
Furniture and home furnishings
Gasoline service stations
General merchandise
Liquor stores

Wholesaling
Alcoholic beverages
Drugs
Dry goods
Electrical goods
Farm products
Groceries
Hardware, plumbing and heating equipment
Lumber and construction materials
Machinery
Metals and minerals
Motor vehicles
Paper and its products
Petroleum and its products

Manufacturing
Apparel
Chemicals and allied products
Electrical supplies and equipment
Fabricated metal products
Food products (bakery products, beverage industries, canned goods, dairy
    products, grain mill products, meats, and sugar)
Furniture and fixtures
Leather and its products
Lumber and wood products
Machinery
Motor vehicles and equipment
Ordnance, except guided missiles
Paper and allied products
Petroleum refining
Primary metal industries
Printing and publishing
Rubber and miscellaneous plastics products
Scientific industries
Stone, clay, and glass products
Textile mill products
Tobacco
Transportation equipment

Services, Transportation and Communications
Advertising
Air transportation
Automobile parking, repair and service
Business services
Electrical companies and systems
Hotels
Medical services
Motion picture production
Motion picture theaters
Personal services
Pipeline transportation
Radio and television broadcasting
Railroad transportation
Repair services
Telephone and telegraph services
Trucking and warehousing
Water supply and other sanitary services
Water transportation

Finance, Insurance, and Real Estate

Agriculture and Mining

Robert Morris Associates
Philadelphia National Bank Building
Philadelphia, Pennsylvania 19107

Manufacturing
Advertising displays and devices
Apparel and other finished fabric products:
  Canvas products
  Children's clothing
  Curtains and draperies
  Men's, youths' and boys' suits, coats and overcoats
  Women's dresses
  Women's suits, skirts, sportswear and coats
  Women's undergarments and sleepwear
Beverages:
  Flavoring extracts and syrups
  Malt liquors
  Wines, distilled liquor and liqueurs
Caskets and burial supplies
Chemicals and allied products:
  Drugs and medicines
  Fertilizers
  Industrial chemicals
  Paint, varnish and lacquer
  Perfumes, cosmetics and other toilet preparations
  Plastic materials and synthetic resins
  Soap, detergents and cleaning preparations
Food and kindred products:
  Bread and other bakery products
  Candy and dried fruits and vegetables
  Dairy products
  Flour and other grain mill products
  Frozen fruits, fruit juices, vegetables, and specialties
  Meat packing
  Prepared feeds for animals and poultry
  Vegetable oils
Furniture and fixtures:
  Mattresses and bedsprings
  Metal household furniture
  Store, office, bar and restaurant fixtures
  Wood furniture—except upholstered
  Wood furniture—upholstered

Jewelry, precious metals
House furnishings
Leather and leather products:
    Footwear
    Furs
    Hats
    Men's and boys' sport clothing
    Men's work clothing
    Men's, youths' and boys' separate trousers
    Men's, youths' and boys' shirts, collars and nightwear
    Luggage and special leather products
Tanning, currying, and finishing
Lumber and wood products:
    Millwork
    Prefabricated wooden buildings and structural members
    Sawmills and planing mills
    Veneer, plywood, and hardwood
    Wooden boxes and containers
Machinery, equipment and supplies—electrical:
    Air conditioning
    Electronic components and accessories
    Equipment for public utilities and industrial use
Machinery, except electrical equipment:
    Ball and roller bearings
    Construction and mining machinery and equipment
    Farm machinery and equipment
    General industrial machinery and equipment
    Industrial and commercial refrigeration equipment and complete air conditioning units
    Machine shops—jobbing and repair
    Machine tools and metal working equipment
    Measuring, analyzing, and controlling instruments
    Oil field machinery and equipment
    Special dies and tools, die sets, jigs and fixtures
    Special industry machinery
Metal industries—primary:
    Iron and steel forgings
    Iron and steel foundries
    Non-ferrous foundries
Metal products—fabricated (except ordnance, machinery, and transportation equipment):
    Coating, engraving and allied services
    Cutlery, hand tools and general hardware
    Enameled iron, metal sanitary ware and plumbing supplies
    Fabricated plate ware
    Fabricated structural steel
    Heating equipment, except electric

Metal cans
Metal doors, sash, frames, molding and trim
Metal stampings
Miscellaneous fabricated wire products
Miscellaneous non-ferrous fabricated products
Screw machine products, bolts, nuts, screws, rivets and washers
Sheet metal work
Valves and pipe fittings, except plumbers' brass goods
Paper and allied products:
Envelopes, stationery and paper bags
Paperboard containers and boxes
Pulp, paper and paperboard
Printing, publishing and allied industries:
Book printing
Bookbinding and miscellaneous related work
Books: publishing
Commercial printing, lithographic
Newspapers: publishing and printing
Periodicals
Typesetting
Rubber and miscellaneous plastics products:
Miscellaneous plastics products
Rubber footwear and fabricated rubber products
Stone, clay and glass products:
Brick and structural clay tile
Concrete brick, block and other products
Minerals and earths, ground or otherwise treated
Pressed and blown glass and glassware
Ready-mixed concrete
Textile mill products:
Broad woven fabric—cotton, silk and synthetic
Broad woven fabric—woolens and worsteds
Dyeing and finishing
Hosiery—anklets—children's, men's and boys'
Hosiery—women's—full fashioned and seamless
Knitting—cloth, outerwear and underwear
Narrow fabrics and other smallwares
Yarn—cotton, silk and synthetic
Toys, amusement, sporting and athletic goods:
Games and toys, except dolls and children's vehicles
Sporting and athletic goods
Transportation equipment:
Aircraft parts (except electric)
Motor vehicle parts and accessories
Motor vehicles
Ship and boat building and repairing

Wholesaling
Automotive equipment and supplies:
   Automobiles and other motor vehicles
   Automotive equipment
   Tire and tubes
Beauty and barber supplies and equipment
Drugs, drug proprietaries and druggists' sundries
Electrical equipment:
   Electrical supplies and apparatus
   Electronic parts and supplies
   Radios, refrigerators and electrical appliances
Flowers and florists' supplies
Food, beverages and tobacco:
   Coffee, tea and spices
   Confectionery
   Dairy products and poultry
   Fish and sea foods
   Frozen foods
   Fruits and vegetables
   General groceries
   Grains
   Meats and meat products
   Tobacco and tobacco products
   Tobacco leaf
   Wine, liquor and beer
Furniture and home furnishings:
   Floor coverings
   Furniture
General merchandise
Iron, steel, hardware and related products:
   Air conditioning and refrigeration equipment and supplies
   Hardware and paints
   Metal products
   Metal scrap
   Plumbing and heating equipment and supplies
   Steel warehousing
Lumber, building materials and coal:
   Building materials
   Coal and coke
   Lumber and millwork
Machinery and equipment:
   Agricultural equipment
   Heavy commercial and industrial machinery and equipment
   Laundry and dry cleaning equipment and supplies
   Mill supplies
   Professional equipment and supplies
   Restaurant and hotel supplies, fixtures and equipment
   Transportation equipment and supplies, except motor vehicles

Paper and paper products:
   Printing and writing paper
   Wrapping or coarse paper and products
Petroleum products:
   Fuel oil
   Petroleum products
Scrap and waste materials:
   Textile waste
Sporting goods and toys
Textile products and apparel:
   Dry goods
   Footwear
   Furs
   Men's and boys' clothing
   Women's and children's clothing
   Wool

Retailing
Aircraft
Apparel and accessories:
   Family clothing stores
   Furs
   Infants' clothing
   Men's and boys' clothing
   Shoes
   Women's ready-to-wear
Boat dealers
Books and office supplies:
   Books and stationery
   Office supplies and equipment
Building materials and hardware:
   Building materials
   Hardware stores
   Heating and plumbing equipment dealers
   Lumber
   Paint, glass and wallpaper stores
Cameras and photographic supplies
Department stores and general merchandise:
   Department stores
   Dry goods and general merchandise
Drugs
Farm and garden equipment and supplies:
   Cut flowers and growing plants
   Farm equipment
   Feed and seed—farm and garden supply
Food and beverages:
   Dairy products and milk dealers
   Groceries and meats
   Restaurants

Fuel and ice dealers:
  Fuel, except fuel oil
  Fuel oil dealers
Furniture, home furnishings and equipment:
  Floor coverings
  Furniture
  Household appliances
  Radio, TV, and record players
Jewelry
Liquor
Luggage and gifts
Motor vehicle dealers:
  Autos—new and used
  Gasoline service stations
  Mobile homes
  Motorcycles
  Tires, batteries, and accessories
  Trucks—new and used
Musical instruments and supplies
Road machinery equipment
Sporting goods
Vending machine operators, merchandise

Services
Advertising agencies
Auto repair shops
Auto and truck rental and leasing
Bowling alleys
Cable television
Car washing
Commercial research and development laboratories
Data processing
Direct mail advertising
Engineering and architectural services
Farm products warehousing
Funeral directors
Insurance agents and brokers
Intercity bus lines
Janitorial services
Laundries and dry cleaners
Linen supply
Local trucking
Local trucking—without storage
Long distance trucking
Motels, hotels, and tourist courts
Nursing homes
Outdoor advertising
Photographic studios

Radio broadcasting
Real estate holding companies
Refrigerated warehousing, except food lockers
Refuse systems
Telephone communications
Transportation on rivers and canals
Travel agencies
Television stations
Water utility companies

Contractors

Not Elsewhere Classified
Beef cattle raisers
Bituminous coal mining
Bottlers—soft drinks
Commercial feed lots
Construction, sand and gravel
Crude petroleum and natural gas mining
Horticultural services
Poultry, except broiler chickens
Seed companies (vegetable and garden)

Accounting Corporation of America
Research Department
1929 First Avenue
San Diego, California 92101

Apparel, children's and infants
Apparel, men's specialty
Apparel, men's and women's
Apparel, women's specialty
Appliance stores
Auto parts and accessories
Bakeries
Beauty shops
Cocktail lounges
Confectionery stores
Contractors—building
Contractors—specialty
Dairies
Dentists
Doctors of medicine
Dry cleaning shops
Drug stores
Feed and seed stores
Florists
Food stores—combination

Food stores—specialty
Furniture stores
Garages
Gift and novelty stores
Hardware stores
Jewelry stores
Laundromats and hand laundries
Laundries, plant
Liquor stores
Lumber and building material
Machine shops
Meat markets
Motels
Music stores
New car dealers
Nursery and garden supplies
Paint, glass and wallpaper
Photographic supply stores
Plumbing and heating equipment
Printing shops

Professional—others
Repair services
Restaurants
Service stations
Shoe stores
Sporting goods stores

Taverns
TV radio sales and service
Transportation
Used car dealers
Variety stores

National Cash Register Company

Apparel stores
Appliance and radio-TV dealers
Automobile dealers
Auto parts dealers
Beauty shops
Book stores
Building material dealers
Cocktail lounges
Department stores
Dry cleaners
Feed stores
Florists
Food stores
Furniture stores
Garages
Gift, novelty and souvenir stores
Hardware stores
Hotels
Jewelry stores
Laundries

Liquor stores
Mass merchandising stores
Meat markets
Men's wear stores
Motels and motor inns
Music stores
Novelty stores
Nursery and garden supply stores
Photographic studio and supply
  stores
Professional services
Repair services
Restaurants
Service Stations
Shoe stores (family)
Sporting goods stores
Supermarkets
Transportation and service
Variety stores

TRADE ASSOCIATIONS

Associations which have published
ratio studies in the past include the following:

American Association of Advertising Agencies, 666 Third Avenue, New
  York, NY 10017
American Camping Association, Bradford Woods, Martinsville, IN 46151
American Jewelry Distributors Association, 1900 Arch Street, Philadelphia,
  PA 19103
American Meat Institute, 1700 North Moore Street, Arlington, VA 22209
American Paper Institute, 260 Madison Avenue, New York, NY 10016
American Society of Association Executives, 1575 Eye Street, N.W., Wash-
  ington, D.C. 20005
American Supply Association, 221 North LaSalle Street, Chicago, IL 60601
Bowling Proprietors Association of America, Box 5802, Arlington, TX 76011

Building Owners and Managers Association, International, 1221 Massachusetts Avenue, N.W., Washington, D.C. 20005

Door and Hardware Institute, 7711 Old Springhouse Road, McLean, VA 22102

Florists Transworld Delivery Association/Interflora, 29200 Northwestern Highway, Southfield, MI 48076

Food Marketing Institute, Suite 700, 1750 K Street, N.W., Washington, D.C. 20006

Foodservice Equipment Distributors Association, 332 South Michigan Avenue, Chicago, IL 60604

Independent Insurance Agents of America, 100 Church Street, New York, NY 10007

Laundry and Cleaners Allied Trade Association, 543 Valley Road, Upper Montclair, NJ 07043

Material Handling Equipment Distributors Association, 201 Route 45, Vernon Hills, ILL 60061

Mechanical Contractors Association of America, 5530 Wisconsin Avenue, N.W., Suite 750, Chevy Chase, MD 20815

Menswear Retailers of America, Suite 600, 2011 Eye Street, N.W., Washington, D.C. 20006

Motor and Equipment Manufacturers Association, 222 Cedar Lane, Teaneck, NJ 07666

National American Wholesale Grocers Association, 201 Park Washington Court, Falls Church, VA 20046

National Art Materials Trade Association, 178 Lakeview Avenue, Box 739, Clifton, NJ 07015

National Association of Accountants, 919 Third Avenue, New York, NY 10022

National Association of Electrical Distributors, 600 Summer Street, Stamford, CT 06901

National Association of Furniture Manufacturers, Suite 530, 5515 Security Lane, Rockville, MD 20852

National Association of Music Merchants, Inc., 500 North Michigan Avenue, Chicago, IL 60611

National Association of Plastics Distributors, Gilson Road, Jaffrey, NH 03452

National Association of Retail Dealers of America, 5105 Tallview Drive, Rolling Meadows, IL 60008

National Association of Textile and Apparel Wholesalers, 401 Seventh Ave., New York, NY 10001

National Association of Tobacco Distributors, 17th Floor, 630 Third Ave., New York, NY 10017

National Beer Wholesalers Association of America, Suite 505, 5205 Leesburg Pike, Falls Church, VA 22041

National Confectioners Association of the United States, Suite 514, 7900 Westpark Drive, McLean, VA 22102

National Consumer Finance Association, 4th Floor, 1101 Fourteenth Street, Washington, D.C. 20005

National Decorating Products Association, 1050 North Lindburgh Boulevard, St. Louis, MO 63132

National Electrical Contractors Association, Inc., 7315 Wisconsin Avenue, 13th Floor, Bethesda, MD 20814

National Electrical Manufacturers Association, 2101 L Street, N.W., Washington, D.C. 20037

National Farm and Power Equipment Dealers Association, 10877 Watson Road, St. Louis, MO 63127

National Grocers Association, Suite 820, 1825 Samuel Morse Drive, Reston, VA 22090

National Home Furnishings Association, 405 Merchandise Mart Plaza, Chicago, IL 60654

National Kitchen Cabinet Association, 136 Saint Matthew Avenue, Louisville, KY 40207

National Lumber and Building Material Dealers Association, 40 Ivy Street, S.E., Washington, D.C. 20036

National Machine Tool Builders Association, 7901 Westpark Drive, McLean, VA 22102

National Office Products Association, 301 North Fairfax Street, Alexandria, VA 22314

National Oil Jobbers Council, Inc., 1707 H Street, N.W., 11th Floor, Washington, D.C. 20006

National Paint and Coatings Association, 1500 Rhode Island Avenue, N.W., Washington, D.C. 20005

National Paper Box and Packaging Association, 231 Kings Highway East, Haddonfield, NJ 08033

National Paper Trade Association, Inc., 111 Great Neck Road, Great Neck, NY 11021

National Parking Association, 2000 K Street, N.W., Washington, D.C. 20006

National Restaurant Association, 311 First Street, N.W., Washington, D.C. 20001

National Retail Hardware Association, 770 North High School Road, Indianapolis, IN 46224

National Retail Merchants Association, 100 West 31st Street, New York, NY 10016

National Shoe Retailers Association, 200 Madison Avenue, New York, NY 10016

National Soft Drink Association, 1101 16th Street, N.W., Washington, D.C. 20036

National Sporting Goods Association, 1699 Wall Street, Mt. Prospect, IL 60056

National Tire Dealers and Retreaders Association, 1343 L Street, N.W., Washington, D.C. 20005

National Wholesale Druggists Association, 105 Oronoco Street, Alexandria, VA 22314

National Wholesale Hardware Association, 1900 Arch Street, Philadelphia, PA 19103

Northamerican Heating and Airconditioning Wholesalers Association, 1661
West Henderson Road, Columbus, OH 43220

North American Wholesale Lumber Association, Inc., Suite 680, 2340 South
Arlington Heights Road, Arlington Heights, IL 60005

Northeastern Retail Lumbermens Association, 180 Linden Street, Wellesley,
MA 02181

Optical Laboratories Association, 6935 Wisconsin Avenue, Suite 200, Chevy
Chase, MD 20815

Painting and Decorating Contractors of America, 7223 Lee Highway, Falls
Church, VA 22406

Petroleum Equipment Institute, Box 2380, Tulsa, OK 74101

Printing Industries of America, Inc., 1730 North Lynn Street, Arlington, VA
22209

Scientific Apparatus Makers Association, Suite 300, 1101 Sixteenth Street,
N.W., Washington, D.C. 20036

Shoe Service Institute of America, 154 West Hubbart Street, Chicago, IL
60610

Society of the Plastics Industry, Inc., The, 355 Lexington Avenue, New York,
NY 10017

Textile Care Allied Trades Association, 543 Valley Road, Upper Montclair,
NJ 07043

United Fresh Fruit and Vegetable Association, North Washington & Madison
Streets, Alexandria, VA 22134

Urban Land Institute, Suite 300, 1090 Vermont Avenue, N.W., Washington,
D.C. 20005

Wine and Spirit Wholesalers of America, Inc., Suite 400, 2003 M Street,
N.W., Washington, D.C. 20036

APPENDIX B

SMALL BUSINESS DEVELOPMENT CENTERS

University of Alabama
Small Business Development Center
1000 South Twelfth St., Suite F
Birmingham, AL 35294
(205) 934-6760

University of Arkansas
Small Business Development Center
P.O. Box 3017
Little Rock, AR 72203
(501) 371-5381

University of Connecticut
Small Business Development Center
School of Business Administration
Box U-41D
Storrs, CT 06268
(203) 486-4135

Howard University
Small Business Development Center
2361 Sherman Ave., NW
Washington, D.C. 20059
(202) 636-7187

University of West Florida
Small Business Development Center
School of Business Administration
Pensacola, FL 32504
(904) 476-9500, Ext. 2908

University of Georgia
Small Business Development Center
Brooks Hall, Room 348
Athens, GA 30602
(404) 542-5760

Iowa State University
Small Business Development Center
Center for Industrial Research and
  Service
Room 205—Engineering Annex
Ames, IA 50011
(515) 294-3420

University of Kentucky
Small Business Development Center
Commerce Building, Room 415
Lexington, KY 40506
(606) 257-1751

University of Massachusetts
Small Business Development Center
School of Business Administration
Amherst, MA 01003
(413) 549-4930, Ext. 304

University of Southern Maine
Small Business Development Center
246 Deering Avenue
Portland, ME 04102
(207) 780-4432

St. Thomas College
Small Business Development Center
2115 Summit Ave.
St. Paul, MN 55105
(612) 697-5840

University of Mississippi
Small Business Development Center
1855 Eastover Dr.
Jackson, MS 39211
(601) 982-6684

St. Louis University
Small Business Development Center
School of Business and Administration
3674 Lindell Blvd.
St. Louis, MO 63108
(314) 658-3826

University of Nebraska—Omaha
Small Business Development Center
1313 Farnam-on-the-Mall
Omaha, NE 68182
(402) 554-3291

Rutgers University
Small Business Development Center
3rd Floor—Ackerson Hall
180 University St.
Newark, NJ 07102
(201) 648-5621

University of Pennsylvania
Small Business Development Center
The Wharton School
413 Centenary Dr.
Philadelphia, PA 19104
(215) 243-4861, Ext. 228

University of South Carolina
Small Business Development Center
Basic Service Center
College of Business Administration
Columbia, SC 29208
(803) 777-5118

University of Utah
Small Business Development Center
Graduate School of Business
Salt Lake City, UT 84112
(801) 581-7905

Small Business Development Center
of Vermont, Inc.
Chace Mill, One Mill St.
Burlington, VT 05401
(802) 862-0200

Washington State University
Small Business Development Center
441 Todd Hall
Pullman, WA 99164
(509) 335-1576

University of Charleston
Small Business Development Center
2300 MacCorkle Ave. SE
Charleston, WV 25304
(304) 346-9471

University of Wisconsin
Small Business Development Center
One South Park St.
Madison, WI 53706
(608) 263-2221

394

APPENDIX C

FREE MANAGEMENT ASSISTANCE PUBLICATIONS (SBA)

The **Management Aids (MAs)** recommend methods and techniques for handling management problems and business operations.

Small Business Bibliographies (SBBs) list key reference sources for many business management topics.

Starting Out Series (SOSs) are one page fact sheets describing financial and operating requirements for selected manufacturing, retail, and service businesses.

MAs

Financial Management and Analysis

__ MA 1.001	The ABC's of Borrowing.
__ MA 1.002	What Is the Best Selling Price?
__ MA 1.003	Keep Pointed Toward Profit
__ MA 1.004	Basic Budgets for Profit Planning
__ MA 1.005	Pricing for Small Manufacturers
__ MA 1.006	Cash Flow in a Small Plant
__ MA 1.007	Credit and Collections
__ MA 1.008	Attacking Business Decision Problems With Breakeven Analysis
__ MA 1.009	A Venture Capital Primer for Small Business
__ MA 1.010	Accounting Services for Small Service Firms
__ MA 1.011	Analyze Your Records to Reduce Costs
__ MA 1.012	Profit by Your Wholesalers' Services
__ MA 1.013	Steps in Meeting Your Tax Obligations
__ MA 1.014	Getting the Facts for Income Tax Reporting
__ MA 1.015	Budgeting in a Small Business Firm
__ MA 1.016	Sound Cash Management and Borrowing
__ MA 1.017	Keeping Records in Small Business
__ MA 1.018	Check List for Profit Watching
__ MA 1.019	Simple Breakeven Analysis for Small Stores
__ MA 1.020	Profit Pricing and Costing for Services

Planning

__ MA 2.002	Locating or Relocating Your Business
__ MA 2.004	Problems in Managing a Family-Owned Business
__ MA 2.005	The Equipment Replacement Decision
__ MA 2.006	Finding a New Product for Your Company
__ MA 2.007	Business Plan for Small Manufacturers
__ MA 2.008	Business Plan for Small Construction Firms
__ MA 2.009	Business Life Insurance
__ MA 2.010	Planning and Goal Setting for Small Business
__ MA 2.011	Fixing Production Mistakes
__ MA 2.012	Setting Up a Quality Control System

Miscellaneous

— MA 7.002   Association Services for Small Business
— MA 7.003   Market Overseas With U.S. Government
             Help

SBBs

— 1. Handcrafts
— 2. Home Businesses
— 3. Selling By Mail Order
— 9. Marketing Research Procedures
— 10. Retailing
— 12. Statistics and Maps for National Market Analysis
— 13. National Directory for Use in Marketing
— 15. Recordkeeping Systems—Small Store and Service
     Trade
— 18. Basic Library Reference Sources
— 20. Advertising—Retail Store
— 31. Retail Credit and Collection
— 37. Buying for Retail Stores
— 72. Personnel Management
— 75. Inventory Management
— 85. Purchasing for Owners of Small Plants
— 86. Training for Small Business
— 87. Financial Management
— 88. Manufacturing Management
— 89. Marketing for Small Business
— 90. New Product Development
— 91. Ideas Into Dollars
— 92. Effective Business Communication

SOS

— 0101 Building Service Contracting
— 0104 Radio-Television Repair Shop
— 0105 Retail Florists
— 0106 Franchised Businesses
— 0107 Hardware Store or Home Centers
— 0111 Sporting Goods Store
— 0112 Drycleaning
— 0114 Cosmetology
— 0115 Pest Control
— 0116 Marine Retailers
— 0117 Retail Grocery Stores
— 0122 Apparel Store
— 0123 Pharmacies
— 0125 Office Products
— 0129 Interior Design Services
— 0130 Fish Farming
— 0133 Bicycles
— 0134 Roofing Contractors
— 0135 Printing
— 0137 The Bookstore
— 0138 Home Furnishings
— 0142 Ice Cream
— 0145 Sewing Centers
— 0148 Personnel Referral Service
— 0149 Selling By Mail Order
— 0150 Solar Energy
— 0201 Breakeven Point for Independent Truckers

APPENDIX D

For Sale Management Assistance Publications (SBA)

For-Sale Books

To Order: Complete the Order Form and check off requested publications. Send it with your check or money order to the **Superintendent of Documents,** Government Printing Office, Washington, D.C. 20402. Make check or money order payable to the Superintendent of Documents. Do not send postage stamps or cash. These booklets are not sold by the Small Business Administration. Foreign remittances should be made by international money order payable to the Superintendent of Documents, by draft on an American or Canadian bank located in the U.S. or Canada, or by UNESCO coupons. Orders may be charged to MasterCard, Visa, or Superintendent of Documents deposit accounts. Please include your card number and date of expiration. Prices subject to change without notice.

Small Business Management Series
The books in this series discuss specific management techniques or problems.

No.
1. **An Employee Suggestion System for Small Companies**
9. **Cost Accounting for Small Manufacturers**
   Assists managers of small manufacturing firms establish accounting procedures that help control production and business costs.
15. **Handbook of Small Business Finance**
20. **Ratio Analysis for Small Business**
22. **Practical Business Use of Government Statistics**
   Available only from SBA.
25. **Guides for Profit Planning**
   Guides for computing and using the breakeven point, the level of gross profit, and the rate of return on investment.
27. **Profitable Community Relations for Small Business**
28. **Small Business and Government Research and Development.** Includes a discussion of the procedures necessary to locate and sell to Government agencies.
29. **Management Audit for Small Manufacturers**
   A questionnaire for manufacturers.
30. **Insurance and Risk Management for Small Business**
31. **Management Audit for Small Retailers**
   149 questions to review business operations.
32. **Financial Recordkeeping for Small Stores**
33. **Small Store Planning for Growth**
   Covers merchandising, advertising and display, and provides checklists to increase sales.

35. **Franchise Index/Profile**
    Presents an evaluation process that may be used to
    investigate franchise opportunities.
36. **Training Salesmen to Serve Industrial Markets**
    Available only from SBA.
37. **Financial Control by Time-Absorption Analysis**
38. **Management Audit for Small Service Firms**
    A questionnaire for service firms.
39. **Decision Points in Developing New Products**
    Provides a path from idea to marketing plan for the
    small manufacturing or R & D firm.
40. **Management Audit for Small Construction Firms**
    A questionnaire for construction firms.
41. **Purchasing Management and Inventory Control for
    Small Business**
42. **Managing the Small Service Firm for Growth and Profit**
43. **Credit and Collections for Small Stores**

Starting and Managing Series

This series is designed to help the small
entrepreneur "to look before leaping" into a
business.

No.
  1. **Starting and Managing a Small Business of Your Own**
101. **Starting and Managing a Small Service Firm**

Nonseries Publications

Export Marketing for Smaller Firms
045–000–00158–0
U.S. Government Purchasing and Sales Directory
A directory for businesses interested in selling to the U.S.
Government. Lists the purchasing needs of various Agencies.
045–000–00153–9
Managing for Profits
Discusses the various management functions. 045–000–00206–3
Buying and Selling a Small Business.
045–000–00164–4
Strengthening Small Business Management
Emphasizes management self-improvement. 045–000–00114–8
The Best of the SBI Review—1973–1979
Management ideas for the small business owner-manager.
045–000–00172–5

Business Basics

Each of the 23 self-study booklets in this series
contains text, questions, and exercises that teach
a specific aspect of small business management.

No.
1001   The Profit Plan
1002   Capital Planning
1003   Understanding Money Sources
1004   Evaluating Money Sources
1005   Asset Management
1006   Managing Fixed Assets
1007   Understanding Costs
1008   Cost Control
1009   Marketing Strategy

1010 Retail Buying Function
1011 Inventory Management–Wholesale/Retail
1012 Retail Merchandise Management
1013 Consumer Credit
1014 Credit and Collections: Policy and Procedures
1015 Purchasing for Manufacturing Firms
1016 Inventory Management—Manufacturing/Service
1017 Inventory and Scheduling Techniques
1018 Risk Management and Insurance
1019 Managing Retail Salespeople
1020 Job Analysis, Job Specifications, and Job Descriptions
1021 Recruiting and Selecting Employees
1022 Training and Developing Employees
1023 Employee Relations and Personnel Policies

Order Form Check List

Small Business Management Series

No.	Stock No.	Price
1.	045–000–00020–6	$3.50
9.	045–000–00162–8	6.00
15.	045–000–00208–0	4.50
20.	045–000–00150–4	4.50
25.	045–000–00137–7	4.50
27.	045–000–00033–8	1.50
28.	045–000–00130–0	4.25
29.	045–000–00151–2	4.25
30.	045–000–00209–8	5.00
31.	045–000–00149–1	4.50
32.	045–000–00142–3	5.50
33.	045–000–00152–1	5.50
35.	045–000–00125–3	4.50
37.	045–000–00134–2	2.75
38.	045–000–00203–9	4.50
39.	045–000–00146–6	4.25
40.	045–000–00161–0	4.25
41.	045–000–00167–9	4.50
42.	045–000–00165–2	4.25
43.	045–000–00169–5	5.00

Business Basics

No.	Stock No.	Price
1001.	045–000–00192–0	$4.50
1002.	045–000–00193–8	4.50
1003.	045–000–00194–6	4.75
1004.	045–000–00174–1	5.00
1005.	045–000–00175–0	2.75
1006.	045–000–00176–8	4.50
1007.	045–000–00195–4	3.25
1008.	045–000–00187–3	4.75
1009.	045–000–00188–1	4.75
1010.	045–000–00177–6	4.50
1011.	045–000–00190–3	4.50
1012.	045–000–00178–4	4.75
1013.	045–000–00179–2	4.50
1014.	045–000–00180–6	4.75
1015.	045–000–00181–4	4.75
1016.	045–000–00182–2	4.75
1017.	045–000–00183–1	4.75
1018.	045–000–00184–9	4.50
1019.	045–000–00189–0	4.75
1020.	045–000–00185–7	4.50
1021.	045–000–00186–5	4.50
1022.	045–000–00191–1	4.50
1023.	045–000–00196–2	4.50

Nonseries Publications

Stock No.	Price
045–000–00158–0	$4.75
045–000–00153–9	7.00
045–000–00206–3	5.50
045–000–00164–4	5.00
045–000–00114–8	4.00
045–000–00172–5	5.50

Starting and Managing Series

No.	Stock No.	Price
1.	045–000–00212–8	4.75
101.	045–000–00207–1	4.50

400

APPENDIX E

SBA FIELD OFFICES

Alabama
908 South 20th Street
Birmingham, AL 35205
(205) 254-1341

Alaska
701 C Street, Box 67, Federal Bldg.
Anchorage, AK 99513
(907) 271-4022

Arizona
3030 North Central Ave., Suite 1201
Phoenix, AZ 85012
(602) 241-2206

Arkansas
P.O. Box 1401, 320 West Capitol Ave.
Suite 601
Little Rock, AR 72201
(501) 378-5277

California
1229 N Street
Fresno, CA 93712
(209) 487-5189

350 South Figueroa St., 6th Floor
Los Angeles, CA 90071
(213) 688-2956

Federal Bldg., Suite 4-S-33
880 Front Street
San Diego, CA 92188
(714) 293-5430

211 Main Street, 4th Floor
San Francisco, CA 94105
(415) 556-7490

Colorado
721 Nineteenth Street
Denver, CO 80202
(303) 837-2607

Connecticut
One Hartford Square, West, 2nd Fl.
Hartford, CT 06106
(203) 244-2511

Delaware
844 King St., Room 5207
Wilmington, DE 19801
(302) 573-6294

Florida
2222 Ponce de Leon Boulevard
5th Floor
Coral Gables, FL 33134
(305) 350-5533

400 West Bay Street, Box 35067
Jacksonville, FL 39201
(904) 791-3100

Georgia
1720 Peachtree Road
Atlanta, GA 30309
(404) 881-4749

Hawaii
P.O. Box 50207
300 Ala Moana
Honolulu, HI 96850
(808) 546-8950

Idaho
1005 Main St.
Boise, ID 83702
(208) 334-1696

Illinois
219 South Dearborn Street
Room 438
Chicago, IL 60604
(312) 353-4528

Indiana
New Federal Bldg., 5th Floor
575 North Pennsylvania Avenue
Indianapolis, IN 46204
(317) 269-7000

Iowa
210 Walnut Street
Des Moines, IA 50309
(515) 284-4567

373 Collins Road Northeast
Cedar Rapids, IA 52402
(319) 399-2580

Kansas
Main Place Bldg.
110 East Waterman Street
Wichita, KS 67202
(316) 269-6566

Kentucky
P.O. Box 3517
600 Federal Place
Louisville, KY 40201
(502) 582-5987

Louisiana
1661 Canal Street
2nd Floor, Ford-Fisk Bldg.
New Orleans, LA 70112
(504) 589-6685

Maine
40 Western Avenue
Augusta, ME 04330
(207) 622-6171

Maryland
Oxford Bldg.
8600 LaSalle Road
Towson, MD 21204
(301) 962-2054

Massachusetts
150 Causeway Street
10th Floor
Boston, MA 02114
(617) 223-4074

Michigan
477 Michigan Avenue
McNamara Bldg., Room 515
Detroit, MI 48226
(313) 226-6000

Minnesota
610C Butler Square
100 North Sixth Street
Minneapolis, MN 55403
(612) 349-3530

Mississippi
New Federal Bldg., Suite 322
100 West Capitol Street
Jackson, MS 30201
(601) 969-4363

Missouri
12 Grand Bldg., 5th Floor
1150 Grand Avenue
Kansas City, MO 64106
(816) 374-5557

815 Olive Street
Room 242
St. Louis, MO 63101
(314) 425-6600

Montana
301 South Park
Room 528
Helena, MT 59601
(406) 449-5381

Nebraska
Empire State Building
Nineteenth and Farnam Streets
Omaha, NE 68102
(402) 221-3620

Nevada
Box 7527
301 East Stewart
Las Vegas, NV 89101
(702) 385-6611

New Hampshire
55 Pleasant Street
Concord, NH 03301
(603) 224-4041

New Jersey
970 Broad Street
Newark, NJ 07102
(201) 645-3580

New Mexico
5000 Marble Avenue Northeast
Patio Plaza Bldg.
Albuquerque, NM 87110
(505) 766-3430

New York
26 Federal Plaza
New York, NY 10007
(212) 264-1318

Federal Bldg.
100 South Clinton St.
Syracuse, NY 13260
(315) 423-5371

North Carolina
230 South Tryon Street
Suite 700
Charlotte, NC 28202
(704) 371-6561

North Dakota
P.O. Box 3086
53 Second Avenue North
Fargo, ND 58102
(701) 237-5131

Ohio
AJC Federal Bldg., Room 317
1240 East Ninth Street
Cleveland, OH 44199
(216) 522-4194

Federal Bldg., U.S. Courthouse
85 Marconi Boulevard
Columbus, OH 43215
(614) 469-6860

Oklahoma
200 Northwest Fifth Street
Suite 670, Federal Bldg.
Oklahoma City, OK 73102
(405) 231-5237

Oregon
Federal Bldg., Room 676
1220 Southwest Third Avenue
Portland, OR 97204
(503) 294-5221

Pennsylvania
One Bala Cynwyd Plaza
231 St. Asaphs Road
Bala Cynwyd, PA 19004
(215) 597-3311

1000 Liberty Avenue
Pittsburgh, PA 15222
(412) 644-2784

Rhode Island
40 Fountain Street
Providence, RI 02903
(401) 528-4586

South Carolina
1835 Assembly Street, 3rd Floor
P.O. Box 2786
Columbia, SC 29201
(803) 765-5373

South Dakota
Security Bldg., Suite 101
101 South Main Avenue
Sioux Falls, SD 57102
(605) 336-2980

Tennessee
Parkway Towers, Room 1012
404 James Robertson Parkway
Nashville, TN 37219
(615) 251-5850

Texas
1100 Commerce Street
Room 3C36
Dallas, TX 75242
(214) 767-0600

222 East Van Buren, Suite 500
Harlingen, TX 78550
(512) 423-4533

2525 Murworth Suite 112
Houston, TX 77002
(713) 660-2409

712 Federal Bldg., & US Courthouse
1205 Texas Avenue
Lubbock, TX 79401
(806) 762-7462

727 East Durango
Room A-513, Federal Bldg.
San Antonio, TX 78206
(512) 229-6105

Utah
125 South State Street
Room 2237
Salt Lake City, UT 84138
(801) 524-5804

Vermont
87 State Street
Montpelier, VT 05602
(802) 229-0538

Virginia
400 North Eighth Street
P.O. Box 1026, Federal Bldg.
Richmond, VA 23240
(804) 771-2741

Washington
915 Second Avenue
Federal Bldg., Room 1744
Seattle, WA 98174
(206) 442-5534

P.O. Box 2167
651 U.S. Courthouse
Spokane, WA 99210
(509) 456-3781

West Virginia
109 North Third Street
Clarksburg, WV 26301
(304) 623-5631

Wisconsin
212 East Washington Avenue
Room 213
Madison, WI 53703
(608) 264-5205

Wyoming
Federal Bldg., Room 4001
100 East B Street
P.O. Box 2839-82602
Casper, WY 82601
(307) 265-5550

District of Columbia
1030 Fifteenth Street Northwest
Washington, D.C. 20417
(202) 634-1805

Puerto Rico
Federal Bldg., Carlos Chardon Ave.
Hato Rey, PR 00919
(809) 753-4218

Virgin Islands
Veterans Drive, Room 283
St. Thomas, VI 00801
(809) 774-8530

APPENDIX F

SMALL BUSINESS ADMINISTRATION

REQUEST FOR MANAGEMENT ASSISTANCE

Please Print

Name of Company	Name of Inquirer	Telephone #

Street	City	State	County	Zip

Employer ID #	Social Security Number	Veteran	Viet Era Veteran
		Yes No	Yes ☐ No ☐
		☐ ☐	Discharged:

Are you presently:	Yes	No	Can you furnish		Yes	No
In Business?	☐	☐	a recent:	Balance Sheet?	☐	☐
Starting a Business?	☐	☐		Profit & Loss Statement?	☐	☐
SBA Borrower?	☐	☐				

Kind of business/services (Please specify)

Retail (Selling) _____   Construction _____

Service (Kind) _____   Wholesale (Selling) _____

Manufacturing (Product) _____   Other (Specify) _____

Check the problem areas for which you seek assistance.

☐ 1. Starting a New Business
☐ 2. Sources of Credit and Financing
☐ 3. Increasing Sales
☐ 4. Advertising & Sales Promotion
☐ 5. Market Research
☐ 6. Selling to the Government
☐ 7. Bidding and Estimating
☐ 8. International Trade

☐ 9. Recordkeeping and Accounting
☐ 10. Financial Statements
☐ 11. Office or Plant Management
☐ 12. Personnel
☐ 13. Engineering and Research
☐ 14. Inventory Control
☐ 15. Purchasing
☐ 16. Credit & Collections

Please describe how SBA may be of assistance.

I request management assistance from the Small Business Administration. I understand that this assistance is free of charge and that I incur no obligation to SBA or its counselor for providing this assistance. I authorize SBA to furnish relevant information to the assigned management counselor although I expect that information to be held in strict confidence by him/her.

I further understand that any counselor has agreed not to: (1) recommend goods or services from sources in which he/she has an interest and (2) accept fees or commissions developing from this counseling relationship. In consideration of SBA's furnishing management or technical assistance, I waive all claims against SBA personnel or counselors arising from this assistance.

Signature and Title of Requestor	Date

SBA Form 641 (10-81) Previous Editions are Obsolete   GPO 884-910

APPENDIX G

U.S. DEPARTMENT OF COMMERCE FIELD OFFICES

Alabama
Suite 200-201
908 S. 20th St.
Birmingham, AL 35205
(202) 254-1331

Alaska
P.O. Box 32
701 C St.
Anchorage, AK 99513
(907) 271-5041

Arizona
2950 Valley Bank Center
201 N. Central Avenue
Phoenix, AZ 85073
(602) 261-3285

Arkansas
Room 635
320 W. Capitol Ave.
Little Rock, AR 72201
(501) 378-5794

California
Room 800
11777 San Vincente Blvd.
Los Angeles, CA 90049
(213) 209-6712

Room 15205 Federal Bldg.
Box 36013
450 Golden Gate Ave.
San Francisco, CA 94102
(415) 556-5860

Colorado
Room 119
U.S. Customhouse
721 19th St.
Denver, CO 80202
(303) 837-3246

Connecticut
Room 610-B, Federal Bldg.
450 Main St.
Hartford, CT 06103
(203) 244-3530

Florida
Room 821, City National Bank Bldg.
25 W. Flagler St.
Miami, FL 33130
(305) 350-5267

Georgia
Suite 600, 1365 Peachtree St., N.E.
Atlanta, GA 30309
(404) 881-7000

222 U.S. Courthouse
P.O. Box 9746
12529 Bull St.
Savannah, GA 31412
(912) 944-4204

Hawaii
Federal Bldg.
300 Ala Moana Blvd.
P.O. Box 50026
Honolulu, HI 96850
(808) 546-8694

Illinois
Room 1406, Mid-Continental Plaza
  Bldg.
55 E. Monroe St.
Chicago, IL 60603
(312) 353-4450

Indiana
357 U.S. Courthouse & Federal
  Office Bldg.
46 E. Ohio St.
Indianapolis, IN 46204
(317) 269-6214

Iowa
817 Federal Bldg.
210 Walnut St.
Des Moines, IA 50309
(515) 284-4222

Kansas
Room 1840
601 E. 12th St.
Kansas City, KS 64106
(816) 374-3142

Kentucky
Room 636B
U.S. Post Office & Courthouse Bldg.
Louisville, KY 40202
(502) 582-5066

Louisiana
432 International Trade Mart
2 Canal St.
New Orleans, LA 70130
(504) 589-6546

Maryland
415 U.S. Customhouse
Gay and Lombard Sts.
Baltimore, MD 21202
(301) 962-3560

Massachusetts
10th Floor
441 Stuart St.
Boston, MA 02116
(617) 223-2312

Michigan
445 Federal Bldg.
231 W. Lafayette
Detroit, MI 48226
(313) 226-3650

Minnesota
218 Federal Bldg.
110 S. 4th St.
Minneapolis, MN 55401
(612) 725-2133

Mississippi
Suite 3230
300 Woodrow Wilson Blvd.
Jackson, MS 39213
(601) 960-4388

Missouri
120 S. Central Ave.
St. Louis, MO 63105
(314) 425-3302

Nebraska
Empire State Bldg., 1st Floor
300 S. 19th St.
Omaha, NE 68102
(402) 221-3664

Nevada
1755 East Plum Lane
Room 152
Reno, NV 89502
(702) 784-5203

New Jersey
240 West State St.
8th Floor
Trenton, NJ 08608
(609) 989-2100

New Mexico
505 Marquette Ave., N.W.
Room 1015
Albuquerque, NM 87102
(505) 766-2386

New York
1312 Federal Bldg.
111 W. Huron St.
Buffalo, NY 14202
(716) 846-4191

37th Floor, Federal Office Bldg.
26 Federal Plaza, Foley Sq.
New York, NY 10278
(212) 264-0634

North Carolina
203 Federal Bldg.
W. Market St.
P.O. Box 1950
Greensboro, NC 27402
(919) 378-5345

Ohio
10504 Federal Bldg.
550 Main St.
Cincinnati, OH 45202
(513) 684-2944

Room 600
666 Euclid Ave.
Cleveland, OH 44114
(216) 522-4750

Oklahoma
4024 Lincoln Blvd.
Oklahoma City, OK 73105
(405) 231-5302

Oregon
Room 618
1220 S. W. 3rd Ave.
Portland, OR 97204
(503) 221-3001

Pennsylvania
9448 Federal Bldg.
600 Arch St.
Philadelphia, PA 19106
(215) 597-2866

2002 Federal Bldg.
1000 Liberty Ave.
Pittsburgh, PA 15222
(412) 644-2850

Puerto Rico
Room 659, Federal Bldg.
Chardon Ave.
San Juan, PR 00918
(809) 753-4555, Ext. 555

South Carolina
Strom Thurmond Federal Bldg.
1835 Assembly St.
Columbia, SC 29201
(803) 765-5345

Tennessee
Suite 1427, One Commerce Place
Nashville, TN 37239
(615) 251-5161

Texas
Room 7A5
1100 Commerce St.
Dallas, TX 75242
(214) 767-0542

2625 Federal Bldg.
515 Rusk St.
Houston, TX 77002
(713) 226-4231

Utah
Room 340
U.S. Post Office & Courthouse Bldg.
350 S. Main St.
Salt Lake City, UT 84104
(801) 524-5116

Virginia
8010 Federal Bldg.
400 N. 8th St.
Richmond, VA 23240
(804) 771-2246

Washington
706 Lake Union Bldg.
1700 Westlake Ave., North
Seattle, WA 98109
(206) 442-5616

West Virginia
3000 New Federal Office Bldg.
500 Quarrier St.
Charleston, WV 25301
(304) 343-6181, Ext. 375

Wisconsin
605 Federal Bldg.
517 E. Wisconsin Ave.
Milwaukee, WI 53202
(414) 291-3473

Wyoming
8007 O'Mahoney Federal Center
2120 Capitol Ave.
Cheyenne, WY 82001
(307) 772-2151, Ext. 2151

APPENDIX H

MINORITY BUSINESS DEVELOPMENT AGENCY (MBDA)

MBDA Regional Office
450 Golden Gate Avenue
Room 36114
San Francisco, CA 94102
(415) 556-7234

MBDA Regional Office
1730 K Street, N. W.
Suite 420
Washington, D.C. 20006
(202) 634-7897

MBDA Regional Office
1371 Peachtree Street, N. E.
Suite 505
Atlanta, GA 30309
(404) 881-4091

MBDA Regional Office
55 East Monroe Street
Suite 1440
Chicago, IL 60603

MBDA Regional Office
26 Federal Plaza
Room 36-116
New York, NY 10278
(212) 264-3262

MBDA Regional Office
1100 Commerce Street
Room 7B19
Dallas, TX 75242
(214) 767-8001

MBDA District Office
2500 Wilshire Boulevard
Room 908
Los Angeles, CA 90057
(213) 688-7175

MBDA District Office
333 West Coleax Avenue
3rd Floor
Denver, CO 80204
(303) 837-2767

MBDA District Office
216 Federal Building
Miami, FL 33130
(305) 350-5054

MBDA District Office
P.O. Box 570
441 Stuart Street
7th Floor
Boston, MA 02116
(617) 223-3726

MBDA District Office
Federal Building
911 Walnut
Suite 501
Kansas City, MO 64106
(816) 374-3381

MBDA District Office
9436 W. J. Green Federal Building
Philadelphia, PA 19106
(215) 597-9236

APPENDIX I

This is a revised form of the original yellow **PASS** booklet. If you have already filled this out, you need not send back this form but why not **PASS** it on to a friend?

PROCUREMENT AUTOMATED SOURCE SYSTEM — COMPANY PROFILE

IDENTIFICATION PASS is designed only for small businesses which are organized for profit and independently owned and operated

COMPANY NAME_____

MAILING ADDRESS_____
CITY_____ STATE_____ ZIP_____
CONTACT PERSON _____ TITLE _____

EMPLOYER IDENTIFICATION NO. (if avail.)_____
NO. OF EMPLOYEES _____
TOTAL SALES LAST FISCAL YEAR _____
YEAR BUSINESS ESTABLISHED_____
PHONE ____ Area Code ____ Number

PASS is divided into 4 types of businesses. Please estimate the percentage of your business allocated to the following (total must equal 100%) and complete the appropriate section(s).

MANUFACTURING/SUPPLIES CHECK ONE ☑ ___%

☐ MANUFACTURER   ☐ DEALER   ☐ WHOLESALE DISTRIBUTOR
MANUFACTURING FACILITY   SIZE _____ SQ FT

CONSTRUCTION ___%

MAXIMUM CURRENT BONDING LEVEL $_____ (if applicable)
MAXIMUM OPERATING RADIUS _____ MILES
ANYWHERE IN U.S., ENTER 3999 ABOVE
ANYWHERE IN THE WORLD, ENTER 9999 ABOVE

RESEARCH and DEVELOPMENT ___%

No. of engineers & scientists_____
Expertise of key personnel_____

SERVICES ___%

MAXIMUM CURRENT BONDING LEVEL $_____ (if applicable)
MAXIMUM OPERATING RADIUS _____ MILES
ANYWHERE IN U.S., ENTER 3999 ABOVE
ANYWHERE IN THE WORLD, ENTER 9999 ABOVE

CAPABILITIES (limit 32 words — avoid abbreviations)

List products and services offered and special capabilities.
_____
_____
_____
_____

OWNERSHIP CHECK ALL APPLICABLE BOXES ☑

Company is at least
51% OWNED, CONTROLLED and ACTIVELY MANAGED BY:

☐ VETERAN(S)
☐ CHECK IF ANY SERVICE WAS IN VIETNAM ERA (1964-1975)
☐ WOMAN/WOMEN
☐ MINORITY PERSON(S)

IF MINORITY OWNER, CHECK ☑

☐ BLACK
☐ NATIVE AMERICAN (Includes American Indian, Eskimo, Aleut & Native Hawaiian)
☐ HISPANIC AMERICAN
☐ ASIAN PACIFIC AMERICAN (Includes Oriental)

EXPORTS CHECK ONE BOX ☑ FOR INTERNATIONAL TRADE INTEREST

☐ ACTIVE EXPORTER   ☐ INTERESTED IN EXPORTS   ☐ NOT INTERESTED IN EXPORTS

SIGNATURE Important! Signature is required!

INFORMATION CONTAINED IN THIS PROFILE MAY BE DISCLOSED BY THE SMALL BUSINESS ADMINISTRATION

Please sign here

_____   _____   _____
Signature of Company Officer   Title   Date   (for SBA Use)

Questions? Contact your regional or district U.S. Small Business Administration Office for answers.

FILL OUT .... SEAL .... AND MAIL TODAY! IT'S EASY!

SBA Form 1167-Revised 10/80 OMB Clearance No 100R0089-March1983

APPENDIX J

ALABAMA
    Contact:

Office of State Planning and Federal Programs
State Capitol
Montgomery, Alabama 36130
Telephone: (205) 832-6400

ALASKA
    Contact:

Alaska Permit Information Center
Alaska Department of Environmental
Conservation
P.O. Box 2420
Juneau, Alaska 99803
Telephone: (907) 465-2615

ARIZONA
    Contact:

Governor's Office of Small Business
Development
1700 W. Washington Street, Room 810
Phoenix, Arizona 85007
Telephone: (602) 255-3301

ARKANSAS
    Contact:

Small and Minority Business Enterprise
Division
Arkansas Department of Commerce
Little Rock, Arkansas 72201
Telephone: (501) 371-1060

CALIFORNIA
    Contact:

Office of Small Business Development
Department of Economic and Business
Development
Sacramento, California 95814
Telephone: (916) 445-6545

COLORADO
    Contact:

Office of Regulatory Reform
Business Information Center
1525 Sherman Street, Room 110
Denver, Colorado 80203
Telephone: (303) 866-3933

CONNECTICUT
    Contact:

Connecticut Department of Economic
Development

                                        Office of Small Business Affairs
                                        Hartford, Connecticut 06106
                                        Telephone: (203) 566-4051

DELAWARE
   Contact: Delaware Development Office
                                        State Office Building
                                        Wilmington, Delaware 19801
                                        Telephone: (302) 736-4271

FLORIDA
   Contact: Florida Department of Commerce
                                        Bureau of Business and Community
                                        Development
                                        107 W. Gaines Street
                                        Room B26
                                        Tallahassee, Florida 32301
                                        Telephone: (904) 488-9357
                                        Toll-free: (800) 342-0771

GEORGIA
   Contact: Senate Small Business Study Committee
                                        State Capitol
                                        Atlanta, Georgia 30334
                                        Telephone: (404) 656-6029

HAWAII
   Contact: Office of the Governor
                                        State Capitol
                                        Honolulu, Hawaii 96813
                                        Telephone: (808) 548-2211

IDAHO
   Contact: Division of Economic and Community
                                        Development
                                        Room 108
                                        Capitol Building
                                        Boise, Idaho 83720
                                        Telephone: (208) 334-2470

ILLINOIS
   Contact: Division of Business Services
                                        Illinois Department of Commerce and
                                        Community Affairs
                                        310 Michigan Boulevard
                                        Chicago, Illinois 60604
                                        Telephone: (312) 793-3130
                                        Hotline (in state): (800) 252-2923
                                        (out of state): (800) 637-8000

INDIANA
   Contact: Ombudsman Office
                                     Forms Management Division
                                     Commission on Public Records
                                     501 State Office Building
                                     Indianapolis, Indiana 46204
                                     Telephone: (317) 232-3375

IOWA
   Contact: Call-One Program
                                     Iowa Development Commission
                                     250 Jewett Building
                                     Des Moines, Iowa 50309
                                     Telephone: (515) 281-8310; or
                                                (515) 281-8324
                                     Call-One: (800) 532-1216

KANSAS
   Contact: Kansas Department of Economic Development
                                     503 Kansas Avenue
                                     Topeka, Kansas 66603
                                     Telephone: (913) 296-3338

KENTUCKY
   Contact: Small Business Development Section
                                     Kentucky Department of Economic
                                     Development
                                     2329 Capital Plaza Tower
                                     Frankfort, Kentucky 40601
                                     Telephone: (502) 564-2064

LOUISIANA
   Contact: Small Business Assistance Program
                                     Office of Commerce and Industry
                                     Louisiana Department of Commerce
                                     P.O. Box 44185
                                     Baton Rouge, Louisiana 70804
                                     Telephone: (504) 343-5366

MAINE
   Contact: State Development Office
                                     Small Business Assistance Division
                                     State House Station 59
                                     Augusta, Maine 04333
                                     Telephone: (207) 289-2656

MARYLAND
   Contact: Office of Business Liaison
                                     Maryland Department of Economic and
                                     Community Development

1123 N. Utah Street
Baltimore, Maryland 21201
Telephone: (301) 269-3514

MASSACHUSETTS
Contact:

Massachusetts Department of Commerce
Small Business Assistance Division
100 Cambridge St., 13th Floor
Boston, Massachusetts 02202
Telephone: (617) 727-4005

MICHIGAN
Contact:

Michigan Department of Commerce
Office of Economic Development
Small Business Development Division
P.O. Box 30225
5th Floor, Law Building
Lansing, Michigan 48909
Telephone: (517) 373-0637
Toll-free in state: (800) 292-9544

MINNESOTA
Contact:

Small Business Assistance Center
Minnesota Department of Energy, Planning and
Development
480 Cedar Street
St. Paul, Minnesota 55101
Telephone: (612) 296-5011
Toll-free in state: (800) 652-9747

MISSISSIPPI
Contact:

Small Business Assistance Department
Mississippi Department of Economic
Development
P.O. Box 849
Jackson, Mississippi 39205
Telephone: (601) 354-6487

MISSOURI
Contact:

Existing Business Development Office
Missouri Division of Community and
Economic Development
P.O. Box 118
Jefferson City, Missouri 65102
Telephone: (314) 751-4982

MONTANA
Contact:

Development Bureau
Division of Economic and Community
Development

Montana Department of Commerce
Capital Station
1424 9th Avenue
Helena, Montana 59620
Telephone: (406) 449-3494

NEBRASKA
Contact:

Small Business and Community Assistance
Section
Division of Industrial Development
Nebraska Department of Economic
Development
P.O. Box 94666
301 Centennial Mall South
Lincoln, Nebraska 68509
Telephone: (402) 471-3118

NEVADA
Contact:

Department of Economic Development
Capitol Complex
Carson City, Nevada 89710
Telephone: (702) 885-4322

NEW HAMPSHIRE
Contact:

New Hampshire Business Service Center
P.O. Box 856
Concord, New Hampshire 03306
Telephone: (603) 271-3610
Hotline (in state): (800) 852-3782

NEW JERSEY
Contact:

Office of Small Business Assistance
New Jersey Department of Commerce and
Economic Development
Trenton, New Jersey 08625
Telephone: (609) 984-4442

NEW MEXICO
Contact:

Economic Development Division
New Mexico Department of Commerce and
Industry
Bataan Memorial Building
Santa Fe, New Mexico 87503
Telephone: (505) 827-3301

NEW YORK
Contact:

Division of Small Business Services
New York Department of Commerce
230 Park Avenue
New York, New York 10017
Telephone: (212) 949-9303

WASHINGTON
Contact:

Office of Small Business
Department of Commerce and Economic
Development
101 General Administration Building
Olympia, Washington 98504
Telephone: (206) 753-5614

Washington Department of Licensing
Business Licensing Center
Olympia, Washington 98504
Telephone: (206) 754-2784
In-state: (800) 562-8203

WEST VIRGINIA
Contact:

Small Business Service Unit
Governor's Office of Economic and
Community Development
Building 6, Suite 5-531
Capitol Complex
Charleston, West Virginia 25305
Telephone: (304) 348-2960

WISCONSIN
Contact:

Small Business Ombudsman
Wisconsin Department of Development
123 West Washington Avenue
P.O. Box 7970
Madison, Wisconsin 53707
Telephone: (608) 266-9465

Minority Business Development Agency
Wisconsin Department of Development
123 West Washington Avenue
P.O. Box 7970
Madison, Wisconsin 53707
Telephone: (608) 266-8380

WYOMING
Contact:

Wyoming Department of Economic Planning
and Development
Industrial Development Division
Barratt Building
Cheyenne, Wyoming 80220
Telephone: (307) 777-7284

PUERTO RICO
Contact:

Puerto Rico Department of Commerce
Box 4275
San Juan, Puerto Rico 00905
Telephone: (809) 724-0542

The Office of Business Permits
A. E. Smith Office Bldg., 17th Floor
Albany, New York 12225
Telephone: (518) 474-8275
In state: (800) 343-3464

NORTH CAROLINA
Contact:

Small Business Development Section
Business Assistance Division
North Carolina Department of Commerce
430 N. Salisbury Street
Raleigh, North Carolina 27611
Telephone: (919) 733-6254

NORTH DAKOTA
Contact:

North Dakota Economic Commission
1050 East Interstate Avenue
Bismarck, North Dakota 58501
Telephone: (701) 224-2810

OHIO
Contact:

Office of Small Business
Ohio Department of Development
30 E. Broad, 23rd Floor
Columbus, Ohio 43215
Telephone: (614) 466-4945
In state: (1-800) 282-1085

OKLAHOMA
Contact:

Office of the Governor
Department of Economic Development
Industrial Division
Existing Industry Engineer
P.O. Box 53424
4024 North Lincoln Blvd.
Oklahoma City, Oklahoma 73152
Telephone: (405) 521-2401 Ext. 28

OREGON
Contact:

Office of Business Development
Oregon Department of Economic Development
155 Cottage Street, N.E.
Salem, Oregon 97310
Telephone: (503) 373-1200

PENNSYLVANIA
Contact:

Office of Small Business
Pennsylvania Department of Commerce
416 South Office Building
Harrisburg, Pennsylvania 17120
Telephone: (717) 787-2048

Small Business Action Center
Pennsylvania Department of Commerce
400 South Office Building
Harrisburg, Pennsylvania 17120
Telephone: (717) 783-5700

RHODE ISLAND
  Contact:

Department of Economic Development
Seven Jackson Walkway
Providence, Rhode Island 02903
Telephone: (401) 277-2601

SOUTH CAROLINA
  Contact:

Office of the Governor
Division of Rural Development
Office of Small and Minority
Business Assistance
1205 Pendleton St., Third Floor
Columbia, South Carolina 29201
Telephone: (803) 758-7804

South Carolina Chamber of Commerce
P.O. Box 11278
Columbia, South Carolina 29211
Telephone: (803) 799-4601

SOUTH DAKOTA
  Contact:

South Dakota Department of Commerce and
Tourism
State Capitol Building
Pierre, South Dakota 57501
Telephone: (605) 773-3177

TENNESSEE
  Contact:

Small Business Office
Tennessee Department of Economic and
Community Development
1025 Andrew Jackson State Office Building
Nashville, Tennessee 37219
Telephone: (615) 741-5020
In state: (800) 342-8470
Out-of-state: (800) 251-8594

Existing Industry Services
1025 Andrew Jackson Building
Nashville, Tennessee 37219
Telephone: (615) 741-2626
In state: (800) 342-8470
Out-of-state: (800) 251-8594

Office of Minority Business Enterprise
1025 Andrew Jackson Building
Nashville, Tennessee 37219
Telephone: (615) 741-2545
In state: (800) 342-8470
Out-of-state: (800) 251-8594

Industrial Development Office
1021 Andrew Jackson Building
Nashville, Tennessee 37219
Telephone: (615) 741-3282
In state: (800) 342-8470
Out-of-state: (800) 251-8594

TEXAS
  Contact:

Business Development Department
Texas Industrial Commission
P.O. Box 12728
Capitol Station
410 East 5th Street
Austin, Texas 78711
Telephone: (512) 472-5059

UTAH
  Contact:

Division of Economic and Industrial
Development
Utah Department of Community and
Development
Economic Development
200 South Main, Suite 620
Salt Lake City, Utah 84101
Telephone: (801) 533-5325

VERMONT
  Contact:

Director of Industrial Development
Economic Development Department
109 State Street
Montpelier, Vermont 05602
Telephone: (802) 828-3221

VIRGINIA
  Contact:

Virginia State Office of Minority
Business Enterprise
1028 9th Street Office Building
Richmond, Virginia 23219
Telephone: (804) 786-5560

VIRGIN ISLANDS
  Contact: Small Business Development Agency
                                  Virgin Islands Department of Commerce
                                  P.O. Box 2058
                                  St. Thomas, Virginia Islands 00801
                                  Telephone: (809) 774-8784

APPENDIX K

IRS PUBLICATIONS

Accounting Periods and Methods, Publication 538.
Business Expenses, Publication 535.
Basis of Assets, Publication 551.
Tax Information on Corporations, Publication 542.
Depreciation, Publication 534.
Employment Taxes, Publication 539.
Employer's Tax Guide (Circular E), Publication 15.
Your Federal Income Tax, Publication 17.
Tax Guide for Small Business, Publication 334.
Tax Calendars for 1983, Publication 509.
Investment Credit, Publication 572.
Net Operating Losses and the At-Risk Limits, Publication 536.
Tax Information on Partnerships, Publication 541.
Self-Employment Tax, Publication 533.

APPENDIX L

SURVEY CHART OF THE FIFTY STATES

[1] on informal basis
[2] pending program
[3] existing business liaison

	Small Business Assistance Office	Loan Program	Advisory Board	Procurement Program	Complaint Handling	Other Significant Programs	Legislative Activity
ALABAMA				X			
ALASKA	X	X					
ARIZONA	X[1]			X	X		
ARKANSAS	X			X	X		
CALIFORNIA	X	X	X	X		X	X
COLORADO	X		X				
CONNECTICUT	X	X		X	X	X	
DELAWARE							
FLORIDA	X		X		X		
GEORGIA			X	X			
HAWAII		X					
IDAHO							
ILLINOIS	X	X		X	X		X
INDIANA				X	X	X	
IOWA					X^2	X	X
KANSAS				X			X
KENTUCKY	X	X	X^2	X	X		X
LOUISIANA	X^2			X	X^2		
MAINE		X				X	
MARYLAND	X[3]	X		X			
MASSACHUSETTS	X	X		X	X	X	X
MICHIGAN	X	X^2		X	X	X	
MINNESOTA	X	X^2		X	X	X	X
MISSISSIPPI	X	X		X		X	
MISSOURI	X	X				X	

SURVEY CHART OF THE
FIFTY STATES (cont'd)

[1] on informal basis
[2] pending program
[3] existing bus. liaison

	Small Business Assistance Office	Loan Program	Advisory Board	Procurement Program	Complaint Handling	Other Significant Programs	Legislative Activity
MONTANA	X	X	X	X	X		
NEBRASKA	X^3						
NEVADA							
NEW HAMPSHIRE		X					
NEW JERSEY	X	X			X	X	
NEW MEXICO	X^3				X	X	
NEW YORK	X		X	X	X	X	X
NORTH CAROLINA			X^2	X			
NORTH DAKOTA		X	X				
OHIO	X	X	X		X	X	X
OKLAHOMA		X				X	
OREGON	X				X	X	
PENNSYLVANIA	X		X	X^2	X	X	
RHODE ISLAND		X	X		X	X	X
SOUTH CAROLINA							
SOUTH DAKOTA							
TENNESSEE	X^2	X	X^2				
TEXAS	X	X	X	X			
UTAH	X				X	X	
VERMONT	X^{23}	X					
VIRGINIA	X^3						
WASHINGTON	X			X	X	X	
WEST VIRGINIA	X		X		X	X	X
WISCONSIN			X	X	X	X	X
WYOMING							
PUERTO RICO		X					
VIRGIN ISLANDS	X	X					

APPENDIX M

PROFESSIONAL ASSOCIATIONS REPRESENTING SMALL BUSINESSES

Active Corps of Executive
c/o Small Business Administration
1441 L Street, N.W.
Room 602H
Washington, D.C. 20416

American Association of Small Research Companies
8794 West Chester Pike
Upper Darby, PA 19082

American Business Women's Association
P.O. Box 8728
9100 Ward Parkway
Kansas City, MO 64114

American Federation of Small Business
407 S. Dearborn Street
Chicago, IL 60605

Center for Family Business
P.O. Box 24268
Cleveland, OH 44124

Conference of American Small Business Organizations
407 S. Dearborn Street
Chicago, IL 60605

Continental Association of Resolute Employers
1800 Lincoln Avenue
San Rafael, CA 94901

International Council for Small Business
3550 Lindell Boulevard
St. Louis, MO 63103

International Entrepreneurs Association
2311 Pontius Avenue
Los Angeles, CA 90064

National Association of Women Business Owners
2000 P Street, N.W.
Suite 410
Washington, D.C. 20036

National Association of the Self Employed
Denton, TX

National Business League
4324 George Avenue, N.W.
Washington, D.C. 20011

National Family Business Council
1000 Vermont Avenue, N.W.
Washington, D.C. 20005

National Federation of Independent Business
150 W. 20th Avenue
San Mateo, CA 94403

National Small Business Association
NSB Building
1604 K Street, N.W.
Washington, D.C. 20006

Service Corps of Retired Executives Association
c/o Small Business Administration
1441 L Street, N.W.
Room 100
Washington, D.C. 20416

Smaller Business Association of New England
69 Hickory Drive
Waltham, MA 02154

Small Business Legislative Council
1604 K Street, N.W.
Washington, D.C. 20006

Small Business Service Bureau, Inc.
544 Main Street
P.O. Box 1441
Worcester, MA 01601

Support Service Alliance, Inc.
Crossroads Building
Two Times Square
New York, NY 10036

United States Chamber of Commerce
1615 H Street, N.W.
Washington, D.C. 20062

Women Entrepreneurs
3061 Fillmore Street
San Francisco, CA 94123

APPENDIX N

THE BANK OF AMERICA

The Small Business Reporter
Department 3120
P.O. Box 37000
San Francisco, California

Apparel Stores
Auto Parts
Bars
Bicycle Stores
Book Stores
Building Maintenance Services
Independent Camera Stores
Proprietary Day Care Centers
Independent Drug Stores
Coin Operated Dry Cleaning Stores
Business Equipment Rental
Convenience Food Stores
The Handicraft Business
Health Food Stores

Home Furnishing Stores
Independent Liquor Stores
Mail Order Enterprises
Mobile Home and Recreation Dealers
Independent Pet Shops
Plant Shops
Small Job Printing Shops
Repair Services
Restaurants and Food Services
Service Stations
Sewing and Needlecraft Shops
Shoe Stores
Independent Sporting Goods
Toy and Hobby Craft Stores

APPENDIX O

PUBLICATIONS EMPHASIZING SMALL BUSINESS TOPICS

Barter News
P.O. Box 3024
Mission Viejo, CA 92690

The Business Owner
383 South Broadway
Hicksville, NY 11801

Entrepreneur Magazine
2311 Pontius Avenue
Los Angeles, CA 90064

Entrepreneurial Manager's Newsletter
311 Main Street
Worcester, MA 01608

Inc. Magazine
38 Commercial Wharf
Boston, MA 02110

Journal of Applied Management
1700 Ygnacio Valley Road, Suite 222
Walnut Creek, CA 94598

Journal of Small Business Management
Bureau of Business Research
West Virginia University
Morgantown, West Virginia 26506

Managing, the Entrepreneur's Guide to Success
757 Third Avenue
New York, NY 10017

Small Business Report
497 Lighthouse Avenue
Monterey, CA 93940

Venture Magazine
35 W. 45th Street
New York, NY 10037

APPENDIX P

ASSOCIATIONS REPRESENTING VENTURE CAPITAL FIRMS

National Venture Capital Association
1225 19th Street, N.W. Suite 750
Washington, D.C. 20036
(202) 659-5756

Western Association of Venture Capitalists
3000 Sand Hill Road
Building 2, Suite 260
Menlo Park, California 94025
(415) 854-1322

New York Venture Capital Forum
c/o AMEV Capital Corporation
2 World Trade Center, Suite 9766
New York, New York 10048
(212) 755-1912

Connecticut Venture Group
P.O. Box 2451
Darien, Connecticut 06820
(203) 323-3143

New England Venture Capital Association
183 Essex Street
Boston, Massachusetts 02111
(617) 423-4355

Venture Capital Club of New Mexico
524 Camino del Monte Sol
Santa Fe, New Mexico 87501
(505) 983-1769

APPENDIX Q

ASSOCIATIONS REPRESENTING SMALL BUSINESS INVESTMENT COMPANIES

National Association of Small Business Investment Companies
618 Washington Building, N.W.
Washington, D.C. 20005
(202) 638-3411

American Association of Minority Enterprise Small Business Investment
Companies
915 15th Street, N.W.
Washington, D.C. 20005
(202) 347-8600

APPENDIX R

National Commercial Finance Conference
One Penn Plaza
New York, New York 10001
(212) 594-3490

American Association of Equipment Lessors
1700 North Moore Street
Suite 1930
Arlington, Virginia 22209

APPENDIX S*

OUTLINE OF AN INVESTMENT AGREEMENT

What follows is a detailed outline of the contents of a venture investment agreement. The main sections of a typical agreement are briefly described and many of the terms that might appear in each section are noted. However, not all of the terms listed will appear in an investment agreement. Venture capital investors select terms from among those listed (and some not listed) to best serve their needs in a particular venture-investment situation.

1. Description of the Investment

This section of the agreement defines the basic terms of the investment. It includes descriptions of the:

a. Amount and type of investment.
b. Securities to be issued.
c. Guarantees, collateral subordination and payment schedules associated with any notes.
d. Conditions of closing: time, place, method of payment.

When investment instruments are involved that carry warrants, or debt conversion privileges, the agreement will completely describe them. This description will include the:

a. Time limits on the exercise of the warrant or conversion of the debt.
b. Price and any price changes that vary with the time of exercise.
c. Transferability of the instruments.
d. Registration rights on stock acquired by the investor.
e. Dilution resulting from exercise of warrants or debt conversion.
f. Rights and protections surviving after conversion, exercise, or redemption.

2. Preconditions to Closing

This section covers what the venture must do or what ancillary agreements and documents must be submitted to the investor before the investment can be closed. These agreements and documents may include:

a. Corporate documents; e.g., by-laws, articles of incorporation, resolutions authorizing sale of securities, tax status certificates, list of stockholders, and directors.
b. Audited financial statements

*Reprinted with the permission of Jeffry A. Timmons and Paul T. Babson, from their book entitled, *New Venture Creation* (pp. 599-602), published by Richard D. Irwin, Inc., Homewood, Illinois. © copyright 1977.

c. Any agreements for simulataneous additional financing from another source or for lines of credit.

d. Ancillary agreements; e.g., employment contracts, stock option agreements, key man insurance policies, stock repurchase agreements.

e. Copies of any leases or supply contracts.

3. Representations and Warranties by the Venture

This section contains legally binding statements made by the venture's officers that describe its condition on or before the closing date of the investment agreement. The venture's management will warrant:

a. That it is a duly organized corporation in good standing.

b. That its action in entering into an agreement is authorized by its directors, allowed by its by-laws and charter, legally binding upon the corporation and not in breach of any other agreements.

c. If a private placement, that the securities being issued are exempt from registration under the Securities Act of 1933 as amended, under state securities law, and that registration is not required under the Securities Exchange Act of 1934.

d. That the capitalization, shares, options, directors, and shareholders of the company are as described (either in the agreement or an exhibit).

e. That no trade secrets or patents will be used in the business that are not owned free and clear or if rights to use them have not been acquired.

f. That no conflicts of interest exist in their entering the agreement.

g. That all material facts and representations in the agreement and exhibits are true as of the date of closing (includes accuracy of business plan and financials).

h. That the venture will fulfill its part of the agreement so long as all conditions are met.

i. That any patents, trademarks, or copyrights owned and/or used by the company are as described.

j. That the principal assets and liabilities of the company are as described in attached exhibits.

k. That there are no undisclosed obligations, litigations or agreements of the venture of a material nature not already known to all parties.

l. That any prior year income statements and balance sheets are accurate as presented and have been audited. And that there have been no adverse changes since the last audited statements.

m. That the venture is current on all tax payments and returns.

4. Representations and Warranties by the Investor

This section contains any legally binding representations made by the investor. They are much smaller in number than those made by the company. The investor may warrant:

a. If a corporation, that it is duly organized and in good standing.

b. If a corporation, that its action in entering into an agreement with the venture is authorized by its directors, allowed by its by-laws and charter, legally binding upon the corporation, and not in breach of any existing agreements.

c. If a private placement, that the stock being acquired is for investment and not with a view to or for sale in connection with any distribution.

d. The performance of his or her part of the contract if all conditions are met.

5. Affirmative Covenants

In addition to the above representations and warranties, the company in which the investor invests usually has a list of affirmative covenants with which it must comply. These could include agreeing to:

a. Pay taxes, fees, duties, and other assessments promptly.

b. File all appropriate government or agency reports.

c. Pay debt principal and interest.

d. Maintain corporate existence.

e. Maintain appropriate books of accounts and keep a specified auditing firm on retainer.

f. Allow access to these records to all directors and representatives of the investor.

g. Provide the investor with periodic income statements and balance sheets.

h. Preserve and provide for the investor's stock registration rights as described in the agreement.

i. Maintain appropriate insurance, including key man life insurance with the company named as beneficiary.

j. Maintain minimum net worth, working capital, or net assets levels.

k. Maintain the number of investor board seats prescribed in the agreement.

l. Hold prescribed number of directors' meetings.

m. Comply with all applicable laws.

n. Maintain corporate properties in good condition.

o. Notify the investor of any events of default of the investment agreement within a prescribed period of time.

p. Use the investment proceeds substantially in accordance with a business plan that is an exhibit to the agreement.

6. Negative Covenants

These covenants define what a venture must not do, or must not do without prior investor approval; such approval not to be unreasonably withheld. A venture usually agrees not to do such things as:

a. Merge, consolidate with, acquire, or invest in any form of organization.

b. Amend or violate the venture's charter or by-laws.

c. Distribute, sell, redeem, or divide stock except as provided for in the agreement.

d. Sell, lease, or dispose of assets whose value exceeds a specified amount.

e. Purchase assets whose value exceeds specified amount.

f. Pay dividends.

g. Violate any working capital or net worth restrictions described in the investment agreement.

h. Advance to, loan to, or invest in individuals, organizations, or firms except as described in the investment agreement.

i. Create subsidiaries.

j. Liquidate the corporation.

k. Institute bankruptcy proceedings.

l. Pay compensation to its management other than as provided for in the agreement.

m. Change the basic nature of the business for which the firm was organized.

n. Borrow money except as provided for in the agreement.

o. Dilute the investors without giving them the right of first refusal on new issues of stock.

7. Conditions of Default

This section describes those events that constitute a breach of the investment agreement if not corrected within a specified time and under which an investor can exercise specific remedies. Events that constitute default may include:

a. Failure to comply with the affirmative or negative covenants of the agreement.

b. Falsification of representations and warranties made in the investment agreement.

c. Insolvency or reorganization of the venture.

d. Failure to pay interest or principal due on debentures.

8. Remedies

This section describes the actions available to an investor in the event a condition of default occurs. Remedies depend on the form an investment takes. For a common stock investment the remedies could be:

a. Forfeiture to the investor of any stock of the venture's principals that was held in escrow.

b. The investor receiving voting control through a right to vote some or all of the stock of the venture's principals.

c. the right of the investor to "put" his stock to the company at a predetermined price.

For a debenture, the remedies might be:

a. The full amount of the note becoming due and payable on demand.

b. Forfeiture of any collateral used to secure the debt.

In the case of a preferred stock investment, the remedy can be special voting rights (e.g., the right to vote the entrepreneurs' stock) to obtain control of the Board of Directors.

9. Other Conditions

A number of other clauses that cover a diverse group of issues often appear in investment agreements. Some of the more common issues covered are:

a. Who will bear the costs of closing the agreement; this is often borne by the company.
b. Who will bear the costs of registration of the investors' stock; again, the investors like this to be borne by the company for the first such registration.
c. Right of first refusal for the investor on subsequent company financings.

APPENDIX T

Form Approved
OMB No. 3245—0016

U.S. Small Business Administration

APPLICATION FOR BUSINESS LOAN

I. Applicant

30

Trade Name of Borrower
32

Street Address
34

City	County	State	Zip	Tel. No. (Inc. A/C)
36		37	39	

Employers ID Number	Date of Application	Date Application Received by SBA	Number of Employees (including subsidiaries and affiliates)
33		5	

Type of Business

Date Business Established

- [ ] Existing Business
- [ ] New Business
- [ ] Purchase Existing Business

At Time of Application ____

If Loan is Approved ____

Bank of Business Account

II. Management (Proprietor, partners, officers, directors and stockholders owning 20% or more of outstanding stock)

Name	Address	% Owned	Annual Comp.	*Military Service From	*Military Service To	*Race	*Sex
			$				
			$				
			$				
			$				

*This data is collected for statistical purposes only. It has no bearing on the credit decision to approve or decline this application.

III. Use of Proceeds:
(Enter Gross Dollar Amounts Rounded to Nearest Hundreds)

	Loan Requested	SBA USE ONLY Approved
5 Land Acquisition	$	
6 New Plant or Building Construction		
7 Building Expansion or Repair		
8 Acquisition and/or Repair of Machinery and Equipment		
9 Inventory Purchase		

2	SBA Office Code	1	1	SBA Loan Number

IV. Summary of Collateral:

If your collateral consists of (A) Land and Building, (D) Accounts Receivable and/or (E) Inventory, fill in the appropriate blanks. If you are pledging (B) Machinery and Equipment, (C) Furniture and Fixtures, and/or (F) Other, please provide an itemized list (labeled Exhibit A) that contains serial and identification numbers for all articles that had an original value greater than $500. Include a legal description of Real Estate offered as collateral.

	Present Market Value	Present Mortgage Balance	Cost Less Depreciation
A. Land and Building	$	$	$
B. Machinery & Equipment			
C. Furniture & Fixtures			
D. Accounts Receivable			
E. Inventory			
F. Other			
Total Collateral	$	$	$

10. Working Capital (Including Accounts Payable)

11. Acquisition of all or part of Existing Business

12a. Payoff SBA Loan

12b. Payoff Bank Loan (Non SBA Associated)

12c. Other Debt Payment (Non SBA Associated)

13. All Other

14. Total Loan Requested $

Term of Loan

V. Previous Government Financing: If you or any principals or affiliates have ever requested Government Financing (including SBA), complete the following :

Name of Agency	Amount	Date of Request	Approved or Declined	Balance	Status
	$			$	
	$			$	
	$			$	

Previous SBA Financing (Check One)
(1) No ☐   (2) Repaid/Other ☐   (3) Present Borrower ☐   (4) Loan Number of 1st SBA Loan

VI. Indebtedness: Furnish the following information on all installment debts, contracts, notes, and mortgages payable. Indicate by an asterisk (*) items to be paid by loan proceeds and reason for paying same (present balance should agree with latest balance sheet submitted).

To Whom Payable	Original Amount	Original Date	Present Balance	Rate of Interest	Maturity Date	Monthly Payment	Security	Current or Delinquent
	$		$			$		
	$		$			$		
	$		$			$		
	$		$			$		

SBA Form 4 (11–82) REF SOP 50 10   PREVIOUS EDITIONS ARE OBSOLETE   (OVER)

All Exhibits must be signed and dated by person signing this form.

1. Submit SBA Form 912 (Personal History Statement) for each person e.g. owners, partners, directors, major stockholders, etc; the instructions are on SBA Form 912.

2. Furnish a signed current personal balance sheet (SBA Form 413 may be used for this purpose) for each stockholder (with 20% or greater ownership), partner, officer, and owner. Social Security number should be included on personal financial statement. Label this Exhibit B.

3. Include the statements listed below: 1, 2, 3 for the last three years; also 1, 2, 3, 4 dated within 90 days of filing the application; and statement 5, if applicable. This is Exhibit C (SBA has Management Aids that help in the preparation of financial statements.)

   1. Balance Sheet   2. Profit and Loss Statement
   3. Reconciliation of Net Worth
   4. Aging of Accounts Receivable and Payable
   5. Earnings projections for at least one year where financial statements for the last three years are unavailable or where requested by District Office.

   (If Profit and Loss Statement is not available, explain why and substitute Federal Income Tax Forms.)

4. Provide a brief history of your company and a paragraph describing the expected benefits it will receive from the loan. Label it Exhibit D.

5. Provide a brief description of the educational, technical and business background for all the people listed in Section II under Management. Please mark it Exhibit E.

6. Do you have any co-signers and/or guarantors for this loan? If so, please submit their names, addresses and personal balance sheet(s) as Exhibit F.

7. Are you buying machinery or equipment with your loan money? If so, you must include a list of the equipment and the cost. This is Exhibit G.

8. Have you or any officers of your company ever been involved in bankruptcy or insolvency proceedings? If so, please provide the

AGREEMENTS AND CERTIFICATIONS

Agreement of Nonemployment of SBA Personnel: I/We agree that if SBA approves this loan application I/We will not, for at least two years, hire as an employee or consultant anyone that was employed by the SBA during the one year period prior to the disbursement of the loan.

Certification: I/We certify: (a) I/We have not paid anyone connected with the Federal Government for help in getting this loan. I/We also agree to report to the SBA Office of Security and Investigations, 1441 L Street N.W., Washington, D.C., 20416 any Federal Government employee who offers, in return for any type of compensation, to help get this loan approved.

(b) All information in this application and the Exhibits is true and complete to the best of my/our knowledge and is submitted to SBA so SBA can decide whether to grant a loan or participate with a lending institution in a loan to me/us. I/We agree to pay for or reimburse SBA for the cost of any surveys, title or mortgage examinations, appraisals etc., performed by non-SBA personnel provided I/We have given my/our consent.

(c) I/We give the assurance that we will comply with sections 112 and 113 of Title 13 of the Code of Federal Regulations. These Code sections prohibit discrimination on the grounds of race, color, sex, religion, marital status, handicap, age, or national origin by recipients of Federal financial assistance and require appropriate reports and access to books and records. These requirements are applicable to anyone who buys or takes control of the business. I/We realize that if I/We do not comply with these nondiscrimination requirements SBA can call, terminate, or accelerate repayment of my/our loan. As consideration for any Management and Technical Assistance that may be provided, I/We waive all claims against SBA and its consultants.

I/We understand that I/We need not pay anybody to deal with SBA. I/We have read and understand Form 394 which explains SBA policy on representatives and their fees.

For Guaranty Loans please provide an original and one copy (Photocopy is Acceptable) of the Application Form, and all Exhibits to the participating lender. For Direct Loans submit one original copy of application and Exhibits to SBA.
It is against SBA regulations to charge the applicant a percentage

details as Exhibit H. If none, check here ☐

9. Are you or your business involved in any pending lawsuits? If yes, provide the details as Exhibit I. If none, check here ☐

10. Do you or your spouse or any member of your household, or anyone who owns, manages, or directs your business or their spouses or members of their households work for the Small Business Administration, Small Business Advisory Council, SCORE or ACE, any Federal Agency, or the participating lender? If so, please provide the name and address of the person and the office where employed. Label this Exhibit J. If none, check here ☐

11. Does your business have any subsidiaries or affiliates? If yes, please provide their names and the relationship with your company along with a current balance sheet and operating statement for each. This should be Exhibit K.

12. Do you buy from, sell to, or use the services of any concern in which someone in your company has a significant financial interest? If yes, provide details on a separate sheet of paper labeled Exhibit L.

13. If your business is a franchise, include a copy of the franchise agreement and a copy of the FTC disclosure statement supplied to you by the Franchisor. Please include it as Exhibit M.

CONSTRUCTION LOANS ONLY

14. Include in a separate exhibit (Exhibit N) the estimated cost of the project and a statement of the source of any additional funds.

15. File all the necessary compliance documents (SBA Form-Series 601). The loan officer will advise which forms are necessary.

16. Provide copies of preliminary construction plans and specifications. Include them as Exhibit O. Final plans will be required prior to disbursement.

DIRECT LOANS ONLY

17. Include two bank declination letters with your application. These letters should include the name and telephone number of the persons contacted at the banks, the amount and terms of the loan, the reason for decline and whether or not the bank will participate with SBA. In cities with 200,000 people or less, one letter will be sufficient.

SBA Form 4 (11-82)

---

of the loan proceeds as a fee for preparing this application.

ASSISTANCE

List the names of attorneys, accountants, appraisers, agents, or other persons rendering assistance in preparation of this form. Check here if none: ☐

Name and Occupation	Total Fees Paid
Address	Fees Due
Name and Occupation	Total Fees Paid
Address	Fees Due

If you make a statement that you know to be false or if you over value a security in order to help obtain a loan under the provisions of the Small Business Act, you can be fined up to $5,000 or be put in jail for up to two years, or both.

Signature of Preparer if Other Than Applicant

Print or Type Name of Preparer

Address of Preparer

If Applicant is a proprietor or general partner, sign below:

By: _____ Date _____

If Applicant is a corporation, sign below:

Corporate Seal _____ Date _____

By: _____
     Signature of President

Attested by: _____
     Signature of Corporate Secretary

U.S. GOVERNMENT PRINTING OFFICE : 1982   O—394-355

Return Executed Copies 1, 2, and 3 to SBA

Please Read Carefully - Print or Type

Each member of the small business concern requesting assistance or the development company must submit this form in TRIPLICATE for filing with the SBA application. This form must be filled out and submitted:

1. If a sole proprietorship, by the proprietor;
2. If a partnership, by each partner;
3. If a corporation or a development company, by each officer, director, and additionally, by each holder of 20% or more of the voting stock;
4. Any other person, including a hired manager, who has authority to speak for and commit the borrower in the management of the business.

United States of America

SMALL BUSINESS ADMINISTRATION

STATEMENT OF PERSONAL HISTORY

Name and Address of Applicant (Firm Name)(Street, City, State and ZIP Code)

SBA District Office and City

Amount Applied for:

1. Personal Statement of: (State name in full, if no middle name, state (NMN), or if initial only, indicate initial). List all former names used, and dates each name was used. Use separate sheet if necessary.

First   Middle   Last

2. Date of Birth: (Month, day and year)

3. Place of Birth: (City & State or Foreign Country)

U.S. Citizen? ☐ yes ☐ no

If no, give alien registration number:

#

4. Give the percentage of ownership or stock owned or to be owned in the small business concern or the Development Company.

Social Security No.

5. Present residence address

From   To   Address

City   State

Home Telephone No. (Include A/C)

Business Telephone No. (Include A/C)

Immediate past residence address

From   To   Address

BE SURE TO ANSWER THE NEXT 3 QUESTIONS CORRECTLY BECAUSE THEY ARE IMPORTANT.

THE FACT THAT YOU HAVE AN ARREST OR CONVICTION RECORD WILL NOT NECESSARILY DISQUALIFY YOU. BUT AN INCORRECT ANSWER WILL PROBABLY CAUSE YOUR APPLICATION TO BE TURNED DOWN.

6. Are you presently under indictment, on parole or probation?

☐ Yes ☐ No   If yes, furnish details in a separate exhibit. List name(s) under which held, if applicable.

7. Have you ever been charged with or arrested for any criminal offense other than a minor motor vehicle violation?

☐ Yes ☐ No   If yes, furnish details in a separate exhibit. List name(s) under which charged, if applicable.

8. Have you ever been convicted of any criminal offense other than a minor motor vehicle violation?

☐ Yes ☐ No   If yes, furnish details in a separate exhibit. List name(s) under which convicted, if applicable.

9. Name and address of participating bank

The information on this form will be used in connection with an investigation of your character. Any information you wish to submit, that you feel will expedite this investigation should be set forth.

Whoever makes any statement knowing it to be false, for the purpose of obtaining for himself or for any applicant, any loan, or loan extension by renewal, deferment or otherwise, or for the purpose of obtaining, or influencing SBA toward, anything of value under the Small Business Act, as amended, shall be punished under Section 16(a) of that Act, by a fine of not more than $5000, or by imprisonment for not more than 2 years, or both.

Signature	Title	Date

SBA FORM 912 (1-81) SOP 50 10 1 EDITION OF 3-79 WILL BE USED UNTIL STOCK IS EXHAUSTED

Form Approved
OMB No. 3245-0017

PERSONAL FINANCIAL STATEMENT

As of _____, 19___.

Return to:

Small Business Administration

For SBA Use Only

SBA Loan No.

Complete this form if 1) a sole proprietorship by the proprietor; 2) a partnership by each partner; 3) a corporation by each officer and each stockholder with **20%** or more ownership; 4) any other person or entity providing a guaranty on the loan.

Name and Address, Including ZIP Code   *(of person and spouse submitting Statement)*

This statement is submitted in connection with S.B.A. loan requested or granted to the individual or firm, whose name appears below:

Name and Address of Applicant or Borrower, Including ZIP Code

SOCIAL SECURITY NO. _____

Business *(of person submitting Statement)*

Please answer all questions using "No" or "None" where necessary

ASSETS		LIABILITIES	
Cash on Hand & In Banks . . . . $		Accounts Payable . . . . $	
Savings Account in Banks		Notes Payable to Banks	
U. S. Government Bonds		*(Describe below - Section 2)*	
Accounts & Notes Receivable		Notes Payable to Others	
Life Insurance-Cash Surrender Value Only . .		*(Describe below - Section 2)*	
Other Stocks and Bonds		Installment Account (Auto)	
(Describe - reverse side - Section 3)		Monthly Payments $	
Real Estate		Installment Accounts (Other)	
(Describe - reverse side - Section 4)		Monthly Payments $	
Automobile - Present Value		Loans on Life Insurance	
Other Personal Property		Mortgages on Real Estate	
(Describe - reverse side - Section 5)		*(Describe - reverse side - Section 4)*	
Other Assets		Unpaid Taxes	
(Describe - reverse side - Section 6)		*(Describe - reverse side - Section 7)*	
		Other Liabilities	
		(Describe - reverse side - Section 8)	
		Total Liabilities	
		Net Worth	
Total . . . . $		Total . . . . $	

Section I. Source of Income

(Describe below all items listed in this Section)

Salary	$
Net Investment Income	
Real Estate Income	
Other Income (Describe) *	

CONTINGENT LIABILITIES

As Endorser or Co-Maker	$
Legal Claims and Judgments	
Provision for Federal Income Tax	
Other Special Debt	

Description of items listed in Section I

* **Not necessary** to disclose alimony or child support payments in "Other Income" unless it is desired to have such payments counted toward total income.

Life Insurance Held *(Give face amount of policies - name of company and beneficiaries)*

SUPPLEMENTARY SCHEDULES

Section 2. Notes Payable to Banks and Others

Name and Address of Holder of Note	Amount of Loan		Terms of Repayments	Maturity of Loan	How Endorsed, Guaranteed, or Secured
	Original Bal.	Present Bal.			
	$	$	$		

SBA FORM 413 (12-78) REF: SOP 50 50   Edition of 8-67 May Be Used Until Stock Is Exhausted

Section 3. Other Stocks and Bonds: Give listed and unlisted Stocks and Bonds (Use separate sheet if necessary)

No. of Shares	Names of Securities	Cost	Market Value Statement Date	
			Quotation	Amount

Section 4. Real Estate Owned. (List each parcel separately. Use supplemental sheets if necessary. Each sheet must be identified as a supplement to this statement and signed). (Also advises whether property is covered by title insurance, abstract of title, or both).

Title is in name of _____

Type of property _____

Address of property (City and State)

Original Cost to (me) (us) $ _____
Date Purchased _____
Present Market Value $ _____
Tax Assessment Value $ _____

Name and Address of Holder of Mortgage (City and State)

Date of Mortgage _____
Original Amount $ _____
Balance $ _____
Maturity _____
Terms of Payment _____

Status of Mortgage, i.e., current or delinquent. If delinquent describe delinquencies

Section 5. Other Personal Property. (Describe and if any is mortgaged, state name and address of mortgage holder and amount of mortgage. terms of payment and if delinquent, describe delinquency.)

Section 6. Other Assets. (Describe)

Section 7. Unpaid Taxes. (Describe in detail, as to type, to whom payable, when due, amount, and what, if any, property a tax lien, if any, attaches)

Section 8. Other Liabilities. (Describe in detail)

(I) or (We) certify the above and the statements contained in the schedules herein is a true and accurate statement of (my) or (our) financial condition as of the date stated herein. This statement is given for the purpose of: (Check one of the following)

☐ Inducing S.B.A. to grant a loan as requested in application, of the individual or firm whose name appears herein, in connection with which this statement is submitted.

☐ Furnishing a statement of (my) or (our) financial condition, pursuant to the terms of the guaranty executed by (me) or (us) at the time S.B.A. granted a loan to the individual or firm, whose name appears herein.

_____   _____   _____
Signature   Signature   Date

SBA FORM 413 (12-78) REF: SOP 50 50   Page 2   GPO: 1982 O—392-391

INDEX

Finances, managing, 170
Financial control, as factor in business, 198
Financial information, means of comparing, 45
Financial institutions, and managerial assistance, 65
Financial statements, 45-46, 170
Financing:
  application procedures for, 126-127
  by banks, 109-110
  bridge, 98-99
  capital needs for existing business, 92
  capital requirements for new business, 92
  capital shortages, 96
  by certified development companies, (CDCs), 126
  by commercial finance companies, 113-114
  debt, 100
  equity, 100
  external, 99
  factoring, 114-115
  by family and friends, 108-109
  by government sources. See Financing, government sources of
  internal, 99-100
  by investment bankers (underwriters), 116-117
  leasing, 113-114
  by life insurance companies, 116
  by local development companies (LDCs), 126
  outlets, 107-126
  by pension funds, 116
  self-, 107-108
  rejection of request for, 163-166
  by venture capital companies, 111-112
Financing, government sources of:
  Bureau of Indian Affairs, 123
  Commodity Credit Corporation (CCC), 121
  Department of Energy (DOE), 122
  Economic Development Administration (EDA), 121-122
  Export/Import Bank (Eximbank), 123-124
  Farm Credit Administration (FCA), 120-121

Financing, sources of (cont'd.):
  Farmers Home Administration (FmHA), 119-120
  Federal Reserve Board (FRB), 124
  Geological Survey, 123
  local, 125
  Maritime Administration, 122
  Minority Enterprise Small Business Investment Companies (MESBICs), 113
  National Science Foundation (NSF), 124
  Overseas Private Investment Corporation (OPIC), 124
  Small Business Administration (SBA), 117-119
  Small Business Investment Corporations (SBICs), 112-113
  state, 125
  State Development Companies (SDCs), 125
Fire insurance, 180-183
First stage, of capital evolution, 98
Foreign Credit Insurance Association, 123
Forms of business. See Organization, forms of
Fourth stage (bridge financing), of capital evolution, 98-99
Franchise organizations, 33-34
Franchises:
  acquiring, 26
  advantages of, 30-31
  books on, 33
  disadvantages of, 31
  evaluation of, 31-32
  organizations monitoring, 33-34
  questions concerning reputability of, 32
  questions to ask before acquiring, 34-38
Friends, family and associates, managerial assistance from, 66
  financing by, 108-109
Funding. See Financing
Funding negotiations, 160-163
  rejection, 24 reasons for, 163-166
Funds, kinds of, 100-101

General partnership, 75-77
Glass insurance, 186